T0305678

INTERDISCIPLINARY PERSPECTIVES ON PLANETARY WELL-BEING

This book proposes a paradigm shift in how human and nonhuman well-being are perceived and approached. In response to years of accelerated decline in the health of ecosystems and their inhabitants, this edited collection presents planetary well-being as a new cross-disciplinary concept to foster global transformation towards a more equal and inclusive framing of well-being.

Throughout this edited volume, researchers across the humanities, social sciences, and natural sciences apply and reflect on the concept of planetary well-being, showcasing its value as an interdisciplinary, cross-sectoral changemaker. The book explores the significance of planetary well-being as a theoretical and empirical concept in sustainability science and applies it to discipline-specific cases, including business, education, psychology, culture, and development. Interdisciplinary perspectives on topical global questions and processes underpin each chapter, from soil processes and ecosystem health to global inequalities and cultural transformation, in the framework of planetary well-being.

The book will appeal to academics, researchers, and students in a broad range of disciplines including sustainability science, sustainable development, natural resources, and environmental humanities. Calling readers to assess, challenge, and rethink the dominant perceptions of well-being and societal activities, this rich resource that explores the interconnection between human and nonhuman well-being serves as a tool to foster transformative action towards a more sustainable society.

Merja Elo is a postdoctoral researcher of community ecology at University of Jyväskylä, Finland, covering topics from macroecology to conservation biology and restoration ecology.

Jonne Hytönen is a research coordinator at University of Jyväskylä and a postdoctoral researcher at Aalto University Department of Built Environment. He conducts research on sustainability transition in spatial planning.

Sanna Karkulehto is a professor of literature at University of Jyväskylä, Finland, whose most recent publications include the ESCL Collaborative Research Award Finalist *Reconfiguring Human, Nonhuman and Posthuman in Literature and Culture* (2020, Routledge, ed. with A-K. Koistinen and E. Varis).

Teea Kortetmäki is a senior researcher in social sciences and philosophy at University of Jyväskylä, Finland. She conducts research on environmental ethics, climate policy, and sustainability transitions.

Janne S. Kotiaho is a professor of ecology and director of the School of Resource Wisdom at University of Jyväskylä, Finland. He is the chair of the Finnish Nature Panel and a scientific advisor to the government of Finland in issues related to biodiversity and ecosystem restoration.

Mikael Puurtinen is a research coordinator at the School of Resource Wisdom at University of Jyväskylä, Finland. He conducts evolutionary ecology research and coordinates interdisciplinary sustainability education at his home university.

Miikka Salo is a senior lecturer at University of Jyväskylä, Finland. He conducts research on energy politics and environmental governance and citizenship.

Routledge Studies in Sustainable Development

This series uniquely brings together original and cutting-edge research on sustainable development. The books in this series tackle difficult and important issues in sustainable development including: values and ethics; sustainability in higher education; climate compatible development; resilience; capitalism and degrowth; sustainable urban development; gender and participation; and well-being.

Drawing on a wide range of disciplines, the series promotes interdisciplinary research for an international readership. The series was recommended in the *Guardian*'s suggested reads on development and the environment.

Interdisciplinary Perspectives on Socio-Ecological Challenges
Sustainable Transformations Globally and in the EU
Edited by Anders Siig Andersen, Henrik Hauggaard-Nielsen, Thomas Budde Christensen and Lars Hulgaard

Sustainable Development Goal 16 and the Global Governance of Violence
Critical Reflections on the Uncertain Future of Peace
Edited by Timothy Donais, Alistair D. Edgar, and Kirsten Van Houten

Interdisciplinary Perspectives on Planetary Well-Being
Edited by Merja Elo, Jonne Hytönen, Sanna Karkulehto, Teea Kortetmäki, Janne S. Kotiaho, Mikael Puurtinen, and Miikka Salo

For more information about this series, please visit: www.routledge.com/ Routledge-Studies-in-Sustainable-Development/book-series/RSSD

INTERDISCIPLINARY PERSPECTIVES ON PLANETARY WELL-BEING

Edited by Merja Elo, Jonne Hytönen, Sanna Karkulehto, Teea Kortetmäki, Janne S. Kotiaho, Mikael Puurtinen, and Miikka Salo

This volume is a joint project and edited in collaboration. The editors are listed alphabetically to indicate that they have contributed equally to the project and want to attribute an equal share of credit to each editor. Funding by Academy of Finland (project number 333366) has enabled Jonne Hytönen to take part in editing this book.

Routledge
Taylor & Francis Group
London and New York

from Routledge

Designed cover image: © Eva Kaján

First published 2024
by Routledge
4 Park Square, Milton Park, Abingdon, Oxon OX14 4RN

and by Routledge
605 Third Avenue, New York, NY 10158

Routledge is an imprint of the Taylor and Francis Group, an informa business

British Library Cataloguing-in-Publication Data
A catalogue record for this book is available from the British Library

Library of Congress Cataloging-in-Publication Data
Names: Elo, Merja, editor; Hytönen, Jonne, editor; Karkulehto, Sanna, editor; Kortetmäki, Teea, editor; Kotiaho, Janne S., editor; Puurtinen, Mikael, editor; Salo, Miikka, editor.
Title: Interdisciplinary perspectives on planetary well-being / edited by Merja Elo, Jonne Hytönen, Sanna Karkulehto, Teea Kortetmäki, Janne S. Kotiaho, Mikael Puurtinen and Miikka Salo.
Description: Abingdon, Oxon ; New York, NY : Routledge, 2024. | Series: Routledge studies in sustainable development | Includes bibliographical references and index.
Identifiers: LCCN 2023009437 (print) | LCCN 2023009438 (ebook) | ISBN 9781032368283 (hardback) | ISBN 9781032368269 (paperback) | ISBN 9781003334002 (ebook)
Subjects: LCSH: Sustainable development. | Environmentalism. | Well-being.
Classification: LCC HC79.E5 I52879 2024 (print) | LCC HC79.E5 (ebook) | DDC 338.9/27—dc23/eng/20230323
LC record available at https://lccn.loc.gov/2023009437
LC ebook record available at https://lccn.loc.gov/2023009438

ISBN: 978-1-032-36828-3 (hbk)
ISBN: 978-1-032-36826-9 (pbk)
ISBN: 978-1-003-33400-2 (ebk)

DOI: 10.4324/9781003334002

Typeset in Times New Roman
by codeMantra

CONTENTS

FIGURES

CONTRIBUTORS

Valtteri A. Aaltonen; Researcher in Management and Leadership, University of Jyväskylä, Finland

Nerea Abrego; Academy Research Fellow, University of Jyväskylä, Finland

Atte Arffman; PhD Candidate in Environmental History, University of Jyväskylä, Finland

Riikka Aro; Postdoctoral Researcher in Sociology, University of Jyväskylä, Finland

Stefan Baumeister; Senior Lecturer and Adjunct Professor, Program Director in Corporate Environmental Management, University of Jyväskylä, Finland

Ilze Brila; PhD Researcher in Ecology, University of Oulu, Finland

Gonzalo Cortés-Capano; Wisdom Research Fellow in Sustainability Science, University of Jyväskylä, Finland

Jessie Do; Doctoral Researcher in Sustainable Business, University of Jyväskylä, Finland

Rémi Duflot; Senior Researcher in Landscape Ecology, University of Jyväskylä, Finland

Sami El Geneidy; Doctoral Researcher in Corporate Environmental Management, University of Jyväskylä, Finland

Merja Elo; Postdoctoral Researcher in Community Ecology, University of Jyväskylä, Finland

Teppo Eskelinen; Senior Lecturer in Social Sciences, University of Eastern Finland, Finland

Kyle Eyvindson; Associate Professor in Forest Planning, Norwegian University of Life Sciences, Norway

Miia Grénman; Postdoctoral Researcher in Business and Economics, University of Jyväskylä, Finland

Jari Haimi; Senior Lecturer in Bio- and Environmental Science, University of Jyväskylä, Finland

Panu Halme; Senior Lecturer in Conservation Biology, University of Jyväskylä, Finland

Anni M. Hämäläinen; Postdoctoral Researcher in Evolutionary Ecology, University of Jyväskylä, Finland

Pilvi Hämeenaho; University Lecturer in Ethnology and Anthropology, University of Jyväskylä, Finland

Hannu L.T. Heikkinen; Professor of Education, University of Jyväskylä, Finland

Kari Heimonen; Professor in Economics, University of Jyväskylä, Finland

Mikko Hiljanen; University Teacher in Pedagogy of Sustainability, University of Jyväskylä, Finland

Hanna-Mari Husu; Associate Professor in Social Sciences, LUT School of Engineering Science, Finland

Suvi Huttunen; Leading Researcher in Environmental Policy, Finnish Environment Institute, Finland

Jonne Hytönen; Research Coordinator, University of Jyväskylä; Postdoctoral Researcher in Spatial Planning, Aalto University, Finland

Katriina Hyvönen; Senior Researcher, Institute of Rehabilitation, Jamk University of Applied Sciences, Finland

Toni Jernfors; Postdoctoral Researcher in Environmental Microbiology, University of Jyväskylä, Finland

Veera Joro; Doctoral Student in Development Studies, University of Jyväskylä, Finland

Juha Junttila; Professor in Economics, University of Jyväskylä, Finland

Eva R. Kallio; Senior Lecturer in Cell and molecular biology, University of Jyväskylä, Finland

Sanna Karkulehto; Professor in Literature, University of Jyväskylä, Finland

Saana Kataja-aho; University Teacher in Bio- and Environmental Science, University of Jyväskylä, Finland

Minna Käyrä; University Teacher in Corporate Environmental Management, University of Jyväskylä, Finland

Jenni Kesäniemi; Postdoctoral Researcher in Evolutionary Biology, University of Jyväskylä, Finland

Kirsi E. Keskinen; Postdoctoral Researcher in Sport and Health Sciences and Gerontology, University of Jyväskylä, Finland

Aino-Kaisa Koistinen; Senior Researcher in Contemporary Culture Studies, University of Jyväskylä, Finland

Kaisa Kortekallio; Postdoctoral Researcher in Literature, University of Jyväskylä, Finland

Teea Kortetmäki; Senior Research Fellow in Philosophy, University of Jyväskylä, Finland

Esa Koskela; Senior Lecturer in Evolutionary Ecology, University of Jyväskylä, Finland

Janne S. Kotiaho; Professor in Ecology, University of Jyväskylä, Finland

Irene Kuhmonen; Project Researcher in Corporate Environmental Management, University of Jyväskylä, Finland

Inari Kulmunki, PhD in Art History, University of Jyväskylä, Finland

xvi Contributors

Anton Lavrinienko; Postdoctoral Researcher in Microbial Ecology, University of Jyväskylä, Finland

Heidi Layne; Senior Lecturer in Global and Sustainable Education, University of Jyväskylä, Finland

Heikki Lehkonen; PhD. University Researcher, University of Jyväskylä, Finland

Anna Lehtonen; Postdoctoral Researcher in Sustainability Education, University of Jyväskylä, Finland

Meri Löyttyniemi; Doctoral Researcher in Corporate Environmental Management, University of Jyväskylä, Finland

Marileena Mäkelä; Senior Lecturer in Corporate Environmental Management, University of Jyväskylä, Finland

Tuuli Mäkinen; Assistant Teacher in Corporate Environmental Management, University of Jyväskylä, Finland

Risto-Matti Matero; PhD Candidate in General History, University of Jyväskylä, Finland

Aila-Leena Matthies; Professor in Social Work, University of Jyväskylä, Kokkola University Consortium Chydenius, Finland

Niina Mykrä; Postdoctoral Researcher in Sustainability Education, University of Jyväskylä, Finland

Kati Närhi; Professor in Social Work, University of Jyväskylä, Finland

Annukka Näyhä; Academy Research Fellow in Corporate Environmental Management, University of Jyväskylä, Finland

Godfred Obeng; Doctoral Student in Development Studies, University of Jyväskylä, Finland

Mari-Anne Okkolin; Associate Professor and Lead Expert in Peace Education Institute, Finland

Tiina Onkila; Associate Professor in Corporate Environmental Management, University of Jyväskylä, Finland

Jane-Veera Paakkolanvaara; Project Researcher, Institute of Rehabilitation, Jamk University of Applied Sciences, Finland

Tommi Perälä; Senior Researcher in Computational Ecosystem Sciences, University of Jyväskylä, Finland

Jenna Purhonen; Researcher in Community Ecology, University of Jyväskylä, Finland

Mikael Puurtinen; Coordinator in Sustainability Education, University of Jyväskylä, Finland

Kaisa J. Raatikainen; Postdoctoral Researcher in Sustainability Science, University of Jyväskylä, Finland

Juulia Räikkönen; Postdoctoral Researcher in Biodiversity Unit, University of Turku, Finland

Liia-Maria Raippalinna; Doctoral Researcher in Ethnology and Anthropology, University of Jyväskylä, Finland

Satu Ranta-Tyrkkö, Senior Lecturer in Social Work, University of Jyväskylä

Eleanor Ratcliffe; Lecturer in Environmental Psychology, University of Surrey, UK

Mitra Salimi; Doctoral Researcher in Sustainable Business, University of Jyväskylä, Finland

Jelena Salmi; Postdoctoral Researcher in Anthropology, University of Jyväskylä, Finland

Miikka Salo; Senior Lecturer in Sociology, University of Jyväskylä, Finland

Kirsi Salonen; Postdoctoral Research Fellow in Welfare Sciences, Tampere University, Finland

Minna Santaoja; Project Researcher, University of Eastern Finland, Finland

Milla Sarja; Project Researcher in Corporate Environmental Management, University of Jyväskylä, Finland

Bhavesh Sarna; University Teacher in Corporate Environmental Management, University of Jyväskylä, Finland

Katri Savolainen; Senior Lecturer in Psychology, University of Jyväskylä, Finland

Tiffany Scholier; Doctoral Researcher in Evolutionary Genomics, University of Jyväskylä, Finland

Ingo Stamm; Postdoctoral Researcher in Social Work, University of Jyväskylä, Kokkola University Consortium Chydenius, Finland

Johanna Suikkanen; Researcher in Product's Environmental Performance, Finnish Environment Institute, Finland

Outi Uusitalo; Professor and Head of Marketing, University of Jyväskylä, Finland

Anu S. Virtanen; Doctoral Researcher in Philosophy, University of Jyväskylä, Finland

Yingying Wang; Postdoctoral Researcher in Disease Ecology, University of Jyväskylä, Finland

Phillip C. Watts; Professor in Evolutionary Genetics, University of Jyväskylä, Finland

Terhi-Anna Wilska; Professor in Sociology, University of Jyväskylä, Finland

ACKNOWLEDGEMENTS

We would like to warmly thank all living systems who contributed to and helped in completing this project. We are especially grateful to the multidisciplinary group of chapter authors for their enthusiasm and insightful effort as well as patience during the process. We would also like to express our gratitude to Māris Grunskis for preparing the figures and our research assistant Otto Snellman for his skillful, competent, and invaluable assistance in finalizing the book. We are especially thankful to the Routledge Studies in Sustainability series and the anonymous peer-reviewers for believing in the need and significance of a new concept of planetary well-being in the field of sustainability science. We would also like to thank *Human and social sciences communications* journal for the possibility to use our original research article "Planetary well-being" as a reprint in this book. The final thanks go to the whole JYU.Wisdom research community at the University of Jyväskylä, Finland, where this book has been planned and prepared and where we have enjoyed numerous discussions that have supported the creation of this book.

INTRODUCTION TO INTERDISCIPLINARY PERSPECTIVES ON PLANETARY WELL-BEING

Merja Elo, Jonne Hytönen, Sanna Karkulehto, Teea Kortetmäki, Janne S. Kotiaho, Mikael Puurtinen and Miikka Salo

Life matters. Life on Earth emerged about 3.7 billion years ago and what we call diversity of life is the result of genetic information passing from one generation to the next and diversifying in the process. The metaphor of the tree of life captures how all life is intertwined: Imagine leaves growing from the twigs of a tree. Each leaf is a species connected to others through the branches and the trunk of the tree. One of the leaves among millions is our species. We are all the same yet different—we are all different forms and shapes of the life that once emerged.

Thousands of scientific papers and reports have documented the human-induced devastation of the diversity of life and destruction of whole ecosystems, testifying to our inadequate care for the planet. The creation of the unprecedented current material wealth of the high-consumption societies has converted natural ecosystems to agricultural fields, cities, and other infrastructures; exploited renewable natural resources more quickly than they can regenerate; changed the atmospheric composition too rapidly for many life forms to adapt; polluted and poisoned; and has moved non-native species to areas where they overrun vulnerable native species. We humans shake the tree of life heavy-handedly: Twigs are breaking and leaves are falling.

All life has intrinsic value, and our moral obligation is to respect and cherish, not destroy, its diversity. Even though the contribution of different peoples and nations to the present crisis is highly uneven on a global scale, we humans together hold the knowledge and capacities, and the equal but differentiated responsibility, to repair the damage done to human and nonhuman well-being.

This volume strives to secure the preservation of the diversity of life and the prospects of well-being for all on Earth. It is a manifestation of an ambitious goal to establish the new, non-anthropocentric, and holistic concept of *planetary well-being*. At its core, planetary well-being insists that the planet's life-sustaining

DOI: 10.4324/9781003334002-1

systems remain sufficiently undamaged by human activities so as to allow all species and populations to survive and thrive. Planetary well-being is a novel cross-disciplinary concept coined to foster global transformation to a more inclusive and equal expression of well-being for all. As such, it pushes for a paradigm shift in how human and nonhuman well-being are perceived and approached. The concept has grown from an understanding that preservation of the diversity of life demands an urgent reversal of the deterioration of Earth and ecosystem processes threatening the existence and well-being of so many of Earth's inhabitants. The concept stems from theoretically and ethically critical stances that call into question the anthropocentric biases of Western scientific and political thought as well as the dualistic idea of human–nonhuman relations. It brings new perspectives to the ethical discussions on sustainability, justice and responsibility, and well-being.

Despite decades of work on sustainability and sustainable development, the planet's life-supporting systems are failing. While explanations for this can be offered at multiple levels, what matters now is whether the harmful trajectories can be changed. As moral agents, we humans are responsible for changing these trajectories. We believe that the actors who deliberate, plan, and enact the change need new conceptualizations to make their decisions and actions effectively transformative. By adopting process-oriented and systems-focused thinking and by unifying human and nonhuman well-being, planetary well-being offers a new conceptual framework for theoretical, methodological, and empirical research in the field of sustainability science, and for stimulating actions to preserve well-being on Earth.

In this edited volume, researchers across human, social, and natural sciences apply and reflect on the concept of planetary well-being, showcasing its value as an interdisciplinary, cross-sectoral changemaker. The objective of this volume is to scrutinize the meaning, position, and significance of planetary well-being as a theoretical and empirical concept in sustainability science. We apply it to discipline-specific domains including anthropology, art and culture, business, financing and corporate environmental management, consumption, development, ecology, education, history, philosophy, planning, psychology, and social work. These discipline-specific and interdisciplinary explorations, while far from being exhaustive, cover a variety of theoretical and methodological approaches. In addition to addressing the consequences of the degradation of ecosystem processes, such as climate change and biodiversity loss, the volume tackles other global threats and challenges facing humanity, such as economic inequality, uneven power structures, and social injustice. This way, planetary well-being serves as a tool to sharpen and broaden the analytical outlook beyond the conventional frameworks of sustainability transformation, just transition, and sustainable development.

Many contributions in this volume also address methodological questions related to the use of planetary well-being in research: How can it be operationalized for different purposes, and what aspects of human and nonhuman well-being are highlighted, omitted, or sometimes purposefully obscured in various methodological as well as societal contexts? The ultimate objective is to reflect on how planetary well-being as a non-anthropocentric and holistic framework can be used to promote transformative action towards a world where all forms of life, humans and beyond, would have the opportunity to achieve well-being.

The organization of the volume

This book is divided into five parts that each approach planetary well-being differently. The first part focuses on introducing and defining the concept by presenting its theoretical, contextual, and ethical backgrounds. The opening chapter, "Planetary well-being", is a verbatim reproduction of a research article originally published in *Humanities and Social Sciences Communications*, where planetary well-being was conceptualized for the first time. The chapter critically discusses the problems of the existing conceptual frameworks within sustainability science and well-being and introduces planetary well-being as a needed addition to address the root causes of ecological crises. Chapter 2, demonstrates how planetary well-being is positioned in the broader ontological and ethical-theoretical landscape, owing to its process-oriented perspective and non-anthropocentric normative grounds. Chapter 3, encourages more attention to ontological questions as well as openness to differences and transdisciplinary and multi-ontological co-researching in the pursuit of planetary well-being.

After the introductory part, the book continues examining theoretical, methodological, empirical, contextual, and political questions on planetary well-being, with a division of four parts. Each part approaches the concept and puts it into use and practice in certain spheres of urgency that are key when aiming at collective sustainability transformation: The second part deals with the urgency to assess ecological processes as constituents of planetary well-being and to change the direction of humanity's impact on them; the third part covers the urgency to challenge and revise economic structures and practices; the fourth part underlines the urgency to rethink and contest anthropocentric ideas of well-being; and the fifth part focuses on the urgency to find solutions to foster cultural and societal transformation towards planetary well-being.

Part 2, lays the groundwork for planetary well-being by exploring many of those processes whose integrity contributes to planetary well-being but are currently threatened or undermined by the harmful impact of human activities, driven especially by high-consumption societies. Chapter 4, argues that human activities such as overexploitation of natural resources, ecosystem degradation, and global trade have had severe consequences for the prevalence and spread of pathogens in human and wildlife communities. The chapter outlines how human activities can provide favourable conditions for pandemics and trigger cascading consequences for ecosystems worldwide. Chapter 5, argues that landscape approaches hold transformative potential for the managing of socio-ecological systems and offer an opportunity to put planetary well-being into practice. Chapter 6, maintains that soils are closely interlinked with planetary well-being as they are related directly or indirectly to nearly all critical ecosystem processes on Earth, including energy flows, element and water cycles, and interactions between living organisms. The chapter proposes that by taking care of the soil health humans can actively contribute to planetary well-being.

Part 3, consists of chapters that aim at revealing how societies organized around economic motives have harmed and continue to harm both human and nonhuman well-being. The chapters also propose alternative ways how our present economy-driven society might be changed to better take into consideration ecological and social sustainability as well as planetary well-being more generally. Chapter 7, analyses why ecocentric ideas of well-being have not been adopted more widely and argues that economic and political incentives, or path-dependencies, have hindered attempts to understand well-being in more ecologically balanced terms. Chapter 8, demonstrates how the critical development studies perspective is significant in the conceptualization and usage of planetary well-being by virtue of its analysis of the connection between global injustice and local ecological knowledge.

Chapters 9 and 10 introduce examples of the ways in which the current economic imperative could be exposed and challenged. Chapter 9, discusses sustainable marketing and consumption from the perspective of planetary well-being, and Chapter 10, presents a critical analysis of selected sustainable business concepts and practices by using planetary well-being as a conceptual framework. Chapter 9 begins with the bold claim that the current marketing and consumption system is a threat to planetary well-being. The chapter even challenges the concept of sustainable marketing, which it regards as an oxymoron. The authors call for structural and cultural transformations and systemic changes in our everyday consumption practices, with the aim being to reduce consumption levels and to incorporate a non-anthropocentric and systemic view of planetary well-being into business structures and economic systems.

Chapter 10 for its part continues challenging the existing economic system by maintaining that a range of current sustainable business concepts and practices have critical shortcomings when analyzed from the viewpoint of planetary well-being; despite of their aim and reputation as sustainability promoters they are still based on a business logic dominated by profitability and shareholder wealth. Therefore, Chapter 10 arrives at a similar kind of conclusion as the previous chapter: "In order to truly achieve planetary well-being, the whole economic system (not only individual companies) should shift the focus from economic perspective (i.e., continuous economic growth) to environmental and social perspectives."

Part 4, offers a continuation of Part 3 by exploring ways to enable systemic and structural changes and transformations by changing mindsets, especially regarding perceptions of human well-being. Chapter 11, proceeds by challenging the assumptions guiding current mainstream marketing and consumer research. It discusses planetary well-being from the perspective of moral philosophy, transformative consumer research and positive psychology, and emphasizes the premises of Aristotelian *eudaimonia*, which encompasses pursuing a life of meaning, virtue, and excellence instead of "ever-increasing production and consumption", transmitting the message that "the goods life" is the path to "the good life". While Chapter 11 argues that transformative consumption on the individual level requires also systemic and structural transformation of markets and marketing, Chapter 12, focuses on individual change by demonstrating the significance of people's mental well-being in changing their behaviour towards promoting planetary well-being. According to the chapter, the needed transformation "requires the reshaping of human–nature relationships and restoring the view of humans and human minds as part of nature, not separate from it".

Sharing a similar focus on individuals, Chapter 13, emphasizes that social work must step back from the systems-processes level and embrace the individual level when discussing and promoting planetary well-being. This is because social work—both as an academic discipline and a practice-oriented profession—is involved in the daily lives of individuals, families, and groups, and their social problems. Nevertheless, planetary well-being can help social work researchers and professionals to reconsider their role regarding the well-being of other species and entire ecosystems. In this way, social work appears as one more sphere of social practice in which adopting the concept of planetary well-being becomes crucial.

Part 5, explores possibilities for initiating and guiding transformation away from unsustainable societal practices towards ones that are in line with the objectives of planetary well-being. Chapter 14, reviews the disappointing track record of multilateral biodiversity agreements and suggests that assignable targets are necessary to secure progress in global biodiversity conservation. The chapter proposes that country-level extinction risk indices are promising tools for motivating actions and tracking progress towards planetary well-being.

Chapter 15, argues that transition towards planetary well-being in organizations requires a deeper integration of environmental values in financial accounting and reporting. Such integration at the level of financial valuation is critical to ensure that environmental impacts begin to influence the management decisions of the organizations. Chapter 16, discusses the role that financial markets may play in steering economic production towards planetary well-being. The chapter proposes changes in financial incentives that, via influencing the cost of financial capital, would lead to exclusion of non-environmentally friendly production and tilt financial flows towards less harmful production, thereby promoting planetary well-being.

The last two chapters of the book approach perhaps the two most consequential arenas of human communities with respect to enabling paradigmatic change: culture and education. Chapter 17, argues that the role of art and culture is indispensable in challenging, preventing, and changing destructive human practices that cause ecological and well-being crises. The chapter focuses on the capacity of contemporary art to foster cultural transformation towards planetary well-being and presents a new concept of "culture as planetary well-being" to reflect the required cultural transformation, which it sees as a large-scale change in shared knowledges, lifestyles, traditions, beliefs, morals, laws, customs, values, institutions, and worldviews. Likewise, in the final chapter of the volume, a new theoretical concept is introduced as a pathway for replacing the traditional anthropocentric view with a wiser form of humanity.

Nurturing a new beginning

The protection of well-being on Earth calls for a paradigmatic policy reform. We believe that sustainability science and policy need a conception of well-being that is built on systemic and non-anthropocentric grounds. Human development needs to be re-evaluated based on its impact on planetary well-being. We hope that this book opens the floor and inspires researchers across the globe to continue research on planetary well-being and to explore topics only touched upon in this volume. Our aim has been to seed a new beginning in sustainability science. While the endeavour for planetary well-being is a shared task that we hope will encourage and connect humans across the planet, it is crucial to acknowledge the historical and current stark inequalities and the differentiated role of various communities that have contributed to the present plight. Responsibilities for planetary well-being are shared yet differentiated, and it is only fair that the greatest burden should fall on the shoulders of the well-off communities and people who have much more than what they need; they, including us the editors, owe it to the present peoples, future generations, and nonhuman life in all its diversity.

PART I

Grounding the concept

1

PLANETARY WELL-BEING[1]

*Teea Kortetmäki, Mikael Puurtinen, Miikka Salo, Riikka Aro,
Stefan Baumeister, Rémi Duflot, Merja Elo, Panu Halme,
Hanna-Mari Husu, Suvi Huttunen, Katriina Hyvönen,
Sanna Karkulehto, Saana Kataja-aho, Kirsi E. Keskinen,
Inari Kulmunki, Tuuli Mäkinen, Annukka Näyhä, Mari-
Anne Okkolin, Tommi Perälä, Jenna Purhonen, Kaisa J.
Raatikainen, Liia-Maria Raippalinna, Kirsi Salonen,
Katri Savolainen and Janne S. Kotiaho*

Introduction[2]

Human activities dominate Earth: Less than one-quarter of the land area remains free from significant direct human impact, and by 2050 this area is projected to shrink to <10% (Watson *et al.*, 2016; the Intergovernmental Science-Policy Platform on Biodiversity and Ecosystem Services (IPBES), 2018). Nearly three-quarters of freshwater areas and over half of marine areas are exploited for food production (Díaz *et al.*, 2019; IPBES, 2019). The biomass of wild mammals has fallen by 82% since prehistory (Bar-On, Phillips and Milo, 2018), and it is projected that by 2050 humans will have eliminated 38–46% of all biodiversity (measured as mean species abundance) from the planet (van der Esch *et al.*, 2017; IPBES, 2018).

Human actions threaten to cause irreversible changes in the Earth system, with critical safety limits (planetary boundaries) exceeded for biosphere integrity, biochemical flows, climate change, and land system change (Rockström *et al.*, 2009; Steffen *et al.*, 2015a; O'Neill *et al.*, 2018; IPCC, 2019). Crossing such boundaries may lead to irreversible changes in the Earth system (Steffen *et al.*, 2015a; O'Neill *et al.*, 2018). The scale of these pressures has evoked a proposal for labelling the current geological epoch the Anthropocene, an era where humans shape the geosphere and biosphere evolution (*e.g.*, Crutzen and Stoermer, 2000; Dryzek and Pickering, 2018). The negative anthropogenic impact on the Earth system has thus reached a point where the future of human societies and the flourishing of life, in general, are threatened. On the other hand, attributing the aforementioned negative impacts on the whole of humanity, "Anthropos", is overgeneralizing: It dismisses that only a fraction of the humanity is historically responsible for most of the environmental harm and that the extent of harmful impacts varies significantly depending on the particular processes of production and consumption (Malm and

DOI: 10.4324/9781003334002-3

Hornborg, 2014). According to the historical graphs, these developments have "been almost entirely driven by a small fraction of the human population, those in developed countries" (Steffen *et al.*, 2015b).

Global inequalities among humanity are stark regarding who receives the benefits of environmentally damaging actions and who has to bear their detrimental impacts. Around the world, nations' top 10% of earners capture 37–61% of national income; globally, the share of the top 10% of global income is between 53% and 60% depending on the method of measurement (Alvaredo *et al.*, 2018). The costs of ecosystem degradation and climate change, on the other hand, hurt the well-being of at least 3.2 billion less affluent people (IPBES, 2018; UN Environment, 2019). Retaining the present standard of living in the wealthiest countries necessitates structures that maintain globally unequal, exploitative labour division, and ecological exchange (Hornborg, 1998; Newsome *et al.*, 2015). Transformative changes to social, economic, and technological systems are increasingly called for to change the course towards a more sustainable future in both environmental and social terms (*e.g.*, Díaz *et al.*, 2019; Kohler *et al.*, 2019; Willemen *et al.*, 2020).

The above described environmental and social problems have generated a broad spectrum of discourses and action, from the sustainable development framework and goals (United Nations (UN), 2015; World Commission on Environment and Development (WCED), 1987) to the foundations of social justice (Nussbaum and Sen, 1993) (for key frameworks, see the Supplementary Material in Kortetmäki *et al.*, 2021). From the ecological viewpoint especially, a serious challenge is that a majority of the frameworks focus on the human perspective and consider nonhuman well-being important only to the extent it contributes to human well-being (*e.g.*, Dryzek, 2005, p. 157). Solely human-focused ethos of many conceptualizations of sustainability is typical of Western science, contrary to some other knowledge systems (for example, some forms of Indigenous and non-Western knowledge) that emphasize balance and collaboration with nature (Díaz *et al.*, 2015).

Another challenge with the existing frameworks is that they seldom focus on the systems and processes that support life, well-being, and biodiversity at different spatial scales. Although sustainability studies have recognized the interconnectedness of the social, economic, and ecological aspects of life, and the importance of studying processes as taking place in complex socio-ecological systems (Ostrom, 2009), the mainstreaming of such thinking to well-being studies has been slower. Lack of a systems-oriented and multiscalar outlook can result in a fragmentary view of the problems and their solutions. Many frameworks aim to overcome either anthropocentrism or the lack of systemic and multiscalar outlook, but few attempt both and do that with the viewpoint of well-being. For example, the widely used notion of ecosystem services is focused on the instrumental values of nonhuman nature to humanity, which reduces nonhuman nature into capital and has even been suggested to be the "Trojan Horse" of anthropocentrism within the community of conservation (Washington, 2020). In Supplementary Material in Kortetmäki *et al.* (2021), we list the widely acknowledged concepts that address the ecological crisis, sustainable well-being or the environmental impacts of human actions, and we shortly describe how these notions differ from the concept that we propose in this paper.

The need to conceptualize well-being in a way that is non-anthropocentric and encourages a systems-oriented, multi-scalar outlook, raises a fundamental question: What is well-being? In human psychology, the focus is traditionally on subjective, experienced well-being: Persons with subjectively high well-being are satisfied with life, experience positive feelings, are able to fulfil personal aspirations, have favourable relations, and are in good mental health (Keyes, 2005; Kokko *et al.*, 2013). The subjective accounts of well-being have also been criticized from the environmental sustainability view-point: If experienced well-being depends on the fulfilment of seemingly limitless human desires and wants (instead of limited needs) with manifold direct and indirect material impacts, this poses unsustainably high material criteria for well-being (Gough, 2015). To address this problem, ecopsychology (as well as the ecosocial approach to well-being, see the Supplementary Material in Kortetmäki *et al.*, 2021) argues that human beings are simply a part of nature (Winter and Koger, 2004). From this perspective, nature and humanity are ineradicably linked and high levels of well-being can only be achieved through the experiential realization of nature connectedness and exposure to nonhuman nature (Roszak, Gomes and Kanner, 1995; Mayer and Frantz, 2004; Brymer, Cuddihy and Sharma-Brymer, 2010). Especially from the viewpoint of social justice as an equal opportunity to achieve well-being, nearby nature which anybody can access is important. In spite of that, focus on subjective well-being is problematic from the viewpoint of social justice and equality even when the ecological inter-connectedness is incorporated. Underprivileged people can adapt to their circumstances (demonstrating "malleable preferences") and may be unable to articulate their experiences of lower well-being and satisfaction of life, whereas minor losses of the privileged groups can get overemphasized (Nussbaum and Sen, 1993; Nussbaum, 2011).

In social sciences, consequently, well-being is often approached nonsubjectively and understood to depend on the satisfaction of basic human needs, such as the need for material subsistence, protection, affection, understanding, and autonomy, which contribute to physical and mental health, and to the abilities for social participation (*e.g.*, Doyal and Gough, 1984; Rice, 2013; Gough, 2017; see also Nussbaum and Sen, 1993). The argument is that these universal human needs persist through cultures and time, even while the strategies and means to satisfying the needs, and thresholds for adequate needs satisfaction, can change (Gough, 2017). Needs-based approaches thereby conceptualize well-being in a way that is more suitable (than subjective experiences of well-being) for public policy planning and implementation.

Needs-based, objective accounts of well-being are also used in the context of nonhumans, since studying their experienced well-being is challenging (Wemelsfelder, 1997). This newer strand of literature alleviates the anthropocentric orientation of the well-being discourse by acknowledging that it is not only humans who can gain or lose well-being. Most of the literature on nonhuman well-being focuses on nonhuman animals and maintains that they have species-typical physical and behavioural needs, the satisfaction of which is crucial for their well-being (*e.g.*, Broom, 1991; Bartussek, 1999; Singer, 2002; Nussbaum, 2006). Nevertheless, the concept of well-being (also referred to as thriving or flourishing) has been applied to other organisms, too: Populations, species or lineages, and even ecosystems. Ecosystem well-being, for example, has been defined as the functional integrity of an ecosystem and its capacity to retain its typical functionings and characteristics (Schlosberg, 2007; Kortetmäki, 2017; see also Prescott-Allen, 2001), including succession and adaptation. The well-being of species or lineages is addressed via regenerative capacities that are related to functional integrity: To be well, species must be able to maintain self-sustaining capacities and to adapt to environmental changes (Kortetmäki, 2018).

In sum, the theoretical and conceptual research literature on well-being has expanded much. It has advanced from disconnected and subjective accounts to interconnected ecopsychological and ecosocial views, to objective and needs-based conceptualizations that help to address well-being from the social equality and public policy-related aspects, and finally also to the well-being beyond humans. Nevertheless, the contributions typically focus on one level or aspect at a time, be it the human–nonhuman connections, sentient animals, or collective nonhuman entities. The challenge of connecting different levels and domains has remained insufficiently addressed. Although the conflicts between the well-being of different organisms have been acknowledged and reflected upon (*e.g.*, Nussbaum, 2006; Schlosberg, 2007 for the predator–prey relations), these reflections have also received criticism (*e.g.*, Cripps, 2010; Hailwood, 2012), and interactions between well-being at different levels are articulated mainly in parentheses,[3] lacking the multiscalar approach. Contributions cannot be easily integrated, as the criticism has pointed out.

We propose a new concept, *planetary well-being*, to address the above discussed need for a non-anthropocentric, systemic conceptualization of well-being that takes into account the multiple scales of interaction. Planetary well-being acknowledges the value of both human and nonhuman well-being for their own sake (intrinsic value): The moral right for both humans and nonhumans to exist, to have their needs satisfied, and to realize their typical characteristics and capacities. The needs of organisms—both human and nonhuman—are interconnected so that the satisfaction of the needs of various entities creates both synergies and conflicts. Hence, the concept transcends the level of individual organisms and focuses on the integrity of Earth system and ecosystem processes underlying the well-being of all forms of life. It also serves as a framework that ties together ecological and social equality considerations. As a concept, planetary well-being facilitates scientific and political discussions by using the same vocabulary to address the impacts of human activities on the well-being of human and nonhuman nature.

To derive and propose a non-anthropocentric concept means that we openly commit to certain normative views on moral considerability. Morally considerable beings and collectives have moral value for their own sake (inherent or intrinsic value), regardless of whether they have instrumental value for humans. Consequently, the well-being of morally considerable entities matters for their own sake. We adopt a pluralist or multicriterial approach to moral valuation; it grounds the moral considerability of entities on several criteria (Warren, 1997). The pluralist valuing grants moral considerability to human and nonhuman individuals but extends the sphere of moral considerability beyond them: Species or lineages and ecosystems that can be well or flourish and have self-regulative capacities (*e.g.*, Rolston, 1985, 2002; Schlosberg, 2007) are also morally considerable (hereafter, the term "living entities" denotes this diverse ensemble of morally considerable individuals and non-individual entities). While our normative viewpoint may not be shared by all, we believe that responding to ecological crisis adequately requires adopting a non-anthropocentric normative approach where nonhuman nature is valued also for its own sake, not only due to its importance for human prosperity.

Conceptualization of planetary well-being

We ground the concept of planetary well-being in accounts that link well-being with the satisfaction of basic needs as they are perceived from a neutral, nonsubjective viewpoint. As described above, the needs-based accounts of well-being have been previously applied to human well-being (Doyal and Gough, 1984; Max-Neef, 1991; Rice, 2013; Gough, 2015, 2017), animal well-being (*e.g.*, Broom, 1991; Bartussek, 1999; Singer, 2002; Nussbaum, 2006) and the well-being of populations and ecosystems (*e.g.*, Schlosberg, 2007; Kortetmäki, 2017). Yet, the overall diversity and number of different needs of various life forms prevents the integration of those views easily into a singular calculus of well-being—or at least renders the possible results hardly applicable in practice. Therefore, instead of focusing on needs themselves, we propose a focus on the systems and processes that are necessary for the satisfaction of the needs of diverse life forms on Earth. The focus on life-supporting systems and processes enables the integration of human and nonhuman well-being into a single framework.

A systems-oriented approach (Bunge, 2003, 2004) allows conceptualizing well-being at a general level (see Table 1.1). We utilize this approach to define planetary well-being in a way that links well-being across levels of biological hierarchies, from organisms (including humans) and populations and lineages to ecosystems—these all can be considered as *systems*—and to Earth system and ecosystem processes. In general, life on Earth can be understood as a set of interlinked, interdependent systems, and well-being at any level as the integrity of that particular system (be it an individual organism, population, or ecosystem). Crucially, the functional integrity of any system (*i.e.*, its well-being) is dependent on the satisfaction of its needs. Need satisfiers are usually products of, or comprise, interactions between other systems. In other words, the well-being of any particular system depends on inputs provided by other systems.

TABLE 1.1 The generic systems-oriented conceptual framework for well-being

System	A system is an entity that is comprised of its components, that can be impacted by the environment, has characteristic relations and interactions between its components, and has system-specific characteristics and capacities that stem from the system processes.
Critical system processes	System processes are recurring interactions between system components. Interactions require inputs to function. Critical system processes are those without which the system cannot continue its existence and realize its system-specific characteristics and capacities.
Needs and need satisfiers	Needs are conditions of dependence on inputs (need satisfiers). Needs must be satisfied for the critical system processes to function.
Well-being	Well-being is the functional integrity of the system, or in other words, the integrity of the critical system processes, that allows the system to continue its existence and realize its system-specific characteristics and capacities.

The conceptualization of well-being as the functional integrity of a system could, in principle, be applied also to human artefacts (like motors), or to socially constructed systems (like economic systems). However, as we do not consider such entities or systems to have moral considerability (value of their own that does not depend on their value for humans), the well-being of artefacts and socially constructed systems falls outside the scope of this manuscript.

The consideration of life on Earth as comprised of interlinked and interacting systems directs attention to how the needs and well-being of different species and ecosystems are connected. For example, the needs of organisms have evolved over their evolutionary history in the context of the ecosystems they inhabit. All organisms participate in many interactions. Some of the interactions are critical for their well-being (such as feeding), while others may be detrimental and even lethal for them (like being fed upon), yet critical for the well-being of some other organism(s). Interactions take place in ecosystems that in turn are dependent on the functioning of other, larger-scale processes (such as climatic processes that affect temperatures and rainfall). Ecosystems further interact with other ecosystems; the examples of teleconnections between ecosystems include precipitation in terrestrial areas, which in large part depends on evapotranspiration in distant forested areas (van der Ent *et al.*, 2010) and transport of energy and nutrients from marine to terrestrial ecosystems by migratory fish (Cederholm *et al.*, 1999).

We define planetary well-being as a state in which the integrity of Earth system and ecosystem processes remains unimpaired to a degree that lineages can persist to the future as parts of ecosystems, and organisms (including humans) can realize their typical characteristics and capacities (see Table 1.2). Planetary well-being puts the emphasis on the integrity of Earth system processes (such as the global climate and biogeochemical cycles of elements) and ecosystem-level processes (such as succession and pollination) instead of organismal well-being, because at the organismal level life is rife with conflicts such as predator–prey relations, and consequently not all organisms can "be well" all the time. Death and senescence are also normal life processes although they may demonstrate the lack of organismal well-being. However, the integrity of Earth system and ecosystem processes is fundamental for the survival and evolutionary potential of species and lineages— and for the existence and well-being of organisms and ecosystems they inhabit. We intend planetary well-being as a concept to promote respectful ways of cohabiting Earth with all forms of life so that both humans and nonhumans can achieve well-being in all parts of the world.

By the integrity of Earth system and ecosystem processes, we refer to the integrity of those flows of energy and matter on Earth and biotic interactions in ecosystems that are critical for the satisfaction of the needs of various organisms, populations, and communities.[4] These processes are manifold, and while there is a reasonable understanding about several important processes, such as nutrient cycles or pollination, it would be foolhardy to assume that all important processes are known inside out. For example, the ozone layer depletion following the emission of chlorofluorocarbons came as a surprise to the scientific community (Rowland, 2006). Thus, all actions that significantly impact the flows of energy and matter are a serious concern for planetary well-being, be it by resource use such as the human appropriation of 38% of the net primary production on Earth (Running, 2012), or by the release of nutrients, greenhouse gases, or other chemicals with possibly

TABLE 1.2 Key concepts of planetary well-being

Organismal (human and nonhuman) well-being	Organismal well-being is a state where an organism can realize its typical characteristics and capacities.
Organismal needs and need satisfiers	Organismal needs are conditions of dependence on inputs (need satisfiers). Needs must be satisfied for an organism to realize its typical characteristics and capacities. Needs depend on the evolutionary history of the lineage an organism belongs to.
Lineages, species, populations	A group of organisms with a shared genetic ancestry that is distinct from other such groups constitutes a lineage. For sexually reproducing organisms, species and populations constitute lineages at global and local scales, respectively.
Ecosystems	Ecosystems are communities of organisms that interact with each other and the abiotic environment.
Earth system and ecosystem processes	Processes relating to the flows of energy and matter on Earth and to biotic interactions in ecosystems.
Planetary well-being	Planetary well-being is a state in which the integrity of Earth system and ecosystem processes remains unimpaired to a degree that lineages can persist to the future as parts of ecosystems, and organisms (human and nonhuman) can realize their typical characteristics and capacities.

unknown effects. Similarly, excessive interference with natural ecosystems (by, for example, the destruction of natural habitats or overharvesting of natural populations) is likely to harm planetary well-being by impacting the integrity of crucial processes.

While we (as the research community) have an incomplete understanding of specific processes, we also have limited knowledge about interactions between and among the Earth's geophysical systems, ecosystems, and human-created systems (*e.g.*, Reid *et al.*, 2010; Liu *et al.*, 2015, 2018). Many of these interactions are likely to magnify each other: The risks of causing irreversible changes to the Earth system are higher in studies that consider interactions between systems or processes (*e.g.*, Lade *et al.*, 2019). Given that there are profound uncertainties regarding the consequences of human interference with the Earth system and ecosystem processes, abstinence from potential harm even in the absence of the *proof of harm*—the precautionary principle (*e.g.*, Cameron and Abouchar, 1991)—is often a safer strategy to avoid worsening global environmental problems.

The definition of planetary well-being underscores the persistence of lineages (*e.g.*, species and populations) as parts of ecosystems for both instrumental and normative reasons. As discussed above, the processes contributing to the satisfaction of the needs of various living systems are not fully understood. However, it is possible to monitor the status of populations and species, and this gives a good indication of whether the needs of lineages and organisms within them can be adequately satisfied. For example, if population sizes show unusual persistent declines, this usually indicates a failure of some critical process(es) relating to need satisfaction (of also individual organisms). The viability of species and populations thus indicates the integrity of the critical, but sometimes intractable, processes that underpin well-being at all levels.

As a non-anthropocentric and systemic concept, planetary well-being aligns with views that consider the survival of lineages to be an end in itself (Rolston, 1985). The present human exploitation of and interference with ecosystems harm vast numbers of other species and populations, with the estimated number of species considered to be at risk of extinction being up to 1 million (IPBES, 2019). However, humans also have needs that have to be satisfied for human well-being. The satisfaction of some of these needs—like the need for adequate nutrition—is practically impossible without some interference with ecosystems and, consequently, lineages. From the planetary well-being point of view, the level of human interference with ecosystems must not compromise the ability of other species and lineages to persist in these ecosystems to the future (*i.e.*, it must not put them at the risk of extinction). The importance of lineages has significant impacts on the consideration of, for example, the impacts of human-managed food system activities. Achieving planetary well-being necessitates that human basic needs are satisfied in a way that does not compromise the capacity for nonhuman entities to achieve well-being. An important step in this direction is to prioritize the satisfaction of basic human needs over the satisfaction of desires and wants that have a negative impact on nonhuman nature.

Putting the concept to use

Planetary well-being is not purported to simply replace the existing concepts, many of which are valuable in their particular domains of application. However, by integrating the systemic, process-oriented view and the concept of well-being with the needed ethical transformation away from anthropocentrism, planetary well-being provides a fruitful analytical and discursive lens for many domains of addressing—thinking about, researching, and acting upon—the ecological crisis. In academia, it has the potential to advance research on transformational changes (sustainability transition) and advance sustainability sciences by encouraging the non-anthropocentric framing of future research questions (*cf.*, Kates *et al.*, 2001). Outside academia, the notion of planetary well-being contributes to discussing and acting upon the ecological crisis at several levels: In addressing the trade-offs between different needs and desires, in setting targets and measures for decision-making, and in bridging divergent worldviews. We reflect upon these next in more detail.

Reconciling human needs with planetary well-being

The idea of needs and need satisfiers is integral to the concept of planetary well-being. While the satisfaction of needs is necessary for the well-being of any system, the relationship between the needs and need satisfiers is contingent: Needs can often be satisfied in various ways. When it comes to securing the satisfaction of the needs of nonhuman nature, the human action mainly concerns safeguarding or not harming the Earth system and ecosystem processes as far as possible. Active measures are often unnecessary; the well-being of "wild" nonhuman nature is often best served by "deconstructing the impediments to nature's own capabilities [or capacities] to fully and continually function" (Schlosberg, 2007, p. 150). Domesticated animals and ecosystems (gardens, for example) on the other hand depend on human provision for their continued existence. While we do not discuss the status of domesticated nature (that raises distinct normative questions) here, we note that many domesticated animals are not able to realize their characteristics and capacities, and ecosystem modification (*e.g.*, building a garden) may interfere with ecosystem processes that are critical for the satisfaction of the needs of wild nonhuman nature.

When it comes to the satisfaction of human needs, it is necessary to reflect upon what the quality of life—as associated with well-being—entails, especially regarding the consumption of material goods (IPBES, 2019). Humans are complex social beings and different scientific fields provide different accounts of human well-being with varying emphasis. However, when the question is how societies can organize and operate in ways that best support human well-being, it is necessary to approach well-being in a way that is institutionally applicable and meaningful to governance and policymaking. This directs attention to the needs-based, nonsubjective conceptions of human well-being. They are grounded on the assumption that all humans, like all organisms, have certain universal basic needs that have to be satisfied in order to avoid harm and have a good life including the ability to act fully in life: The satisfaction of needs is a necessary (though not necessarily sufficient) condition for well-being. Although the articulation of the needs varies between different authors (*e.g.*, Doyal and Gough, 1984; Max-Neef, 1991; Rice, 2013; Gough, 2017) and some accounts emphasize the capabilities to achieve various functionings that contribute to needs satisfaction over the actual outcome of needs satisfaction (Nussbaum and Sen, 1993; Nussbaum, 2011), they all have as key elements the need for physical and mental health, for relationships, and for autonomy in action and thought. Satisfaction of these key elements may require, for example, adequate nutrition, safety, and at least some kind of health care and education. When approached from a human perspective, planetary well-being is a state in which the organization of human systems simultaneously allows human needs to be met, and the impact on Earth and ecosystem processes is limited so that lineages can persist to the future as parts of ecosystems and organisms can realize their typical characteristics and capacities.

Needs-based approaches to human well-being have several features that are relevant to discussions about sustainability (Gough, 2017). First, many human needs are objective: Regardless of subjective experiences, it is empirically verifiable that, for example, malnourishment or the lack of caring relationships causes serious harm to individuals (this is not to deny that needs are still subjectively interpreted at the individual level). Second, human needs are plural: They include material, social, and psychological aspects. Third, human needs are non-substitutable: It is not possible to satisfy, for example, a need for healthy nutrition with more education. Fourth, human needs are in principle satiable: It is possible to identify a level of needs satisfaction that would suffice for adequate well-being. However, in consumerist societies, being able to "live without shame" requires a level of consumption that matches—or exceeds—the consumption of others, which drives ever-increasing consumption. Yet, at the societal level, this does not lead to increasing social well-being but to fragmentation and anomie (Jackson, 2017, p. 124). Fifth, needs are substantially universal and apply to people in different places and at different times although the ways of satisfying them vary in different times and cultures: Even the objective and universal needs are not "absolute" but involve relative, context-specific aspects. The precise level where a need is satisfied may vary across individuals and contexts (consider the differentiated needs for nutrition or, for example, belongingness); and some space of choice for needs satisfaction and actual doings in one's individual life are required for freedom (Nussbaum and Sen, 1993). The conception of universal needs and average requirements for their satisfaction at individual level, nevertheless, provides a useful tool for guiding and evaluating societal activities in directions that support human well-being. This gives a foundation for considering the well-being of both present and future generations in such arenas.

The idea of satiable human needs means that good, fulfilling, and dignified life can be achieved with limited consumption sufficient to meet the material needs, together with the satisfaction of non-material needs like significant primary relationships, leisure, and social participation (Max-Neef, 1991; Gough, 2017). Acknowledged, the levels of subjectively experienced well-being in such scenarios of reduced material consumption are not well known although similar changes have historically occurred in societies, especially during the post-war periods. Suggestions for achieving well-being with significantly lesser material consumption, however, are difficult. They are in stark contrast with consumerist and materialistic societies, where ever-increasing production and consumption fuel the dynamics of the economy, where well-being is understood as the realization of insatiable human preferences, and where the good life is understood as the rising material standard of living. Planetary well-being does not require the reduction of well-being but calls for reducing the consumption of material goods that are not relevant to human needs or that directly harm well-being. Global and regional equality considerations necessitate a focus on the satisfaction of both material and non-material needs of all, instead of increased (assumed) well-being for the already privileged. There are successful examples of participatory well-being workshops that utilize the needs-based approach to human well-being and help communities critically discuss what is needed for well-being, what is not, and what are the obstacles to achieving well-being in ecologically less harmful ways in the societies (*e.g.*, Guillen-Royo, Guardiola and Garcia-Quero, 2017). We suggest that planetary well-being could be put into use in citizen deliberation and policy-making arenas in similar ways, which would produce the benefit of expanding the well-being considerations beyond humans.

It is also important to note that human material needs can be satisfied in many ways (by different need satisfiers), with significantly differing impacts on planetary well-being. This directs attention to the processes of production. One relevant example that has received much research attention is the human need for protein, which can be satisfied in various ways that differ in their impacts on planetary well-being. When there are multiple ways of fulfilling human needs, those with the least harmful impacts on planetary well-being and the most beneficial impacts on needs satisfaction globally, between and within human communities, should be prioritized to move towards planetary well-being. Simultaneously, it should be kept in mind that the best need satisfiers may be different in different locations and societies and should hence remain open to community-level reflections and some level of individual freedom of choice (*cf.*, Nussbaum and Sen, 1993) because of the importance of autonomy for human well-being. Understanding and propping up the factors that promote pro-environmental behaviour (including lower material consumption) at individual levels is also crucial. Related behaviour patterns are influenced by, for example, institutional, economic, social, emotional, motivational, value, attitude, and awareness factors (Kollmuss and Agyeman, 2002). The multiscalar view of processes calls for attending to the dynamics between different levels, such as the impact of global processes on the needs satisfaction, and preferences within different communities, from the viewpoint of planetary well-being.

Measures and targets for decision-making

The fact that more than 25% of the 134,425 assessed species are threatened with extinction (The International Union for Conservation of Nature (IUCN), 2021) manifests the lack of well-being of nonhuman life on Earth today. Improving planetary well-being necessitates halting or transforming the harmful human activities and fostering actions to restore the integrity of Earth system and ecosystem processes that have been impaired by past actions. Ecological remediation, rehabilitation, and restoration advance this aim at local levels (Gann *et al.*, 2019). Data about the national and regional drivers of extinction threats can be a valuable source of information to identify those human practices (such as livestock farming and ranching, logging and wood harvesting, and the release of effluents) that are most damaging to planetary well-being at regional and national scales, and to justify urgent changes in these actions. This information about the direct drivers of extinction threat is available in the national/regional IUCN Red Lists although the coverage is not yet global. Information from the IUCN Red Lists also helps to identify those ecosystems and processes that require the most urgent protection and restoration actions to improve the viability of threatened species and populations.

From Red Lists, it is also possible to construct indices that can be used as surrogate measures for regional and global states and trends in planetary well-being, at least as far as nonhuman nature is concerned. As we have pointed out earlier, the status of populations and species can serve as a good indicator for the integrity of processes that are critical for the satisfaction of the needs of various living systems. The Red List Index (RLI) calculates the average threat status of the set of species included in the index. RLI takes values between 0 (all species extinct) and 1 (all species in the "Least Concern" category). As we define planetary well-being also in terms of the persistence of lineages to the future (see Table 1.2), RLIs for well-chosen sets of species at regional and global scales could be used to measure the status of planetary well-being at different scales (however, extinction threats due to nonhuman causes, such as volcanic eruptions and natural diseases, should not count negatively to the score of planetary well-being). Regional and global RLI values approaching 1 could also serve as intuitive, specific, and measurable targets for efforts to stop and reverse current declines in biodiversity, like the UNFCCC target of limiting global warming to 1.5 °C.

Progress towards planetary well-being ultimately depends on the ability of human societies to organize the systems for satisfying human needs so that they do not compromise the integrity of Earth system and ecosystem processes. Societal goals and targets, and the indicators of progress, should thus be aligned with the aim of maintaining and restoring the integrity of the processes that are constitutive for planetary well-being while providing for the satisfaction of human needs. The first step in this direction could be the adoption of indicators that emphasize sufficiency and the meeting of basic material, social and psychological needs while depreciating environmentally and socially harmful development (see *e.g.*, Rogers *et al.*, 2012; Hickel, 2020).

Bridging divergent worldviews

We believe that planetary well-being could enrich the conceptual toolbox to foster transformation to a world that promotes well-being more equally by unifying systems-thinking and both human and nonhuman well-being to a single, intuitively appealing concept. Unlike many related concepts, planetary well-being avoids anthropocentrism and allows for discussions onhuman and nonhuman well-being in a common framework. The emphasis on well-being as the satisfaction of basic needs helps draw attention to the plight of underprivileged human communities and socio-economic groups and to the literally existential plight of nonhuman nature.

The concept speaks to different scientific disciplines, which we have tested during the process of writing this work, and it is approachable to different domains in the public sector, at different levels, as well as to civil society and private sector actors whose cooperation is required for solving the ecological crisis. The concept of planetary well-being does not aim to replace previous conceptual frameworks everywhere but, rather, to supplement them by providing a multiscalar and non-anthropocentric approach to discussing the pressing questions of environmental and social challenges. Planetary well-being—the opportunity for both humans and nonhumans to have their needs satisfied now and in the future—can, and should, become the ultimate goal of human activities and cooperation.

Acknowledgements

Writing has been supported by the following grants: the Kone Foundation (RD, ME, JP); Strategic Research Council Finland grants 327284 (TK) and 313015 (MS); and ERC grant COMPLEX-FISH 770884 (TP).

Notes

1 Originally published as an article (including Supplementary Material): Kortetmäki *et al.* (2021).
2 JYU.Wisdom community: This paper is a result of a collective effort and intense trans-disciplinary discussions by the JYU.Wisdom community. All authors contributed to the work significantly and are listed in alphabetical order, except for the first three and the last author, who are together considered as the shared first author.
3 For example, Schlosberg (2007, p. 148) notes: "It is simply not possible to talk about the flourishing of individual animals without reference to the environment in which this flourishing is to occur. Systems are living entities with their own integrity; atomizing nature into isolated animals devalues a form of life, and the way that this form of life flourishes". He acknowledges how the integrity of larger systems contributes to the functioning of individuals and proposes it meaningful to talk about flourishing at both levels. However, in Schlosberg's account, it seems that individuals are after all "subjugated" to the functioning integrity of the larger system; moreover, he does not clarify which non-individual systems can flourish (be well) except for doubting that species may not be able to have well-being (see Kortetmäki, 2018), which is a problematic potential exclusion. Moreover, the theoretical and unidisciplinary nature of Schlosberg's work lacks the explanation what he means by systems and the way in which their flourishing is interconnected, which he (2007, p. 157) leaves to be the task of interdisciplinary work—which we are doing now.

4 It is possible to suggest and think about the well-being of the Earth system as a whole, understood as a stable geophysical state of the system (and potentially some other conditions). There are two reasons we do not address this further. First, high planetary well-being would also imply the well-being of the Earth system because the Earth system comprises Earth's interacting processes the integrity of which is constitutive to planetary well-being. Second, the normative viewpoint that we have adopted here would not in any case attach inherent value to the well-being of the Earth system. It is too unclear what it would mean for the Earth system to "realise its system-specific characteristics and capacities" (part of the definition of well-being used in this work, see Table 1.1). Consequently, we consider that the potential well-being of the Earth system as a stable geophysical state is sufficiently covered by planetary well-being.)

References

Alvaredo, F. *et al.* (2018) *World Inequality Report 2018.* Cambridge, MA: Belknap Press.

Bar-On, Y.M., Phillips, R. and Milo, R. (2018) 'The biomass distribution on Earth', *PNAS*, 115(25), pp. 6506–6511. https://doi.org/10.1073/pnas.1711842115

Bartussek, H. (1999) 'A review of the animal needs index (ANI) for the assessment of animals' well-being in the housing systems for Austrian proprietary products and legislation', *Livestock Production Science*, 61(2–3), pp. 179–192. https://doi.org/10.1016/S0301-6226(99)00067-6

Broom, D.M. (1991) 'Animal welfare: concepts and measurement', *Journal of Animal Science*, 69(10), pp. 4167–4175. https://doi.org/10.2527/1991.69104167x

Brymer, E., Cuddihy, T.F. and Sharma-Brymer, V. (2010) 'The role of nature-based experiences in the development and maintenance of wellness', *Asia-Pacific Journal of Health, Sport and Physical Education*, 1(2), pp. 21–27. https://doi.org/10.1080/18377122.2010.9730328

Bunge, M. (2003) *Emergence and Convergence: Qualitative Novelty and the Unity of Knowledge.* Toronto: University of Toronto Press.

Bunge, M. (2004) 'How does it work? The search for explanatory mechanisms', *Philosophy of the Social Sciences*, 34(2), pp. 182–210. https://doi.org/10.1177/0048393103262550

Cameron, J. and Abouchar, J. (1991) 'The precautionary principle: A fundamental principle of law and policy for the protection of the global environment', *Boston College International and Comparative Law Review*, 14(1), pp. 1–27.

Cederholm, C. J. *et al.* (1999) 'Pacific salmon carcasses: Essential contributions of nutrients and energy for aquatic and terrestrial ecosystems', *Fisheries*, 24(10), pp. 6–15. https://doi.org/10.1577/1548-8446(1999)024<0006:Psc>2.0.Co;2

Cripps, E. (2010) 'Saving the polar bear, saving the world: Can the capabilities approach do justice to humans, animals and ecosystems?', *Res Publica*, 16, pp. 1–22. https://doi.org/10.1007/s11158-010-9106-2

Crutzen, P.J. and Stoermer, E.F. (2000) 'The 'Anthropocene'', *IGBP Global Change Newsletter*, 41, pp. 17–18.

Díaz, S. *et al.* (2015) 'The IPBES Conceptual Framework—connecting nature and people', *Current Opinion in Environmental Sustainability*, 14, pp. 1–16. https://doi.org/10.1016/j.cosust.2014.11.002

Díaz, S. *et al.* (2019) 'Pervasive human-driven decline of life on Earth points to the need for transformative change', *Science*, 366(6471), eaax3100. https://doi.org/10.1126/science.aax3100

Doyal, L. and Gough, I. (1984) 'A theory of human needs', *Critical Social Policy*, 4(10), pp. 6–38. https://doi.org/10.1177/026101838400401002

Dryzek, J.S. (2005) *The Politics of the Earth: Environmental Discourses.* 2nd edn. Oxford: Oxford University Press.

Dryzek, J. S. and Pickering, J. (2018) *The Politics of the Anthropocene.* Oxford: Oxford University Press. https://doi.org/10.1093/oso/9780198809616.001.0001

Gann, G.D. *et al.* (2019) 'International principles and standards for the practice of ecological restoration. Second edition', *Restoration Ecology,* 27(S1), pp. S3–S46. https://doi.org/10.1111/rec.13035

Gough, I. (2015) 'Climate change and sustainable welfare: the centrality of human needs', *Cambridge Journal of Economics,* 39(5), pp. 1191–1214. https://doi.org/10.1093/cje/bev039

Gough, I. (2017) 'Recomposing consumption: defining necessities for sustainable and equitable well-being', *Philosophical Transactions of the Royal Society A Mathematical, Physical and Engineering Sciences,* 375(2095), 20160379. https://doi.org/10.1098/rsta.2016.0379

Guillen-Royo, M., Guardiola, J. and Garcia-Quero, F. (2017) 'Sustainable development in times of economic crisis: A needs-based illustration from Granada (Spain)', *Journal of Cleaner Production,* 150, pp. 267–276. https://doi.org/10.1016/j.jclepro.2017.03.008

Hailwood, S. (2012) 'Bewildering Nussbaum: Capability justice and predation', *Journal of Political Philosophy,* 20(3), pp. 293–313. https://doi.org/10.1111/j.1467-9760.2010.00392.x

Hickel, J. (2020) 'The sustainable development index: measuring the ecological efficiency of human development in the anthropocene', *Ecological Economics,* 167, 106331. https://doi.org/10.1016/j.ecolecon.2019.05.011

Hornborg, A. (1998) 'Towards an ecological theory of unequal exchange: Articulating world system theory and ecological economics', *Ecological Economics,* 25(1), pp. 127–136. https://doi.org/10.1016/S0921-8009(97)00100-6

IPBES (2018) *Summary for Policymakers of the Assessment Report on Land Degradation and Restoration of the Intergovernmental Science-Policy Platform on Biodiversity and Ecosystem Services.* Zenodo. https://doi.org/10.5281/zenodo.3237411

IPBES (2019) *Summary for Policymakers of the Global Assessment Report on Biodiversity and Ecosystem Services of the Intergovernmental Science-Policy Platform on Biodiversity and Ecosystem Services.* Zenodo. https://doi.org/10.5281/zenodo.3553579

IPCC (2019) *Climate Change and Land: An IPCC Special Report on Climate Change, Desertification, Land Degradation, Sustainable Land Management, Food Security, and Greenhouse Gas Fluxes in Terrestrial Ecosystems.* IPCC.

IUCN (2021) *The Red* List. Available at: https://www.iucnredlist.org/ (Accessed: 7 August 2021).

Jackson, T. (2017) *Prosperity without Growth: Foundations for the Economy of Tomorrow.* 2nd edn. Abingdon: Routledge.

Kates, R.W. *et al.* (2001) 'Environment and development. Sustainability Science', *Science,* 292(5517), pp. 641–642. https://doi.org/10.1126/science.1059386

Keyes, C.L. (2005) 'Mental illness and/or mental health? Investigating axioms of the complete state model of health', *Journal of Consulting & Clinical Psychology,* 73, pp. 539–548. https://doi.org/10.1037/0022-006X.73.3.539

Kohler, F. *et al.* (2019) 'Embracing diverse worldviews to share planet Earth', *Conservation Biology,* 33(5), pp. 1014–1022. https://doi.org/10.1111/cobi.13304

Kokko, K. *et al.* (2013) 'Structure and continuity of well-being in mid-adulthood: A longitudinal study', *Journal of Happiness Studies,* 14, pp. 99–114. https://doi.org/10.1007/s10902-011-9318-y

Kollmuss A. and Agyeman, J. (2002) 'Mind the gap: Why do people act environmentally and what are the barriers to pro-environmental behavior?', *Environmental Education Research*, 8(3), pp. 239–260. https://doi.org/10.1080/13504620220145401

Kortetmäki, T. (2017) 'Applying the capabilities approach to ecosystems: Resilience as ecosystem capability', *Environmental Ethics*, 39(1), pp. 39–56. https://doi.org/10.5840/enviroethics20179263

Kortetmäki, T. (2018) 'Can species have capabilities, and what if they can?', *Journal of Agricultural and Environmental Ethics*, 31(3), pp. 307–323. https://doi.org/10.1007/s10806-018-9726-7

Kortetmäki, T. *et al.* (2021) 'Planetary well-being', *Humanities and Social Sciences Communications*, 8, 258. https://doi.org/10.1057/s41599-021-00899-3

Lade, S.J. *et al.* (2019) 'Human impacts on planetary boundaries amplified by Earth system interactions', *Nature Sustainability*, 3, pp. 119–128. https://doi.org/10.1038/s41893-019-0454-4

Liu, J. *et al.* (2015) 'Sustainability. Systems integration for global sustainability', *Science*, 347(6225), 1258832. https://doi.org/10.1126/science.1258832

Liu, J. *et al.* (2018) 'Nexus approaches to global sustainable development', *Nature Sustainability*, 1(9), pp. 466–476. https://doi.org/10.1038/s41893-018-0135-8

Malm, A. and Hornborg, A. (2014) 'The geology of mankind? A critique of the Anthropocene narrative', *The Anthropocene Review*, 1(1), pp. 62–69. https://doi.org/10.1177/2053019613516291

Max-Neef, M.A. (1991) *Human Scale Development: Conception, Application and Further Reflections*. New York: The Apex Press.

Mayer, F.S. and Frantz, C.M. (2004) 'The connectedness to nature scale: A measure of individual's feeling in community in nature', *Journal of Environmental Psychology*, 24, pp. 503–515. https://doi.org/10.1016/j.jenvp.2004.10.001

Newsome, K., Taylor, P., Bair, J., and Rainnie, A. (2015) *Putting Labour in its Place: Labour Process Analysis and Global Value Chains*. London: Palgrave.

Nussbaum, M.C. (2006) *Frontiers of Justice: Disability, Nationality, Species Membership*. Cambridge, MA: Harvard University Press.

Nussbaum, M.C. (2011) *Creating Capabilities: The Human Development Approach*. Cambridge, MA: Harvard University Press.

Nussbaum, M.C. and Sen, A. (eds.) (1993) *The Quality of Life*. Oxford: Clarendon Press.

O'Neill, D.W. *et al.* (2018) 'A good life for all within planetary boundaries', *Nature Sustainability*, 1(2), pp. 88–95. https://doi.org/10.1038/s41893-018-0021-4

Ostrom, E. (2009) 'A general framework for analyzing sustainability of social-ecological systems', *Science*, 325(5939), pp. 419–422. https://doi.org/10.1126/science.1172133

Prescott-Allen, R. (2001) *The Wellbeing of Nations*. Washington, DC: Island Press.

Reid, W.V. *et al.* (2010) 'Environment and development. Earth system science for global sustainability: Grand challenges', *Science*, 330(6006), pp. 916–917. https://doi.org/10.1126/science.1196263

Rice, C.M. (2013) 'Defending the objective list theory of well-being', *Ratio*, 26, pp. 196–211. https://doi.org/10.1111/rati.12007

Rockström, J. *et al.* (2009) 'A safe operation space for humanity', *Nature*, 461, pp. 472–475.

Rogers, D.S. *et al.* (2012) 'A vision for human well-being: Transition to social sustainability', *Current Opinion in Environmental Sustainability*, 4, pp. 61–73. https://doi.org/10.1016/j.cosust.2012.01.013

Rolston, H.I. (1985) 'Duties to endangered species', *BioScience*, 35, pp. 718–726. https://doi.org/10.2307/1310053

Rolston, H.I. (2002) 'What do we mean by the intrinsic value and integrity of plants and animals', in *Genetic Engineering and the Intrinsic Value and Integrity of Plants and Animals* [workshop]. Edinburg: Royal Botanic Garden, 18–21 September.

Roszak, T., Gomes, M.E. and Kanner, A.D. (1995) *Ecopsychology: Restoring the Earth, Healing the Mind.* San Francisco, CA: Sierra Club Books.

Rowland, F.S. (2006) 'Stratospheric ozone depletion', *Philosophical Transactions of the Royal Society B Biological Sciences,* 361(1469), pp. 769–790. https://doi.org/10.1098/rstb.2005.1783

Running, S.W. (2012) 'Ecology. A measurable planetary boundary for the biosphere', *Science,* 337(6101), pp. 1458–1459. https://doi.org/10.1126/science.1227620

Schlosberg, D. (2007) *Defining Environmental Justice: Theories, Movements, and Nature.* Oxford: Oxford University Press. https://doi.org/10.1093/ACPROF:OSO/9780199286294.001.0001

Singer, P. (2002) *Animal Liberation.* 1st Ecco paperback ed. New York: Ecco.

Steffen, W. *et al.* (2015a) 'Sustainability. Planetary boundaries: Guiding human development on a changing planet', *Science,* 347(6223), 1259855. https://doi.org/10.1126/science.1259855

Steffen, W. *et al.* (2015b) 'The trajectory of the Anthropocene: The Great Acceleration', *Anthropocene Review,* 2(1), pp. 81–98. https://doi.org/10.1177/2053019614564785

UN (2015) *Transforming Our World: The 2030 Agenda for Sustainable Development.* A/RES/70/1. Geneva: United Nations General Assembly.

UN Environment (2019) *Global Environment Outlook – GEO-6: Healthy Planet, Healthy People.* Cambridge: Cambridge University Press. https://doi.org/10.1017/9781108627146

van der Ent, R.J. *et al.* (2010) 'Origin and fate of atmospheric moisture over continents', *Water Resources Research,* 46(9). https://doi.org/10.1029/2010WR009127

van der Esch, S. *et al.* (2017) 'Exploring future changes in land use and land condition and the impacts on food, water, climate change and biodiversity: Scenarios for the UNCCD Global Land Outlook'. The Hague: PBL Netherlands Environmental Assessment Agency.

Warren, M.A. (1997) *Moral Status: Obligations to Persons and Other Living Things.* Oxford: Clarendon Press.

Washington, H. (2020) 'Ecosystem services—a key step forward or Anthropocentrism's 'Trojan Horse' in conservation?', in Kopnina, H. and Washington, H. (eds.) *Conservation.* Cham: Springer, pp. 73–88. https://doi.org/10.1007/978-3-030-13905-6_6

Watson, J.E.M. *et al.* (2016) 'Catastrophic declines in wilderness areas undermine global environment targets', *Current Biology,* 26(21), pp. 2929–2934. https://doi.org/10.1016/j.cub.2016.08.049

WCED (1987) *Our Common Future [Brundtland Report].* A/42/427. Geneva: United Nations General Assembly.

Wemelsfelder, F. (1997) 'The scientific validity of subjective concepts in models of animal welfare', *pplied Animal Behaviour Science,* 53(1–2), pp. 75–88. https://doi.org/10.1016/S0168-1591(96)01152-5

Willemen, L. *et al.* (2020) 'How to halt the global decline of lands', *Nature Sustainability,* 3(3), pp. 164-166. https://doi.org/10.1038/s41893-020-0477-x

Winter, D.D.N. and Koger, S.M. (2004) *The Psychology of Environmental Problems.* 2nd edn. New York: Psychology Press.

2

PLANETARY WELL-BEING

Ontology and ethics

*Teea Kortetmäki, Mikael Puurtinen, Miikka Salo,
Gonzalo Cortés-Capano, Sanna Karkulehto and
Janne S. Kotiaho*

Introduction

Planetary well-being is defined as "a state in which the integrity of Earth system and ecosystem processes remains unimpaired to a degree that lineages can persist to the future as parts of ecosystems, and organisms (including humans) can realize their typical characteristics and capacities" (Kortetmäki *et al.*, 2021, p. 4). This "state" is a dynamic rather than a static condition: Planetary well-being may increase and decline, and human activities influence it greatly. Understanding these dynamics necessitates grounding the ontology and ethics of planetary well-being. In this chapter, we examine how the conceptualization of planetary well-being is grounded and positioned in the broader theoretical landscape, both in ontological and ethical terms. We also reflect upon the overall conceptual underpinnings of planetary well-being and its implications for the different well-being frames that are used for guiding societal development and policy-making, hoping to encourage further research. It should be noted that we limit our normative reasoning to human activities: Although large-scale natural events might also affect planetary well-being by disrupting large-scale processes, only humans are *morally responsible* for their activities' impacts on planetary well-being.

Ontology behind planetary well-being: Systems and processes

Ontologically, planetary well-being takes a systems- and process-oriented approach. Planetary well-being commits to the Bungean type of systemism (see *e.g.*, Bunge, 2000) where every "thing" is a system or a component of one (Kortetmäki *et al.*, 2021). Ontologically speaking, a system is an entity that consists of interacting components and has structures and processes that are characteristic of

DOI: 10.4324/9781003334002-4

the given kind of system. All systems are situated in a context (environment) where they interact with other systems.

Most systems are material and independent of human and nonhuman minds.[1] Communication systems as well as human-made complex systems, such as schools, financial systems, and preservable semiotic and symbolic systems (texts and images), may be partially immaterial but their immaterial parts have causal effects only through cognition and action, *i.e.*, through the material neural system (Elder-Vass, 2010a). For example, money does nothing unless humans believe it does and agree with (and act upon) the rules determining what money can do.

Systems have both aggregative and emergent properties. Aggregative properties result from the simple addition of the properties of the parts. A classic example of an aggregative property is mass (*ibid.*). Emergent properties are those novel properties that emerge particularly due to the ordering and interaction of the components in a system (Bunge, 2000). Emergent properties are those that make the system "greater than the sum of its parts": Its components do not have such properties in themselves, nor in aggregate. Certain emergent properties, such as the ability of systems to reproduce and preserve themselves, and sentience, also add to the properties of a system in a way that is relevant to moral considerations (see the section on ethical underpinnings).

Emergent properties constitute the basis for a view of the stratified nature of reality. Various phenomena have physical, chemical, biological, psychological, and social levels. Various scientific disciplines have also specialized in the research of a specific level of reality. While scientific activities may often be most fruitful when a level is studied with the concepts, theories, and methods developed for that particular level, it is also possible and sometimes valuable to combine tools or apply them at different levels. For example, psychological level phenomena can be viewed through psychology but also approached with the tools of neurobiology (a lower level), or with social psychology and sociology (a higher level). Phenomena in complex systems, such as societies, can only be explained comprehensively by studying them with multi- and interdisciplinary approaches.

In the planetary well-being framework, the well-being of a system is understood in a nonsubjective way, as the functional integrity of that system. Well-being means meeting the needs conveyed through critical processes at the biological, mental, and social levels. This understanding is in line with the above-described systems- and process-oriented approach where also non-conscious entities can gain or lose well-being. In the case of conscious entities such as sentient animals (those who can feel pain and suffer), consciousness does not always capture all critical processes. Also, some subjects with rich imagination and tendencies to comparison (many human beings) may consider some non-critical processes hastily as critical to their well-being. Hence, the subjective experience of well-being—although generally a good indicator of, for example, experienced human well-being—is not necessarily accurate or a comprehensive description of the state of well-being of an individual in the sense of the definition relevant to planetary well-being.

Processes and relations

Planetary well-being is rooted in the idea that all living systems come into existence (emerge), develop, and behave in ways that result from complex sets of causal relations and patterns of species association (assemblages/communities of species) (Banitz *et al.*, 2022; DeLanda, 2016). Relations and feedbacks between interacting entities generate emergent properties: Many ecological processes are produced by the interactions between species (Folke *et al.*, 2016). For example, pollination as an ecological process often emerges from the relations between animal pollinators and the plants they pollinate (see also Chapter 6 for soil processes). These processes are mostly contingent: If the interactions end, animal pollination as an emergent process would cease to exist (DeLanda, 2016). The integrity of ecological processes in turn is vital for the continuity and well-being of the members of the communities, that is species and organisms (Levin *et al.*, 2013).

It is important to note that in many relations between the entities (*e.g.*, species) and the emergent systems they belong to (*e.g.*, ecosystems), entities maintain their relative autonomy and are not fused together into a homogeneous whole (DeLanda, 2016). For example, individuals can be connected to each other in many ways yet also remain as individuals in their community. Acknowledging the relative autonomy of entities as parts-of-wholes implies in some cases replaceability or functional redundancy within processes: A pollination process can (at least in many cases) continue even if the current pollinator species is replaced with other species, local or exotic, or robot brushes, as long as the replaced entities realize the same functions in the system. However, very rarely does a species have only one role in an ecosystem. Pollinators, for example, also interact in numerous other assemblages beyond pollination such as comprising a food source for other species in that system. This overall complexity of relationships means that precautionary measures and preventive action should be adopted to avoid potential harm to the integrity of larger ecological systems, and hence, to planetary well-being.

Knowledge about the interactions between and among Earth's geophysical systems, ecosystems, and human-created systems is still very limited (*e.g.*, Mastrángelo *et al.*, 2019). The ontological basis of planetary well-being implies the need for interdisciplinary work to make sense of the connections between different processes that comprise planetary well-being. This also necessitates acknowledging epistemic humility: We humans will likely never be able to know, and thus take into account, all relevant relations and interactions between different species. To avoid too simplistic ontological or epistemic assumptions, it is important to recognize the social dimensions of such knowledge, while asserting the reality of the material dimension of the problems (Bhaskar *et al.*, 2010).

The ontological position taken in planetary well-being challenges traditional dualisms between humans and nature and the assumption that humans' interactions with (the use of) nonhuman entities or materials could be considered in isolation from their ecosystems and processes. Planetary well-being emphasizes that humans are part of co-evolving systems and participants in multispecies processes in nature, not external to the rest of the natural world (*cf.*, Berkes and Folke, 1998). The processual viewpoint in planetary well-being also highlights the presence of agency throughout nature, as life is intertwined in these processes in myriad ways: Humans are not the active agent using and managing passive nature, but a participant in the webs of actants. However, moral agency—the capacity to think of (and shape) one's actions with an ethical perspective—and, thus, also the responsibility to act ethically, is specific only to humans. As the technological capacity of humans to use nonhuman world and interfere with its processes has grown, the concept of moral agency has also become more important since human actions can have such huge and far-reaching effects on planetary well-being.

Notably, the ontological basis of planetary well-being described here leaves room for different, more detailed ontological perceptions. For example, it is possible to emphasize the different levels of complexity in the existence of entities. Moreover, questions about how inter-entity relations are constitutive of the entities engaged in such relations, remain open to different characterizations. This, we believe, allows the engagement with planetary well-being from different perspectives and worldviews (see also Chapters 3 and 8).

The ethical underpinnings of planetary well-being

Planetary well-being is based on certain normative premises, some of which are influenced by the above-described ontology, that constitutes the ethical underpinnings of planetary well-being. By "underpinnings", we emphasize that such considerations still leave room for the diversity of further ethical elaborations. In our treatment, we adhere to scientific realism about values. Scientific realism

> commits one to treating values as socially produced and historically contingent. This does not, however, prevent us from reasoning about values, nor from developing critiques by combining ethical reasoning with a theoretical understanding of the social world and its possibilities.
>
> *(Elder-Vass, 2010b, p. 33)*

Most importantly, planetary well-being transcends human-prioritizing value hierarchies (moral anthropocentrism) for more inclusive and equal valuation. The more inclusive stance is known as moral non-anthropocentrism or more-than-human ethics (*e.g.*, Puig de la Bellacasa, 2017; see also Kohler *et al.,* 2019) and broadens the sphere of moral considerability. Morally considerable entities have a particular moral status and moral (intrinsic or non-instrumental) value regardless of their utility for humans. The value of nonhuman well-being is not derived from its importance to humans (without denying such importance): In the planetary well-being framework, both human and nonhuman well-beings are morally worthy for their own sake.

The basic sphere of moral considerability in planetary well-being grounds moral value in the self-regulative and self-regenerative capacity of living entities, extending moral considerability beyond humans (Kortetmäki *et al.*, 2021, p. 3). This is closely connected to the functional integrity, the well-being, of such entities. Understood this way, well-being as a morally relevant idea also extends beyond individuals. However, since individuals' striving for well-being unavoidably generates continuous conflicts between organisms, and because the organisms are so vast in their number, it would be extremely difficult or even impossible to adequately capture ethical concern for all well-being by paying attention to each individual. Thus, planetary well-being seeks to focus on another level to capture the moral concern for all well-being in a way that is meaningful and applicable to guiding societal development and policy evaluation. To succeed in this, planetary well-being takes a dual standpoint to moral valuation: First, it takes lineages (a group of organisms with a shared genetic ancestry) as the key entities of moral concern, and second, it embraces a multicriterial valuation that is relevant for addressing the diversity in how well-being is manifested in different life forms.

Focusing on lineages (*e.g.*, species and populations) is a theoretically and pragmatically satisfactory way to capture the moral concern for all nonhuman well-being. This is for two reasons. First and foremost, lineages as species possess particularly weighty value. Each species manifests a unique historical continuum and story of evolving life; many lineages have existed for thousands, even millions of years, and many of them will continue to exist far beyond the duration of human communities. However, if a species is driven into extinction by human activities, it is likely lost forever; the irreversibility of the harm and the piece of history lost due to it makes the harm particularly severe (Rolston, 1985). Second, pragmatic reasons also favour the focus on lineages. The status of lineages indicates well the overall state of affairs regarding the possibility of nonhuman entities to satisfy their needs and strive for well-being. Population declines or the increased number of endangered species are signs that some critical processes are failing and compromising planetary well-being (see Chapter 14).

Another ethically focal acknowledgement in planetary well-being, already highlighted, is that both human and nonhuman well-being are valuable for their own sake. The well-being of various humans and nonhumans requires sufficient integrity of Earth system and ecosystem processes (shared preconditions for all well-being) but also the satisfaction of species-specific needs. This implies that planetary well-being is inclusive of multicriterial approaches to moral considerability where the moral status can be grounded in several criteria. The multicriterial approach also has the advantage of being much better equipped to explain some of the carefully considered ethical intuitions that are illustrated by the range of problem cases used to test various moral approaches. For example, single-criterion approaches that attribute moral value only to an entity's characteristic of having a life would not explain why we might have special (additional) duties to the individuals of endangered species (Warren, 2000, pp. 172–173). The use of multiple criteria also helps distinguish and clarify why we have such different duties to different morally considerable entities: Our duties to fellow human beings are different from our duties to nonhuman individuals, let alone the duties to non-individual entities such as species or populations.

In multicriterial moral valuation, different criteria constitute together the overall sphere of moral considerability, which is comprised of different (overlapping) spheres of morally considerable entities. Different spheres set different demands and limitations to acceptable human behaviour, depending on the features of the systems. Sentience, for example, constitutes one feature-specific sphere of moral considerability. The well-being of sentient creatures sets some additional well-being related requirements because sentience influences the behavioural and physical needs of these beings. Many of those activities that are wrong towards sentient beings (such as industrialized meat production) would not, to our current knowledge, harm non-sentient beings and would therefore be wrong only when practised towards sentient beings. This way, multicriterial valuation is also compatible with the view that we human beings owe some species-specific duties to fellow human beings.

The broadest sphere of moral considerability includes all entities that can have well-being and have self-regenerative capacities. This broadest sphere is relevant for the framing of well-being in contexts that aim to guide overall societal development. Planetary well-being, thus, means a paradigmatic change in how well-being should be framed in such contexts. The inclusive notion of well-being broadens the scope of consideration when the well-being impacts of societal development are to be assessed (or when policy planning and implementation aim to improve the overall well-being or more equal well-being). As a non-anthropocentric notion, planetary well-being requires that a society-guiding conception of well-being is framed in a way that considers nonhuman well-being for its own sake, not only as a factor that influences human well-being. This implies that the possibilities of non-humans to satisfy their needs, now and in the future, must not be undermined when societies strive to increase well-being or promote development that is assumed to increase well-being indirectly.

The needs-based understanding of well-being also highlights the universality of human needs, which has ramifications on the appropriate framing of human well-being in societal contexts. Ramifications concern universality and inclusiveness. Regarding universality, an objective approach to well-being—a conception where well-being is neither defined nor usually measured by subjective experiences but by external criteria—is necessary for considering social contexts and inequalities adequately (*e.g.*, Nussbaum, 2011).[2] Objective approaches have a strong foothold in justice and social policy studies (*e.g.*, Doyal and Gough, 1984; Nussbaum, 2011). Protecting the opportunity of all humans to satisfy their needs and strive for a good life is a condition for minimum social justice (*e.g.*, Nussbaum, 2011). This condition of considering *all* humans is quite demanding: The needs fulfilment of current generations should take the global perspective and must not compromise the possibility of future generations to fulfil their needs (Max-Neef, 1991; the

World Commission on Environment and Development (WCED), 1987). The needs-based understanding of well-being is thereby also more attentive (than subjective accounts) to the situation of disadvantaged human communities and groups. It urges the prioritization of the satisfaction of universal human needs before investing in the fulfilment of desires that stem from the increased standard of living in high-income communities and consumerist marketing processes (see also Chapters 9 and 10), even though such desires might be perceived locally as important to sub-jective well-being. Overall, an objective approach to well-being provides a tangible set of criteria for conceptualizing well-being for societal development purposes in a more suitable and morally acceptable way than subjective approaches do (*e.g.*, Doyal and Gough, 1984; Kortetmäki *et al.*, 2021; Nussbaum, 2011; Rice, 2013).

The objective approaches to well-being also allow the moral inclusiveness that planetary well-being seeks to promote. Some approaches already extend inclusive-ness beyond human well-being and thus provide a compatible platform for fur-ther theorizing about the politics of planetary well-being. They have addressed the well-being of nonhuman animals (*e.g.*, Broom, 1991; Nussbaum, 2011), other organisms, and even species and ecosystems (Kortetmäki, 2017; Schlosberg, 2007; see also Prescott-Allen, 2001). Adopting the non-anthropocentric, inclusive fram-ing of well-being to guide societal development makes a big difference for the consideration of legitimate and illegitimate societal actions, policies, and develop-ment trajectories. It renders the nonhuman world from a background resource and service provider into an ensemble of active recipients, beneficiaries, and sufferers, of societal development. The relevant community affected by societal development and policies always includes the biotic community (Dryzek and Pickering, 2018).

Planetary well-being and moral duties

Assigning at least some moral value to well-being for its own sake means that moral duties related to well-being arise in relation to any entities that may gain or lose well-being. Such duties, however, are not identical towards all morally consid-erable entities. Negative duties, or duties to avoid causing harm, comprise the cor-nerstone of environmental ethical duties to nonhuman nature. Because planetary well-being comprises processes whose functioning is the general precondition for the well-being of morally considerable entities, the primary duty for planetary well-being would be the negative duty to avoid impairing those processes. However, the impairments already caused—and the consequent harm to nonhuman and human well-being at all levels—suggest that positive duties to restore the prospects of nonhumans to strive for well-being can be justifiably demanded. We see this kind of positive duty, or a duty to actively promote good, as crucial. The moral obliga-tion to aim at restoring the impaired Earth and ecosystem processes is an important ethical implication of the idea of planetary well-being.

May positive duties also imply duties to advance planetary well-being even in situations where the impairment is not human-originated? The quick answer intuitively appears to be "no": Humans are unlikely to have duties to compensate the impacts of volcanic eruptions to nonhuman species. However, the actual question is more complex since it is increasingly hard to tell whether the negative impacts from "nonhuman activities" are exacerbated by human activities. For example, volcanic eruptions might today induce greater harm to nonhuman well-being because the human-induced habitat degradation prevents nonhumans from migrating to new places from areas damaged by the eruption. Addressing the question of positive duties beyond restoration goes, in its complexity, beyond this chapter's scope. Here it can be noted that even for now, the positive duty to restore processes that comprise planetary well-being but have been degraded by human activities is so significant that taking it seriously implies transformative changes to human activities.

When it comes to duties to individuals, the planetary well-being framework goes beyond individualistic approaches in its framing of moral considerability. This does not need to render the well-being of individuals unmeaningful or value-less. Both individuals and entities beyond individuals, such as species or ecosystems, are acknowledged to be morally considerable. Yet, the duties for planetary well-being must be imposed on levels higher than the individual to make the obligations feasible. The ethical framework that underpins planetary well-being allows the integration of various approaches with the attribution of moral considerability (also inherent value) in environmental ethics. Yet, the requirements set by planetary well-being limit the range for the approaches that planetary well-being embracing pluralism can accommodate. Moral obligations to individuals, whatever they comprise (depending on the chosen ethical approach), must not require actions that would cause societies to undermine planetary well-being.

Mapping planetary well-being in environmental ethics

How is the normative core commitment of planetary well-being positioned within environmental ethics? Inclusive approaches that grant moral considerability to non-humans comprise three stances where moral considerability is grounded in different attributes (*e.g.*, Goodpaster, 1978; Schweitzer, 1969; Taylor, 1981; for a good summary, see Warren, 2000): sentientism, biocentrism, and ecocentrism. Sentientism (*e.g.*, Nussbaum, 2011; Singer, 2002) only considers sentient animals. Biocentrism grants moral considerability to individual organisms that act as teleological systems so that something can be good or bad for them.[3] It has also been proposed that biocentric moral considerability is grounded in the state of being alive as the ultimate goal or good, for which all other goals are instrumental. Ecocentrism, in turn, emphasizes the stability and integrity of ecosystems and/or ecological entities (such as lineages) more broadly but essentially beyond individuals who are not of primary concern in ecocentric approaches (Callicott, 1986; Leopold, 1949; Naess, 2008). The most-cited articulation of an ecocentric viewpoint is Leopold's (1949, pp. 224–225) land ethic thesis: "A thing is right when it tends to preserve the integrity, stability, and beauty of the biotic community. It is wrong when it tends otherwise."

Ecological dynamics entail that individuals' striving for well-being creates constant conflicts. Thus, even if an individual's well-being is valuable for its own sake, we align planetary well-being in the camp of approaches which posit that individualist non-anthropocentrism cannot meaningfully ground normative guidance for societal development. Despite works that attempt to resolve these conflicts in different ways by, for example, determining certain simple rules (such as choosing the action with the least number of harmed individuals) or principles for making prioritizations for certain goods to be protected or harms to be avoided (*e.g.*, Taylor, 1981; Wienhues, 2017), there is an overwhelming number of conflicting demands. Attempts to include and navigate all the claims between different kinds of individuals, let alone the claims between ecosystem-, species-, and organism-levels, have been heavily criticized as prone to fail (*e.g.*, Cripps, 2010). We agree with the criticism that creating a conflict-generating approach is unlikely to successfully guide societal action: It is important to find a way to consider all well-being without considering all possible claims at all levels. More-than-individualistic environmental ethics, such as ecocentrism, usually ground moral considerability in the self-regulative and self-regenerative capacities of living entities (*e.g.* Kortetmäki, 2017; Rolston, 2002; Schlosberg, 2007) and planetary well-being aligns well with them.

There is also another reason why planetary well-being must reach beyond individualistic ethics: The moral considerability of non-individual entities is not reducible to individuals. We agree with Callicott (1986) and Rolston (1985) that the loss of a species due to human action is morally reprehensible for its own sake and not just due to the suffering it causes to individual beings. The extinction of lineages are exceptionally grave and morally reprehensible losses because of the timeframe of evolutionary history that reaches up to millions of years to the past and could have reached equal periods in the future without human interruption. Thus, planetary well-being aligns with those normative views where the survival of lineages is an end in itself (Naess, 1989, 2008; Rolston, 1985). This is a huge issue since the currently estimated number of species under risk of extinction due to human-originating interference is around 1 million (based on a rough but informed extrapolation, IPBES, 2019).

Amongst the established environmental ethics approaches, deep ecology is the most resemblant to planetary well-being. Deep ecology is grounded in a relational and holistic approach and considers human and nonhuman flourishing as morally valuable for their own sake. This implies that "[h]umans have no right to reduce this [nonhuman] richness and diversity except to satisfy vital needs" (Naess, 1989, p. 29; "vital needs" remains a vague notion but is not restricted to biological survival needs). Planetary well-being differs from deep ecology by paying more attention to socio-ecological systems, relations, and processes. This is in line with socio-ecological sustainability and transformations research, thereby providing a more elaborate basis for the examination of societal development and for creating non-anthropocentric framings of sustainable development (see United Nations (UN), 2015; WCED, 1987 for the recent and original framings). Second, planetary well-being gives a more process-oriented definition for the limits of permissible harm by focusing on process integrity. This might also imply differences between deep ecology and planetary well-being approaches in the permissibility of some actions deep ecology and planetary well-being find morally permissible, but an examination of them is beyond the scope of this chapter. It must be, however, emphasized that planetary well-being is meant to complement, not to replace social ethics that further guides the promotion of equal well-being among humans and the organization of human societies.

Since planetary well-being addresses large-scale processes (see section Introduction in this chapter), it may become confused with the planetary boundaries framework that is also systemic and process-oriented. The planetary boundaries framework was introduced (Rockström *et al.*, 2009) as a framework to help maintain the Holocene, the stable environmental conditions on Earth. The essential difference between planetary boundaries and planetary well-being is both epistemic and normative. Planetary boundaries are measurable thresholds, the crossing of which could lead to irreversible changes and unstable environmental conditions, threatening safe human existence. It highlights the importance of avoiding the crossing of "tipping points" (and thus staying within stricter boundaries of safe action) that could lead to the abrupt changes or collapse of crucial processes. In contrast, planetary well-being focuses on functional integrity. These thresholds differ greatly: Consider, analogously, the difference between avoiding the crossing of a human individual's tipping point (physical or psychological collapse) vs. securing their functional integrity (well-being). Protecting one's functional integrity requires more than simply avoiding the crossing of a safety boundary; admittedly, however, the state of integrity is also fuzzy. Moreover, planetary boundaries are defined with reference to human safety: The framework is thus explicitly anthropocentric in normative terms. This also shows in the status of biodiversity loss rate as just one of the safety boundaries. In the planetary boundaries framework, extinctions are not a concern *per se* but due to their impacts on the safe existence of humans and stability of the Holocene. Planetary well-being sets more demanding limits for permissible activities: Increasing the risk of extinctions is a concern as such, and some disruptions that are insignificant for planetary boundaries can be very significant for planetary well-being.

Finally, one central ethical aspect of planetary well-being is the shift of attention from actual well-being outcomes to the *opportunities* to achieve well-being, to avoid paralysis in front of unavoidable conflicts between individuals in their realization of well-being. Planetary well-being focuses on factors that are constitutive of the opportunity of almost any living entity to achieve well-being. In its focus on the opportunities to achieve well-being, the ethical grounding of planetary well-being resembles the influential capabilities approach to justice and development (Nussbaum, 2011; Nussbaum and Sen, 1993). The capabilities approach focuses on evaluating the capabilities of humans—what they can do and be in terms of striving for a dignified and worthy life—rather than the actual outcomes of each individual or their perception of well-being. Although the initial capabilities approach was limited to humans, social justice literature expanded it to sentient animals (Nussbaum, 2006) and ecological justice literature even to ecosystems and species, asking whether such entities are able to maintain their functional integrity and what impediments to that goal human activities are causing (*e.g.*, Kortetmäki, 2017; Schlosberg, 2007).

Ethics of moderate and severe scarcity

Opportunities for achieving well-being depend on numerous goods. Many of them are scarce in one way or another. This very fact of scarcity has, in the first place, given rise to various theories of justice that aim to define (among other things) appropriate criteria for the just distribution of goods. However, almost all approaches to justice—even those that speak about justice for nature—assume that scarcity is only *moderate* and that there are enough goods to provide everyone what they need (Wienhues, 2020). However, the present world manifests significant or severe scarcity for many nonhumans (*ibid.*): They barely survive or even face extirpation as populations or extinction as species. The basic moral imperative of planetary well-being is to strive towards circumstances where Earth and ecosystem processes function so well that nonhuman entities have the opportunity to achieve well-being. This is to be pursued alongside the production of greater equality of well-being among human beings.

Of course, one thing needing clarification is whether the scarcity concerns all potential need satisfiers that could satisfy the species-specific needs of humans, or whether it is caused by unbearably burdensome/consuming need satisfiers. Severe scarcity would urge promoting the availability of the least harmful need satisfiers that can provide well-being to humans and the rejection of the more harmful ones. The prospects for planetary well-being would then be maximized by shifting to the least burdensome human need satisfiers. For example, standards for adequate housing, the availability of fuelled traffic vehicles and the composition of adequate diets differ greatly in their impacts on planetary well-being. But what if scarcity is too severe for combining such goals: What if the needs of all humans cannot be satisfied due to scarcity, or what if satisfying all human needs necessarily hampers the prospects of nonhumans to achieve well-being?

Speaking of equality remains relevant also with relation to well-being and to "survival" (existence deprived of well-being). Insofar as there are enough goods to support survival, there are still prospects to reach "back" to well-being later. This happens, for example, when human communities face acute catastrophes but get over them and recover. Below the threshold of survival, however, speaking of equal distribution becomes meaningless. If a ship is sinking and there are life jackets only for half of the passengers, cutting life jackets in half (if the half-jacket does not increase the likelihood of survival) for equality would not make sense: Everyone would die. To avoid tragedies that are analogous to this metaphor, realizing the need for urgent transformations and communicating this urgency in action-encouraging ways is crucially important. From the viewpoint of survival, helping species stay existent until their prospects to be well are secured again is a meaningful goal.

Planetary well-being can provide a hopeful vision also for the ethics of scarcity by suggesting a focus on thinking about the preconditions of well-being, which constitutes a broadly embraced value and thus a common overarching vision across times and even groups of deep differences (Rogers *et al.*, 2012). The above-described considerations of just distribution do, however, also raise unavoidably questions about human population size in the long term. What share of goods are we, as one species, entitled to use on the planet whose goods we share with millions of other species?

Planetary well-being as a bridging concept

The relational notions underpinning the concept of planetary well-being acknowledge the importance of fundamental, life supporting processes and relationships for the survival and well-being of both humans and nonhumans. By overcoming human—nature dualisms, these relational notions resonate with both Western and non-Western considerations that take into account traditional knowledge, Indigenous views, and diverse forms of experience (Muraca, 2011) and may facilitate understanding of the diverse ways human societies relate to and interact with nonhuman nature (Köhler *et al.*, 2019). The critique of Enlightenment-based Cartesian, Eurocentric, and anthropocentric humanism has generated calls for the recognition of pluralism in, for example, biodiversity conservation (Cortés-Capano *et al.*, 2022). Planetary well-being as a framework might resonate with the plurality of ethical-theoretical approaches such as feminist, gender, and queer studies; postcolonial, indigenous, and critical race studies; human—animal studies, new materialism, and posthumanism; virtue ethics, and ethics of care. In the case of planetary well-being, the framing of well-being around the idea of needs and combining the consideration of human and nonhuman needs (non-anthropocentrism) could support the identification of boundaries against unlimited desires and wants driving the crisis, and for finding ways forward to foster just sustainability transformations.

Conclusion: The imperative for planetary well-being

Planetary well-being addresses the need for a morally inclusive and systemic conceptualization of well-being that considers the multiple levels of interaction between the different living systems and the processes they co-create and co-maintain. Planetary well-being acknowledges the value of both human and nonhuman well-being for their own sake: The moral right for both humans and nonhumans to exist, to have their needs satisfied, and to realize their typical characteristics and capacities.

The satisfaction of the needs of various entities creates both synergies and conflicts. Hence, the concept transcends the level of individual organisms and focuses on the integrity of Earth system and ecosystem processes underlying the well-being of all forms of life.

As a concept, planetary well-being facilitates scientific, political, and ethical discussions by using the same vocabulary to address the impacts of human activities on both human and nonhuman well-beings. Of course, one concept alone cannot do the work. Transdisciplinary collaboration is needed to understand how planetary well-being can help humans, both as individuals and in their collective efforts, in transforming worldviews, values, and assumptions towards a direction that promotes sustainable well-being for all. It is crucial to analyze the prevalent societal structures and power relations in terms of how they maintain or prevent striving towards planetary well-being and the equal prospects of different species and human communities to achieve it.

Planetary well-being calls for transformative changes in how we think and discuss well-being, deliberate and create policies for well-being, and how the various inhabitants of the planet are incorporated and valued in these discussions. In the common framings of sustainable development, the minimum threshold for "sustainability" is that to be sustainable, human activities must retain the opportunity of present and future human generations to satisfy their needs. In contrast, planetary well-being implies that human activities, to be sustainable, must retain the opportunity of all types of living entities on Earth to satisfy their needs now and in the future. Planetary well-being makes a difference to how we think about sustainability and well-being.

Planetary well-being does not require compromising human well-being but urges finding other ways to achieve it than those which currently dominate in high-consumption societies. Various human need satisfiers differ greatly in their impacts on planetary well-being: This calls for studying how the processes of production and consumption influence the satisfaction of universal human needs (Gough, 2017) *and* planetary well-being. The central question is: How to organize human systems to simultaneously allow meeting human needs while retaining Earth and ecosystem process integrity so that both humans and nonhumans—with particular attention to those who now are unable to achieve well-being—have the opportunity to strive for well-being, now and in the future?

Notes

1 Scientific materialism, or philosophical materialism, refers to ontological thinking where "the real world is composed exclusively of material things"; scientific realism refers here to the epistemic view where scientific knowledge can—and attempts to—represent reality (Bunge, 1981). Such views can be embraced in varying degrees and planetary well-being does not involve commitment to the "pure" stances of these views. Instead, the conceptualization of planetary well-being resonates more closely with many ideas presented in the new materialism that "is cross-fertilized by both the human and natural sciences" and emphasizes the processual nature and the self-organizing capacities of matter (*e.g.*, Yi Sencindiver, 2017).

2 For example, long oppression might lead humans to internalize their "inferior" status in which case the oppression is not reflected in subjective reports about experienced well-being. Long privileged status, in turn, might lead humans to internalize their well-off status so that even minor impairment in, let us say, access to luxury goods might be reflected strongly in subjective reports about experienced well-being. Thus, the subjective experiences of privileged groups get easily overemphasized in subjective reports about well-being.

3 Those things that are good for an entity are also often called its interests. Having interests does not require mental awareness of those interests; human infants also demonstrate this case (Taylor, 1986).

References

Banitz, T. *et al.* (2022) 'Visualization of causation in social-ecological systems', *Ecology and Society*, 27(1), p. 31. https://doi.org/10.5751/ES-13030-270131

Berkes, F. and Folke, C. (1998) *Social and Ecological Systems: Management Practices and Social Mechanisms for Building Resilience.* New York: Cambridge University Press.

Bhaskar, R. *et al.* (eds.) (2010) *Interdisciplinarity and Climate Change: Transforming Knowledge and Practice.* Abingdon: Routledge.

Broom, D.M. (1991) 'Animal welfare: Concepts and measurement', *Journal of Animal Science*, 69, pp. 4167–4175. https://doi.org/10.2527/1991.69104167X

Bunge, M. (1981) *Scientific Materialism.* Dordrecht: R. Reidel Publishing Company.

Bunge, M. (2000) 'Systemism: The alternative to individualism and holism', *The Journal of Socio-Economics*, 29, pp. 147–157. https://doi.org/10.1016/S1053-5357(00)00058-5

Callicott, J.B. (1986) 'On the intrinsic value of nonhuman species', in Norton, B.G. (ed.) *The Preservation of Species.* Princeton, NJ: Princeton University Press, pp. 138–172. https://doi.org/10.1515/9781400857869

Cortés-Capano, G. *et al.* (2022) 'Ethics in biodiversity conservation: The meaning and importance of pluralism', *Biological Conservation*, 275, 109759. https://doi.org/10.1016/j.biocon.2022.109759

Cripps, E. (2010) 'Saving the polar bear, saving the world: Can the capabilities approach do justice to humans, animals and ecosystems?', *Res Publica*, 16, pp. 1–22. https://doi.org/10.1007/s11158-010-9106-2

DeLanda, M. (2016) *Assemblage Theory.* Edinburgh: Edinburgh University Press.

Doyal, L. and Gough, I. (1984) 'A theory of human needs', *Critical Social Policy*, 4, pp. 6–38. https://doi.org/10.1177/026101838400401002

Dryzek, J.S. and Pickering, J. (2018) *The Politics of the Anthropocene.* Oxford: Oxford University Press. https://doi.org/10.1093/oso/9780198809616.001.0001

Elder-Vass, D. (2010a) *The Causal Power of Social Structures: Emergence, Structure and Agency.* Cambridge: Cambridge University Press.

Elder-Vass, D. (2010b) 'Realist critique without ethical naturalism and moral realism', *Journal of Critical Realism*, 9, pp. 33–58. https://doi.org/10.1558/jcr.v9i1.33

Folke, C. *et al.* (2016) 'Social-ecological resilience and biosphere-based sustainability science', *Ecology and Society*, 21(3), p. 41. https://doi.org/10.5751/ES-08748-210341

Goodpaster, K.E. (1978) 'On being morally considerable', *Journal of Philosophy*, 75(6), pp. 308–325. https://doi.org/10.2307/2025709

Gough, I. (2017) 'Recomposing consumption: Defining necessities for sustainable and equitable well-being', *Philosophical Transactions of the Royal Society A: Mathematical, Physical and Engineering Sciences*, 375, 20160379. https://doi.org/10.1098/rsta.2016.0379

IPBES (2019) *Summary for Policymakers of the Global Assessment Report on Biodiversity and Ecosystem Services of the Intergovernmental Science-Policy Platform on Biodiversity and Ecosystem Services*. Zenedo. https://doi.org/10.5281/zenodo.3553579

Kohler, F. *et al.* (2019) 'Embracing diverse worldviews to share planet Earth', *Conservation Biology*, 33(5), pp. 1014–1022. https://doi.org/10.1111/cobi.13304

Köhler, J. *et al.* (2019) 'An agenda for sustainability transitions research: State of the art and future directions', *Environmental Innovation and Societal Transitions*, 31, pp. 1–32. https://doi.org/10.1016/j.eist.2019.01.004

Kortetmäki, T. (2017) 'Applying the capabilities approach to ecosystems: Resilience as ecosystem capability', *Environmental Ethics*, 39, pp. 39–56. https://doi.org/10.5840/ENVIROETHICS20179263

Kortetmäki, T. *et al.* (2021) 'Planetary well-being', *Humanities and Social Sciences Communications*, 8, p. 258. https://doi.org/10.1057/s41599-021-00899-3

Leopold, A. (1949) *A Sand County Almanac, and Sketches Here and There*. Oxford: Oxford University Press.

Levin, S. *et al.* (2013) 'Social-ecological systems as complex adaptive systems: Modeling and policy implications', *Environment and Development Economics*, 18, pp. 111–132. https://doi.org/10.1017/S1355770X12000460

Mastrángelo, M.E. *et al.* (2019) 'Key knowledge gaps to achieve global sustainability goals', *Nature Sustainability*, 2, pp. 1115–1121. https://doi.org/10.1038/s41893-019-0412-1

Max-Neef, M.A. (1991) *Human Scale Development: Conception, Application and Further Reflections*. New York: The Apex Press.

Muraca, B. (2011) 'The map of moral significance: A new axiological matrix for environmental ethics', *Environmental Values*, 20, pp. 375–396. https://doi.org/10.3197/096327111X13077055166063

Naess, A. (1989) *Ecology, Community and Lifestyle: Outline of an Ecosophy*. Cambridge: Cambridge University Press. https://doi.org/10.1017/CBO9780511525599

Naess, A. (2008) in Devall B. and Drengson, A. (eds.) *Ecology of Wisdom: Writings by Arne Naess*. New York: Counterpoint.

Nussbaum, M.C. (2006) *Frontiers of Justice: Disability, Nationality, Species Membership*. Cambridge, MA: Harvard University Press.

Nussbaum, M.C. (2011) *Creating Capabilities: The Human Development Approach*. Cambridge, MA: Harvard University Press.

Nussbaum, M.C. and Sen, A. (eds.) (1993) *The Quality of Life*. Oxford: Clarendon Press.

Prescott-Allen, R. (2001) *The Wellbeing of Nations*. Washington, DC: Island Press.

Puig de la Bellacasa, M. (2017) *Matters of Care: Speculative Ethics in More Than Human Worlds*. Minneapolis: University of Minnesota Press.

Rice, C.M. (2013) 'Defending the objective list theory of well-being', *Ratio*, 26, pp. 196–211. https://doi.org/10.1111/rati.12007

Rockström, J. *et al.* (2009) 'A safe operation space for humanity', *Nature*, 461, pp. 472–475.

Rogers, D.S. *et al.* (2012) 'A vision for human well-being: Transition to social sustainability', *Current Opinion in Environmental Sustainability*, 4, pp. 61–73. https://doi.org/10.1016/j.cosust.2012.01.013

Rolston, H.I. (1985) 'Duties to endangered species', *BioScience*, 35, pp. 718–726. https://doi.org/10.2307/1310053

Rolston, H.I. (2002) 'What do we mean by the intrinsic value and integrity of plants and animals', in *Genetic Engineering and the Intrinsic Value and Integrity of Plants and Animals* [workshop]. Edinburg: Royal Botanic Garden, pp. 18–21 September. Available at: https://mountainscholar.org/bitstream/handle/10217/39371/Ifgene-updated.pdf (Accessed: 14 January 2023).

Schlosberg, D. (2007) *Defining Environmental Justice: Theories, Movements, and Nature*. Oxford: Oxford University Press. https://doi.org/10.1093/ACPROF:OSO/9780199286294.001.0001

Schweitzer, A. (1969) *Reverence for Life*. New York: Harper & Row.

Singer, P. (2002) *Animal Liberation*. 1st Ecco paperback ed. New York: Ecco.

Taylor, P.W. (1981) 'The ethics of respect for nature', *Environmental Ethics*, 3, pp. 197–218. https://doi.org/10.5840/ENVIROETHICS19813321

Taylor, P.W. (1986) *Respect for Nature: A Theory of Environmental Ethics*. Princeton, NJ: Princeton University Press. https://doi.org/10.2307/j.ctt7sk1j

UN (2015) *Transforming Our World: The 2030 Agenda for Sustainable Development*. A/RES/70/1. Geneva: United Nations General Assembly. Available at: https://sdgs.un.org/2030agenda (Accessed: 14 January 2023).

Warren, M.A. (2000) *Moral Status: Obligations to Persons and Other Living Things*. Oxford: Clarendon Press.

WCED (1987) *Our Common Future [Brundtland Report]*. A/42/427. Geneva: United Nations General Assembly. Available at: https://digitallibrary.un.org/record/139811?ln=en (Accessed: 14 January 2023).

Wienhues, A. (2017) 'Sharing the earth: A biocentric account of ecological justice', *Journal of Agricultural and Environmental Ethics*, 30(3), pp. 367–385. https://doi.org/10.1007/S10806-017-9672-9

Wienhues, A. (2020) *Ecological Justice and the Extinction Crisis: Giving Living Beings their Due*. Bristol: Bristol University Press. https://doi.org/10.46692/9781529208528

Yi Sencindiver, S. (2017) 'New materialism', *Oxford Bibliographies Online in Literary and Critical Theory*. https://doi.org/10.1093/OBO/9780190221911-0016

3

ONTOLOGICAL DIFFERENCES AND THE PURSUIT OF PLANETARY WELL-BEING

Liia-Maria Raippalinna, Pilvi Hämeenaho and Jelena Salmi

Introduction

Scientific concepts and methods not only characterize and analyze worlds but also shape them. Global systemic concepts born and raised in Western universities may appear to be neutral and unbiased abstractions floating above the complexity of the world, but they reflect the worldviews of their makers. Indeed, human perception, including scientific knowledge, is socially and culturally produced (Latour and Woolgar, 1986; Said, 1978) and takes part in the shaping of realities (Law and Urry, 2004).

Planetary well-being draws attention to the integrity of ecosystem and Earth system processes that are vital to the well-being of all organisms, species, populations, lineages, and ecosystems. The concept addresses the need for an ethically inclusive and systemic conceptualization of well-being that takes into account the multiple dimensions of interaction between divergent entities (see Chapter 2). It also works as a tool for bridging different worldviews to make the concept globally applicable (see Kortetmäki *et al.*, 2021). This chapter approaches the notion of planetary well-being as a dynamic, political process that develops through transdisciplinary collaboration, which brings together viewpoints, concepts, and methods from both natural and human sciences. We contribute to the development of planetary well-being by discussing its cross-cultural applicability and suggesting how to make the concept more open to difference and, hence, better able to resonate with perceptions that differ from mainstream Western (scientific) thinking. Our suggestions aim to support the goal of promoting planetary well-being through transdisciplinary and decolonizing research.

One possible way of enhancing the cross-cultural reach of planetary well-being is to open it to divergent ontologies. By ontologies we mean various understandings

DOI: 10.4324/9781003334002-5

of what exists, and the constitutive relations of diverse kinds of beings. Ontologies are enacted and performed through an array of practices, including discourses, scientific methods, and everyday mundane tasks (Gad, Jensen and Winthereik, 2015); thus, we start from the premise that *practices shape realities*. Planetary well-being is a particular kind of practical ontology that both perceives and enacts the world as a range of ecological processes and categorizes all beings as biological species and mutually exclusive biological organisms that are part of ecosystems. While this is an appealing way of apprehending existence within the scientific domain, biological species and ecosystems may not be meaningful or sufficient organizing categories in all ontologies. Furthermore, not all ontologies are based on a human–nonhuman dichotomy or other Cartesian dichotomies such as culture (social)/nature, material/immaterial, mind/matter, and animate/inanimate. While planetary well-being, faithful to scientific realism and materialism, perceives ecosystems as material and independent of the human mind (Chapter 2), ecosystems can also be approached as dynamic material-discursive wholes, which change and develop through practices such as ecosystem conservation programs. From this perspective, the human mind-body is embedded within the ecosystem and "nature" more generally.

Western, Eurocentric science tends to view the world from an "exterior observational point" (Barad, 2003, p. 828), thereby enacting a category of pure Nature existing independently of human cognition. Here, however, we do not seek to reproduce the dichotomy of "the West" and "the rest", but recognize that "the West", too, is ontologically multiple (Jensen, 2021, p. 100) and that ontologies interact and entangle. In fact, the coming together of divergent ontologies *as equals* is necessary for a common world that enables planetary well-being to be realized. This does not require their becoming the same; rather, it involves respecting difference (Verran, 2002). Ontological dialogue starts with the recognition that the dominant scientific ontology is not an objective view coming from a detached, external nowhere.

The great divide of nature and culture is deeply embedded in scientific theories and Western thought dating back to the age of Enlightenment and René Descartes, or all the way to the emergence of mainstream monotheistic traditions in the Middle East (Ginrich, 2014). While nature and the material world have been to a significant extent excluded from social theory, the social and the human have been correspondingly excluded from natural sciences (Tsing, 2014). We have ended up with a separation of the human and natural worlds, as if human culture was not part of nature. While sometimes represented as overlapping and interrelated, they are still conceptualized as two distinct realities. Another outcome of these Cartesian dualisms is anthropocentrism, which lies at the root of the current environmental and climate crises, since nature and other entities have been valued merely as resources for human beings to utilize. The concept of planetary well-being defeats normative anthropocentrism by prioritizing the intrinsic value of nonhuman populations, species, and lineages over their instrumental value for human prosperity (Kortetmäki *et al.*, 2021). Thus, it puts humans back to nature by rendering *Homo sapiens* a species among others.

We argue that to promote and achieve planetary well-being, we also need to recognize that culture is not a separate entity but *enmeshed within nature*. Instead of framing human practices merely as a threat to biological systems, it is important to analyze how they may maintain, enhance, and even create biodiversity (Maffi, 2007, 268; see also Pretty *et al.*, 2009) and planetary well-being. For example, the concept of biocultural[1] diversity views biology, culture, and language as dialectically and inextricably intertwined (Franco, 2022; Maffi, 2005, 2007; Skutnabb-Kangas, Maffi and Harmon, 2003). According to Luisa Maffi (2007, p. 269), biocultural diversity is based on three key elements. Firstly, it recognizes that the diversity of life is made up not only of the diversity of plants and animal species, habitats, and ecosystems found on the planet, but also of the diversity of human cultures and languages. Secondly, it acknowledges that these diversities do not exist in separate and parallel realms but affect one another in complex ways. Thirdly, it notes that the links among these diversities have developed over time through mutual adaptation between humans and the environment at the local level. In sum, biocultural diversity realizes that biological, cultural, and linguistic diversity co-occur and mutually support one another. They are also threatened by the same forces. To maintain the resilience of social-ecological systems on the long run, it is imperative to maintain diversity in all its forms (Pretty *et al.*, 2009).

Focusing on biocultural diversity highlights cultural differences in the satisfaction of basic needs, central to the notion of planetary well-being (Kortetmäki *et al.*, 2021). However, instead of perceiving difference only in terms of culturally varying need satisfaction, the concept of biocultural diversity encourages sensitivity towards ontological difference and related perceptions of needs and well-being: Determining what well-being means requires openness to different ontologies (Hiemstra, Subramanian and Verschuuren, 2014). But how, then, could ontological multiplicity be addressed in the development and implementation of planetary well-being?

John Law and John Urry (2004) encourage researchers to ask what kinds of realities we make with our concepts and methodologies, and what kinds of realities we would wish to make with them. Taking these questions as our starting point, we propose that the pursuit of planetary well-being be geared towards cultivating divergent biocultural realities. This requires that ontological difference is appreciated by means of "softening" the realisms of biology (Law and Joks, 2019, p. 441). We seek the means to do this by drawing on ontological politics, discussed in the following section. After that, we propose some conceptual and methodological tools that open up a space for interdisciplinary and cross-cultural dialogue on planetary well-being. Anthropologist Anna Tsing's (2017) conceptual pair of *multispecies resurgence* and *Anthropocene proliferation* is helpful in envisioning planetary well-being from the point of view of biocultural diversity grounded in and emerging from particular landscapes. Her approach to landscapes as *more-than-human assemblages* enables investigation of how multiple world-making practices—ranging from those of plants and fungi to industrial landscape projects, Indigenous cosmology, and scientific classification—come together. In other words, landscapes are open-ended and constantly changing gatherings. Their livability depends on how well the gatherings succeed in cultivating biocultural diversity and well-being. Tsing's conceptual tools, we argue, are hospitable to different realities, including the scientific ontology of planetary well-being.

Enacting realities

Within the social sciences and humanities, the core concepts of culture and society are subjects of constant debate. The concern with cultural and social differences relies on a conception of the world as one, while "culture" implies only a specific kind of perspective on the one world. In other words, epistemologies (ways of making sense of the world) vary, but there is only one ontology (what kinds of things exist and their constitutive relations) (Heywood, 2017). Conventionally, the task of anthropologists has been to study people's cultural perceptions—that is, epistemologies—of the one world. However, the Western notion of culture takes its ontological status for granted as it relies on the dualism of nature and culture (Blaser, 2013, p. 550). Therefore, we need to move beyond "cultures" in thinking about difference.

Western science tends to treat Indigenous and other realities as cultural takes on a single natural world, the one reality. Politics, then, comes to be about negotiating individual and collective rights and duties within the social realm, a "politics of who" (Mol, 2002, p. 166). Marisol de la Cadena (2010, p. 360) calls this "politics as usual", referring to "power disputes within a singular world." But what if we start from a position that the common world is not pregiven, that semiotic and material practices do not just reflect knowledge of the one world but enact and perform diverse realities or ontologies?

A sensibility known as *ontological politics* assumes that the making of reality is open-ended, contested, and shaped within mundane practices (Law, 2002; Mol, 1999). Approached from this perspective, science's single Nature loses its purported objectivity, and "multiculturalism" turns into "multinaturalism" (Latour, 2011; Lorimer, 2012). Multiple natures, however, are not different kinds of human perspectives, but emerge from embodied entanglements of human and nonhuman agents including plants, animals, materials, and technologies, which make these knowledge communities more-than-human. Furthermore, differing natures are not stable and mutually exclusive totalities; rather, different kinds of enactments clash and collaborate (Mol, 1999, p. 88). Therefore, it is more fruitful to focus on world-making *practices* than on "orders" that locate actors within impermeable worlds (Gad, Jensen and Winthereik, 2015). Indigenous peoples, for instance, do not live in closed and pure "indigenous worlds." Their knowledge and practices cannot be separated from the larger world of media, science, and political and economic systems or ignore the impact of (uneven) power relations within these global systems of localities (see, *e.g.*, Hastrup, 2015; Kottak, 1999). For instance, economic globalization has resulted in changes in many indigenous contexts, including that of turning traditional practices into commercial activity (Kopnina 2012, p. 131).

Abandoning mononaturalism in favour of multinaturalism opens the possibility of attending to the ways in which ontological difference is recognized and handled. For example, in their analysis of the enactment of the Deatnu River and its salmon by the Norwegian state and Indigenous Sámi people, John Law and Solveig Joks (2019, p. 440) argue that the former tends to be intolerant of different realities. Although the Norwegian state recognizes traditional ecological knowledge in theory, genuine dialogue between divergent realities has not been achieved in practice, leading to the gradual disappearance of Sámi fishing practices and the realities that go with them. The "settler" way of ignoring ontological differences is a form of colonial politics (*ibid.*). A more successful case of ontological dialogue has been presented by Helen Verran (2002) who has studied how Yolngu Aboriginal landowners and environmental scientists in Australia relate their respective fire-control strategies, *worrk* and prescribed burning, in workshops involving lectures, seminar-type discussions, and practical demonstrations of fire control. Verran argues that a postcolonial knowledge space resulting from the workshops enables the participants to see how their strategies are both the same and profoundly different. The common world, then, is not a pregiven solid ground, but "a risky and highly disputable goal that remains very far in the future" (Latour, 2011, p. 9). Yet, despite being extremely difficult to obtain, the common world is an existential and ethical imperative, which necessitates co-researching and collective experiments (Latour, 2011). As Wim Hiemstra, Suneetha M. Subramanian, and Bas Verschuuren (2014, p. 24) posit, "a plurality of ways of knowing is better able to find ways of flourishing within ecological limits than one mainstream way of knowing on its own."

From the perspective of ontological politics, the methodological choices of natural and human scientists are not objective or innocent. They are political and performative, taking part in the shaping of realities (Law and Urry, 2004). In global research, it is important to understand divergent ontologies and avoid imposing concepts and categorizations that may not be relevant outside the West or which may even reproduce colonialist attitudes and power structures. Anthropology's historical complicity in the colonial project (*e.g.*, Asad, 1973; Hymes, 1969) has led to a heightened awareness of how research practices may reproduce systems of oppression. Decolonizing science means engaging in critical reflection on questions of power in knowledge production, how we teach, and how we frame our research questions and relate to the people with whom we work (McGranahan and Rizvi, 2016). All this starts from recognizing and reflecting on one's own ontological presuppositions and position within intersecting structures of power—a prerequisite of ethical research.

Promoting planetary well-being, however, requires both understanding diversity and supporting the struggles needed to sustain it (see Brightman and Lewis, 2017, p. 22). The fight against the erasure of differences, an instantiation of colonial politics, amounts to "resistance against territorial expropriation, against institutional disaggregation, and against ontological erosion" (de Almeida, 2017, p. 283). As scholars, we need to be cognizant of the fact that our concepts shape the worlds that they describe. Choosing and using certain methods, concepts, and (underlying) ontologies are world-making practices, since they outline how the world will be categorized and represented, and what will be left out of the inquiry. In the following section, we present some conceptual tools that assist in approaching divergent world-making practices and cultivating a postcolonial sensibility in striving for planetary well-being.

Tools for bringing culture back to nature

Reconciling human interests with nonhuman well-being poses challenges. For instance, most conservation and development projects seek to preserve either nature or cultures (Kopnina, 2012), something visible in struggles over who decides the aims and ways of preservation and the opportunities local people have to be involved in these negotiations (see Chapter 8). Nature preservation plans have been seen as neo-imperialist since they have sometimes ignored the rights and/or ways of life of local residents and Indigenous communities in favour of endangered species (Kohler and Brondizio, 2017; Kottak, 1999). Correspondingly, prioritizing the social, cultural, and economic rights of human communities over biodiversity and the rights of nonhuman species has been criticized for enacting elite-imposed concepts such as development and human rights that support the anthropocentric line of thought (Kopnina, 2012, p. 141).

A focus on biocultural diversity helps to reconcile these challenges (Kopnina, 2012; Pretty *et al.*, 2009). As Tove Skutnabb-Kangas, Louisa Maffi, and David Harmon (2003, p. 42) have stated, "fostering the health and vigour of ecosystems is one and the same goal as fostering the health and vigour of human societies, their cultures, and their languages." The study of biocultural diversity also assists in addressing ways of protecting natural places that have endured over generations and that value certain sites as sacred (Pretty *et al.*, 2009); these are not based on scientific ontologies but on spiritual connection to the more-than-human environment. While Indigenous and local lifeways must not be romanticized, they provide diverse solutions to current environmental crises and help to envision "radically alternative futures" (Chapter 8). Focusing on interactions and relations that occur in divergent environments, the concept of biocultural diversity enables culture[2] to be integrated into interdisciplinary research of planetary well-being. But how can the various relations that contribute to the making of biocultural diversity and particular biocultural realities be approached? How can this be done in a world where ontologies and localities are affected by and involved in global processes?

Several fields of science have sought to overcome the division of nature and culture. Among others, these include cultural geography, with the elaboration of the concept of landscape (see Wylie, 2007); posthumanist, feminist, and new materialist theories that attend to vibrant matter (*e.g.*, Barad, 2003; Bennett, 2010); and philosophies that see the world as composed of assemblages and actor-networks (*e.g.*, Deleuze and Guattari, 2004; Latour, 2005). Anthropologist Anna Tsing builds on Deleuzian assemblage theory to investigate more-than-human histories of places, entities, relations, and multispecies communities on multiple scales. In the following, we present her approach and suggest it as a suitable tool for interdisciplinary investigation of the making and unmaking of biocultural diversity—and, thereby, planetary well-being.[3]

Multispecies resurgence and Anthropocene proliferation

Planetary well-being states that human activities are sustainable if they "retain the opportunity for all types of living entities on Earth to satisfy their needs now and in the future" (Chapter 2). Visioning true and serious sustainability, Tsing (2017) presents a similar idea on a local level, grounding analysis in landscapes: Dynamic gatherings or "assemblages" of more-than-human encounters (Tsing, 2015, pp. 22–23). She claims that human ways of life within particular landscapes are truly sustainable only if they "align themselves with the dynamics of multispecies resurgence" (Tsing, 2017, p. 51). Here resurgence refers to the ability of multispecies communities to regenerate after disturbances through the actions of many organisms, including humans. In the long run, the continuity of human cultures also depends on multispecies resurgence that forms livable landscapes. Tsing uses the term "resurgence" instead of "resilience", because of its polysemy and lack of exact definition. With this conceptual choice, she aims to facilitate open-ended discussion among natural scientists, humanists, and social scientists (*ibid.*, p. 63). Tsing's radical, non-anthropocentric reconceptualization of sustainability encourages us to envision what kinds of worlds we want to enact with planetary well-being. It facilitates the perception of humans as part of multispecies communities and landscape gatherings, and cultural practices as part of their regenerative processes. Consequently, Tsing's approach is useful for researching biocultural diversity and the more-than-human practices and processes increasing and decreasing it.

To describe the making of livable landscapes, Tsing (2017) turns towards the ecological modality of the Holocene, the era starting from the glacial retreat in the northern hemisphere after the Ice Age. Species recolonized land emerging from the ice through the dynamics of succession. Holocene farming encouraged the re-enactment of post-Ice Age succession, such as that of field and woodland species. Some patches of Holocene resurgence where farming practices reproduce resurgence processes and species assemblages typical of the Holocene still exist. Tsing (*ibid.*, pp. 56–57) gives an example from her own research on Japan's Honshu Island, where traditional cultivation produced a biodiverse woodland, the *satoyama* forest. The peasants made intensive use of these forests by cutting down trees for timber and firewood, collecting leaves and humus for fertilizing fields, and gathering products for everyday needs. Farming and subsistence in villages was dependent on the surrounding forests. Meanwhile, human engagement in the forest repeated the pioneering succession where pines that would have died out without human disturbance, smothered by broadleaf trees, colonized bare mineral soil with their companion species, matsutake mushrooms. Without villagers cutting down broadleaf trees, pines would have disappeared from the forests together with the culturally appreciated matsutake. Multispecies resurgence of the *satoyama* forest both depended on and enabled traditional farming as a way of life. Currently, however, these forests have mostly been replaced by timber plantations or transformed after being abandoned by peasants. People have moved to cities and traditional farming practices have been replaced by chemical fertilizers and fossil fuels. Without human engagement, deciduous trees have taken over the forests with species assemblages that no longer support traditional farming; matsutake is now imported from Europe and North America (see Tsing, 2015).

Pretty *et al.* (2009) state that many of the drivers for the loss of biocultural diversity evolve from capitalist economies that stress economic growth. Growth orientation has resulted in a shift in consumption patterns, the globalization of markets, and the commercialization of resources, paving the way to the homogenization of cultures and landscapes. For instance, globalization of the food system leads to loss of ecological knowledge and locally developed skills and practices, and monocultural plantations lead to loss of traditional diets and knowledge of famine foods (*ibid.*, pp. 104–105). Tsing (2017, pp. 51–52) argues that in the Anthropocene, multispecies resurgence has become severely threatened by ecologies of *proliferation*: Simplified, human-made ecologies that are designed to produce assets for future investments and kill off beings not recognized as assets. The Anthropocene is characterized by plantation ecologies, industrial technologies, and large-scale governance projects, as well as capitalist modes of accumulation that drive major changes in landscapes and earth system processes (*ibid.*, p. 53). Its ecological modality produces monocultural proliferation of a few species, separating organisms from their life worlds and companion species. Monocultural plantations and related global trade kill off diversity and enable the unmanageable proliferation of viruses and pathogens (see also Chapter 4). For instance, industrialization of the nursery trade of ash trees led to a dieback of ashes around Europe in the early 1990s as trading and shipping young plants across regions and continents allowed the spread of a fungal pathogen. The dieback of ashes poses a threat to biocultural diversity; in addition to having cultural significance, the ash is a keystone species, supporting many insects, lichens, fungi, molluscs, and birds (Tsing, 2017, p. 59).

Overcoming the ecological crises requires an understanding of the more-than-human histories and socialities of the Anthropocene (for examples, see Tsing *et al.*, 2021) that are killing off biocultural diversity. However, there are still patches where human practices align themselves with regenerative processes that sustain multispecies communities. Spotting and learning from those rare patches may be critical to sustaining a livable world (Tsing, 2017, p. 62) and achieving planetary well-being. In sum, to promote planetary well-being, we need to be aware of the histories in which various more-than-human social relations come into being:

Relations of proliferation (destructive to planetary well-being) as well as relations of resurgence (supportive to planetary well-being).

More-than-human assemblages

A focus on multispecies relations and communities makes Tsing's conceptualization of sustainability well suited to envisioning planetary well-being. Furthermore, and not restricted to biological and ecological relations, her approach to the more-than-human formation of landscape assemblages and multispecies socialities has potential for bridging different ontologies. In assemblages, the lifeways of organisms and non-living ways of being come together and emerge through mutual transformations. They consist of everything that gathers in a place: "Assemblages are just those we find assembled", such as plants growing around each other in a particular landscape, or plants and their symbiotic fungi (Tsing, 2014, pp. 31–32). Both landscape assemblages and entities gathering in them take shape within more-than-human social relations that transform over time.

Investigating what gathers paves the way to noticing underlying relations without making a priori assumptions about what kinds of relations or entities matter. Importantly, the investigation does not have to be restricted to living organisms. Assemblages can include biotic and abiotic, natural and supranatural, material and immaterial, as well as discursive and practical entities, among others. For example, rocks, rivers, gods, ancestors, and sacred places can participate in the making of landscapes, and so can tools, technologies, infrastructures, governance discourses, global economies, and so on. Therefore, Tsing's understanding of assemblage is particularly beneficial in bridging different ontologies and perceptions of well-being in the pursuit of planetary well-being. It attends to what matters in actual more-than-human landscapes where biocultural realities are made.

Assemblages are continuously taking shape, but careful, sensitive, and critical description enables the co-emergence of gathered entities in a landscape to be traced and explored and opens their more-than-human histories to investigation. Various scales and sources from Indigenous cosmology and unwritten histories to scientific reports and observation can be combined when investigating more-than-human landscapes and their historical trajectories, keeping in mind that different sources have different methods of knowing and making the world (Tsing, 2017, p. 62; on Indigenous storytelling as research, see, *e.g.*, Iseke, 2013). Tsing (2014) advises us to start by following people into their landscape. Listening to human informants and perceiving and participating in their actions offer insights into the cultural practices involved in the shaping of landscapes, although it is not human practices as such but the dynamic relations among many species that create the multispecies web of social relations. In addition, landscapes are the products of multiple histories of various scales from microbial to global. For example, *satoyama* forests emerge from local interspecies relations as well as from global timber and fuel markets (*ibid.*, pp. 35–38). Apart from understanding the material and semiotic nature of divergent ecologies, we need to combine observations in particular multispecies communities with broad histories and difficult-to-trace connections (Tsing, 2017, p. 61).

Approaching (landscape) assemblages and entities as products of more-than-human histories enables transdisciplinary work and research that covers multiple aspects of complex realities.[4] Tsing's assemblage approach can be used as a tool for investigating Anthropocene proliferation as well as multispecies resurgence in livable landscapes. Therefore, it has the potential to provide a bridge between the biological relations and ecological processes central to the notion of planetary well-being, and the multiple more-than-human relations that remain outside the scope of the ecological/biological perspective. These include relations to spirits, gods, and ancestors to which planetary well-being does not assign any moral consideration. Undertaking cross-disciplinary and multi-ontological "assemblage studies" through the lens of planetary well-being would benefit both conceptual elaboration and practical implication of the concept. The approach allows the combining of different ontologies and conceptualizations of well-being without forcing them into a unified framework.

While we encourage ontological bridging both on the theoretical plane and in empirical research and development projects, we are not claiming it to be an easy task. Indeed, softening the scientific realism of planetary well-being with assemblage thinking poses challenges. For instance, the assemblage perspective on landscapes as emergent and fluid gatherings undermines the stability of biological and ecological systems and processes that are central to the concept of planetary well-being. Seeking synthesis between different ontologies is problematic, but some promising attempts have been made. In the field of sociology, Timothy Rutzou and Dave Elder-Vass (2019) have sought to combine critical realism with assemblage thinking. The way they integrate critical realist focus on structure, stability, and causality with assemblage theorists' interest in heterogeneity, fluidity, and processes could be useful in further conceptual and theoretical development of planetary well-being. Bridging ontologies will certainly involve (yet unforeseen) problems. Nevertheless, the aim of ethically inclusive well-being requires us to go through the trouble of seeking to broaden the ontological foundations of planetary well-being.

Conclusions

This chapter has focused on recognizing the importance of ontological sensitivity and conceptual choices to the development of the concept of planetary well-being. Enacting a world of mutually exclusive species, lineages, populations, and ecosystems, planetary well-being proposes a predefined, singular domain of Nature (see Lorimer, 2012) removed and abstracted from social and cultural life, or the "human mind" (Chapter 2). However, these categories are not universally meaningful. Hence, we have suggested first acknowledging that *scientific practices shape realities*. Second, we encourage shifting the concept of planetary well-being towards *cultivating biocultural diversity*, which necessitates openness to other realities and ways of knowing and making them. Not only do we think this augments the concept's genuine ability to bridge worldviews, it is also more generally beneficial to the pursuit of planetary well-being.

This chapter has highlighted the importance of considering what kinds of worlds we make—and would wish to make—with our investigations. The concepts, categories, and methodologies that we use are world-making practices. This idea is not news to planetary well-being, with its stated aims of overcoming moral anthropocentrism and building a world where the integrity of earth system processes is retained so that all organisms can be well. Proposed as a tool for policy and governance, the pursuit of planetary well-being seeks to put the concept into practice on a global scale. This, we argue, requires engaging in dialogue with other place-based ontologies. Otherwise, the promotion of planetary well-being risks reproducing Western dichotomies and colonizing different biocultural realities with universalizing notions of reality and well-being. We emphasize the importance of cultivating multiple biocultural worlds instead of a universal one and suggest that an important aim for planetary well-being would be making a *world where different biocultural realities can thrive*.

How should we proceed with this aim in practice? Kortetmäki *et al.* (2021, p. 6) suggest that the first step towards planetary well-being could be "the adoption of indicators that emphasize sufficiency and the meeting of basic material, social, and psychological needs while depreciating environmentally and socially harmful development." We encourage drawing on biocultural diversity in developing indicators grounded in local socio-ecological contexts (Sterling *et al.*, 2017). To be appropriate and relevant, these indicators must respect local ideas of well-being. Some local visions emphasize spiritual connection to the surrounding environment—manifested in the form of sacred sites and ritual practices—apart from material and social connection (Escobar, 2014; Hiemstra, Subramanian and Verschuuren, 2014). Planetary well-being does not currently recognize the importance of spirituality and religion for well-being although both have been shown to have a significant role in facilitating environmental conservation and poverty alleviation (see, *e.g.*, Bhagwat, Dudley and Harrop, 2011; Hiemstra, Subramanian and Verschuuren, 2014).

Ontological dialogue is also a question of social justice. Bringing culture back to nature provides opportunities for more just development plans and outcomes. Furthermore, protecting the existing patches of biocultural diversity is important for the pursuit of planetary well-being, because achieving planetary well-being will require adapting human actions to ecological processes *everywhere*. There exists a real possibility of learning from those patches of biocultural diversity where human action aligns with regenerative processes. This learning means understanding the way "cultural" beings and practices engage in making multispecies communities, ecosystems, and more-than-human landscapes. By committing oneself to a dialogical learning relationship with other ontologies, one may learn new ways of engaging with the world.

Finally, the chapter has discussed how planetary well-being could be enacted without the nature–culture division and suggested some conceptual tools for inter-disciplinary and cross-cultural collaboration and experimentation. It has proposed Tsing's conceptual pair of *multispecies resurgence* and *Anthropocene proliferation* for making sense of how cultural practices can either cultivate or disrupt regenerative processes central to planetary well-being. The chapter has also presented Tsing's assemblage approach to investigating more-than-human histories of landscapes and multispecies communities. On the one hand, the approach is useful in embedding scientific practice within the reality that it analyses; on the other, it helps the researcher to attend to biocultural realities as dynamic products of divergent world-making practices gathering in landscapes, without denying the effect of power asymmetries. Bridging ontologies may not be an easy task. Nevertheless, it is something that is required in the pursuit of *planetary* well-being.

Acknowledgements

Critical feedback on drafts of this paper from editors, especially Miikka Salo, is warmly acknowledged. This work was carried out with financial support from University of Jyväskylä and the Academy of Finland (Decision No. 318782).

Notes

1 Or ecocultural, see Franco (2022).
2 In principle also language, although this remains beyond our focus here.
3 Tsing uses the Deleuzian concept of assemblage (agencement) in her own way. Her use of the concept also differs from other later uses, like that of actor-network theorists (Tsing, 2015, Chapter 1, footnote 8). On a synthesis of assemblage theory and critical realism, see Rutzou and Elder-Vass (2019). On different uses of assemblage, see Buchanan (2021).
4 For examples, see Tsing *et al.* (2021).

References

Asad, T. (1973) *Anthropology and the Colonial Encounter*. New York: Humanities Press.
Barad, K. (2003) 'Posthumanist performativity: Toward an understanding of how matter comes to matter', *Signs*, 28(3), pp. 801–831. https://doi.org/10.1086/345321
Bennett, J. (2010) *Vibrant Matter: A Political Ecology of Things*. Durham: Duke University Press.
Bhagwat, S.A., Dudley, N. and Harrop, S.R. (2011) 'Religious following in biodiversity hotspots: Challenges and opportunities for conservation and development', *Conservation Letters*, 4, pp. 234–240. https://doi.org/10.1111/j.1755-263X.2011.00169.x
Blaser, M. (2013) 'Ontological conflicts and the stories of peoples in spite of Europe: Toward a conversation on political ontology', *Current Anthropology*, 54(5), pp. 547–568. https://doi.org/10.1086/672270
Brightman, M. and Lewis, J. (2017) 'Introduction: The anthropology of sustainability: Beyond development and progress', in Brightman, M and Lewis, J. (eds.) *The Anthropology of Sustainability: Beyond Development and Progress*. New York: Palgrave Macmillan, pp. 1–34. https://doi.org/10.1057/978-1-137-56636-2

Buchanan, I. (2021) *Assemblage Theory and Method*. London: Bloomsbury Academic. https://doi.org/10.5040/9781350015579.0005

de Almeida, M.W.B. (2017) 'Local struggles with entropy: Capoira and other demons' in M. Brightman, A. and Lewis, J. (eds.) *The Anthropology of Sustainability: Beyond Development and Progress*. New York: Palgrave Macmillan, pp. 273–290. https://doi.org/10.1057/978-1-137-56636-2

de la Cadena, M. (2010) 'Indigenous cosmopolitics in the andes: Conceptual reflections beyond 'politics'', *Cultural anthropology*, 25(2), pp. 334–370. https://doi.org/10.1111/j.1548-1360.2010.01061.x

Deleuze, G. and Guattari, F. (2004) *A Thousand Plateaus: Capitalism and Schizophrenia*. London and New York: Continuum.

Escobar, C. (2014) 'Community well-being in Bolivia: An indigenous perspective', in Verschuuren, B., Subramanian, S.M. and Hiemstra, W. (eds.) *Community Well-Being in Biocultural Landscapes: Are We Living Well?* Warwickshire: Practical Action Publishing, pp. 42–57.

Franco, F.M. (2022) 'Ecocultural or biocultural? Towards appropriate terminologies in biocultural diversity', *Biology*, 11(2), p. 207. https://dx.doi.org/10.3390/biology11020207

Gad, C., Jensen, C.B. and Winthereik, B.R. (2015) 'Practical ontology: Worlds in STS and anthropology', *NatureCulture*, 3, pp. 67–86. Available at: https://stsinfrastructures.org/content/practical-ontology-worlds-sts-and-anthropology (Accessed: 14 December 2022).

Ginrich, A. (2014) 'Establishing a 'Third Space'? Anthropology and the potentials of transcending a Great Divide', in Hastrup, K. (ed.) *Anthropology and Nature*. New York, Abingdon, and Oxon: Routledge, pp. 108–124.

Hastrup, K. (2015) 'Comparing climate worlds: Theorizing across ethnographic fields', in Greschke, H. and Tischler, J. (eds.) *Grounding Global Climate Change: Contributions from the Social and Cultural Sciences*. Dordrecht: Springer, pp. 139–154. https://doi.org/10.1007/978-94-017-9322-3

Heywood, P. (2017) 'Ontological turn, the', *The Cambridge Encyclopedia of Anthropology*. Available at: https://www.anthroencyclopedia.com/entry/ontological-turn (Accessed: 14 December 2022).

Hiemstra, W., Subramanian, S.M. and Verschuuren, B. (2014) 'Exploring a new approach to well-being assessment', in Verschuuren, B., Subramanian, S.M. and Hiemstra, W. (eds.) *Community Well-being in Biocultural Landscapes: Are We Living Well?* Warwickshire: Practical Action Publishing, pp. 21–41.

Hymes, D. (1969) 'The use of anthropology: Critical, political, personal', in Hymes, D. (ed.) *Reinventing Anthropology*. New York: Pantheon Books, pp. 3–79.

Iseke, J. (2013) 'Indigenous storytelling as research', *International Review of Qualitative Research*, 6, pp. 559–577. https://doi.org/10.1525/irqr.2013.6.4.559

Jensen, C.B. (2021) 'Practical ontologies redux', *Berliner Blätter*, 84, pp. 93–104. https://doi.org/10.18452/22974

Kohler, F. and Brondizio, E.S. (2016) 'Considering the needs of indigenous and local populations in conservation programs', *Conservation Biology*, 31(2), pp. 245–251. https://doi.org/10.1111/cobi.12843

Kopnina, H. (2012) 'Toward conservational anthropology: Addressing anthropocentric bias in anthropology', *Dialectical Anthropology*, 36, pp. 127–146. https://doi.org/10.1007/s10624-012-9265-y

Kortetmäki, T. *et al.* (2021) 'Planetary well-being', *Humanities and Social Sciences Communications*, 8, 258. https://doi.org/10.1057/s41599-021-00899-3

Kottak, C.P. (1999) 'The new ecological anthropology', *American Anthropologist,* 101(1), pp. 23–35.

Latour, B. (2005) *Reassembling the Social: An Introduction to Actor-Network-Theory.* Oxford: Oxford University Press.

Latour, B. (2011) 'From multiculturalism to multinaturalism: What rules of method for the new socio-scientific experiments?', *Nature and Culture,* 6(1), pp. 1–17. https://doi.org/10.3167/nc.2011.060101

Latour, B. and Woolgar, S. (1986) *Laboratory Life: The Construction of Scientific Facts.* 2nd ed. Princeton, NJ: Princeton University Press.

Law, J. (2002) *Aircraft Stories: Decentering the Object in Technoscience.* Durham, NC: Duke University Press.

Law, J. and Joks, S. (2019) 'Indigeneity, science, and difference: Notes on the politics of how', *Science, Technology, & Human Values,* 44(3), pp. 424–447. https://doi.org/10.1177/0162243918793942

Law, J. and Urry, J. (2004) 'Enacting the social', *Economy and Society,* 33(3), pp. 390–410. https://doi.org/10.1080/0308514042000225716

Lorimer, J. (2012) 'Multinatural geographies for the Anthropocene', *Progress in Human Geography,* 36(5), pp. 593–612. https://doi.org/10.1177/0309132511435352

Maffi, L. (2005) 'Linguistic, cultural, and biological diversity', *Annual Review of Anthropology,* 34, pp. 599–617.

Maffi, L. (2007) 'Biocultural diversity and sustainability', in Pretty, J. *et al.* (eds.) *The SAGE Handbook of Environment and Society.* London: Sage Publications, pp. 267–277.

McGranahan, C. and Rizvi, U.Z. (2016) 'Decolonizing anthropology', *Savage Minds,* 19 April. Available at: https://savageminds.org/2016/04/19/decolonizing-anthropology/ (Accessed: 14 December 2022).

Mol, A. (1999) 'Ontological politics. A word and some questions', in Law, J. and Hassard, J. (eds.) *Actor Network Theory and After.* Oxford: Blackwell Publishers, pp. 74–90.

Mol, A. (2002) *The Body Multiple: Ontology in Medical Practice.* Durham, NC: Duke University Press.

Pretty, J. *et al.* (2009) 'The intersections of biological diversity and cultural diversity: Towards integration', *Conservation and Society,* 7(2), pp. 100–112.

Rutzou, T. and Elder-Vass, D. (2019) 'On assemblages and things: Fluidity, stability, causation stories, and formation stories', *Sociological Theory,* 37 (4), pp. 401–424. https://doi.org/10.1177/0735275119888250

Said, E. (1978) *Orientalism.* New York: Pantheon Books.

Skutnabb-Kangas, T., Maffi, L. and Harmon, D. (2003) *Sharing a World of Difference: The Earth's Linguistic, Cultural and Biological Diversity.* Paris: UNESCO, Terralingua and WWF. Available at: https://unesdoc.unesco.org/ark:/48223/pf0000132384 (Accessed: 14 December 2022).

Sterling, E.J. *et al.* (2017) 'Biocultural approaches to well-being and sustainability indicators across scales', *Nature Ecology & Evolution,* 1, pp. 1798–1806. https://doi.org/10.1038/s41559-017-0349-6

Tsing, A.L. (2014) 'More-than-human sociality: A call for critical description', in Hastrup, K. (ed.) *Anthropology and Nature.* New York, Abingdon, and Oxon: Routledge, pp. 27–42.

Tsing, A.L. (2015) *The Mushroom at the End of the World: On the Possibility of Life in Capitalist Ruins.* Princeton, NJ and Oxford: Princeton University Press.

Tsing, A.L. (2017) 'A threat to holocene resurgence is a threat to liveability', in Brightman, M. and Lewis, J. (eds.) *Anthropology of Sustainability: Beyond Development and Progress*. New York: Palgrave Macmillan US, pp. 51–65. https://doi.org/10.1057/978-1-137-56636-2_3

Tsing, A.L. *et al.* (2021) *Feral Atlas: The More-Than-Human Anthropocene*. Redwood City, CA: Stanford University Press. http://doi.org/10.21627/2020fa

Verran, H. (2002) 'A postcolonial moment in science studies: Alternative firing regimes of environmental scientists and aboriginal landowners', *Social Studies of Science*, 32(5/6), pp. 729–762.

Wylie, J. (2007) *Landscape*. Routledge: New York.

Assessing ecological processes as constituents of planetary well-being

PART II

4

ECOSYSTEM HEALTH AND PLANETARY WELL-BEING

*Ilze Brila, Anni M. Hämäläinen, Toni Jernfors,
Eva R. Kallio, Jenni Kesäniemi, Esa Koskela,
Anton Lavrinienko, Tiffany Scholier, Yingying Wang
and Phillip C. Watts*

Ecosystem degradation decreases planetary well-being

Properly functioning *ecosystems* support diverse processes that sustain life, ranging from climate regulation and oxygen production to maintaining biodiversity. A healthy ecosystem may be defined as a sustainable and resilient system that maintains its function despite external stress (Costanza and Mageau, 1999). A healthy ecosystem provides key services to its biota, and disturbances to the system may impact the *health* and/or abundance of key members of its assemblage, such that they can no longer perform their ecological roles. In this chapter, we discuss the cascading effects that ecosystem degradation has on the health of wildlife, humans, and entire ecosystems and the consequent threat to planetary well-being.

Overexploitation of natural resources by humans has resulted in widespread ecosystem degradation: More than half of all ecosystems on Earth have deteriorated because of human actions (Myers, 2017; Song *et al.*, 2018). This degradation has negatively impacted a range of ecological functions with notable adverse consequences for the well-being of *wildlife* (undomesticated animals and plants inhabiting natural environments) and humans. Environmental change has, for example, directly increased *infectious disease prevalence* in humans and other organisms by facilitating the spread of invasive species, *disease vectors* (organisms that carry and transmit *pathogens* to other organisms), and pathogens (Parmesan and Yohe, 2003).

The interplay between ecosystem, human, and nonhuman health is recognized by several well-established health-related concepts, such as Conservation Medicine (Aguirre *et al.*, 2002), EcoHealth (Charron, 2012), One Health (Gibbs, 2014), and Planetary Health (Lerner and Berg, 2017). These concepts all share the recognition that humans share the Earth with wildlife and the

DOI: 10.4324/9781003334002-7

need for interdisciplinarity to safeguard health. Nonetheless, they tend to be anthropocentric and emphasize the protection of human health, whereas planetary well-being aims to identify humans as only a part of ecosystems and recognize the needs of nonhuman organisms. Similarly, infectious disease research is biased towards pathogens that cause illness in humans or in economically important species such as livestock. Meanwhile, the potentially devastating effects of *pathogens* (organisms that can cause disease by invading another organism) in nonhuman organisms generally receive less attention. Wildlife disease research is largely directed towards *reservoir hosts* (organisms in which pathogens can reproduce and that serve as a source of infection to other *hosts*) of *zoonotic* pathogens (infections that can be transmitted between humans and other animals). Because of this knowledge bias, the patterns of disease dynamics are best known for vertebrates and their pathogens (reflected also in this chapter), but the general patterns can be expected to extend to other taxa.

In this chapter, we present the role of ecosystem health in the well-being of all organisms. We demonstrate that (1) the health of ecosystems is declining worldwide due to human actions, (2) ecosystem degradation has complex adverse effects on the health of humans and nonhuman organisms by affecting disease dynamics, (3) planetary well-being and the health of ecosystems are interconnected. While planetary well-being is unattainable without sustaining healthy ecosystems, the planetary well-being concept offers a useful approach for finding solutions for global disease burden, for example through improved ecosystem management.

Disease as a part of a healthy ecosystem

All organisms have evolved in contact with a certain ecological community, including beneficial symbiotic organisms as well as *parasites* that exploit the host's resources, causing loss of health or mortality. These organisms, including pathogens, are important for proper ecosystem function, for example as a means of naturally controlling host population size (Fischhoff *et al.*, 2020). As such, in healthy ecosystems the well-being of parasites is equally important as the well-being of their hosts, however, ecosystem functioning can suffer from a shifting balance of host-parasite associations. Pathogens and their hosts are engaged in an evolutionary "arms race" between the hosts' immune defences and the diverse solutions evolved by pathogens to bypass the host defences. Many pathogens have a higher rate of evolution than their host, which limits the capacity of hosts to avoid or eliminate pathogens completely. Thus, disease is a natural feature of ecosystem dynamics, but the introduction of a novel pathogen into an ecosystem can have unpredictable consequences when the pathogen is transmitted to a new or sensitive host. A host encountering novel pathogens may be vulnerable to infection due to the lack of evolved defence mechanisms, possibly leading to a more severe disease. For example, when a large proportion of a population is simultaneously in poor health, there can be a concomitant decline in their function within the ecosystem.

Disease spread and disease burden increase due to anthropogenic impacts

Anthropogenic impacts on disease burden in ecosystems

Human impacts on ecosystems, for example, through changes in climate, land use (*e.g.,* agriculture, and growth of urban areas), pollution, and exploitation of natural resources, have caused profound and unpredictable changes in the ecology of pathogens, hosts, and host communities (Figure 4.1). Human activities can impact the infectious disease burden of nonhuman organisms by affecting the distribution and interactions of hosts and vectors, and the susceptibility of individuals and ecosystems to disease. These processes are outlined below.

Changes in the distribution of vector and host species

Human activities and climate change alter the geographic ranges of vectors, hosts, and pathogens on local and global scales (Parmesan and Yohe, 2003),

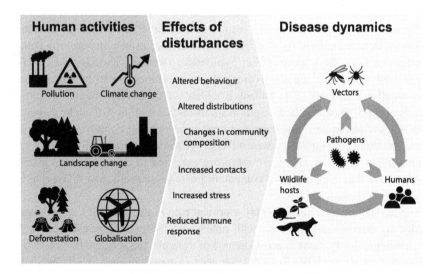

FIGURE 4.1   Disease dynamics of animals and humans are altered due to anthropogenic impacts on changes in the distributions, communities, and susceptibility of organisms to pathogens. Increase in disease risk of wildlife will, in turn, threaten human health and well-being through human–animal–vector interactions. Figure created by Māris Grunskis/@PHOTOGRUNSKIS.

potentially impacting the distribution and emergence of many diseases (Cohen *et al.*, 2020). Changes in the distribution and abundance of vector or reservoir species were implicated in nearly 10% of the 100 largest zoonotic disease outbreaks in the last 47 years (Stephens *et al.*, 2021). For example, some tick species have extended their distribution in the northern hemisphere and thus altered the prevalence and geographic distribution of tick-borne diseases (*e.g.*, anaplasmosis, babesiosis, Lyme disease, and tick-borne encephalitis) (Bouchard *et al.*, 2019). Similarly, there are concerns that certain mosquito species originating from tropical and subtropical areas, such as *Aedes albopictus,* a vector of dengue virus and Chikungunya virus, may be able to thrive in temperate regions in the near future (Caminade, McIntyre and Jones, 2019). Indeed, climate change has been implicated in increasing human malaria infections in Southern Europe and altering the distribution of avian malaria in wild birds (Garamszegi, 2011). At local scales, animals may also change their typical movement behaviours to escape a degraded habitat or new competitors or predators, concurrently spreading pathogens to new communities.

Altered community composition and ecological interactions among species

Changes in the species composition of a community (*e.g.*, through biodiversity loss or spread of invasive species), can influence key ecological interactions and thus impact disease dynamics in wildlife communities and humans (Keesing *et al.*, 2010; Keesing and Ostfeld, 2021). A high-species diversity is thought to reduce disease risk in a community, whereas the loss of species can increase the pathogen burden (*i.e.*, the dilution effect hypothesis; (Keesing and Ostfeld, 2021)). Large mammals (*e.g.*, top carnivores) are more vulnerable to human impacts than smaller mammals (*e.g.*, rodents), which often thrive in human-disturbed ecosystems (Gibb *et al.*, 2020). Certain small-bodied and short-lived host species also support pathogen replication and transmission exceptionally well, making them particularly competent reservoir hosts (Cronin, Rúa and Mitchell, 2014). Human-disturbed ecosystems are therefore expected to have increased disease risk because they support more competent hosts (*e.g.*, small mammals) relative to undisturbed communities.

Human actions can likewise play a critical role in the dynamics of pathogens carried by domesticated species, with potentially far-reaching consequences for host-pathogen interactions in ecosystems. For example, the accidental introduction of canine parvovirus on Isle Royale, USA, led to a major decline in wolf abundance and consequently released moose populations from predation pressure (Wilmers *et al.*, 2006). The introduction of domestic (and thus feral) cats to many ecosystems is responsible for numerous extinctions (Doherty *et al.*, 2017) and for the spread of new pathogens, such as the protozoan *Toxoplasma gondii,* which causes disease or even death in humans, livestock, and diverse wildlife (Dubey, 2008). In contrast, the eradication of cattle plague by humans led to such a significant increase in wildebeest populations in the Serengeti, Tanzania, that its ecosystem impacts include substantially reduced fires, higher tree density, and increased carbon storage in the area (Holdo *et al.*, 2009). Thus, human-associated species can mediate and amplify the effects of human activities on disease dynamics, with diverse and unpredictable ecosystem-level effects.

Immune system functioning and susceptibility to disease

Stressors linked to human activities (*e.g.,* urbanization, pollution, habitat loss, and fragmentation) affect wildlife and human health, including immune system dysregulation and a reduced host *resistance* to pathogens (Martin *et al.*, 2010; Lee and Choi, 2020). For example, in Australia, deforestation has led to the establishment of populations of *Pteropus* bats (flying foxes) in urban gardens. In addition to a change in distribution and movement, the high-density, isolated urban populations of flying foxes appear to have an altered pattern of herd immunity to Hendra virus, characterized by less frequent but larger disease outbreaks (Plowright *et al.*, 2011); this is cause for broader concern as Hendra virus can be fatal for humans and horses.

Increased human–wildlife encounters and pathogen exchange

Human activities promote the spillover of pathogens from host animals to humans through increased contact rates at the "animal-vector-human interface" in interaction with environmental, ecological, and social processes (Jones *et al.*, 2013; Destoumieux-Garzón *et al.*, 2022). Human–animal interactions occur through (wild) animal trade and (wild) meat consumption, or indirectly through humans living in increasingly close vicinity to wildlife due to the growth of urban areas, intensive farming, and unsustainable exploitation of natural resources (Magouras *et al.*, 2020). Several disease outbreaks in humans have been traced back to contacts with wildlife, including Ebola (Marí Saéz *et al.*, 2015) and SARS-CoV-2 (cause of the COVID-19 pandemic (Holmes *et al.*, 2021)).

Disease dynamics at the socio-ecological interface

Human social and economic systems are broadly intertwined with the state of natural systems, including but not limited to a shared disease burden. For example, the COVID-19 pandemic has been presented as a result of the complex dynamic system incorporating human population growth, culture, and actions that altered ecological processes, including climate change (Thoradeniya and Jayasinghe, 2021). Socioeconomic inequality, as well as political and economic disturbances, influence the pressure placed on ecosystems and create conflicts between the needs of humans and nonhuman organisms. For example, threats to human food security due to loss of crops or trade (*e.g.*, disruption of global supply chains following COVID-19 restrictions (Erokhin and Gao, 2020)), or socioeconomic hardship may increase contacts at the human–animal interface, such as increased harvesting of wildlife (Golden *et al.*, 2016). Profit-driven, intensive animal husbandry has resulted in the mass rearing of livestock in conditions that expose animals to suffering and generate opportunities for further disease outbreaks (Jones *et al.*, 2013). Additionally, there is an elevated risk of zoonotic infectious disease emergence and spread among humans in high-density urban hubs near wildlife habitats or agricultural areas, particularly in the absence of effective public health infrastructure (Santiago-Alarcon and MacGregor-Fors, 2020).

Global travel and trade have transformed the spread of pathogens, vectors, and hosts

Few human activities have transformed disease dynamics and distribution of pathogens as fundamentally as the increased human mobility and trade on a global scale. Human mobility across countries and continents has a long history of facilitating infectious disease spread, but high-volume air travel has multiplied that potential (Findlater and Bogoch, 2018). For example, air travel has been implicated in the global distribution of *Aedes aegypti* and *A. albopictus* mosquitos, important vectors of many infectious diseases (Kraemer *et al.*, 2015). Global trade of live and dead animals and plants has dramatically transformed the way pathogens and vectors can spread to new geographical locations, causing many infectious and zoonotic diseases to spread across continents (Jones *et al.*, 2013; Can, D'Cruze and Macdonald, 2019). The globalized scale of disease spread has resulted in profound consequences, such as increased *morbidity* and mortality and economic losses, as well as threatening the well-being of many species, populations, and entire ecosystems (examples in Table 4.1).

The COVID-19 pandemic has exemplified the effects of human mobility on the spread of infectious diseases. Initially detected in a single location in China, the SARS-CoV-2 virus rapidly spread in human populations around the globe, aided by international travel and trade (Sigler *et al.*, 2021). More than 585 million cases and 6.4 million deaths have been confirmed in humans (as of August 2022; World Health Organization (WHO), 2022). This pandemic has likewise emphasized the inequalities present in the globalized world, for example, low vaccine availability in low and lower-middle-income countries and the lack of human preparedness to deal with large disease outbreaks. Additionally, spillback of SARS-CoV-2 from humans to wildlife (Chandler *et al.*, 2021) and domestic animals (Shi *et al.*, 2020) have been observed, further highlighting the global-scale interconnectedness of human and animal health.

TABLE 4.1 Examples of the *globalization* of disease dynamics by human activities and consequences for ecosystems

Disease name	Pathogen type, species	Host organism and area affected	Outcome	Anthropogenic factors affecting the disease spread or outcome	References
NA	Bacterium. *Xylella fastidiosa*	Hundreds of plant species. Global	Local biodiversity loss and loss of crops → economic loss	Introduced to Europe from North America	Godefroid et al. (2019)
Bovine tuberculosis	Bacterium, zoonotic. *Mycobacterium tuberculosis*	Domestic cow (*Bos taurus*), European badger (*Meles meles*). United Kingdom	Slaughter of infected cows, extensive culling of wild badgers	Wild animal culling as zoonotic disease management—badgers were culled to slightly lower tuberculosis prevalence in cattle and lower the economic loss	Downs et al. (2019)
Chytridio-mycosis	Fungus. *Batrachochytrium dendrobatidis, B. salamandrivorans*	>500 species of amphibians. Global	90 species confirmed or suspected extinct, more experience severe population declines	Pathogen distribution facilitated by global trade of various amphibian species	Fisher and Garner (2020)
White-nose syndrome	Fungus. *Pseudogymnoascus destructans*	Bats (Chiroptera). North America	Decimation of populations	Disease spread by cavers, bat researchers, and tourists	Hoyt et al. (2021)
Chestnut blight	Fungus. *Cryphonectria parasitica*	American chestnut (*Castanea dentata*). North America	Near wipe-out of American chestnut, previously the dominant tree species in Eastern USA	Imported with seedlings from Asia	Jacobs (2007)
NA	Nematode. *Anguillicoloides crassus*	European eel (*Anguilla anguilla*). Europe	Population decline	Import of the parasite's native host, Japanese eel (*Anguilla japonica*), exposing the European eel, a novel host species, to the pathogen	Currie et al. (2020)

(Continued)

TABLE 4.1 (Continued)

Disease name	Pathogen type, species	Host organism and area affected	Outcome	Anthropogenic factors affecting the disease spread or outcome	References
Crayfish plague	Oomycete (fungus-like pathogen). *Aphanomyces astaci*	Many native crayfish species. Eurasia and Australia	Decimation of populations	Legal and illegal crayfish trade from North America	Martin-Torrijos *et al.* (2021)
NA	Virus. *Varroa destructor* mite vector for deformed wing virus	European honey bee (*Apis mellifera*). North America and Europe	Colony collapse	Asian honey bee *Apis cerana* transported from Asia together with *V. destructor*. European honey bee—a novel host.	Nazzi *et al.* (2012)
African Swine fever	Virus. African swine fever virus	Domestic and wild pigs. Global	Mass mortality of domestic and wild pigs, economic losses via loss of domestic pigs	Legal and illegal trade of pigs and swine products	Beltran-Alcrudo *et al.* (2019)
Myxomatosis	Virus. *Myxoma virus*	European rabbit (*Oryctolagus cuniculus*). Europe	Severe population declines	Introduction of new species as pest control. Virus from South America was purposefully introduced to control rabbits in Australia but then spread to rabbits in Europe.	Kerr (2012)

Harnessing principles of disease ecology as ecosystem health indicators for planetary well-being

Human activities that prioritize human needs over ecosystem health have led to a worldwide disruption of disease dynamics, with severe consequences for planetary well-being. The rapid evolution of microbes allows pathogens to effectively take advantage of beneficial conditions created by human actions to spread and infect susceptible hosts. The failure of disease control mechanisms in disrupted ecosystems can lead to a cascade of altered disease dynamics through socio-ecological systems at a global scale.

The recognition of these dynamics raises a difficult question: Is it possible for modern human societies to integrate as part of healthy ecosystems? Such assimilation may be achievable when small human societies use natural resources sustainably and locally, but in the globalized world most ecosystems that are affected by humans are linked to practically all other ecosystems on the planet. This facilitates potential universal sharing of pathogens among those ecosystems, risking both nonhuman and human health and well-being all over the world. This potential for global negative impacts begs questions such as whether it is ethical to allow any human activity within the relatively few thus-far undisturbed ecosystems, even when such activity is beneficial for human individuals and has no immediate destructive effects. Reaching comprehensive solutions requires shifting the focus away from the satisfaction of human needs and towards the well-being of whole ecosystems, in line with the planetary well-being approach.

Tools and data are needed to evaluate the impacts of different policies and practices on pathogen spread and changing pathogen burden, including pathogens with no immediate economic significance. Tools such as the Red List Index, an integrative measure of species extinction risk (Kortetmäki et al., 2021) could serve as a proxy measure of planetary well-being from the perspective of disease burden, as (novel) pathogens and diseases not only threaten organismal well-being but also induce population declines, increase species extinction risk, and can have cascading effects in communities and ecosystems. Tools are also being developed that allow decision makers to estimate the economic cost through public health costs of altering habitat (see examples in Myers (2017)). These approaches could be complemented with indicators of (1) ecosystem health and functioning, such as measures of biodiversity, resilience, and pathogen or disease prevalence in the system; (2) societal characteristics (urbanization, socioeconomic equality, healthcare, etc.); and (3) risk factors for the spread of invasive species and pathogens (e.g., global travel and trade). Developing reliable and compatible indicators for these complex issues is challenging but increasingly important because the combined information from such indicators could help in navigating trade-offs between human and nonhuman needs, supporting decision-making.

Training public health experts and decision makers with the use of such tools and applying the planetary well-being perspective is a potentially effective way to improve human and wildlife well-being. For example, the objectives of evidence-based ecological restoration policies could include both higher biodiversity and lower disease risk. The approaches under such policies might include *e.g.,* reintroductions of top predators, which have a demonstrated positive effect on community functioning and eventually reduced disease burden (Rey Benayas *et al.*, 2009). Solutions for reducing risky contacts among humans and domesticated or wild animals include reducing the use of animal-origin foods in human diets and ending the practice of keeping live animals in crowded conditions in live markets by developing improved monitoring and cold storage (Naguib *et al.*, 2021). At the same time, contacts with healthy natural ecosystems can benefit humans in terms of *e.g.,* beneficial microbes, clean air, nutrition, and mental health (Andersen, Corazon and Stigsdotter, 2021), with possible feedback through an increased commitment to protecting healthy ecosystems.

References

Aguirre, A.A. *et al.* (2002) *Conservation Medicine: Ecological Health in Practice*, *Conservation Medicine: Ecological Health in Practice*. New York: Oxford University Press.

Andersen, L., Corazon, S.S. and Stigsdotter, U.K. (2021) 'Nature exposure and its effects on immune system functioning: A systematic review', *International Journal of Environmental Research and Public Health*, 18(4), pp. 1–42. https://doi.org/10.3390/ijerph18041416

Beltran-Alcrudo, D. *et al.* (2019) 'Transboundary spread of pig diseases: The role of international trade and travel', *BMC Veterinary Research*, 15(1), pp. 1–14. https://doi.org/10.1186/s12917-019-1800-5

Bouchard, C. *et al.* (2019) 'Increased risk of tick-borne diseases with climate and environmental changes', *Canada Communicable Disease Report*, 45(4), pp. 83–89. https://doi.org/10.14745/ccdr.v45i04a02

Caminade, C., McIntyre, K.M. and Jones, A.E. (2019) 'Impact of recent and future climate change on vector-borne diseases', *Annals of the New York Academy of Sciences*, 1436(1), pp. 157–173. https://doi.org/10.1111/nyas.13950

Can, Ö.E., D'Cruze, N. and Macdonald, D.W. (2019) 'Dealing in deadly pathogens: Taking stock of the legal trade in live wildlife and potential risks to human health', *Global Ecology and Conservation*, 17. https://doi.org/10.1016/j.gecco.2018.e00515

Chandler, J.C. *et al.* (2021) 'SARS-CoV-2 exposure in wild white-tailed deer (Odocoileus virginianus)', *Proceedings of the National Academy of Sciences of the United States of America*, 118(47), pp. 1–3. https://doi.org/10.1073/pnas.2114828118

Charron, D.F. (2012) 'Ecohealth: Origins and approach', in Charron, D.F. (ed.) *Ecohealth Research in Practice: Innovative Applications of an Ecosystem Approach to Health*. New York: Springer, pp. 1–32. https://doi.org/10.4000/vertigo.14935

Cohen, J.M. *et al.* (2020) 'Divergent impacts of warming weather on wildlife disease risk across climates', *Science*, 370(6519). https://doi.org/10.1126/science.abb1702

Costanza, R. and Mageau, M. (1999) 'What is a healthy ecosystem?', *Aquatic Ecology*, 33, pp. 105–115.

Cronin, J.P., Rúa, M.A. and Mitchell, C.E. (2014) 'Why is living fast dangerous? Disentangling the roles of resistance and tolerance of disease', *American Naturalist*, 184(2), pp. 172–187. https://doi.org/10.1086/676854

Currie, H.A.L. *et al.* (2020) 'A mechanical approach to understanding the impact of the nematode Anguillicoloides crassus on the European eel swimbladder', *Journal of Experimental Biology*, 223(17). https://doi.org/10.1242/jeb.219808

Destoumieux-Garzón, D. *et al.* (2022) 'Getting out of crises: Environmental, social-ecological and evolutionary research is needed to avoid future risks of pandemics', *Environment International*, 158. https://doi.org/10.1016/j.envint.2021.106915

Doherty, T.S. *et al.* (2017) 'Impacts and management of feral cats Felis catus in Australia', *Mammal Review*, 47(2), pp. 83–97. https://doi.org/10.1111/mam.12080

Downs, S.H. *et al.* (2019) 'Assessing effects from four years of industry-led badger culling in England on the incidence of bovine tuberculosis in cattle, 2013–2017', *Scientific Reports*, 9(1), pp. 24–29. https://doi.org/10.1038/s41598-019-49957-6

Dubey, J.P. (2008) 'The history of Toxoplasma gondii – The first 100 years', *Journal of Eukaryotic Microbiology*, 55(6), pp. 467–475. https://doi.org/10.1111/j.1550-7408.2008.00345.x

Erokhin, V. and Gao, T. (2020) 'Impacts of COVID-19 on trade and economic aspects of food security: Evidence from 45 developing countries', *International Journal of Environmental Research and Public Health*, 17(16), pp. 1–28. https://doi.org/10.3390/ijerph17165775

Findlater, A. and Bogoch, I.I. (2018) 'Human mobility and the global spread of infectious diseases: A focus on air travel', *Trends in Parasitology*, 34(9), pp. 772–783. https://doi.org/10.1016/j.pt.2018.07.004

Fischhoff, I.R. *et al.* (2020) 'Parasite and pathogen effects on ecosystem processes: A quantitative review', *Ecosphere*, 11(5). https://doi.org/10.1002/ecs2.3057

Fisher, M.C. and Garner, T.W.J. (2020) 'Chytrid fungi and global amphibian declines', *Nature Reviews Microbiology*, 18(6), pp. 332–343. https://doi.org/10.1038/s41579-020-0335-x

Garamszegi, L.Z. (2011) 'Climate change increases the risk of malaria in birds', *Global Change Biology*, 17(5), pp. 1751–1759. https://doi.org/10.1111/j.1365-2486.2010.02346.x

Gibb, R. *et al.* (2020) 'Zoonotic host diversity increases in human-dominated ecosystems', *Nature*, 584(7821), pp. 398–402. https://doi.org/10.1038/s41586-020-2562-8

Gibbs, E.P.J. (2014) 'The evolution of one health: A decade of progress and challenges for the future', *Veterinary Record*, 174(4), pp. 85–91. https://doi.org/10.1136/vr.g143

Godefroid, M. *et al.* (2019) 'Xylella fastidiosa: Climate suitability of European continent', *Scientific Reports*, 9(1), pp. 1–10. https://doi.org/10.1038/s41598-019-45365-y

Golden, C.D. *et al.* (2016) 'Ecosystem services and food security: Assessing inequality at community, household and individual scales', *Environmental Conservation*, 43(4), pp. 381–388. https://doi.org/10.1017/S0376892916000163

Holdo, R.M. *et al.* (2009) 'A disease-mediated trophic cascade in the Serengeti and its implications for ecosystem C', *PLoS Biology*, 7(9). https://doi.org/10.1371/journal.pbio.1000210

Holmes, E.C. *et al.* (2021) 'The origins of SARS-CoV-2: A critical review', *Cell*, 184(19), pp. 4848–4856. https://doi.org/10.1016/j.cell.2021.08.017

Hoyt, J.R., Kilpatrick, A.M. and Langwig, K.E. (2021) 'Ecology and impacts of white-nose syndrome on bats', *Nature Reviews Microbiology*, 19(3), pp. 196–210. https://doi.org/10.1038/s41579-020-00493-5

Jacobs, D.F. (2007) 'Toward development of silvical strategies for forest restoration of American chestnut (Castanea dentata) using blight-resistant hybrids', *Biological Conservation*, 137(4), pp. 497–506. https://doi.org/10.1016/j.biocon.2007.03.013

Jones, B.A. *et al.* (2013) 'Zoonosis emergence linked to agricultural intensification and environmental change', *Proceedings of the National Academy of Sciences of the United States of America*, 110(21), pp. 8399–8404. https://doi.org/10.1073/pnas.1208059110

Keesing, F. *et al.* (2010) 'Impacts of biodiversity on the emergence and transmission of infectious diseases', *Nature*, 468(7324), pp. 647–652. https://doi.org/10.1038/nature09575

Keesing, F. and Ostfeld, R.S. (2021) 'Dilution effects in disease ecology', *Ecology Letters*, 24(11), pp. 2490–2505. https://doi.org/10.1111/ele.13875

Kerr, P.J. (2012) 'Myxomatosis in Australia and Europe: A model for emerging infectious diseases', *Antiviral Research* 93(3), pp. 387–415. https://doi.org/10.1016/j.antiviral.2012.01.009

Kortetmäki, T. *et al.* (2021) 'Planetary well-being', *Humanities and Social Sciences Communications*, 8(1), pp. 1–8. https://doi.org/10.1057/s41599-021-00899-3

Kraemer, M.U.G. *et al.* (2015) 'The global distribution of the arbovirus vectors Aedes aegypti and Ae. Albopictus', *eLife*, 41–18. https://doi.org/10.7554/eLife.08347

Lee, G.H. and Choi, K.C. (2020) 'Adverse effects of pesticides on the functions of immune system', *Comparative Biochemistry and Physiology Part – C: Toxicology and Pharmacology*, 235, 108789. https://doi.org/10.1016/j.cbpc.2020.108789

Lerner, H. and Berg, C. (2017) 'A comparison of three holistic approaches to health: One health, ecohealth, and planetary health', *Frontiers in Veterinary Science*, 4, pp. 1–7. https://doi.org/10.3389/fvets.2017.00163

Magouras, I. *et al.* (2020) 'Emerging zoonotic diseases: Should we rethink the animal–human interface?', *Frontiers in Veterinary Science*, 7, 1–6. https://doi.org/10.3389/fvets.2020.582743

Marí Saéz, A. *et al.* (2015) 'Investigating the zoonotic origin of the West African Ebola epidemic', *EMBO Molecular Medicine*, 7(1), pp. 17–23. https://doi.org/10.15252/emmm.201404792

Martin, L.B. *et al.* (2010) 'The effects of anthropogenic global changes on immune functions and disease resistance', *Annals of the New York Academy of Sciences*, 1195, pp. 129–148. https://doi.org/10.1111/j.1749-6632.2010.05454.x

Martín-Torrijos, L. *et al.* (2021) 'Tracing the origin of the crayfish plague pathogen, Aphanomyces astaci, to the Southeastern United States', *Scientific Reports* 1–11. https://doi.org/10.1038/s41598-021-88704-8

Myers, S.S. (2017) 'Planetary health: Protecting human health on a rapidly changing planet', *The Lancet*, 390(10114), pp. 2860–2868. https://doi.org/10.1016/S0140-6736(17)32846-5

Naguib, M.M. *et al.* (2021) 'Live and wet markets: Food access versus the risk of disease emergence', *Trends in Microbiology* 29(7), pp. 573–581. https://doi.org/10.1016/j.tim.2021.02.007

Nazzi, F. *et al.* (2012) 'Synergistic parasite-pathogen interactions mediated by host immunity can drive the collapse of honeybee colonies', *PLoS Pathogens*, 8(6). https://doi.org/10.1371/journal.ppat.1002735

Parmesan, C. and Yohe, G. (2003) 'A globally coherent fingerprint of climate change', *Nature*, 421, pp. 37–42.

Plowright, R.K. *et al.* (2011) 'Urban habituation, ecological connectivity and epidemic dampening: The emergence of hendra virus from flying foxes (Pteropus spp.)', *Proceedings of the Royal Society B: Biological Sciences*, 278(1725), pp. 3703–3712. https://doi.org/10.1098/rspb.2011.0522

Rey Benayas, J.M. *et al.* (2009) 'Enhancement of biodiversity and ecosystem services by ecological restoration: A meta-analysis', *Science*, 8, pp. 1121–1124.

Santiago-Alarcon, D. and MacGregor-Fors, I. (2020) 'Cities and pandemics: Urban areas are ground zero for the transmission of emerging human infectious diseases', *Journal of Urban Ecology*, 6(1), pp. 1–3. https://doi.org/10.1093/jue/juaa012

Shi, J. *et al.* (2020) 'Susceptibility of ferrets, cats, dogs, and other domesticated animals to SARS-coronavirus 2', *Science*, 368(6494), pp. 1016–1020. https://doi.org/10.1126/science.abb7015

Sigler, T. *et al.* (2021) 'The socio-spatial determinants of COVID-19 diffusion: The impact of globalisation, settlement characteristics and population', *Globalization and* Health, pp. 1–14. https://doi.org/10.1186/s12992-021-00707-2

Song, X.P. *et al.* (2018) 'Global land change from 1982 to 2016', *Nature*, 560(7720), pp. 639–643. https://doi.org/10.1038/s41586-018-0411-9

Stephens, P.R. *et al.* (2021) 'Characteristics of the 100 largest modern zoonotic disease outbreaks', *Philosophical Transactions of the Royal Society B: Biological Sciences*, 376(1837). https://doi.org/10.1098/rstb.2020.0535

Thoradeniya, T. and Jayasinghe, S. (2021) 'COVID-19 and future pandemics: A global systems approach and relevance to SDGs', *Globalization and* Health, pp. 1–10. https://doi.org/10.1186/s12992-021-00711-6

WHO (2022) *WHO Coronavirus (COVID-19) Dashboard*. Available at: https://covid19.who.int/ (Accessed: 12 August 2022).

Wilmers, C.C. *et al.* (2006) 'Predator disease out-break modulates top-down, bottom-up and climatic effects on herbivore population dynamics', *Ecology Letters*, 9(4), pp. 383–389. https://doi.org/10.1111/j.1461-0248.2006.00890.x

5

A LANDSCAPE APPROACH TO PLANETARY WELL-BEING

Rémi Duflot, Kirsi E. Keskinen, Kyle Eyvindson and Kaisa J. Raatikainen

Introduction: Landscapes as geographic interfaces between humans and nonhuman beings

Landscape as a place-based socio-ecological system

A landscape can be defined as a perceivable place of living for human and nonhuman beings. Organisms interact selectively with their surroundings, depending on their characteristics and behaviours. People's influence on nonhuman nature is most acute and prevalent on the landscape level, and landscapes also reciprocally affect human activities (Antrop, 2000). For this reason, landscapes provide a conceptual and actual space for human–nature interactions that support planetary well-being, as we argue throughout this chapter. Human perceptions of and actions on landscapes are deeply rooted in culture, spirituality, history, and the human–nature relationship, leading to incredibly diverse worldviews and practices (for example, Chapter 3). Ultimately, a great diversity of landscapes has evolved out of these everyday socio-ecological interactions.

In this chapter, we approach landscapes as place-based socio-ecological systems (Wu, 2021). Applying the landscape approach within a system analysis involves (at least) three aspects that are also crucial from the planetary well-being perspective. First, the landscape approach emphasizes the spatial nature of various phenomena linked to planetary well-being. For instance, biodiversity loss, which decreases planetary well-being, always occurs somewhere. Second, landscapes are the space where human and nonhuman beings realize and evolve their typical characteristics and capacities in relation to one another and their shared environment. Third, the landscape approach acknowledges the importance of various scale domains, such as the spatial, temporal, and organizational, and is thus able to analyze multiple

DOI: 10.4324/9781003334002-8

scales simultaneously (for example, to evaluate the long-term persistence and spatial distribution of organisms under human influence). This incorporation of multiple scales is crucial to the planetary well-being perspective, as the concept assumes that Earth system and global processes are linked to lower-level phenomena (organismal need satisfaction) and has a temporal dimension (persistence of evolutionary lineages).

The purpose of this chapter is to exemplify how the landscape approach integrates spatial thinking into planetary well-being framework, allowing for studies of the interconnectedness of humans, nonhuman organisms, and abiotic nature while placing them in a temporally evolving spatial context. This allows researchers to investigate how decisions relating to the main dimensions of landscape—biophysical elements, processes, and actors—affect both human and nonhuman need satisfaction. Within this conceptualization (Figure 5.1), we specifically emphasize the ecological dimension of landscapes.

The ecological characteristics of landscapes

Ecologists consider landscapes as consisting of spatially organized, temporally evolving, and interacting biophysical elements. These biophysical elements can be viewed as land uses from the human perspective or as habitat patches from a nonhuman-species perspective (Figure 5.1). Land-use types and intensity reflect human activities, affect the ecological characteristics of the landscape, and, ultimately, determine the suitability of the landscape as a place of living for nonhuman species. Land uses directly impact the heterogeneity of a landscape, which is based on its composition and configuration. The term "composition" refers to the types, relative amounts, and the diversity of biophysical elements in the landscape, whereas "configuration" denotes the spatial organization of these biophysical elements (Fahrig et al., 2011). Landscape composition determines the types of ecosystems and diversity of organisms that can be present in a landscape. Landscape configuration affects landscape-level processes that link ecosystems and species communities across the landscape through fluxes of energy and nutrients, as well as the movement of organisms (Forman and Godron, 1981).

As a result, landscapes are studied as systems of interacting elements that are linked by various processes. These processes are ecological functions that operate within and between ecosystems and can be perceived as ecosystem services by humans when they contribute to human activities (Figure 5.1). Processes are co-produced by actors, i.e., the humans and nonhuman organisms, present in the landscape and supported by the biophysical elements. Certain biophysical elements and processes within landscapes are essential in meeting organismal needs. Therefore, their existence is a prerequisite for planetary well-being (Figure 5.1). A prime example of this is pollination, a process performed by pollinators (actors) in habitat patches with flowering plants (biophysical elements). It is essential for the reproduction of many plants and the feeding of many insects, as well as being

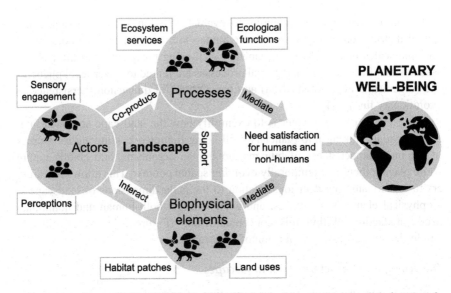

FIGURE 5.1 Conceptualization of a landscape approach to planetary well-being. Landscapes are an operational arena for planetary well-being because the biophysical elements and processes that meet human and nonhuman needs are situated in landscapes, as are the human and nonhuman beings themselves (hereafter referred to as: Actors). The three basic dimensions of a landscape (actors, processes, and biophysical elements) can be seen from the human and nonhuman perspective (icons). This chapter focuses on the biophysical elements and processes that mediate need satisfaction for humans and nonhumans. Figure created by Māris Grunskis/@PHOTOGRUNSKIS.

an important ecosystem service for humans, as 75% of the world's food crops are at least partially dependent on pollination (Food and Agriculture Organization of the United Nations (FAO), 2016).

Pollination illustrates how landscapes host socio-ecological processes. The humans involved in and influenced by any landscape process are commonly termed stakeholders. They are important in land-use planning, *i.e.*, targeting the use of land in a spatially explicit and meaningful manner (Antrop, 2000). The best environmental practices often require collaboration between stakeholders to create functional landscape features that ensure the persistence of nonhuman species and their associated functions and simultaneously meet the objectives of the stakeholders (Vialatte *et al.*, 2019). To illustrate the transformative potential of the landscape approach to planetary well-being, we present three examples of land-use planning principles that acknowledge the role of landscape-level processes and support planetary well-being. In the following sections, we examine the benefits of agro-ecological farming, urban green infrastructure, and multi-objective forest management zoning approaches to planetary well-being. These examples show how to put planetary well-being into practice (Figures 5.2–5.4).

Agroecological farming systems: From field to landscape levels

Decades of farming intensification and landscape homogenization have substantially decreased biodiversity in agricultural landscapes (Benton, Vickery and Wilson, 2003). In contrast to industrialized farming systems, which are based on agrochemicals and mechanization, the agroecological approach relies on biodiversity-driven ecological functions to support food production (Jeanneret *et al.*, 2021). Key ecological functions, which are perceived as ecosystem services by humans, include soil fertility (Chapter 6), natural pest control and pollination. Importantly, agroecological practices build on and benefit from the local diversity of species and their biotic and abiotic interactions which maintain ecological functions (Dainese *et al.*, 2019). Given the very large extent of agricultural land on Earth and the vital societal importance of agriculture, the agroecological landscape approach has tremendous potential to enhance planetary well-being by supporting biodiversity and various ecosystem services. Figure 5.2 shows how the agroecological landscape approach is linked to planetary well-being, with a focus on organism food provisioning.

The biodiversity of agricultural landscapes (including species that co-produce processes useful to humans) depends on the provision of resources needed by the

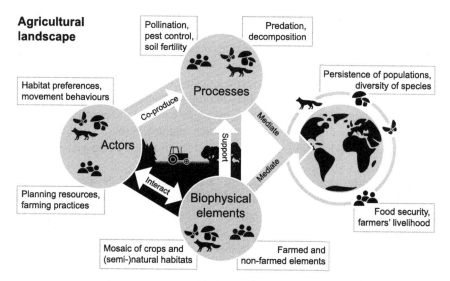

FIGURE 5.2   Conceptualization of a land-use planning principle of agroecological farming, as a landscape approach to planetary well-being, with a focus on food provisioning for humans and nonhuman species. The three basic dimensions of a landscape (actors, processes, and biophysical elements) can be seen from the human and nonhuman perspective (icons). This chapter focuses on the biophysical elements and processes that mediate need satisfaction for humans and nonhumans. Figure created by Māris Grunskis/@ PHOTOGRUNSKIS.

species, such as feeding, shelter, and reproduction and overwintering sites. These are often not available within the crop fields but, rather, in their surroundings. Thus, the central process is the movement of species between semi-natural habitats and crop fields or between crop fields of different types, enabling species to access their required resources at different places and time and adapt to recurrent disturbances (Blitzer *et al.*, 2012). At the field level, the intensity of farming practices, *e.g.*, related to the amount of pesticides, determine the suitability of a crop for hosting diverse species and supporting associated ecological functions (Duflot *et al.*, 2022). Typically, organically farmed fields have higher species diversity and abundance (Puech *et al.*, 2014). At the landscape level, most organisms rely on resources provided by semi-natural habitats (*e.g.*, floral resources or overwintering sites), therefore, landscapes with a high percentage of such non-crop habitats have higher biodiversity and ecological functions (Duarte *et al.*, 2018).

Because most species in agricultural landscapes are very mobile, the agroecological approach acknowledges the need to maintain adequate ecological conditions at both the local-field and landscape levels (Jeanneret *et al.*, 2021). The synergetic influence of landscape heterogeneity and farming intensity on biodiversity and the associated functions (Ricci *et al.*, 2019) suggests that environmentally friendly practices are required at both the field and landscape levels. Practices such as less intense soil management (*e.g.*, no tillage and direct seeding), longer and more diversified crop rotations, and crop mixtures have significant potential to maintain biodiversity, functional agroecosystems, and productive farming systems (Duru *et al.*, 2015). At the landscape level, increasing the proportion of semi-natural habitats, crop diversity, and reducing field size promote biodiversity and ecological functions that contribute to crop production (Sirami *et al.*, 2019). Complex configuration pattern with many edges between different habitat types and smaller fields will facilitate species access to multiple resources and, therefore, further enhance biodiversity, related ecological functions, and crop yields (Martin *et al.*, 2019).

Agroecological approach also provides a socio-ecological perspective to food production and highlights the leading role of farmers and the importance of self-sufficient farms for sustainable landscape management (Jeanneret *et al.*, 2021). For this purpose, agri-environment-climate policy schemes (such as a part of the EU Common Agricultural Policy) subsidize a selection of agroecological practices aimed at reducing field-level intensity of practices and restoring some form of landscape heterogeneity (*e.g.*, through implementation of grassy or flower strips). While reducing farmers' dependency on agrochemicals and promoting biodiversity, the implementation of such agri-environment-climate schemes remains limited due to lack of institutional support and financial resources (Pe'er *et al.*, 2020). As agricultural landscapes consist of spatially intermingled networks of farmers and non-farmers, and corresponding farms, fields, field margins and other landscape elements, such schemes would, however, also benefit from additional strategies for integrated landscape-level cooperation (*e.g.*, through collective contracts; Jeanneret *et al.*, 2021; Vialatte *et al.*, 2019).

Green infrastructure in urban design: Restoring processes in heavily modified ecosystems

Over 55% of the world's human population live in urban landscapes, with further urbanization being projected (United Nations (UN), 2019). Moreover, urban area is increasing twice as fast as the urban population, spreading into other valuable land uses, and is expected to quadruple globally by 2050 as compared to 2000. Urban expansion transforms vegetated land covers into artificial surfaces within urban areas and their surroundings. Urban landscapes are heavily modified by humans, with an altered biophysical environment and ecosystem functioning, thereby compromising planetary well-being. For instance, urbanization increases the fragmentation and shrinking of green areas, which result in dramatic decline in biodiversity in urban landscapes (Lepczyk *et al.*, 2017). It also disrupts important ecosystem fluxes, as artificial surfaces prevent water infiltration, which creates a dry environment and flooding risks (Chapter 6), and increases solar energy absorption and storage, which increases the air temperature in cities (IPBES, 2019). The development of urban landscapes with green infrastructure, *i.e.*, an interconnected network of nature-based elements (hereafter green spaces), provides various benefits for both humans and nonhumans (*ibid.*) and may, thus, support planetary well-being. Figure 5.3 shows how the effects of green infrastructure are linked to planetary well-being, with a focus on organism mobility.

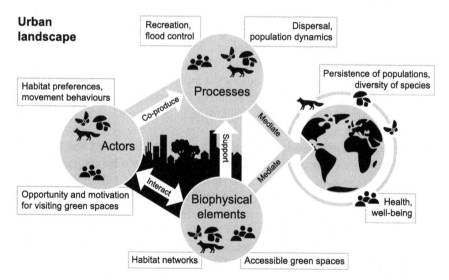

FIGURE 5.3   Conceptualization of a land-use planning principle of urban green infrastructure, as a landscape approach to planetary well-being, with a focus on human and nonhuman organism mobility. The three basic dimensions of a landscape (actors, processes, and biophysical elements) can be seen from the human and nonhuman perspective (icons). This chapter focuses on the biophysical elements and processes that mediate need satisfaction for humans and nonhumans. Figure created by Māris Grunskis/@PHOTOGRUNSKIS.

Urban green infrastructures offer a variety of habitats, ranging from remnants of native vegetation, vacant land, and gardens to green roofs and managed parks (Lepczyk et al., 2017). In urban landscapes, habitat patches are typically small, and species' habitat selection is often governed by patch size and landscape heterogeneity (e.g., Pithon et al., 2021). Therefore, green infrastructure is commonly planned in the form of habitat networks, consisting of multiple habitat patches that are connected by corridors to allow organisms to move within the network (Lepczyk et al., 2017). The ability to move is based on landscape connectivity, which is considered a major factor in species survival and the long-term persistence of biodiversity (Crooks and Sanjayan, 2006). Thus, urban biodiversity is best supported by the careful spatial planning of green spaces and their land uses, including specific habitat management actions (e.g., infrequent grass mowing). Urban green infrastructure can support populations of species that can adapt to urban environments and provide complementary habitats for species threatened by intensive farming and commercial forestry in rural areas (e.g., Selonen and Mäkeläinen, 2017). Biodiversity also supports ecosystem functioning in urban areas, thereby, promotes planetary well-being.

Recreation in green areas benefits human health via three main pathways (Markevych et al., 2017): (1) Reducing harm, e.g., reducing exposure to heat and noise; (2) restoring capacities, e.g., relieving stress (Tyrväinen et al., 2014) and producing positive psychological effects (see Chapter 12); and (3) building capacities, e.g., supporting immune balance (Haahtela, 2019), facilitating social cohesion, and encouraging physical activity. Simultaneously, elements of green infrastructure provide ecosystem services to humans, e.g., by reducing water runoff, they provide peak flow control and flood alleviation for intense rainfalls and stormwater management (Li et al., 2019). Ideally, green infrastructure is developed at the landscape level during the urban development planning phase. However, elements of green infrastructure can be added to existing urban landscapes. For example, setting aside vacant land to unmanaged or less intensively maintained green areas is shown to be a cost-efficient way to increase green infrastructure and increase access to green spaces (McKinney and VerBerkmoes, 2020). Furthermore, encouraging residents to turn their yards into gardens with native species can contribute greatly to green infrastructure and support multiple processes (Cameron et al., 2012). Involving stakeholder groups in green infrastructure development and management may increase knowledge for decision-making, as well as empowering citizens and the local community to take agency (Grêt-Regamey et al., 2021), but it also requires the consideration of social inclusiveness and the reconciliation of differing views.

Multi-objective forest management: Improvements through landscape zoning

Managing forest resources while balancing the ecological needs of species living in forested landscapes require a specific focus on the frequency and intensity of forest management. Traditionally, forest management has prioritized timber profits (Faustmann, 1849), operating on homogenous parcels of forest land. This timber-oriented management aims at sustained timber extraction, that is, maximizing forest growth while ensuring an even flow of timber for the forest industry. Meanwhile, the habitat needs of species living in the forest have been largely ignored in practice, harming forest biodiversity. Innovative management practices intended to enhance the quality and amount of suitable forest habitats strive to mimic natural disturbances and the associated variability of forest structures, *i.e.*, habitat heterogeneity (Kuuluvainen *et al.*, 2021). To reconcile human interests and biodiversity conservation, the division of forest landscape into intensive use, extensive use, and reserve zones has been proposed (Himes *et al.*, 2022). This landscape approach plans and conducts forest operations at multiple levels, first via landscape zones, with each of them prioritizing a specific objective (*i.e.*, timber production, multiple use, and conservation), and then via locally applying diverse management practices, with varied harvesting intensities and cutting methods (*e.g.*, continuous cover forestry or delayed clear-cut harvests). Such land-use planning of forest management focuses on balancing the societal demand for raw material and energy with the needs of nonhuman species and ecosystems, that is, contributing to planetary well-being itself. Multi-objective forest management zoning is shown in Figure 5.4, which describes how human active and passive management of the forest landscape impacts planetary well-being, focusing on maintaining resource extraction while preserving the processes of the forest ecosystem.

The processes of natural disturbance-succession dynamics, *i.e.*, the progress of forest regrowth after partial or total nonhuman tree destruction, is crucial to forest biodiversity, as various species groups depend on the diversity of successional stages and the structure created by disturbances, *e.g.*, deadwood (Hilmers *et al.*, 2018; Tikkanen *et al.*, 2006). Prioritizing biodiversity conservation will, therefore, require a transformation of how we manage human-modified forest landscapes (Arroyo-Rodríguez *et al.*, 2020). The forest management zoning strategy allows landscape processes to proceed along differing disturbance-succession dynamics. Extensive forest management aims at maintaining some level of forest complexity locally and of heterogeneity at landscape level. This can be achieved through substantial adjustments in how forestry is applied and the diversification of management practices (Duflot, Fahrig and Mönkkönen, 2022). However, managed forests are not comparable with natural forests, because the tree species composition, tree age structure, and characteristics of deadwood composition differ considerably, even if forests are managed extensively. Thus, forest reserves must be included in the land-use plan to allow ecological processes without human interference.

Meanwhile, some proportion of carefully located areas of intensive forestry, primarily oriented towards timber production, could be used to meet human needs. Intensive extractive activities in the forest landscape can provide an even flow of timber, allowing for a shift away from non-renewable resources (*e.g.*, fossil fuels),[1] indirectly contributing to enhanced planetary well-being (*e.g.*, climate

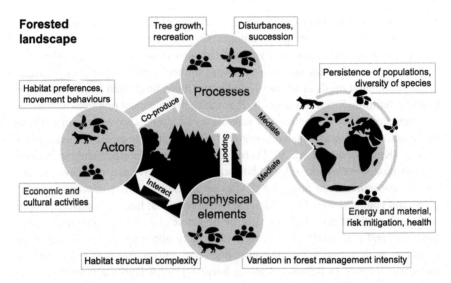

FIGURE 5.4 Conceptualization of a land-use planning principle of forest management zoning, as a landscape approach to planetary well-being, with a focus on sustained forest management. The three basic dimensions of a landscape (actors, processes, and biophysical elements) can be seen from the human and nonhuman perspective (icons). This chapter focuses on the biophysical elements and processes that mediate need satisfaction for humans and nonhumans. Figure created by Māris Grunskis/@PHOTOGRUNSKIS.

change mitigation). Intensive timber extraction can conflict with, and reduce, the availability of other forest benefits for both humans and nonhumans (Eyvindson et al., 2021). Human activities in the forest disrupt the natural functioning of forest ecosystems, leading to a substantially reduced long-term ecological value for biodiversity and ecosystem services (Pohjanmies et al., 2021). Extensive management focused on multiple uses, including non-timber services (e.g., water quality and recreation) can have synergies with the ecological functioning of the forest landscape. For example, for recreational areas, humans prefer subtlety managed forest so as to ease access and create places to enjoy landscape vistas (Pukkala, Lähde and Laiho, 2012).

Determining the relative proportion and spatial distribution of the management zones is challenging (Himes et al., 2022). Forested landscapes are often dominated by human activities, with the intensity of management being defined by the human demand for timber and non-timber resources. This human-centric perspective must shift towards a focus on planetary well-being. This can be accomplished by wisely managing the forest in a way that minimizes damage to the ecological system, e.g., choosing the management plan with most similarity with the natural disturbance-succession dynamics (Côté et al., 2010). The specific distribution and organization of the zones should also be carefully considered, as improved ecological outcomes (*e.g.*, representativeness and connectivity of protected area networks) are possible at a relatively low economic cost (Tittler *et al.*, 2015).

Conclusion

As illustrated by the above land-use planning principles, landscapes host conflicts and synergies between human and nonhuman nature, providing an opportunity to put planetary well-being in practice. The availability of suitable biophysical elements and their spatial organization in a landscape are important aspects of each of our examples, demonstrating how the existence of life-supporting processes depends on the ability of organisms to co-occupy the landscape. Ecological processes, such as dispersal and succession, are impacted by intensive land use. To relax the human-induced pressures faced by nonhuman nature and facilitate ecological functioning, the planning of land uses at the landscape level must be done carefully. Landscapes are the arena in which human actions take place; thus, landscapes are the operational level to achieve planetary well-being. Because they have transformative potential, landscapes can act as an interface across various disciplines and stakeholders, providing a shared representation of space as maps, which are powerful tools to guide human activities towards planetary well-being.

However, all landscape approaches have two main limitations that may hinder their ability to enhance planetary well-being. First, landscapes are open systems subject to external influences. Thus, not all problems can be solved at the landscape level if they originate from outside of the system. Landscapes are embedded in larger entities, such as ecological regions, cultures, or economic and institutional contexts, which impact the organization and dynamics of landscapes. Transforming negative impacts into planetary well-being positive will also require actions beyond the landscape level. In addition, what is done in a landscape may "leak" elsewhere. For example, planning for less dense cities with more green spaces will likely promote further urban expansion. That being said, the challenges resulting from the unboundedness of landscapes can be somewhat controlled for by considering context dependencies in landscape analyses.

Second, landscape approaches often elude ethical consideration; the presented examples offer no principles regarding how to balance between human and nonhuman needs. They do not define legitimate or just actions via which to meet the basic needs of organisms, except the presumption that supporting biodiversity, as a manifestation of evolution, is desirable. The lack of a unified ethics on planetary well-being-oriented land uses is reflected in the provided examples, which differentiate ecosystem services (human needs) from biodiversity conservation (nonhuman needs).

Although land-use planning is generally a process that has been conducted primarily by and for humans, it provides an opportunity to look for synergies between ecosystem services and biodiversity conservation. We argue that land-use planning based on knowledge about ecosystem and landscape processes can strongly benefit both human and nonhuman organisms and ultimately promote planetary well-being. Landscape approaches are powerful in detecting such mutual benefits given that nonhuman species are equally considered as actors in landscape-level processes. In that sense, the concept of planetary well-being might trigger a revolution in land-use planning by giving equal moral significance to human and nonhuman species.

Acknowledgement

Rémi Duflot was financially supported by a postdoctoral grant from the Kone Foundation. Kirsi E. Keskinen was financially supported by a grant from Juho Vainio Foundation. Kyle Eyvindson was partially financially supported from the Norwegian Research Council (NFR project 302701 Climate Smart Forestry Norway). Kaisa J. Raatikainen was a postdoctoral fellow of the School of Resource Wisdom. The study sponsors had no role in designing or writing the book chapter.

Note

1 Studies exploring the potential displacement of carbon emissions from wood substitution highlight that, in general, substitution of wood decreases GHG emissions (Myllyviita *et al.*, 2021).

References

Antrop, M. (2000) 'Background concepts for integrated landscape analysis', *Agriculture, Ecosystems & Environment*, 77, pp. 17–28. https://doi.org/10.1016/S0167-8809(99)00089-4

Arroyo-Rodríguez, V. *et al.* (2020) 'Designing optimal human-modified landscapes for forest biodiversity conservation', *Ecology Letters*, 23, pp. 1404–1420. https://doi.org/10.1111/ele.13535

Benton, T.G., Vickery, J.A. and Wilson, J.D. (2003) 'Farmland biodiversity: Is habitat heterogeneity the key?', *Trends in Ecology & Evolution*, 18, pp. 182–188. https://doi.org/10.1016/S0169-5347(03)00011-9

Blitzer, E.J. *et al.* (2012) 'Spillover of functionally important organisms between managed and natural habitats', *Agriculture, Ecosystems & Environment*, 146, pp. 34–43. https://doi.org/10.1016/j.agee.2011.09.005

Cameron, R.W.F *et al.* (2012) 'The domestic garden—Its contribution to urban green infrastructure', *Urban Forestry & Urban Greening*, 11(2), pp. 129–137. https://doi.org/10.1016/j.ufug.2012.01.002

Côté, P. *et al.* (2010) 'Comparing different forest zoning options for landscape-scale management of the boreal forest: Possible benefits of the TRIAD', *Forest Ecology and Management*, 259(3), pp. 418–427. https://doi.org/10.1016/j.foreco.2009.10.038

Crooks, K.R. and Sanjayan, M. (2006) *Connectivity Conservation, Conservation biology*. New York: Cambridge University Press.

Dainese, M. *et al.* (2019) 'A global synthesis reveals biodiversity-mediated benefits for crop production', *Science Advances*, 5, eaax0121. https://doi.org/10.1126/sciadv.aax0121

Duarte, G.T. *et al.* (2018) 'The effects of landscape patterns on ecosystem services: Meta-analyses of landscape services', *Landscape Ecology*, 33, pp. 1247–1257. https://doi.org/10.1007/s10980-018-0673-5

Duflot, R., Fahrig, L. and Mönkkönen, M. (2022) 'Management diversity begets biodiversity in production forest landscapes', *Biological Conservation*, 268, 109514. https://doi.org/10.1016/j.biocon.2022.109514

Duflot, R. *et al.* (2022) 'Farming intensity indirectly reduces crop yield through negative effects on agrobiodiversity and key ecological functions', *Agriculture, Ecosystems & Environment*, 326, 107810. https://doi.org/10.1016/j.agee.2021.107810

Duru, M. *et al.* (2015) 'How to implement biodiversity-based agriculture to enhance ecosystem services: A review', *Agronomy for Sustainable Development*, 35, pp. 1259–1281. https://doi.org/10.1007/s13593-015-0306-1

Eyvindson, K. *et al.* (2021) 'High boreal forest multifunctionality requires continuous cover forestry as a dominant management', *Land Use Policy*, 100, 104918. https://doi.org/10.1016/j.landusepol.2020.104918

Fahrig, L. *et al.* (2011) 'Functional landscape heterogeneity and animal biodiversity in agricultural landscapes', *Ecology Letters*, 14(2), pp. 101–112. https://doi.org/10.1111/j.1461-0248.2010.01559.x

FAO (2016) 'Pollinators vital to our food supply under threat', 26 February. Available at: https://www.fao.org/news/story/en/item/384726/icode/ (Accessed: 28 April 2022).

Faustmann, M. (1849) 'Berechnung des Werthes, welchen Waldboden, sowie noch nicht haubare Holzbestande fur die Waldwirthschaft besitzen [Calculation of the value which forest land and immature stands possess for forestry]', *Allgemeine Fotst- und Jagd-Zeitung*, 25, pp. 441–455.

Forman, R.T.T. and Godron, M. (1981) 'Patches and structural components for a landscape ecology', *Bioscience*, 31(10), pp. 733–740. https://doi.org/10.2307/1308780

Grêt-Regamey, A. *et al.* (2021) 'Harnessing sensing systems towards urban sustainability transformation', *npj Urban Sustainability*, 1, p. 40. https://doi.org/10.1038/s42949-021-00042-w

Haahtela, T. (2019) 'A biodiversity hypothesis', *Allergy*, 74, pp. 1445–1456. https://doi.org/10.1111/all.13763

Hilmers, T. *et al.* (2018) 'Biodiversity along temperate forest succession', *Journal of Applied Ecology*, 55(6), pp. 2756–2766. https://doi.org/10.1111/1365-2664.13238

Himes, A. *et al.* (2022) 'Perspectives: Thirty years of triad forestry, a critical clarification of theory and recommendations for implementation and testing', *Forest Ecology and Management*, 510, 120103. https://doi.org/10.1016/j.foreco.2022.120103

IPBES (2019) *Global Assessment Report on Biodiversity and Ecosystem Services of the Intergovernmental Science-Policy Platform on Biodiversity and Ecosystem Services.* Zenodo. https://doi.org/10.5281/zenodo.5517154

Jeanneret, Ph. *et al.* (2021) 'Agroecology landscapes', *Landscape Ecology*, 36, pp. 2235–2257. https://doi.org/10.1007/s10980-021-01248-0

Kuuluvainen, T. *et al.* (2021) 'Natural disturbance-based forest management: Moving beyond retention and continuous-cover forestry', *Frontiers in Forests and Global Ghange*, 4. https://doi.org/10.3389/ffgc.2021.629020

Lepczyk, C.A. *et al.* (2017) 'Biodiversity in the city: Fundamental questions for understanding the ecology of urban green spaces for biodiversity conservation', *BioScience*, 67(9), pp. 799–807. https://doi.org/10.1093/biosci/bix079

Li, C. *et al.* (2019) 'Mechanisms and applications of green infrastructure practices for stormwater control: A review', *Journal of Hydrology*, 568, pp. 626–637. https://doi.org/10.1016/j.jhydrol.2018.10.074

Markevych, I. *et al.* (2017) 'Exploring pathways linking greenspace to health: Theoretical and methodological guidance', *Environmental Research*, 158, pp. 301–317. https://doi.org/10.1016/j.envres.2017.06.028

Martin, E.A. *et al.* (2019) 'The interplay of landscape composition and configuration: New pathways to manage functional biodiversity and agroecosystem services across Europe', *Ecology Letters*, 22, pp. 1083–1094. https://doi.org/10.1111/ele.13265

McKinney, M.L. and VerBerkmoes, A. (2020) 'Beneficial health outcomes of natural green infrastructure in cities', *Current Landscape Ecology Reports*, 5, pp. 35–44. https://doi.org/10.1007/s40823-020-00051-y

Myllyviita, T. *et al.* (2021) 'Wood substitution potential in greenhouse gas emission reduction–review on current state and application of displacement factors', *Forest Ecosystems*, 8, p. 42. https://doi.org/10.1186/s40663-021-00326-8

Pe'er, G. *et al.* (2020) 'Action needed for the EU Common Agricultural Policy to address sustainability challenges', *People and Nature*, 2(2), pp. 305–316. https://doi.org/10.1002/pan3.10080

Pithon, J.A. *et al.* (2021) 'Grasslands provide diverse opportunities for bird species along an urban-rural gradient', *Urban Ecosystems*, 24, pp. 1281–1294. https://doi.org/10.1007/s11252-021-01114-6

Pohjanmies, T. *et al.* (2021) 'Forest multifunctionality is not resilient to intensive forestry', *European Journal of Forest Research*, 140, pp. 537–549. https://doi.org/10.1007/s10342-020-01348-7

Puech, C. *et al.* (2014) 'Organic vs. conventional farming dichotomy: Does it make sense for natural enemies?', *Agriculture, Ecosystems & Environment*, 194, pp. 48–57. https://doi.org/10.1016/j.agee.2014.05.002

Pukkala, T., Lähde, E. and Laiho, O. (2012) 'Continuous cover forestry in Finland—Recent research results', in Pukkala, T. and von Gadow, K. (eds.) *Continuous Cover Forestry, Managing Forest Ecosystems*. Dordrecht: Springer Netherlands, pp. 85–128. https://doi.org/10.1007/978-94-007-2202-6_3

Ricci, B. *et al.* (2019) 'Local pesticide use intensity conditions landscape effects on biological pest control', *Proceedings of the Royal Society B Biological Sciences*, 286, 20182898. https://doi.org/10.1098/rspb.2018.2898

Selonen, V. and Mäkeläinen, S. (2017) 'Ecology and protection of a flagship species, the Siberian flying squirrel', *Hystrix the Italian Journal of Mammalogy*, 28(2), pp. 134–146. https://doi.org/10.4404/hystrix-28.2-12328

Sirami, C. *et al.* (2019) 'Increasing crop heterogeneity enhances multitrophic diversity across agricultural regions', *PNAS*, 116(33), pp. 16442–16447. https://doi.org/10.1073/pnas.1906419116

Tikkanen, O.-P. *et al.* (2006) 'Red-listed boreal forest species of Finland: Associations with forest structure, tree species, and decaying wood', *Annales Zoologici Fennici*, 43(4), pp. 373–383.

Tittler, R. *et al.* (2015) 'Maximizing conservation and production with intensive forest management: It's all about location', *Environmental Management*, 56, pp. 1104–1117. https://doi.org/10.1007/s00267-015-0556-3

Tyrväinen, L. *et al.* (2014) 'The influence of urban green environments on stress relief measures: A field experiment', *Journal of Environmental Psychology*, 38, pp. 1–9. https://doi.org/10.1016/j.jenvp.2013.12.005

UN (2019) *World Urbanization Prospects 2018: Highlights*. ST/ESA/SER.A/421. Department of Economic and Social Affairs, Population Division. Available at: https://population.un.org/wup/publications/Files/WUP2018-Highlights.pdf (Accessed: 28 April 2022).

Vialatte, A. *et al.* (2019) 'A conceptual framework for the governance of multiple ecosystem services in agricultural landscapes', *Landscape Ecology*, 34, pp. 1653–1673. https://doi.org/10.1007/s10980-019-00829-4

Wu, J. (2021) 'Landscape sustainability science (II): Core questions and key approaches', *Landscape Ecology*, 36, pp. 2453–2485. https://doi.org/10.1007/s10980-021-01245-3

6

SOIL PROCESSES ARE CONSTITUENTS OF PLANETARY WELL-BEING

Saana Kataja-aho and Jari Haimi

Introduction

Soils provide an excellent example of how one part of an ecosystem is both physically and functionally prerequisite for the well-being of all organisms and concomitantly for various interactions between them. Soils are related directly or indirectly to nearly all critical ecosystem processes on Earth. These processes include energy flow, element and water cycles, and interactions between living organisms (Figure 6.1). Hence, soils are closely interlinked with planetary well-being, which refers to the state in which the integrity of the Earth system and of ecosystem processes is unimpaired (Kortetmäki *et al.*, 2021). In addition, soil-centred ecosystem processes demonstrate how fragile and interlinked life-supporting local and global phenomena may be. For example, carbon released in the decomposition of dead organic matter affects the global climate. Understanding the role and functions of soils significantly helps to understand the critical value of planetary well-being for the well-being of all.

What are soils?

Soils form only a thin mantle between the Earth's atmosphere and lithosphere, yet they are integral parts of all terrestrial ecosystems. Synonyms for soil include *dirt, dust, earth, land, ground, substrate, integument of the planet* and *biomantle* (Johnsson and Johnsson, 2010; Oxford English Dictionary, 2021). The term 'soil' is commonly used in its traditional meaning, which Food and Agriculture Organization of the United Nations (FAO) (2021) defines as "the natural medium for the growth of plants". However, the multidimensionality and high variability in space and time make it difficult to define soil unequivocally. Johnsson and Johnsson (2010) summarized the work of soil scientists and ecologists from the last century in the

DOI: 10.4324/9781003334002-9

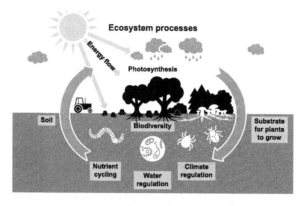

FIGURE 6.1   Significant ecosystem processes related to soil that are a prerequisite for planetary well-being.

following way: "Soil is substrate at or near the surface of Earth and similar bodies altered by biological, chemical, and/or physical agents and processes". Further, the Soil Science Society of America recently agreed on a multifunctional definition for soil: "The layer(s) of generally loose mineral and/or organic material that are affected by physical, chemical, and/or biological processes at or near the planetary surface, and usually hold liquids, gases and biota and support plants" (van Es, 2017; Soil Science Society of America, 2021).

The variability and complexity of the definitions indicate that soils are diverse parts of terrestrial ecosystems. They host multiple functions, but simultaneously appear as a kind of hidden resource. Land covers approximately 29% of Earth's surface and most of it bears some kind of soil (Ritchie and Roser, 2013). Soils have been formed throughout the history of the planet, and although soil formation occurs continuously, it is a slow and diverse process. The quality, quantity, and structure of soil depend on the bedrock quality, topography, climate, and history of the area, including both natural phenomena and human activity (Jenny, 1941). In addition, soil formation is affected by a range of organisms—from microbes and fungi to plants and animals living in the area—and vice versa, meaning soil partly determines which organisms can thrive at a site. Moreover, soils have typically evolved characteristic profiles through interactive climatic, physical, chemical, biological, and landscape processes. As a result, soils consist of mineral materials, dead organic matter of different stages of decay, water and gases in pore spaces, and plant roots, all in varying qualities and quantities (Coleman, Callaham and Crossley, 2018). Together, soils are a precious, non-renewable resource for numerous forms of both human and nonhuman life. The importance of soils has, however, largely been undervalued.

Soil biodiversity

Countless organisms inhabit soils, most of them small (even microscopic) in size. It has been estimated that more than 40% of the present organisms are associated with soil during their life cycle (Wardle, 2002; FAO *et al.*, 2020). The patchy, heterogenous, and three-dimensional spatial structure of soils offers habitats for most organism groups. The belowground environment provides high variation not only in spatial architecture but also in microclimatic, physical, and chemical properties, and the level of specialization in each organism group can be very high. Countless suitable environmental and ecological conditions (niches) are thus available in soils for sufficiently small organisms. All this has reduced competition for resources between organisms (Bardgett, 2005). Most importantly, the diversity of soil organisms produces a high number of different ecosystem functions (Anderson, 2000).

In addition to their diversity, the abundance and biomass of soil organisms are also high. One gram of soil contains millions of bacterial cells and kilometres of fungal filaments. Correspondingly, millions of protistans and nematodes, hundreds of thousands of mites, tens of thousands of springtails and enchytraeids, and hundreds of earthworms, centipedes, millipedes, spiders, and other arthropods are found in a single square metre of forest and meadow soil (Coleman, Callaham and Crossley, 2018). Most of these organisms are functionally classified as decomposers that feed on dead organic matter and microbes living in that matter. Some of the decomposers are specialized in certain microhabitats and food sources, while others are generalists. All, however, have an important role in soil fertility and element fluxes, which are vital ecosystem processes.

Soils are not only the habitat for microbes and animals that are decomposers, but a myriad of other organisms inhabit soils during a certain part of their life cycles (*ibid.*). Some insects are belowground herbivores during their larval stage and feed on plants' roots or mycorrhiza, a vital symbiotic association of the fungus with the roots of plants. When these insects emerge from the soils, they transfer significant amounts of nutrients to aboveground parts of the ecosystems (Callaham *et al.*, 2000). In addition, many invertebrates and vertebrates nest belowground and even more spend unfavourable periods of the year (such as winter or the dry season) in soil, often in an inactive stage. In cold and cool climates, most pollinators (important for reproduction of myriad green plants including human food plants; see Chapter 5) and aboveground herbivores (a major part of terrestrial biodiversity) overwinter in soil. Without an opportunity to seek shelter belowground they would not be able to survive. In sum, the entire soil fauna is tied to the maintenance of soil functioning and concomitantly to many important ecosystem processes (Coleman, Callaham and Crossley, 2018), and hence, to planetary well-being.

Soil functions

Primary production and energy flow

Soils have multiple functions that stem from their diverse and three-dimensional structure (Figure 6.1). Generally, life on Earth depends on energy derived from solar radiation. Plants, algae, and cyanobacteria absorb energy into organic molecules in the process of photosynthesis (also called primary production), and nearly all forms of life, including primary producers themselves, utilize those molecules to fulfil biological requirements such as life-supporting reactions, growth, and reproduction. Most terrestrial primary producers take the water and nutrients needed in the synthesis of biomolecules from soils. In addition, soils offer an essential substrate, or the growth platform, for the majority of plants. Soils, therefore, provide vital support for photosynthesis, the ultimate process of life on Earth, and are essential for all heterotrophic organisms. It is seldom understood that half or even more of the net primary production of plants is allocated belowground (Fogel, 1985; Coleman, Callaham and Crossley, 2018). The fine root production, including the root tissues and root secretion into soil, is requisite for many interactions between soil, plants, and microbes. The thin layer around fine roots, the rhizosphere, strongly mediates microbial communities and biogeochemical element cycles that, in turn, affect the life aboveground (McCormack *et al.*, 2015; Coleman, Callaham and Crossley, 2018).

Decomposition of organic matter and nutrient cycling

Because there are limited amounts of nutrients on the planet, at some point dead organic matter should be decomposed and nutrients recycled. Without decomposition processes, the planet would be covered with organic waste and life would soon wither. Nutrient mineralization (the release of nutrients in the form plants can uptake them) is prerequisite for terrestrial primary production and consequently for other organisms at the higher levels of food webs. A keystone of the decomposition of organic matter and nutrient mineralization is the efficient decomposer food web living in soils. The food web consists of a diverse microbial community and soil fauna (Coleman, Callaham and Crossley, 2018; FAO *et al.*, 2020). Decomposer animals can be classified based on their body size, from the smallest protistans (1–2 μm) to the largest earthworms. The body size of soil fauna is directly related to their microhabitat and role in decomposition processes. Many of the smallest decomposer animals are actually aquatic, inhabiting soil water and living in close interaction with microbes. Large decomposers, in turn, feed on soil organic matter with microbes and, at the same time, strongly modify the soil structure (Coleman, Callaham and Crossley, 2018). Moreover, some decomposers feed on dead plant material (*e.g.*, leaf litter). Hence, the decomposer fauna can be grouped according to how they participate in soil processes and soil formation in different spatial scales.

Decomposers form many functional groups and food webs (*ibid.*). Micro-food webs are composed of microbes and their microfaunal predators, such as nematodes and protistans. Microbes are primary decomposers having enzymes to chemically break down even the most recalcitrant substances. Microbes also finally mineralize most nutrients for reuse by plants. Certain nematodes feed either on bacteria or fungi, and regulate the microbe populations, thus indirectly affecting decomposition and nutrient mineralization. Litter transformers are microarthropods, such as mites and springtails, which chop up dead organic matter and increase the surfaces available for microbes. Ecosystem engineers (organisms that significantly modify or even create their habitat) process the soil habitat by feeding and burrowing activities, such as mixing organic and inorganic materials and affecting soil structure. Earthworms, ants, and termites are often referred to as soil engineers as they significantly modify their habitats. Micro-food webs, litter transformers, and ecosystem engineers operate in the complex soil environment in their own spatial, size and timescales (Wardle, 2002; Coleman, Callaham and Crossley, 2018). All these diverse functional groups contribute to major ecosystem processes such as nutrient cycling, carbon transformation and further to formation and modification of soil structure. In addition, although they live in their own microenvironments, soil organisms strongly interact with the populations of other organisms and eventually affect aboveground biodiversity.

Climate regulation

Nearly 80% of the carbon in Earth's terrestrial ecosystems is found in soils (Lal, 2008; Eglinton *et al.*, 2021). Correspondingly, the soil carbon pool is more than three times larger than that of the atmosphere (Oelkers and Cole, 2008). More than 60% of the soil carbon is organic carbon, dead organic matter at some stage of the decomposition process. The rest is soil inorganic carbon, or elemental carbon and carbonate materials (Lal, 2008). By being the major terrestrial pool of carbon, the soil carbon stock is critical for the global carbon cycle and for regulating Earth's climate (Figure 6.1). Even a small change in the soil carbon pool can cause a large impact on atmospheric CO_2 concentration (Crowther *et al.*, 2016; Bispo *et al.*, 2017). Soil processes also control the emissions and sequestrations of the other significant greenhouse gases, such as methane and nitrous oxide, and release aerosols to the atmosphere. In addition to being the reservoir of carbon, soils with vegetation fix more than a third of anthropogenic carbon emissions to the atmosphere. Further, soils contribute to Earth's radiation balance, either positively or negatively, through evaporation and the albedo of Earth's surface (Lal *et al.*, 2021). Hence, the composition of atmosphere and consequently Earth's climate are strongly related to the structure, composition, and processes of soils.

Water retention and cleaning processes

When rain reaches Earth's surface, the water picks up varying amounts of different impurities, such as particles and chemicals. In rural settings and natural environments, most rainwater infiltrates through the soil. Part of the water is captured along the way down in the soil profile, reserved in soil pore spaces and gradually used by organisms that need water for their metabolism. Water is one raw material in photosynthesis, and nutrients needed in other biosyntheses (such as protein synthesis) are transported into plant tissues in the process of transpiration. As water passes through the soil profile, it is cleaned physically, chemically, and biologically. Soils with many grain sizes contain a matrix of pores of different sizes and can efficiently filter particles out of the infiltrating water (Figure 6.1). Soil organic matter is, however, the most important in removing impurities from water (Ontl and Schulte, 2012). Most soils are negatively charged and hence they capture positively charged ions from soil water. These ions, inorganic forms of nutrients, are available for uptake by green plants and microbes, and also prevented from leaching into groundwater and surface waters. Many other chemicals are removed from the water as they become adsorbed into soil particles, for example through a process of covalent bonding. Moreover, many bacteria and fungi are capable of transforming and decomposing chemicals dissolved in water with appropriate enzymes. Even harmful anthropogenic organic chemicals, such as pesticides and solvents, can be metabolized by certain microbes (Cravo-Laureau *et al.*, 2017; Pesce *et al.*, 2020). Soils detoxify chemicals and prevent their problematic effects on non-target organisms and processes. In this way, they reserve and purify fresh water, which is a vital process for all terrestrial organisms, including human beings.

Degradation and loss of soils

Human impact on the Earth system is continuously intensifying, and land use for agriculture, livestock farming, and commercial forestry speed up the loss of biodiversity and habitat degradation (Vitousek *et al.*, 1997; Goudie, 2019). Agricultural management practices and intensive forestry have also degraded soils physically, chemically, and biologically, for example, through erosion and loss of organic matter (Kaiser, 2004; Ontl and Schulte, 2012). These substantial changes in soil composition and structure may lead to serious inhibition of soil-driven ecosystem processes.

Soil food webs have been shown to be strongly changed and simplified under more intensive management systems, such as increased use of fertilizers and pesticides, intensified tillage, use of larger and heavier vehicles, and higher grazing pressure (Bardgett, 2005). These changes are associated with increased nutrient leaching and carbon losses from the system. It also seems these changes in the soil food web structure may even be irreversible (*ibid.*). However, the reduction of organic matter losses from cultivated soils by using less intensive management practices and the addition of organic amendments could result in positive development in the abundance and diversity of soil biota and the intensity of soil-mediated ecosystem processes (Ontl and Schulte, 2012). Correspondingly, more sustainable management practices in forestry can increase soil health in forests.

The constantly increasing global population and urbanization have drastically decreased the amount of soil that is organically and functionally part of ecosystems. Globally, huge areas of land have been sealed with artificial impenetrable surfaces for housing as well as for transport, industrial, and commercial infrastructure (Liu *et al.*, 2014). Soil sealing leads to serious interference or total inhibition of most ecosystem processes that either take place in the soil or are mediated by soils. This is simply because of the lack of fluxes of water, matter, and elements between belowground and aboveground settings and the disappearance of soil–plant interactions. In urbanized areas, water can flow over the sealed soil surface and transport impurities and nutrients to water courses or surface-water drains. The strain on the water systems may result in eutrophication and pollution of streams and lakes and thereby drastically decrease the quality of these water basins as habitat for aquatic organisms such as fishes, mussels, and plankton. Furthermore, water contamination decreases the quality of human drinking water, while large-scale soil sealing permanently disturbs carbon and nutrient cycling in urban areas (Lu, Kotze and Setälä, 2020). Sealed soils also become unavailable as habitats for any organisms, with the exception of a few microbes.

Soil degradation also affects the mitigation of climate change. The fixation of carbon emissions by vegetated soils is endangered because of human-induced environmental change (Eglinton *et al.*, 2021; Lal *et al.*, 2021). Especially, the amount of soil organic carbon is a critical component which controls soil–atmosphere carbon flux and climate change. Air temperature and precipitation significantly affect soil processes and, consequently, soil organic carbon stocks, while climate change may destabilize these stocks. The feedbacks may be large and unpredictable especially in the soils in northern permafrost regions. In addition, soil organic carbon stocks are prone to human land use changes. As a rule, intensive land use (deforestation, industrial agriculture, increasing mining and construction) increases the release of carbon from the soil to the atmosphere. Thus, all actions that minimize anthropogenic soil disturbance can help to restrain climate change. Sequestration of carbon in soils efficiently mitigates changes in the climate and environment that are evolutionarily too rapid.

Concluding remarks

Soils play a crucial role in numerous ecosystem and global processes that enable the existence and well-being of terrestrial organisms, from microbes and fungi to plants and animals, including humans (Figure 6.1). Conversely, those vital processes do not occur with the proper strength and frequency if organisms living in the soil are disturbed in a way that they are unable to play their roles in their communities. Soil organisms and processes, therefore, are an excellent example of how susceptible and fragile the integrity of the Earth system is and how important certain parts of the ecosystem can be for planetary well-being (Kortetmäki *et al.*, 2021). Although human well-being has not specifically been addressed in this chapter, all soil-driven and soil-mediated processes are also essential for human well-being: Soils provide many of the ecosystem services that humankind (regardless of all technological development) still requires (see Chapter 5).

For example, local populations of pollinators in cool regions depend on overwintering in soil, and human practices that degrade or seal soil with impermeable surfaces harm this overwintering process, which in turn reduces the pollination success of food crops and further decreases food production for both humans and nonhumans. Moreover, the cultivation of food and forage crops requires arable land where soil fertility is maintained by soil structure and processes. If soil in an area is disturbed either physically, chemically, or biologically, vegetation will respond and reciprocally affect soil properties, which undermines beneficial food production conditions, with direct and indirect harmful impacts on human and non-human well-being. Soil disturbances that are strong enough and large enough are reflected also at the landscape level.

If human activity steadily and increasingly degrades soils by, for example, decreasing the amount of soil organic matter and changing the soil structure, soils cannot deliver the ecosystem services they used to offer. Human activities that have a strong negative effect on soil health include, for example, deforestation, intensification of agriculture and livestock farming, and the enlargement of urbanized areas. Soil degradation impairs the typical characteristics and capacities of myriad organisms, not only soil decomposers but also those inhabiting soils during a certain part of their life cycles, to the level where ecosystem-level and global processes do not function properly. At that stage, the integrity of the Earth system could be irreversibly lost. When humanity cares for the health of soil, it is also taking care of the well-being of both human and nonhuman organisms and contributing to planetary well-being.

Acknowledgements

We are grateful to the editorial team for their valuable comments on our earlier versions of this chapter, and Matt Wuethrich for language checking. Thanks to Boost project of Janne Kotiaho for supporting the language check. We thank Photogrunskis for the great illustration they prepared for our chapter.

References

Anderson, J.M. (2000) 'Food web functioning and ecosystem processes: Problems and perceptions of scaling', in Coleman, D.C. and Hendrix, P.F. (eds.) *Invertebrates as Webmasters in Ecosystems*. Wallingford, CT: CAB International, pp. 3–24.

Bardgett, R. (2005) *The Biology of Soils. A Community and Ecosystem Approach*. Oxford: Oxford University Press.

Bispo, A. *et al.* (2017) 'Accounting for carbon stocks in soils and measuring GHGs emission fluxes from soils: Do we have the necessary standards?', *Frontiers in Environmental Science*, 5(41). https://doi.org/10.3389/fenvs.2017.00041

Callaham, M.A. Jr. *et al.* (2000) 'Feeding ecology and emergence production of annual cicadas (Homoptera: Cicadidae) in tallgrass prairie', *Oecologia*, 123, pp. 535–542. https://doi.org/10.1007/s004420000335

Coleman, D.C., Callaham, M.A. Jr. and Crossley, D.A. Jr. (2018) *Fundamentals of Soil Ecology*. 3rd edn. Cambridge, MA: Academic Press, Elsevier.

Cravo-Laureau, C. *et al.* (2017) *Microbial Ecotoxicology*. Cham: Springer International Publishing. https://doi.org/10.1007/978-3-319-61795-4

Crowther, T.W. *et al.* (2016) 'Quantifying global soil carbon losses in response to warming', *Nature*, 540, pp. 104–108. https://doi.org/10.1038/nature20150

Eglinton, T.I. *et al.* (2021) 'Climate control on terrestrial biospheric carbon turnover', *Proceedings of the National Academy of Sciences*, 118(8), e2011585118. https://doi.org/10.1073/pnas.2011585118

FAO (2021) *FAO Soils Portal*. Available at: https://www.fao.org/soils-portal/about/all-definitions/en/ (Accessed: 12 December 2021).

FAO *et al.* (2020) *State of Knowledge of Soil Biodiversity – Status, Challenges and Potentialities*. Rome: FAO. https://doi.org/10.4060/cb1928en

Fogel, R. (1985) 'Roots as primary producers in below-ground ecosystems', in Fitter, A.H. *et al.* (eds.) *Ecological Interactions in Soil: Plants, Microbes and Animals*. Oxford: Blackwell, pp. 23–36.

Goudie, A.S. (2019) *Human Impact on Natural Environment*. 8th edn. Hoboken, NJ: Wiley-Blackwell.

Jenny, H. (1941) *Factors of Soil Formation*. New York: McGraw-Hill Book Company.

Johnsson, D.L. and Johnsson, D.N. (2010) 'A holistic and universal view of soil', *Proceedings of the 19th World Soil Congress*, pp. 1–4. Available at: https://www.iuss.org/19th%20WCSS/Symposium/pdf/0454.pdf (Accessed: 12 December 2021).

Kaiser, J. (2004) 'Wounding earth's fragile skin', *Science*, 304, pp. 1616–1618. https://doi.org/10.1126/science.304.5677.1616

Kortetmäki, T. *et al.* (2021) 'Planetary well-being', *Humanities and Social Sciences Communications*, 8, p. 258. https://doi.org/10.1057/s41599-021-00899-3

Lal, R. (2008) 'Carbon sequestration', *Philosophical Transactions of the Royal Society*, B 363, pp. 815–830. https://doi.org/10.1098/rstb.2007.2185

Lal, R. *et al.* (2021) 'The role of soil in regulating climate', *Philosophical Transactions of the Royal Society*, B 376, 20210084. https://doi.org/10.1098/rstb.2021.0084

Liu, Z. *et al.* (2014) 'How much of the world's land has been urbanized, really? A hierarchical framework for avoiding confusion', *Landscape Ecology*, 29, pp. 763–771. https://doi.org/10.1007/s10980-014-0034-y

Lu, C., Kotze, D.J. and Setälä, H.M. (2020) 'Soil sealing causes substantial losses in C and N storage in urban soils under cool climate', *Science of the Total Environment*, 725, 138369. https://doi.org/10.1016/j.scitotenv.2020.138369

McCormack, M.L. *et al.* (2015) 'Redefining fine roots improves understanding of below-ground contributions to terrestrial biosphere processes', *New Phytologist*, 207, pp. 505–518. https://doi.org/10.1111/nph.13363

Oelkers, E.H. and Cole, D.R. (2008) 'Carbon dioxide sequestration: A solution to the global problem', *Elements*, 4, pp. 305–310. https://doi.org/10.2113/gselements.4.5.305

Ontl, T.A. and Schulte, L.A. (2012) 'Soil carbon storage', *Nature Education Knowledge*, 3(10), p. 35.

Oxford English Dictionary (2021). Available at: https://www.oed.com (Accessed: 30 November 2021).

Pesce, S. *et al.* (2020) 'Editorial: Microbial ecotoxicology', *Frontiers in Microbiology*, 11, 1342. https://doi.org/10.3389/fmicb.2020.01342

Ritchie, H. and Roser, M. (2013) *Land Use*. Available at: https://ourworldindata.org/land-use (Accessed: 5 August 2022).

Soil Science Society of America (2021) *Glossary of Soil Science Terms*. Available at: https://www.soils.org/publications/soils-glossary/# (Accessed: 15 November 2021).

van Es, H. (2017) 'A new definition of soil', *CSA News*, pp. 20–21. https://doi.org/10.2134/csa2017.62.1016

Vitousek, P.M. *et al.* (1997) 'Human domination of Earth's ecosystems', *Science*, 277, pp. 494–499. https://doi.org/10.1126/science.277.5325.494

Wardle, D.A. (2002) *Communities and Ecosystems: Linking the Aboveground and Belowground Components.* Princeton, NJ: Princeton University Press.

PART III

Challenging the economic imperative

7

AN ECONOMIC TAIL WAGGING AN ECOLOGICAL DOG? WELL-BEING AND SUSTAINABLE DEVELOPMENT FROM THE PERSPECTIVE OF ENTANGLED HISTORY

Risto-Matti Matero and Atte Arffman

Introduction

As explained in the introduction of this book, planetary well-being is a state that impartially acknowledges human and nonhuman well-being as a part of healthy Earth systems and ecosystems (Kortetmäki *et al.*, 2021). In this chapter, environmental history is used to add a temporal perspective to understanding planetary well-being. As the realization of planetary well-being requires, for instance, restraints to the human use of natural resources, it is necessary to look into the past and ask, "What has prevented less anthropocentric conceptions of well-being from thriving and why?" This is all the more important since historically, it has been typical for modern industrial societies to promote an understanding of well-being with a sociocentric[1] emphasis with little to no attention paid to the well-being of either other species or future human generations.

This sociocentric emphasis, while often taken for granted, not only simplifies our reality enormously into mere social needs but has also been criticized for easily turning both nature and humans into mere resources for societal (economic) needs (Connolly, 2017). This chapter presents an example of how this tendency can be understood historically in the field of politics, in which the adaptation of a more ecocentric framework for well-being has proven particularly difficult.

Examples of different conceptualizations given to *sustainable development* over time by global and national actors, such as the European Union (EU) and the Green Parties in Finland and Germany, demonstrate how our understanding of well-being develops in time entangled with our social processes. We analyze why the practical implications of a non-anthropocentric understanding of well-being have not flourished and how different path dependencies and social needs provide incentives for a drawback that typically occurs despite good intentions.

DOI: 10.4324/9781003334002-11

As the examples below suggest, these path dependencies are based on perceiving the world sociocentrically and are constructed with discourses that have political incentives. Finally, we consider what it means to break free from the confines that these path dependencies place on political decision-making. We claim, following Mazzucato (2014), that what has really been lacking is the political will to do so. Noticing this requires stepping out of a sociocentric understanding of well-being while keeping the entangled nature of humans and the nonhuman environment in sight. Understanding these cultural mechanisms is a vital part of promoting a planetary, systems-oriented, and non-anthropocentric understanding of well-being.

While environmental history deepens perspectives on planetary well-being, an entanglement-oriented approach also provides new layers of interpretation for historical research. The history scholarship has traditionally focused on humans as the *primus motor* of historical change, with little attention paid to the nonhuman world or the entanglements between the two. Environmental historians have criticized the strict nature–culture dichotomy from the 1960s onwards, and more recent scholarship has created ways to look beyond the more or less imaginary boundary between societies and the environment (McEvoy, 1987; Worster, 1987; Haila and Lähde, 2003; Penna and Rivers, 2013; Rigby, 2015; Carey, 2017; Pritchard and Zimring, 2020; Chakrabarty, 2021). However, till today, many historical accounts are focusing on the societal aspects of human culture and remain oblivious to the nonhuman world—even when addressing environmental politics.

In his influential book *Facing the Planetary*, political theorist William Connolly (2017) called this standpoint as falsely perceiving the human culture as "internal to itself" instead of understanding humans as part of an organic reality through the lens of "entangled humanism". Environmental history enables overcoming the simplistic understanding of reality mentioned above while departing from the more traditional paradigm of historical studies. Humans do not only directly affect nature, but the effect is also created by natural processes reacting to human action; thus, the outcome is a dynamic entanglement of natural phenomena and human activity. These kinds of entanglements are to be found everywhere, as the relationship between humans and the environment is always reciprocal (*ibid.*, pp. 155–157, 168–169).

Furthermore, our conception of well-being guiding our political and economic action is also entangled with deeper interconnected processes that humans and nature share. This understanding has been problematic in political discourse. Connolly (*ibid.*, pp. 9–16) has pointed out how political attempts to formulate more systems-oriented approaches to environmental questions have typically been "dragged down" to mere sociocentric perspectives over time, turning nature into "a deposit of resources". More anthropocentric and materialistic conceptions of well-being that promote, for instance, economic productivity over ecological needs direct human actions in a way that may damage the well-being of ecosystems. These conceptions are typically the consequences of (mal)developments and social path dependencies that run over time and are thus subject to historical research while being closely connected with the entangled actions and responses between human societies and nature. For this reason, the environmental historical framing of questions is useful, as it acknowledges the nonhuman, thus widening the scope of historical research.

The lack of an ecological, systems-oriented conceptualization of well-being becomes more visible from an entangled perspective. Political attempts to resolve one environmental problem often simply create or exacerbate another kind of problem. To use an example of this presented by John Dryzek (2005a), building tall smokestacks to reduce local pollution caused in the end more long-distance pollution, such as acid rain. As environmental issues are solved one problem at a time, separately and from a sociocentric perspective, the events are disconnected from the entangled surroundings from where they occur. When addressing political issues such as the smokestack problem, emphasis has been placed on anthropocentric needs, which led to the harm only being relocated elsewhere, leaving the initial problem unsolved. Paradoxically, acknowledging only human needs causes human well-being to suffer as well. The problems do not disappear but simply tend to be transferred to other areas of life (*ibid.*).

Thus, it is of key importance to understand that human well-being is not separable from the well-being of other living entities and the nonhuman world. It then becomes an intriguing question as to why such a perception of well-being has so often been drawn back to sociocentric standpoints. This entangled perspective opens up new research questions for historical research. Most notably, it raises the need to analyze the different path dependencies behind the aforementioned drawbacks. Understanding social (mal)developments and path dependencies becomes a vital task if we are to understand the mechanisms that prevent us from applying planetary well-being in contexts of action, such as politics, from an entangled perspective. According to historical sociologist James Mahoney, social path dependencies occur when earlier decisions raise expectations of an "increased return" for similar future decisions, turning a chain of decisions into self-reinforcing sequences (Mahoney, 2000, pp. 507–512). As the example below will suggest, these vicious cycles, particularly detectable in politics, have drawn new ecological thinking back to older, more politically convenient, and more anthropocentric modes of understanding well-being.

This explains the abovementioned notion that non-anthropocentric conceptualizations of well-being are "dragged down" to a state of sociocentric normalcy within systems of capitalism, socialism, and nationalism (Connolly, 2017). Through an environmental historical approach, different kinds of chronic path dependencies can be made visible and scrutinized critically in order to reveal how and why such drawbacks occur in the political context. Using the concept of *sustainable development*, we explore the incentives behind this return to normalcy, which tends to inhibit new conceptualizations of well-being.

Sustainable development and the history of entanglements

The adaptation of *sustainable development* marked a new framework for environmental politics from the late 1980s onwards. Analyzing the concept in its political context in the EU reveals how the term has been used as a conceptual tool to draw an understanding of well-being back in more anthropocentric directions. These changes have guided environmental thinking towards a more market-oriented, anthropocentric direction due to political and economic reasons on the national level—for example, in the Finnish and German Green Parties. This new direction was based on social path dependencies which caused, for instance, the Green Parties to de-radicalize their political programmes. We analyze the incentives causing this return to normalcy in political and economic spheres, thus retarding the development of a more holistic and less anthropocentric understanding of well-being. Mapping such path dependencies, which limit the visions of well-being to short-term economic interests, is vital in order to understand the obstacles that our societal and cultural needs place on the advancement of new ideas regarding planetary well-being.

The roots of these debates are in the 1970s, when a variety of rising environmental and grassroots movements presented the public with new radical discourses (Guha, 2000; Radkau, 2011; Mende, 2012). Deep ecological discourses called for a complete abandoning of anthropocentric conceptualizations of well-being; eco-feminists and social-greens noted that human well-being was also jeopardized by the Western mindset of hierarchy, domination, and conquest of nature and should be replaced by a sense of companionship both with other species and between humans (Naess, 1997; Dryzek, 2005b; Radkau, 2005). Still, others were set out to create alternative ways of living with ideals of grassroots democracy, decentralized economic life, and a deeper connection with nature as foundations for a new conceptualization of well-being. All, however, agreed that perceiving nature as a mere resource storage for human well-being was detrimental to both nature and even the survival of human societies. Green parties were typically founded as political representatives for these diverse grassroots movements and their ideals (Dryzek, 2005b; Hockenos, 2007; Milder, 2017; Warde, Libby and Sörlin, 2018).

In the political world, a more moderate discussion arose in an attempt to reconcile the challenges presented by these new discourses on economic needs. Although this discussion had been developing since the early 1970s, the concept of *sustainable development* became a political catchword for moderate environmentalism in 1987, after the United Nations' Brundtland Commission, led by Norwegian Social Democratic Prime Minister Gro Harlem Brundtland, defined the concept. The Commission merged social-democratic themes, economic development, and social equality with the goal of environmental protection (Dryzek, 2005b; Dryzek and Schosberg, 2005; Rumpala, 2011; Warde, Libby and Sörlin, 2018). This was a major turn in the history of environmental discourse. Historian Matthias Schmeltzer pointed out that, despite including *development* in the concept, the point of the concept in 1987 was not mainly to emphasize growth. However, as Schmeltzer (2016, pp. 321–322) put it, "the report's more nuanced analysis and its focus on [...] linking social and ecological questions in a context of global inequalities were soon forgotten". As early as 1989, the OECD's Ministerial Declaration endorsed "sustainable development" while reframing it entirely, with the explicit goal to maintain economic growth within the framework of environmental protection and with the use of optimum market mechanisms (*ibid.*). In the 1992 Earth Summit, the concept was used to promote "global governance" at the expense of local control in favour of free trade and sustainable consumption (Guha, 2000, pp. 140–142; Hinton and Goodman, 2010).

The change in meaning compared to the 1987 Brundtland Commission was notable. The EU soon followed, as the European Commission set its goal of promoting environmentally sustainable industry competitiveness. The stagnant economy in the early 1990s and the liberalization of global markets caused the harmonized environmental regulations of the 1980s to fall out of fashion (Knill and Liefferink, 2007). New "simplified regulation" of the environment was designed to create pressure on industries from below by affecting consumer behaviour, thus effectively re-allocating environmental responsibility from producers to consumers. Britain's Margaret Thatcher in particular was aggressively pursuing the idea of citizens-as-consumers who would make enlightened decisions on the free markets and consequently allow a softer incentive for industries to react to environmental pressure without necessarily hurting their competitiveness with harsh top-down regulations (*ibid.*). By replacing regulations with these market-friendlier measures, the EU was set to compete with the American and Japanese industries, which were ahead in the global markets (Blair, 2010).

Reframing sustainable development for sociocentric needs

Two documents are examined here to fully grasp the environmental discussion in the EU back in the 1990s: The Commission's policy commentaries on the Molitor Report[2] and the 5th Environmental Action Programme (EAP). Knill and Liefferink pointed out that when the 5th EAP was published in 1993, it reflected "a major departure from approaches propagated in earlier programmes", both conceptually and substantially (Knill and Liefferink, 2007, p. 163). Earlier EAPs emphasized forms of hierarchical intervention. Now, the focus was still on legislation to set environmental standards but also on "economic instruments" to encourage the production and use of environmentally friendly products and processes, according to the Commission. Using these instruments was to be studied "in the context of the general economic objectives of the Community, such as employment, competitiveness and growth" (European Commission, 1998, p. 6). Horizontal and financial mechanisms would promote environmentally friendly production by, for example, providing information for the consumer in order to affect behavioural change while providing industries with voluntary possibilities to meet new consumer demands without risking competitiveness or productivity (European Commission, 1993, 1998).

This trend continued two years later with the Molitor Report, formulated by members of "industry, trade unions, academics, and law" (European Commission, 1995, 1b) and led by Bernhard Molitor, an economist and an expert in economic (but not environmental) policies. Tellingly, there is no mention of any environmental experts or scientists belonging to the group that was forging together the outlines of environmental political recommendations for the EU for decades to come, as will be described below. The Commission's new recommendation to start adapting the new deregulatory environmental policy framework on a national level was, in the Commission's own report, portrayed as "an important prerequisite to European industry improving its competitive position" (*ibid.*) and a continuation of questioning the strong top-down environmental regulation because of this economically associated reason (Knill and Liefferink, 2007).

The Molitor Report outlined a market-oriented turn in the EU's environmental political thinking, which member countries soon followed. A human-centred and growth-oriented conceptualization of well-being was visible in the explicit premises of the Report, which focused on the sustainable use of natural resources mainly for human economic benefit. According to the European Commission's statement of the Molitor Report, "legislation or practices hamper the unity of the Community market" (European Commission, 1995, pp. 2–7). Regarding environmental regulation, the report stated that industry "should have flexibility to choose the means of implementations". A "market based [sic] approach" should be used whenever possible, while departure from it should always be separately justified (*ibid.*, p. 27).

The goal of the Commission was to seek the least costly solutions in the framework of simplification of regulation. Both the Molitor Report and the Commission also demanded that, if these voluntary market-based instruments would succeed, better monitoring of the private sector and "full transparency" was needed (*ibid.*, p. 25). In reality, all this would soon come to mean the formation of new market-friendly environmental instruments for voluntary regulation, such as eco-labels and transparent information for consumers, compared to earlier regulation of strict environmental demands, such as pollution control and chimney filters for factories, directed at producers rather than consumers (Knill and Liefferink, 2007).

Ute Collier (1998), who has studied this development in the EU, points out that these formulations were based on the notion of *sustainable development,* giving the concept a very different meaning than the Brundtland Commission had done. The idea was that, through growing green consumption, environmental problems could be solved without hurting economic productivity or industry competitiveness if only the state provided instruments for the markets, such as eco-labels or subsidies to develop ecological technology. Instead of basing environmental responsibility on the ecological effects on the well-being of ecosystems, the responsibility for the environment was thrust on the individual consumer—that is, only at the end spectrum of the production chain (Martell, 1994; Hinton and Goodman, 2010; Akenji,

2019; Olsen, 2019). The recommendations were also objected: Some saw markets as an ineffective tool from an environmental perspective, while one dissident member of the Molitor think tank publicly objected to the outcome of the Molitor Report—and thus the European Commission's recommendations—for perceiving actual environmental protection as a mere obstacle to economic growth that needed to be somehow bypassed in environmental politics (Collier, 1998; Knill and Liefferink, 2007). This controversy, however, was mostly overlooked, as the EU Commission wholeheartedly supported the report.

According to Knill and Liefferink, these recommendations soon caused a "race to the bottom" that emerged in the regulative practices of member countries of the Union. In an open market area, "different environmental regulations in the member states had a direct impact on the economic competitiveness of a country" (Knill and Liefferink, 2007, p. 103). Strict environmental standards caused bigger costs for production, which meant disadvantages in economic competition against countries with looser standards. This threw member states of the open market area into regulatory competition with each other to create favourable competitive conditions. The pressure this situation created for national governments and politicians was immense. As conceptual historian Niklas Olsen (2019) pointed out, even social democrats adapted to the demands of increased consumer responsibility in the 1990s, making consumeristic deregulatory politics a new hegemony. Individual countries started understanding industry competitiveness (measured through economic productivity) as a prerequisite for well-being, placing it at the centre of politics (Kananen, 2008).

This global development strongly affected the Finnish and German Green Parties, studied here as national-level examples of this development. Both Green parties felt tremendous pressure to adapt to the changing situation. In their programmes, both parties criticized the Western way of understanding well-being in an individualistic, materialistic, and economically competitive setting, in which material growth and the consequential extortion of natural resources was a defining feature of well-being. Instead, they promoted a conceptualization of well-being that aimed at a holistic understanding of humans as part of their communities and their natural surroundings. Both warned of the dangers of a centralized and globalized economy that caused irreversible environmental destruction and destroyed possibilities for human well-being as well. Early Green Party programmes thus reveal that the Greens started out extremely critical towards a growth-oriented understanding of well-being based on short-term material gain for the human individual; instead, they promoted holistic models that aimed to understand well-being in more ecocentric ways (Die Grünen, 1980; Vihreä Liitto, 1988, 1990).[3]

This has all changed as a consequence of this global development. The Finnish Greens, for example, emphasized affecting "millions of consumers' product choices" with market-friendly measures in their 1994 programme, something they had scorned before (Vihreä Liitto, 1994, p. 3). The German Greens also thrust environmental responsibility and green growth on "consumer power" in their 2002 programme, although a shift to green growth ideology had already happened in 1991 (Die Grünen, 2002, p. 28). The discussion to radically re-conceptualize the anthropocentric and growth-oriented understanding of well-being disappeared from party programmes, as the focus turned back on an economically oriented understanding of well-being. Finnish Greens were explicitly afraid of losing competitiveness if green technology was not to be developed for exportation (Vihreä Liitto, 1994), using environmental politics as tools for the economy.

The explicit reasons for the turn were notably unideological in nature in Green argumentation: There was a pragmatic need to adapt to a system that demanded certain preconditions to be taken as granted in order to access power. The Finnish Greens felt this harshly in the 1991 government negotiations: During an era of depression, they had no possibilities for governmental cooperation with a growth-critical programme (Isotalo, 2007a). As statements from leading Green politicians reveal, many Green actors were focused on maintaining political influence, which was perceived as a prerequisite to act efficiently in the new paradigm. In Finland, Green environmental minister Pekka Haavisto pointed out how nothing would have been accomplished with the attitude of the NGOs after NGO criticism started to build up towards the Greens' government participation (Isotalo, 2007b); in Germany, *realo* Green Hubert Kleinert was explicitly afraid of the party dying out entirely if they would fail to find "efficient" means to participate in politics (Kleinert, 1991, p. 35). These quotes provide just a few of the many examples in which Green actors thus felt compelled to adapt to the presuppositions of the surrounding discourses in order to become more efficient in the political field.

"Race to the bottom" in a nutshell

In order to understand these development patterns as path-dependent, their outcome would have had to be somewhat predictable, since stepping away from the path would have become increasingly costly. This is precisely the case here. As an initial step, European politicians started demanding the surpassing of state-led industry regulation policies (and other obstacles to economic productivity), with demands of re-allocating responsibility to the consumer. Second, as one country created favourable competitive conditions, others felt compelled to follow, causing a "race to the bottom" that became increasingly difficult to stop. Finally, as Green parties wanted to participate in national-level decision-making, they found themselves in situations in which efficient means to participate in politics were already tied to a path-dependent repetition of promoting industry competitiveness. Thus, the representative political system did not allow decision power to those who drifted too far away from the cultural normalcy of sociocentric premises, causing the focus to shift from ecological to economic perspectives.

The example of what happened to Green parties in the 1990s in the pressure of new market-friendly environmentalism demonstrates the kind of path dependencies that tend to draw radical thinking back towards a state of normalcy when entering the realm of politics. As Mahoney pointed out, changing a system at any given time is more costly than returning to the path-dependent sequences already in use that provide immediate benefits. This is a prime example of a situation where "actors rationally choose to reproduce institutions [...] because any potential benefits of transformation are outweighed by the costs" (Mahoney, 2000, pp. 507–512). Re-allocating responsibility to the individual consumer was the most predictable outcome also among other parties participating in this "race to the bottom". Political actors in individual countries felt compelled to adapt to this changing paradigm (Olsen, 2019). Here, Green parties are examples of the same hegemonic nature of market-oriented thinking in Western political culture[4] that was in the process of strengthening in other parties during the 1980s and 1990s due to the globalization of the economy.

When addressing this development, it is worth noting that these path dependencies are not entirely deterministic, as they take place in the form of "expectations", as mentioned above (Mahoney, 2000). Expectations, however, are thoroughly subjective and discursively constructed. Economist Mariana Mazzucato has claimed that the deregulatory framework associating competitiveness with complete freedom of the markets is based on a "discursive battle", with political incentives driving the discourse that is eventually taken for granted once it has achieved a hegemonic status. These discourses "reproduce stereotypes and images which serve only ideological ends", she claims, as presumed market punishments that supposedly follow market interventions are not true in any empirical sense but merely discursively assumed (Mazzucato, 2014, pp. 1–13). Beliefs play a major role in such discursive games: As John Dryzek (2005a) has pointed out, it has been the *belief* of sustaining investor confidence in fear of market punishments that has driven politicians to emphasize competitiveness over other values that they might personally endorse. Breaking free from such fear-based path dependencies is thus not a question of political realities but of political will.

Conceptually, the emphasis on economic competitiveness has led to a consumerist change in the meanings given to *sustainable development*, as discussed above. Jeremy Caradonna (2018, pp. 154–158) pointed out that even the sustainable development discourse started out as "a radical departure from the status quo of industrial growth", an attempt to reconcile a compromise between the needs of human and nonhuman well-being. When the concept of *sustainable consumption* was developed in political language in the early 1990s, the *sustainable development* discourse had already turned into an attempt to stand by the materialistically understood conception of well-being, although with the add-on of not jeopardizing the needs of future (human) generations (Akenji, 2019). The compromise to start using the concept in a more market-compliant manner linked the whole concept with an anthropocentric and materialistic understanding of well-being, thus turning the focus away from new ideals to the market-oriented framework of growth and competitiveness (Dryzek, 2005b). Furthermore, this compromise created a contradiction between the stated goals and the means used to get there, as environmental responsibility was simultaneously re-allocated to individual consumers in order to enhance industry competitiveness. Based on this development, Lewis Akenji (2019, p. 14) pointed out how green consumerism "lays the responsibility on consumers to undertake the function of maintaining economic growth while simultaneously, contradictorily and with limited agency, bearing the burden to drive the socio-economic system towards ecological sustainability".

Our social conceptualizations of well-being are also connected to entanglements with nature. However, as these conceptualizations are drawn back to anthropocentrism, they tend to blind us from the needs of Earth systems, on which all human well-being is nevertheless still based. This seems to be precisely what occurred in environmental politics in the 1990s. As the social *zeitgeist* of the decade promoted globalization (Kananen, 2008), the needs of the Earth's systems, as well as the threats caused by advancing climate change, desertification, and biodiversity loss, mattered little (Caradonna, 2018). Instead of labelling these decisions "greenwashing", as some scholars (*e.g. ibid.*) have done, we find it more constructive to understand these turns as path dependencies that can be carefully analyzed and understood as rational drawbacks, caused by the understandable need to be effective in the field of politics, and that can be avoided once detected. As politicians are making decisions based on short-term expectations of economic and political benefits, the pressure to adapt to our cultural needs is immensely strong, which is why radical visions of well-being have tended to fall back to a state of sociocentric normalcy. Once these expectations are understood as part of discursive and ideological development, they can be questioned and potentially abandoned. This would require enough political courage and imagination to abandon the everyday presuppositions that have so far guided political decision-making.

Conclusion

Looking at environmental political ideas and concepts from the perspective of entangled history opens up new research questions. There is an increasing need to understand the reasons behind the beliefs and ideas that guide political thinking back to a state of sociocentric normalcy. We have mapped some key elements that affect how well-being is conceptualized in politics and to whom well-being is attributed. As environmental political goals are moving in a more moderate direction while species extinction, desertification, ocean acidity, and climate change, among other issues, are rapidly advancing, we conclude that the key incentives for this development have not lied in ecological needs but rather in economic, human-oriented needs, based on political, social, and economic path dependencies.

The case of sustainable development and its effects on Green parties is merely one example of a much larger phenomenon that environmental history can make visible: Our understanding of well-being being driven back towards a state of anthropocentric normalcy in order to act efficiently within social structures. From the perspective of entanglements, the danger of feeling compelled to return to normalcy in political decision-making is closely connected with the well-being of the nonhuman nature, as the positive effects of political action on the environment can diminish. Therefore, it is of vital importance to detect and analyze the causes of these drawbacks in order to start developing effective strategies on how to manifest *planetary well-being* without losing its paradigm-shifting nature in contexts of action, such as politics.

Approaching the issue this way opens up another, perhaps more important question: How can we break free from these path dependencies? In other words, how can we break free from the deterministic perception of politics that resorts to short-term calculations as a mandatory must in a globalizing world? How can we not let an economic tail wag an ecological dog? The first step in this direction would be to understand that the presumably unavoidable perspectives to politics are, in fact, always discursively constructed and forged to seem as if there are no alternatives to them. In our examples, such assumptions have been taken for granted, causing a drawback in ideas that attempt to escape the *status quo* in the field of politics.

We are reminded of how easily a new set of ideas, no matter how beneficial and innovative, gets drawn back when it is put to use in contexts of action, such as politics, in which effective action is path-dependent on older models of conduct and thought. Stepping out of these models requires stepping out of a sociocentric understanding of well-being. This requires political will, courage, and imagination to look outside the self-created box. Meanwhile, historical research itself can do its part in challenging old ways of thinking by developing a theory embedded in *entangled humanism* rather than in purely anthropocentric grounds.

Notes

1 The term is used somewhat interchangeably with "anthropocentrism", but is also laden with social values, such as the economic measurement of well-being.
2 The Molitor report proposals are directly quoted in the Commission's commentary.
3 This idea was examined more thoroughly in the upcoming dissertation of Risto-Matti Matero (2023) currently in review.
4 Meaning here primarily Western liberal democracies.

Primary sources

Die Grünen (1980) *Das Bundesprogramm* [Federal Programme]. Berlin: Heinrich Böll Stiftung. Available at: https://www.boell.de/sites/default/files/assets/boell.de/images/download_de/publikationen/1980_001_Grundsatzprogramm_Die_Gruenen.pdf (Accessed: 16 December 2022).

Die Grünen (2002) *Die Zukunft ist grün* [The future is green]. Berlin: Heinrich Böll Stiftung. Available at: https://boell.de/sites/default/files/assets/boell.de/images/download_de/publikationen/2002_003_Grundsatzprogramm_Buendnis90DieGruenen.pdf (Accessed: 16 December 2022).

European Commission (1993) "Towards sustainability': The European Community programme of policy and action in relation to the environment and sustainable development', *Official Journal of the European Communities C138*.

European Commission (1995) 'Comments of the Commission on the Report of the Independent Experts Group on legislative and administrative simplification, SEC95 2121 Final'.

European Commission (1998) 'Decision 2179/98/EC', *Official Journal of the European Communities*, L275, pp. 1–13.

Kleinert, H. (1991) 'Ein Anfall von Todessehnsucht' [A seizure of death wish], *Der Spiegel*, 23/1991.

Vihreä Liitto (1988) *Vihreän Liiton yleisohjelma* [General programme of the Green League]. Pohtiva. Available at: https://www.fsd.tuni.fi/pohtiva/ohjelmalistat/VIHR/883 (Accessed: 16 December 2022).

Vihreä Liitto (1990) *Vihreän Liiton puolueohjelma 1990* [Party Programme of the Green League 1990]. Pohtiva. Available at: https://www.fsd.tuni.fi/pohtiva/ohjelmalistat/VIHR/884 (Accessed: 16 December 2022).

Vihreä Liitto (1994) *Vihreän Liiton puolueohjelma* [The Party Programme of the Green League]. Pohtiva. Available at: https://www.fsd.tuni.fi/pohtiva/ohjelmalistat/VIHR/885 (Accessed: 16 December 2022).

References

Akenji, L. (2019) *Avoiding Consumer Scapegoatism: Towards a Political Economy of Sustainable Living*. PhD thesis. University of Helsinki. Available at: http://urn.fi/URN:ISBN:978-951-51-5354-8 (Accessed: 16 December 2022).

Blair, A. (2010) *European Union since 1945*. London: Routledge.

Caradonna, J. (2018) 'An incompatible couple: A critical history of economic growth and sustainable development', in Borowy, I. and Schmeltzer, M. (eds.) *History of the Future of Economic Growth: Historical Roots of Current Debates on Sustainable Degrowth*. London: Routledge, pp. 154–173.

Carey, M. (2017) 'Beyond weather: The culture and politics of climate history', in Isenberg, A. (ed.) *The Oxford Handbook of Environmental History*. New York: Oxford University Press. https://doi.org/10.1093/oxfordhb/9780195324907.001.0001

Chakrabarty, D. (2021) *The Climate of History in a Planetary Age*. Chicago, IL: University of Chicago Press.

Collier, U. (1998) 'The environmental dimension of deregulation: An introduction', in Collier, U. (ed.) *Deregulation in the European Union: Environmental Perspectives*. London: Routledge, pp. 3–22.

Connolly, W. (2017) *Facing the Planetary: Entangled Humanism and the Politics of Swarming*. Durham, NC: Duke University Press. https://doi.org/10.1215/9780822373254

Dryzek, J. (2005a) 'Designs for environmental discourse revisited: A greener administrative state?', in Paehlke, R. and Torgerson, D. (eds.) *Managing Leviathan: Environmental Politics and the Administrative State*. 2nd edn. Toronto: Toronto University Press. https://doi.org/10.3138/9781442602281

Dryzek, J. (2005b) *The Politics of the Earth: Environmental Discourses*. 2nd edn. Oxford: Oxford University Press.

Dryzek, J. and Schosberg, D. (2005) *Debating the Earth: The Environmental Politics Reader*. Oxford: Oxford University Press.

Guha, R. (2000) *Environmentalism: A Global History*. New York: Longman.

Haila, Y. and Lähde, V. (2003) 'Luonnon poliittisuus: Mikä on uutta?', in Haila, Y. and Lähde, V. (eds.) *Luonnon Politiikka*. Tampere: Vastapaino, pp. 7–36.

Hinton, E. and Goodman, M. (2010) 'Sustainable consumption: Developments, considerations and new directions', in Redclift, M. and Woodcate, G. (eds.) *The International Handbook of Environmental Sociology.* 2nd edn. Cheltenham and Northampton: Edward Elgar, pp. 245–261.

Hockenos, P. (2007) *Joschka Fischer and the Making of the Berlin Republic: An Alternative History of Post-War Germany.* Oxford and New York: Oxford University Press.

Isotalo, M. (2007a) 'Hallituspuolueeksi EU-maahan', in Remes, T. and Sohlstén, J. (eds.) *Edellä! Vihreä Liitto 20 vuotta.* Helsinki: Vihreä Sivistysliitto, pp. 131–150.

Isotalo, M. (2007b) 'Vihreät vallan kahvassa', in Remes, T. and Sohlstén, J. (eds.) *Edellä! Vihreä Liitto 20 vuotta.* Helsinki: Vihreä Sivistysliitto, pp. 151–180.

Kananen, J. (2008) 'Kilpailukyky ja tuottavuus 2000-luvun sosiaalipolitiikassa', *Yhteiskuntapolitiikka,* 73(3), pp. 239–249.

Knill, C. and Liefferink, D. (2007) *Environmental Politics in the European Union: Policy-Making, Implementation and Patterns of Multi-Level Governance.* Manchester: Manchester University Press. https://doi.org/10.7228/manchester/9780719075803.001.0001

Kortetmäki, T. *et al.* (2021) 'Planetary well-being', *Humanities and Social Sciences Communications,* 8, p. 258. https://doi.org/10.1057/s41599-021-00899-3

Mahoney, J. (2000) 'Path dependence in historical sociology', *Theory and Society,* 29, pp. 507–548. https://doi.org/10.1023/A:1007113830879

Martell, L. (1994) *Ecology and Society: An Introduction.* Cambridge: Polity Press.

Matero, R. (2023) *From Companionship with Nature to Green Growth: Competing Conceptualisations of Well-Being and The Environment in Finnish and German Green Parties, 1980-2002.* Doctoral Dissertation (forthcoming). Jyväskylä: University of Jyväskylä.

Mazzucato, M. (2014) *The Entrepreneurial State: Debunking Public vs. Private Sector Myths.* New York: Anthem Press.

McEvoy, A. (1987) 'Towards an interactive theory of nature and culture: Ecology, production, and cognition in the California fishing industry', *Environmental Review: ER,* 11, pp. 289–305. https://doi.org/10.2307/3984137

Mende, S. (2012) 'Von der 'Antiparteien-Partei' zur 'Ökologischen Reformpartei' die Grünen und der Wandel des Politischen', *Archiv für Sozialgeschichte,* 52, pp. 273–315.

Milder, S. (2017) *Greening Democracy: The Anti-Nuclear Movement and Political Environmentalism in West Germany and Beyond, 1968–1983.* Cambridge: Cambridge University Press. https://doi.org/10.1017/9781316471401

Naess, A. (1997) 'Pinnallinen ja syvällinen, pitkän aikavälin ekologialiike' [translated from English by Rauhala-Hayes, M.], in Oksanen, M. and Rauhala-Hayes, M. (eds.) *Ympäristöfilosofia: Kirjoituksia ympäristönsuojelun eettisistä perusteista.* Helsinki: Gaudeamus, pp. 138–144.

Olsen, N. (2019) *The Sovereign Consumer: A New Intellectual History of Neoliberalism.* Cham: Palgrave MacMillan. https://doi.org/10.1007/978-3-319-89584-0

Penna, A. and Rivers, J. (2013) *Natural Disasters in a Global Environment.* Chichester: Wiley-Blackwell.

Pritchard, S. and Zimring, C. (2020) *Technology and the Environment in History.* Baltimore, MD: Johns Hopkins University Press.

Radkau, J. (2005) *Nature and Power: A Global History of the Environment.* Washington, DC: Cambridge University Press.

Radkau, J. (2011) *The Age of Ecology.* Cambridge: Polity Press.

Rigby, K. (2015) *Dancing with Disasters: Environmental Histories, Narratives, and Ethics for Perilous Times.* Charlottesville: University of Virginia Press.

Rumpala, Y. (2011) "Sustainable consumption' as a new phase in governmentalization of consumption', *Theory and Society*, 40(6), pp. 669–699. https://doi.org/10.1007/s11186-011-9153-5

Schmeltzer, M. (2016) *The Hegemony of Growth. The OECD and the Making of the Economic Growth Paradigm.* Cambridge: Cambridge University Press. https://doi.org/10.1017/CBO9781316452035

Warde, P., Libby, R. and Sörlin, S. (2018) *The Environment: A History of the Idea.* Baltimore, MD: Johns Hopkins University Press.

Worster, D. (1987) 'Introduction', *Environmental Review: ER,* 11, pp. 251–253. https://doi.org/10.2307/envrev/11.4.251

8

LOCAL KNOWLEDGE AND GLOBAL JUSTICE

From hegemonic development to planetary well-being

Teppo Eskelinen, Veera Joro and Godfred Obeng

Introduction

The planetary well-being approach emphasizes the need to protect vital natural processes in order to secure the well-being of both human and nonhuman nature. While the current hegemonic concept framing the balance between human needs and environmental protection is evidently "sustainable development", planetary well-being departs from this idea, offering a more holistic approach and a stronger emphasis on nonhuman nature (hereafter nature) beyond its instrumental value.

But to tap the full potential of the planetary well-being concept, insights from other disciplines should be used to complement its core ideas. In this chapter, we lay out a perspective from critical development studies. Critical development studies assists us to understand the shortcomings of the sustainable development approach. It highlights how "development" as a practice and a mindset has shaped our understanding of societal problems and solutions, and how current ideas about development (and hence also sustainable development, despite the recent broadening of its agenda) stand in the way of progress towards the aims of planetary well-being. Critical development studies also provides ideas that are complementary to planetary well-being by emphasizing the need to recognize the diversity of knowledge systems and hence of relevant ways of relating to the natural environment, as well as the role of global economic patterns in creating and sustaining inequalities. These insights assist planetary well-being theory to understand the systems of power and inequality which current "development" subtly advocates and operates within, as the theory moves towards addressing the needs of human societies and the planet.

This chapter explicates and illustrates the critical development studies approach and how it can contribute to planetary well-being. We begin with a critical

DOI: 10.4324/9781003334002-12

assessment of the meaning of development, focusing on its role as an epistemic monoculture and hierarchical system. This is done by means of a literature review. Then we apply ideas from the reviewed literature to a case study on climate change and cash crop cultivation, to illustrate the differences between sustainable development and planetary well-being approaches. The chapter closes with a discussion and conclusions.

The problems of development as we know it

As a concept, development appears to capture the human striving for progress, and it describes both a culture of modernity and an economic policy programme. Thanks to these associations, development easily becomes self-justificatory: As development is equated with progress, everything that falls under the label of development can claim to be positive. Moreover, it is the basis for policy interventions. When problems such as persistent poverty and environmental destruction are noted, development emerges as the suggested framework to design the remedies. For these reasons, it is particularly important to scrutinize the concept critically.

Development is traditionally understood as economic growth, and as instrumental in foregrounding the grand target of achieving "the end of poverty" (Sachs, 2005). It is associated with the Enlightenment tradition along with advances in science, transport, healthcare, and the like. But the culture underlying these advances also entails the perception of human beings as superior, "estranged" and "separated" from nature (Diaz Cruz, 2020), leading to attempts to dominate nature as human beings see themselves as the only measure of true value (Purser, Park and Montuori, 1995). Through the process, nature has come to be seen as primarily a resource stock (Abedi-Servastani and Shahvali, 2008), leading to a reckless exploitation of the environment.

Abilities to explain and control the natural world have also impacted upon the attitude of the "developed" towards other knowledge systems (Nygren, 1999). A myriad of cultures and related knowledges about local nature have been deemed "backwards", inferior, or even incapable of reason. During the colonial era, subjects in the colonies faced discrimination as their supposed proximity to nature constituted an excuse for their domination. While less explicit and appearing in a more benevolent guise today, the notion of "the third world" (Escobar, 1995) and the perception of "underdevelopment" as an undignified condition (Esteva, 1992) continue to legitimize interventions among the "underdeveloped" for both the implementers and recipients of this intervention (Escobar, 1995).

Furthermore, justifying policy processes in terms of development has meant the enforcement of market relations and rights, as well as a shift of ownership patterns away from communal ownership (Bryant, 1998). Within cultures of modernity, the state and the market are often seen as mutually exclusive domains, and in practical terms development has meant precisely the enforcement of these two locations of power at the expense of the community.

Not only a process but also a criterion, development became the epistemological basis of how "good quality of life" was understood in terms of a command of goods with market value as well as specific kinds of relationships between states and individuals (Rist, 2007), rendering other relationships invisible. The resulting measures and approaches reflected the attempt to universalize the lifestyles of the global North. Later, these ideas about quality of life were rationalized into technical indicators (Bhuta, Malito and Umbach, 2018), the most prominent being of course the Gross Domestic Product. As the standards and benchmarks used to measure "high quality of life" directly reflect Northern lifestyles, in effect maximizing consumption, they are in direct conflict with many other value systems. Anecdotally, for example, many Andean populations critique Western notions of development as increased material production and consumption (Carbonnier *et al.*, 2017). Rather, there exists the multi-level world theories which influence and enrich the overarching concept of "*buen vivir*" or "good living" which generally depicts development not as an end or achievement of the state but as an ongoing process of enhancing nature-community living (*ibid.*).

In addition to organising and assessing states' performance, development can be also seen as the name and justification for the existing global political order. In this sense it shapes and upholds existing global relations, such as the lock-in of the colonized countries' role as producers of a single unrefined crop. While development is justified as a discourse based on the notion of poorer countries "catching up" economically with wealthier ones, the global economic system has pushed economic disparities to an unprecedented level. Market relations, which are at the heart of cultures of development, mean that distributive logics do not follow human needs but market demands, which is strictly contrary to the idea of planetary well-being. Economic disparities are also intertwined with disparities in political power and epistemological dominance.

Recently, there has been a further expansion of economic relations. The development of the modern market society has meant a globalization of resources and externalities, with negative externalities allocated to already disadvantaged social categories and regions (Hornborg, 2009). The cultural ideas underlying modernity and capitalism, according to which nature can be treated as "resources" or "raw material", have been combined with the globalization of those ideas and the markets for those resources. This has led to new and destructive patterns of relating to nature. Such processes have also paved way for phenomena such as land-grabbing and capture (Abernethy *et al.*, 2017), and the privatization of state property around the global South.

Alternative pathways: Development as usual or something else?

To sum up, despite the progress associated with development, seeing the world as essentially comprising nations at different "development levels" implicitly justifies the downplaying of global hierarchies and a culture that is destructive to the natural environment. Development is both a process and a set of interventions, and to an increasing extent also a governance system. It both solves problems (as interventions and governance) and creates them (as a process), while justifying itself as completely apolitical and technical (Ferguson, 1994). Poverty alleviation is a key goal of development, but development as a process also creates new forms of poverty (Rist, 2007). Environmental protection is at the centre of current development governance, but environmental damage is also a product of the process of development (*e.g.*, Norberg-Hodge, 2009).

From this, there follows a choice between two alternatives: Either the approaches associated with development can be trusted to solve existing problems—if only enough funds are provided, and enough efforts made—or alternatives can be sought. Many will be happy to opt for the first alternative. This is not least because development appears to become an ever-more multifaceted and evolving idea as "non-conventional" development theories form an intellectual current (Peet and Hartwick, 2009) and new definitions of development emerge. Such new approaches have shifted the focus of development to freedoms (Sen, 2000), or have simply aimed to massively broaden the agenda, as is visible in the Sustainable Development Goals (SDGs).

Yet sustainable development (Brundtland, 1987), both as a scientific idea and as a policy programme, also accepts the traditional starting points of development, despite its openness to new definitions and even struggles over definition (Eskelinen, 2021). This means that it confuses a dignified life with a uniform social model, and it accepts the idea of nature as a resource stock. Therefore, sustainable development continues to enforce anthropocentric ideas amid possible ways to formulate human–nature relations (see Chapter 7). It asks how this uniform social model can be maintained, and how the resource stock can be managed responsibly. The primary focus is on "efficiency" by reducing waste and extracting the maximum from non-renewable resources (Eckersley, 1992; for a recent approach, see J. Sachs, 2015), as well as managing various other externalities generated by the contemporary economy. In this process, environmental concerns become assimilated into the rhetoric, dynamics, and power structures of development (W. Sachs, 2015). It has been argued that behind the "noble" intentions of even updated ideas about development lies a design which marginalizes discontent while allowing hierarchies, profit maximization, and "business as usual" (Abernethy *et al.*, 2017; Bryant, 1998).

Practically, an alternative approach would mean noting the variety of epistemologies and undoing hierarchical relations. The first task for research is then to locate and understand the diversity of ways of describing, perceiving, and relating to nature. Some currently marginalized worldviews could inform a healthier relationship with the environment (Dizerega, 1996). But this call for diversity should not be understood only in terms of undoing the destruction of traditional societies (Diaz Cruz, 2020). Indeed, the concept of "grassroots postmodernism", referring to both a diversity of worldviews and a rejection of hierarchies associated with development, has been suggested as an alternative (Esteva and Prakash, 2014). For another possible path, the various conceptualizations of environmental relations offered by the environmental movements of the global South (Martinez-Alier *et al.*, 2014) offer a rich body of grassroots perspectives.

The importance, relevance, and validity of local knowledge have gained increasing recognition and attention (Naess, 2013; Nygren, 1999). Barkin (2010) explains that scientists have come to acknowledge the potential of expanding horizons and looking for insights from premodern sources of knowledge. Martin *et al.* (2016) highlight the importance of recognizing local populations' cultures and identities in environmental conservation. Hinz *et al.* (2020) explain that Indigenous communities in particular often possess knowledge about their immediate environment, accumulated over centuries. These communities have also shown resilience in overcoming adverse situations. They offer "alternative solutions to our contemporary environmental challenges" (Tosam, 2020, p. 283) and can help to identify points of tension and contestation within the dominant knowledge system. When a problem is not framed according to dominant knowledge or perspectives, there is room for new viewpoints and innovative solutions.

It is important not to romanticize local knowledge, or to assume that it is static and inherently conservative. Local knowledge systems do not inherently hold more value, and they may be subject to internal struggles over legitimate representations, just like any other knowledge system. But there should be a balanced view of different knowledge systems, which will allow environmental issues to be assessed from multiple angles. Furthermore, while local knowledge systems cannot be assumed to contain nature-centric approaches, exposure to alternative knowledge systems is nonetheless paramount if we are to break down dominant views of how the world works and ought to work. Exclusively operating within the domain of dominant knowledge systems makes it difficult to envision radically alternative futures, and thus an exploration of local knowledge systems—which may greatly differ from the dominant worldviews—may help us to navigate a critical engagement with planetary well-being. In addition, understanding how development spreads, supports, and maintains a certain form of knowledge dominance can help us to understand where knowledge appropriate for planetary well-being needs to intervene. This is why critical development studies calls for an understanding of various knowledge systems.

Also, it is important to uncover hidden ecological imbalances. The fairness and unfairness of global trade is typically expressed and assessed in monetary terms, downplaying other forms of injustice. Global trade involves ecological inequalities whereby the global South depletes its natural resources and uses its natural world as a dumping ground to satisfy and maintain the lifestyles of the global North (Parks and Roberts, 2010; Rice, 2007). While on the surface the countries of the global North have been successful in reducing their carbon emissions and improving their environmental policies, they continue to be heavily reliant on the extractive economies of the global South (Jorgenson, 2006, 2016; Rice, 2007). In effect, the "wealthy nations offshore the energy-, natural resource- and pollution-intensive stages of production" (Rice, 2007, p. 139). One concept that can take note of hierarchies, for instance, is "climate debt", which refers to the disproportionate level of carbon emissions and flow of resources between the global North and the global South (Parks and Roberts, 2010).

So, while the idea of development suggests that we take states as fundamental units and analyze their development levels, it must be acknowledged that economic hierarchies are first and foremost global, and that they relate not only to resources but also to uneven possibilities to define and affect one's environment. For instance, the conservation paradigm informed by sustainable development has sometimes led to cases where local communities are no longer able to utilize their environments in traditional ways: As governing bodies restrict access to natural resources (Wisner, 2010), communities are unable to define their relationship to nature in appropriate terms.

Furthermore, an alternative approach to environmental protection also means asking questions about what is produced in the first place and who decides about this. Some discussions have pointed out that there is a need to differentiate between luxuries and necessities (cooking, heating, lighting), including in the context of carbon emissions and other environmental damage (Liverman, 2009). Currently, a minority of individuals are driving the extravagant demand for natural resources, with the rest merely functioning to meet that demand. Thus, it is not accurate to blame the entire human species equally for social and environmental destruction. Also, as Räthzel and Uzzell (2009) highlight, it is important to ask questions about who decides what goods are produced and how. Who decides on the accepted social and ecological costs of production? What social categories are involved in this decision-making process? The challenge is not only to point out existing disparities, but also to question the value system that makes the possession of luxuries seem desirable—in other words, to question our understanding of high-quality lifestyles and the unsustainability they promote (Kaijser and Kronsell, 2014). As noted above, quality of life is currently seen mostly in terms of consumption; alternative criteria are needed here. Moreover, even if needs are separated from mere desires, there are still good questions about how needs can be satisfied with less damage to earth systems (see Kortetmäki et al. 2021).

Development as a mode of thought and set of hierarchies is typically not an issue in the ongoing struggles between cultural spheres. Rather, many of the worldviews described above have been largely internalized in the cultures of the global South. This applies especially at the state level, as many Southern countries articulate their goals in terms of economic growth and other ideas originating in development thought. A diversity of epistemologies and relationships to nature exist at the grassroots level and often out of sight, even with difficulties to be articulated; therefore, active anthropological learning is necessary. Critical development studies is an attempt to uncover existing diverse relationships to nature and conceptions of well-being that are currently overlooked. Furthermore, it aims to reveal the patterns of power that impact on the extent to which people have autonomy to alter their environment.

Case example: Organic cocoa farmers in Ghana

Having established the need to recognize patterns of cultural, economic, and political domination as aspects of development, we now go on to present an illustrative case study to highlight how the devaluation of local environmental knowledge is intertwined with global economic inequality. This case study looks at organic cocoa farmers in Ghana and their perceptions of climate change. It is a somewhat typical case for development studies, as it is based in sub-Saharan Africa, is relevant to global economic patterns, and aims for a particular sensitivity to local perceptions. This exemplary case study leans on both a literature review and thematic interviews ($n = 10$) carried out by one of the authors of this chapter, using a qualitative purposive sampling approach.

Cocoa-farming, seen in context, is a typical postcolonial activity in the sense that cocoa is a cash crop for export. Its patterns of production are constructed around the continuity of the colonial division of labour, which employed crop monocultures to serve the imperial economy. For Ghana, cocoa production continues to contribute an estimated 25% of the gross domestic product. The West Africa region accounts for almost 70% of the global production of cocoa. This implies that West Africa generally, Ghana, and a very large number of smallholder farmers are highly dependent on cocoa cultivation. The Ghanaian government has internalized development-framed growth objectives, but it operates within the constraints of the global economy, which make both the increased refinement of raw materials and the diversification of the economy difficult. The government has therefore made efforts to further increase the production of raw cocoa through various farming interventions, such as the supply of fertilizers and the deployment of pollinators to cocoa plantations (COCOBOD, 2021).

These efforts come in the context of climate change, which is causing extreme high temperatures and unpredictable rain patterns that have a massive impact on farming (Derkyi et al., 2018). Economic vulnerability is related to and exacerbated by environmental change and existing inequalities. Cocoa thrives in temperate forest zones, and so climate change affects its sustainable production. Many studies have pointed to the impact of climate change on cocoa production in West Africa, as well as to farmers' awareness and perceptions of the issue (Ameyaw et al., 2018; Hutchins et al., 2015; Ofori-Boateng and Insah, 2014).

Cocoa cultivation is naturally an economic issue. Applying the sustainable development approach would mean asking how production can be maximized given existing environmental constraints and the need to consider the continuity of production. While the SDGs entail a broader perspective, with numerous sub-targets related to environmental protection, this core approach remains. Yet, other vocabularies exist with which to understand these circumstances. The questions emerging from critical development studies that have relevance to planetary well-being are as follows: How do the short-term responses to production challenges such as fertilizer provision influence large-scale processes that are fundamental to human and nonhuman well-being? How is well-being in this case conditioned by global economic structures? What do farmers' perceptions of the change in the natural environment tell us about locally relevant human–nature relationships? And how are these questions related?

Farmers in the region indeed point out an increase in temperatures and occurrences of drought (Ameyaw *et al.*, 2018), changes in rainfall patterns, which cause a high incidence of black pod disease, resulting in low yields (Anim-Kwapong and Frimpong, 2008), and negative effects on soil health and fertility, along with low production (Hutchins *et al.*, 2015). The farmers interviewed for our case study also referred to such experiences, in addition to experiences of poverty and hunger due to the effects of climate change on their livelihoods and environment. Generally, the farmers saw the well-being of natural systems as closely interlinked with their own living conditions, in a sense not restricted to the economy. If bodies of water ran dry, this meant long walks in search of water, which in turn decreased the time available for community development. Changes in the natural environment included the disappearance of living organisms such as plants and mushrooms, less water for animals, and diminishing soil nutrients.

How can people react to such changes in nature and thereby in their lifestyles, even their survival? One possibility is to try to adapt. Much of the sustainable development discourse points in this direction, and "resilience"—referring to the capacities of communities to live through external shocks—has become a fashionable concept. But from the perspective of individual farmers occupying a marginalized position in the global economic system, possibilities for adaptation are limited. They could shift to other economic ventures, an idea expressed by many farmers. Alternative livelihoods include oil palm plantation work, maize and cassava farming, and off-farm activities such as trading or artisanal work such as bricklaying and masonry (Anim-Kwapong and Frimpong, 2008). Even if cocoa cultivation continues, continuity at the level of individual farmers might be very unpredictable. It has been estimated that even though adaptation measures might allow Ghana's current cocoa production level to be sustained until the 2050s, farmland in some areas of the country may become unsuitable (Bunn, Schreyer and Castro, 2018). Some analyses predict a decline in the general production level (Ofori-Boateng and Insah, 2014).

However, the opportunities and constraints with regard to acting and adapting are somewhat unique in the case of organic farmers. Organic farming and labelling is clearly one way to respond to the environmental crisis, a means available to smallholder farmers, and very much in line with the global system of sustainable development governance and market relations. The interviewed farmers expressed a determination to mitigate climate change instead of seeking other subsistence strategies. They mentioned that in order to prevent water scarcity on their farmland and in their community, they were planting trees and vegetative cover to protect bodies of water from drying up. The planting of cover at the local level positively reflects the knowledge that afforestation is one possible way to combat climate change, as it seeks to prevent the intensification of desertification. The farmers also reported that to mitigate climate change and alleviate its local impacts, they had been carrying out many other activities to protect bodies of water on their farmland and in their community, such as protecting the trees on the riverbanks.

But adopting organic agriculture is not only a measure to mitigate climate change; it is also a global standard. As such, it reflects current global governance approaches as well as consumer demand, even if state policies vary. For example, organic cocoa farmers are mandated to practise mixed cropping, and they therefore also need water for other plants such as vegetables. The farmers say they are committed to these practices, despite the hardships involved—for example, not using agrochemicals to control pests and diseases, or bush-burning to control weeds, because of their impacts on biodiversity. But one might ask what epistemological and functional room for manoeuvre are appropriate, who should have the power to oversee production standards, and what are the implications of the postcolonial division of labour on which the production pattern rests. These questions posed by the planetary well-being approach are necessary ones, revealing the limitations of focusing exclusively on optimally large volumes of produce.

Although they had very limited influence, most of the farmers in our data had switched from conventional farming to organic farming as a contribution to combating climate change. Several of the interviewed farmers also interpreted the drivers of climate change through the lens of local changes in nature use—for example, referring to the cutting down of nearby rainforests, the destruction of bodies of water, and observed changes in land use. Despite the global nature of the problems, interpretations of changes in the natural environment are strongly locally mediated. But local sense-making can also mean assuming large responsibilities, despite one's marginal contribution to the environmental problem in question. As people seem to do whatever lies within their power, this responsibility-shifting may have more visible implications in the future. For example, since humanity may soon be approaching the boundaries of global freshwater use (Rockström *et al.*, 2009), questions emerge about exactly whose water use should adapt in response.

All in all, analyzing the intertwining of global power relations and local sense-making as suggested by the planetary well-being approach, helps us to understand the broader problem of sustainable development. Slogans such as "combining people, the planet and profit" (Washington, 2015) say little about the actual possibilities available to farmers, how their interpretations are valued, or how they might undo inequalities. Neither do ideas such as the need to meet human basic needs say much about what would constitute an appropriate action—or even level of action—in these circumstances. It has been suggested that the power an individual or social category is able to exert can be identified through their ability to alter their environment (Kaijser and Kronsell, 2014). A number of scholars (Barkin, 2010; Holden and Linnerud, 2010; Räthzel and Uzzell, 2009) have indeed highlighted that a lack of power or influence over one's environment will hinder one's ability and willingness to change one's behaviour. Moreover, research needs to look at the well-being of specific natural ecosystems in order to understand the conditions of human well-being in specific locations.

The sustainable development approach would mean adapting to existing conditions as far as possible, securing responsible action within the domains under each institution's or individual's control, but accepting the constraints of export orientation, consumer power, and existing systems of trade governance. Farmers could practise mixed cropping, shift to other regions if necessary, and participate in certification schemes that would increase the value of their produce in the eyes of powerful global consumers. Possibly, farmers could also gain access to best practices from other regions. What is omitted in this discourse is questions related to the global division of labour, the allocation of vulnerabilities, local epistemologies, and the room for manoeuvre available to different societal positions. It is also unclear what sustainable development posits as the goal of cocoa farmers. Is there any "catch-up", or just the perennially unequal global organization? Is there increased refinement, new and diverse production methods, or improved food security with more diverse produce? Most importantly, is there any recognized relationship with one's natural environment other than an instrumental one? Planetary well-being, on the other hand, suggests a holistic approach. It respects limits in terms of both planetary boundaries and the protection of local ecosystems, but it also posits the empowerment of producers so that a needs-driven approach will replace existing power structures. If we are trying to understand the conditions of well-being, it is necessary to learn about local perceptions, and to ask questions about the well-being of nature from a non-anthropocentric perspective.

It needs to be noted too that local perceptions matter, beyond confirming what science already tells us. Local environmental knowledge has an important role to play in altering environmentally destructive behaviour, but it might have a limited impact if individuals feel powerless to change the wider system. Farmers construct their relationship with nature based on both the general conditions of cultivation (largely impacted by climate change) and their own approach to farming (for example, opting for organic farming). But it is the broader system of markets that determines what is produced, and most drivers of environmental change are beyond the control of local farmers.

Discussion

Above, we have critically presented the concept and practice of development and the fundamental tension it involves, illustrating our points with a case study. On one hand, development is an effort towards progress: To utilize existing knowledge for the benefit of the whole of humanity. Its achievements need to be noted. Hence, development goals tend to be ambitious and expressed in very ethical rhetoric (Eskelinen, 2018). But development (as both a process and an intervention) can and should also be seen critically as (1) a project to undo locally relevant forms of knowing and relating to the immediate environment, in favour of an epistemological monoculture and an approach that sees nature in terms of resources to be utilized on the global market; (2) a process of universalizing market relations; (3) the making of a set of global hierarchies; (4) the setting of criteria for quality of life that are informed by these relationships and hierarchies. Understanding development entails understanding it both as progress and as a manifestation of all these aspects.

So, what can critical development studies bring to planetary well-being? We need to note that theoretical ideas always carry old patterns of thought, and if not critically scrutinized these old ideas may unintentionally inform the new ideas too. Planetary well-being theory thus risks taking on dominant ideas about development if their roots and impact are not properly recognized. Critical development studies provides tools to analyze these dominant ideas. Not only can development studies help us to find new ways of understanding the root problems of this crisis and to engage with alternative visions, but it can also help to expand discussions of planetary well-being by framing the domain of the issue and where solutions may exist. It sheds light on the power relations that currently exist and need to be unmade if holistic well-being is to be pursued.

While development as a practice and idea is not homogenous, its core ideas persist in subtly justifying a culture that portrays nature as a resource stock and is based on seeing various people and cultures as inferior precisely because of their supposed proximity to nature. Even though ideas evolve, this core of development thinking remains strong. These ideas need to be understood, especially in terms of how they form obstacles to more holistic ideas of well-being and how they creep into ostensibly progressive approaches such as sustainable development. While it needs to be noted that the distinction between business as usual and alternatives is not always clear-cut—for example, resourcist approaches can be incorporated into very critical accounts, such as discussions of ecological boundaries—it is important to understand how development as an idea and practice works. Crucially, even alternative approaches to development reconceptualize the dynamics of human society, rather than human–nature relationships.

But there evidently remain human societies that are unable to even meet basic needs, and therefore there is a genuine need to ensure that all human beings can enjoy a dignified life. This entails an economic aspect: Farmers keep farming to achieve necessary material goods too. While the existence of poverty continues to be the justification for development, it is crucial to rearticulate the need to meet existing wants in accordance with planetary well-being values. Planetary well-being is not about romanticizing poverty, but about showing the connections between the well-being of humans and nonhuman nature—and we can add that it is necessary to see the diversity of possible vocabularies of the good life and progress.

Human beings always contemplate their relationships with nature, use various vocabularies, and attach different meanings to nature. It needs to be asked what kind of knowledge is privileged and recognized as relevant in the fight against environmental destruction (Kaijser and Kronsell, 2014). Environmental protection involves more than state-level environmental policies to meet today's needs without compromising those of the future (Brundtland, 1987), or "resource efficiency": It is a call for human beings to reconsider their relationship with the environment, and various sources of ideas and inspiration are needed for this. Our case study showed that farmers are constantly contemplating changes in nature based on their experience, and seeking solutions with available methods. Yet their room for manoeuvre is curtailed by uneven relations in the global economy, epistemology, environmental damage, and risk allocation. Farmers have some room for manoeuvre, some space for their experiences and interpretations to be heard, and some share of responsibility for mitigating climate change, but this space is limited by economic and epistemological inequalities.

Well-being should be seen not only as a matter of meeting certain baselines, but as a quality and virtue of society, extending from local communities to global society. Seen in this way, the issue is not to overcome poverty, but to overcome material inequalities and epistemological hierarchies. It is necessary to see the various facets of inequality: Wealth, political power, and cultural dominance. Crucially, inequalities are not arbitrary or caused by variations in individual achievements; rather, they are outcomes of long historical processes and economic and cultural structures. In the context of environmental protection, it should be noted that the level of responsibility for environmental damage varies significantly between individuals, groups of people, and nations. The planetary well-being approach helps us to unfold these various and overlapping aspects and understand how they intertwine, rather than managing policy within the system as it exists. The approach emphasizes that the depletion of natural processes also disables human well-being: Critical development studies complements this notion by emphasizing that the means of well-being are dependent on context. Not all means of well-being can be reduced to resources, and hence not even to resource efficiency. Other perceptions of human–nature relationships may be more relevant for promoting general planetary well-being.

References

Abedi-Servastani, A. and Shahvali, M. (2008) 'Ecology and ethics: Some relationships for nature conservation', *Journal of Applied Sciences,* 8(4), pp. 715–718. https://doi.org/10.3923/jas.2008.715.718

Abernethy, P. *et al.* (2017) 'Leverage points for sustainability transformation', *Ambio,* 46, pp. 30–39. https://doi.org/10.1007/s13280-016-0800-y

Ameyaw, L. *et al.* (2018) 'Cocoa and climate change: Insights from smallholder cocoa producers in Ghana regarding challenges in implementing climate change mitigation strategies', *Forests,* 9(12), pp. 742. https://doi.org/10.3390/f9120742

Anim-Kwapong, G.J. and Frimpong, E.B. (2008) 'Climate change on cocoa production', in Agyeman-Bonsu, W. (ed.) *Ghana Climate Change Impacts, Vulnerability and Adaptation Assessments under the Netherlands Climate Assistance Programme (NCAP).* New Tafo Akim: Environmental Protection Agency, pp. 263–298.

Barkin, D. (2010) 'The struggle for local autonomy in a multiethnic society: Constructing alternatives with indigenous epistemologies', in Esquith, S.L. and Gifford, F. (eds.) *Capabilities, Power, and Institutions: Toward a More Critical Development Ethics.* University Park, TX: Penn State University Press, pp. 142–162.

Bhuta, N., Malito, D.V. and Umbach, G. (2018) 'Introduction: Of numbers and narratives: Indicators in global governance and the rise of a reflexive indicator culture', in Malito, D.V., Umbach, G. and Bhuta, N. (eds.) *The Palgrave Handbook of Indicators in Global Governance.* London: Palgrave, pp. 1–29. https://doi.org/10.1007/978-3-319-62707-6

Brundtland, G.H. (1987) *Our Common Future: Report of the World Commission on Environment and Development.* UN Document A/42/427. Geneva: United Nations.

Bryant, R.L. (1998) 'Power, knowledge and political ecology in the third world: A review', *Progress in Physical Geography*, 22(1), pp. 79–94.

Bunn, C., Schreyer, F. and Castro, F. (2018) *The Economic Case for Climate Action in West African Cocoa Production Report.* Cali: CGIAR Research Program on Climate Change, Agriculture and Food Security (CCAFS).

Carbonnier, G., Campodónico, H. and Vázquez, S.T. (eds.) (2017) *Alternative Pathways to Sustainable Development: Lessons from Latin America.* Geneva and Boston, MA: Brill-Nijhoff. https://doi.org/10.1163/9789004351677

COCOBOD (2021) *50th Annual Report and Consolidated Financial Statements.* Available at: https://cocobod.gh/resource_files/50th-annual-report-and-financial-statements-2018-2019.pdf (Accessed: 14 September 2021).

Derkyi, M. *et al.* (2018) 'Smallholder farmers' perception of climatic and socio-economic factors influencing livelihoods in the transition zone of Ghana', *AAS Open Research*, 1(7). https://doi.org/10.12688/aasopenres.12839.1

Diaz Cruz, N. (2020) 'Reimagine the environment implies decolonizing our relationship with nature', *Periódico UNAL*. Available at: https://unperiodico.unal.edu.co/pages/detail/reimagine-the-environment-implies-decolonizing-our-relationship-with-nature/ (Accessed: 17 November 2021).

Dizerega, G. (1996) 'Towards an ecocentric political economy', *The Trumpeter: Journal of Ecosophy* 13(4).

Eckersley, R. (1992) *Environmentalism and Political Theory.* Albany: State University of New York Press.

Escobar, A. (1995) *Encountering Development: The Making and Unmaking of the Third World.* Princeton, NJ: Princeton University Press.

Eskelinen, T. (2018) 'After the millennium development goals: Remarks on the ethical assessment of global poverty reduction success', *Etikk I Praksis: Nordic Journal of Applied Ethics*, 12(1), pp. 61–75. https://doi.org/10.5324/eip.v12i1.2348

Eskelinen, T. (2021) 'Interpreting the sustainable development goals through the perspectives of Utopia and governance', *Forum for Development Studies*, 48(2), pp. 179–197. https://doi.org/10.1080/08039410.2020.1867889

Esteva, G. (1992) 'Development', in Sachs, W. (ed.) *The Development Dictionary: A Guide to Knowledge as Power.* London: Zed Books, pp. 6–25.

Esteva, G. and Prakash, M.S. (eds.) (2014) *Grassroots Post-Modernism: Remaking the Soil of Cultures.* London: Zed Books.

Ferguson, J. (1994) *The Anti-Politics Machine: Development, Depoliticization, and Bureaucratic Power in Lesotho.* Minneapolis: Minnesota University Press.

Hinz, E. *et al.* (2020) 'Indigenous and local knowledge in sustainability transformations research: A literature review', *Ecology and Society*, 25(1). https://doi.org/10.5751/ES-11305-250103

Holden, E. and Linnerud, K. (2010) 'Environmental attitudes and household consumption: An ambiguous relationship', *International Journal of Sustainable Development*, 13(3), pp. 217–231. https://doi.org/10.1504/IJSD.2010.037555

Hornborg, A. (2009) 'Zero-sum world: Challenges in conceptualizing environmental load displacement and ecologically unequal exchange in the world-system', *International Journal of Comparative Sociology*, 50, pp. 237–262. https://doi.org/10.1177/0020715209105141

Hutchins, A. *et al.* (2015) *Assessment of Climate Change Impacts on Cocoa Production and Approaches to Adaptation and Mitigation: A Contextual View of Ghana and Costa Rica*. Washington, DC: Elliott School of International Affairs. Available at: https://elliott.gwu.edu/sites/g/files/zaxdzs2141/f/World%20Cocoa%20Foundation.pdf (Accessed: 19 August 2021).

Jorgenson, A.K. (2006) 'Unequal ecological exchange and environmental degradation: A theoretical proposition and cross-national study of deforestation, 1990-2000', *Rural Sociology*, 71, pp. 685–712. https://doi.org/10.1526/003601106781262016

Jorgenson, A.K. (2016) 'The sociology of ecologically unequal exchange, foreign investment dependence and environmental load displacement: Summary of the literature and implications for sustainability', *Journal of Political Ecology*, 23(1), pp. 334–349. https://doi.org/10.2458/v23i1.20221

Kaijser, A. and Kronsell, A. (2014) 'Climate change through the lens of intersectionality', *Environmental Politics*, 23(3), pp. 417–433. https://doi.org/10.1080/09644016.2013.835203

Kortetmäki, T. *et al.* (2021) 'Planetary well-being', *Humanities and Social Sciences Communications*, 8, p. 258. https://doi.org/10.1057/s41599-021-00899-3

Liverman, D.M. (2009) 'Conventions of climate change: Constructions of danger and the dispossession of the atmosphere', *Journal of Historical Geography*, 35, pp. 279–296. https://doi.org/10.1016/j.jhg.2008.08.008

Martin, A. *et al.* (2016) 'Justice and conservation: The need to incorporate recognition', *Biological Conservation*, 197, pp. 254–261. https://doi.org/10.1016/j.biocon.2016.03.021

Martinez-Alier, J. *et al.* (2014) 'Between activism and science: Grassroots concepts for sustainability coined by environmental justice organizations', *Journal of Political Ecology*, 21, pp. 19–60. https://doi.org/10.2458/v21i1.21124

Naess, L.O. (2013) 'The role of local knowledge in adaptation to climate change', *WIREs Climate Change*, 4, pp. 99–106. https://doi.org/10.1002/wcc.204

Norberg-Hodge, H. (2009) *Ancient Futures: Lessons from Ladakh for a Globalizing World*. San Francisco, CA: Sierra Club Books.

Nygren, A. (1999) 'Local knowledge in the environment-development discourse: From dichotomies to situated knowledges', *Critique of Anthropology*, 19(3), pp. 267–288.

Ofori-Boateng, K. and Insah, B. (2014) 'The impact of climate change on cocoa production in West Africa', *International Journal of Climate Change Strategies and Management*, 6(3), pp. 296–314. https://doi.org/10.1108/IJCCSM-01-2013-0007

Parks, B.C. and Roberts, J.T. (2010) 'Climate change, social theory and justice', *Theory, Culture & Society*, 27(2–3), pp. 134–166. https://doi.org/10.1177/02632764093590

Peet, R. and Hartwick, E. (2009) *Theories of Development: Contentions, Arguments, Alternatives*. New York: Guilford press.

Purser, R.E., Park, C. and Montuori, A. (1995) 'Limits to anthropocentrism: Toward an ecocentric organization paradigm?', *The Academy of Management Review*, 20, pp. 1053–1089.

Räthzel, N. and Uzzell, D. (2009) 'Transformative environmental education: A collective rehearsal for reality', *Environmental Education Research*, 15, pp. 263–277. https://doi.org/10.1080/13504620802567015

Rice, J. (2007) 'Exchange: Consumption, equity, and unsustainable structural relationships within the global economy'. *International Journal of Comparative Sociology* 48 (1), pp. 43–72. https://doi.org/10.1177/0020715207072159

Rist, G. (2007) 'Development as a buzzword', *Development in Practice*, 17(4–5), pp. 485–491. https://doi.org/10.1080/09614520701469328

Rockström, J. (2009) 'Future water availability for global food production: The potential of green water for increasing resilience to global change', *Water Resources Research*, 45(7). https://doi.org/10.1029/2007WR006767

Sachs, J. (2005) *The End of Poverty: Economic Possibilities for Our Time.* New York: Penguin.

Sachs, J. (2015) *The Age of Sustainable Development.* New York: Columbia University Press. https://doi.org/10.7312/sach17314

Sachs, W. (2015) *Planet Dialectics: Explorations in Environment and Development.* 2nd edn. London: Zed Books. https://doi.org/10.5040/9781350221765

Sen, A. (2000) *Development as Freedom.* New York: Anchor books.

Tosam, M.J. (2020) 'Negotiating and overturning the othering of indigenous epistemologies', *Journal of World Philosophies*, 5(1), pp. 282–286. https://doi.org/10.2979/jourworlphil.5.1.18

Washington, H. (2015) *Demystifying Sustainability: Towards Real Solutions.* New York: Routledge. https://doi.org/10.4324/9781315748641

Wisner, B. (2010) 'Climate change and cultural diversity', *International Social Science Journal*, 61, pp. 131–140. https://doi.org/10.1111/j.1468-2451.2010.01752.x

9

CONSUMPTION AND PLANETARY WELL-BEING

Jessie Do, Mitra Salimi, Stefan Baumeister, Milla Sarja, Outi Uusitalo, Terhi-Anna Wilska and Johanna Suikkanen

Unsustainability in consumption and business

Marketing, consumption, and planetary well-being

Consumption or the acquisition of goods and services has reached a level that the planet cannot sustain from the viewpoint of securing long-term human well-being, let alone securing the prospects of nonhuman well-being. Satisfying human needs depletes resources on a scale that compromises the well-being of nonhuman species. Marketing is the engine that stimulates consumption (Kotler, 2011) and, consequently, the use of enormous amounts of natural resources. The interconnected areas of consumption and marketing have important roles in facilitating the transition towards sustainable consumption (McDonagh and Prothero, 2014) that respects planetary well-being (Kortetmäki *et al.*, 2021).

Due to the increasing awareness of the current ecological crisis and the risks it poses, companies integrate sustainability into their strategies and practices. Nevertheless, in the quest for business growth, revenues, and returns on investment, companies continue to feed excessive consumption (Gabler, Landers and Richey, 2021), subordinating ecological concerns to these goals. As marketing and consumption have severe adverse effects on PW, sustainable marketing, which reduces the damage, can even be considered an oxymoron. Concern for nature is seldom present in marketing definitions and practices, with a few exceptions. Macro-level, critical marketing approaches have been called for to foster harmonious relationships between marketing, consumption, and nature (McDonagh and Prothero, 2014). Martin (2013, p. 18) stressed the role of nature by defining sustainable marketing as "a process of creating, communicating and delivering value to customers in ways that ensure maintaining and recovering both natural and human capital".

DOI: 10.4324/9781003334002-13

Apart from emphasizing that marketing should be ecologically sustainable, socially just, and economically enduring, she stated that it has persuasive power and can thus be used to encourage everyone to pay attention to nonhuman needs. Persuasive communicative tools can aid in mainstreaming consumption patterns that do not compromise many species' opportunities to achieve well-being. Instead of endlessly fostering the growth of the demand for and consumption of eco-efficient goods and services, sustainable marketing should acknowledge the systemic view and the delicate balance between human and nonhuman needs to support rather than endanger ecosystem processes.

Companies seeking to comply with the PW premises can take more or less effective alternative routes to marketing. Usually, companies opt to make incremental changes, focusing on single sustainability actions, such as increasing their eco-efficiency or adding green products to their product ranges (Press, 2021). However, single acts would not address the ecological crisis but would signal weak sustainability, which asserts that natural resources can be exploited to increase profits. Assuming that the benefits of economic growth compensate for the loss of natural resources and ecosystem services (*ibid.*), weak sustainability does not lead to changes in the logic of the growth and depletion of resources.

The strong-sustainability approach rejects substitutability and requires maintaining and protecting the natural capital in the ecosystem (Dietz and Neumayer, 2007). This implies creating systemic changes, respecting the intrinsic value of nature in marketing, and altering everyday consumption practices, including reducing consumption levels (Geels *et al.*, 2015; Press, 2021). Awareness of the negative impacts of excessive consumption has catalyzed alternative markets, the use of second-hand items, sharing, recycling, and the circular economy (CE). Deepening concern about nature gives reason to setting conditions for and boundaries to consumers' and marketers' practices. An example of such a norm is sufficiency, defined by Gossen, Ziesemer, and Schrader (2019, p. 252) as "the absolute reduction of the resources and energy used for consumption by questioning the level of demand". Limited consumption can be hard to achieve when consumers expect certain social and cultural patterns of everyday life dictated by the consumerist culture (Kortetmäki *et al.*, 2021). These demands drive consumers to go beyond the level of consumption that only meets their personal needs and that decreases the possibilities of satisfying nonhuman needs. In these cases, taking incremental steps in sustainability can be a practical way of achieving stronger sustainability over the course of time.

Marketing is based on an anthropocentric ideology that is inconsistent with the needs of nature. Reducing the discrepancies between marketing, consumption, and care for nonhuman species is a move towards marketing that acknowledges PW. Structural and cultural transformations are needed to move production, marketing, and consumption from resource depletion to resource maintenance. Viable steps are mitigating unsustainability, reducing waste, improving resource management through circular supply chains, and adopting alternative consumption practices.

Transgressions in marketing

Humans' dominance over the planet causes lasting alterations to ecosystems. The irresponsible practices of companies are among the most serious hazards, putting a variety of ecological and economic functions in jeopardy. Irresponsibility harms both living entities (*e.g.*, humans and nature) and non-living entities (*e.g.*, brands and businesses). These damaging activities in the marketing area are classified as brand transgression (Aaker, Fournier, and Brasel, 2004), brand misconduct (Huber *et al.*, 2010), and corporate social irresponsibility (Lin-Hi and Müller, 2013). "Brand transgression" is a broader term that can cover both "brand misconduct" and "corporate social irresponsibility".

Aaker, Fournier, and Brasel (2004) define brand transgression as a violation of the implicit and explicit rules in the consumer–brand relationship, and it can be related to performance and value (Dutta and Pullig, 2011). Performance-related transgressions pertain to defective goods or services (*e.g.*, product recalls), whereas value-related transgressions pertain to social or ethical concerns inherent in brand values rather than issues directly connected to goods or services. Value-related brand transgressions have ramifications for the concerned brands' perceived symbolic meanings; thus, their consequences on consumers' and nature's well-being can be more lasting and detrimental. A case of value-related transgression is Ryanair's greenwashing news in 2020: The airline claimed that it has the lowest carbon emission rate among the European airlines, but the Advertising Standards Authority revealed that this claim is misleading and far from reality (British Broadcasting Corporation (BBC), 2020). While some instances of greenwashing are inadvertent and arise from a lack of understanding of what environment-friendliness is, it is often carried out on purpose using a variety of marketing and public relations techniques and misinformation.

Among value-related transgressions, social and environmental unsustainability is common and has the most tangible implications for life on Earth; the researched cases of value-related transgressions involved employee mistreatment and workplace discrimination, corporate fraud, sweatshop factories and child labour, environmental harm and animal abuse, and controversial marketing practices and unethical production (*e.g.*, Ouyang, Yao and Hu, 2020; Xu, Bolton and Winterich, 2021). Unsustainability is "institutionalized" in many of the global conventional business structures and economic systems (Ritala, Albareda and Bocken, 2021). Breaking down these institutionalized patterns and acknowledging that nature and humanity are inextricably linked to each other may be the key to a successful transition to a more sustainable economy, ensuring a future for nature and humans. Incorporating the non-anthropocentric and systemic view of PW into business structures and economic systems is necessary for this change as businesses and consumers need to understand that human and nonhuman entities are interconnected, and our planet will not survive unless the needs of diverse forms of life on Earth are satisfied. Both consumers and nature provide input to companies, and nature relies on the benign quality of consumers' and businesses' input to nature to continue to exist and be well.

The current marketing and consumption system is part of the problem that threatens PW. We suggest and emphasize that marketing can become a significant part of the solution if it adopts both incremental and radical methods to pursue planet-friendly outcomes. The second part of this chapter discusses various solutions pointing to the continuum from weak sustainability actions to major, system-level transformations as paths to PW.

Solutions to consumption for planetary well-being

Enhancing sustainable consumer behaviour

Sustainable consumption helps restore natural and human resources and reduce the impacts of human consumption on nonhuman needs by adopting alternatives that use fewer virgin resources. It involves a shift to more efficiently produced need satisfiers (Kortetmäki *et al.*, 2021) via waste reduction, product life extension, and reuse and recycling (Maitre-Ekern and Dalhammar, 2019).

Coming up with solutions to unsustainable consumer behaviour requires an understanding of how needs and desires are culturally and socially determined in different societies. It is also important to understand sustainability in light of consumers' generational values and attitudes. Today, it is generally thought that the youngest consumers are the most environmentally conscious; Generation Z is frequently called Generation Green by the media. However, many studies in different cultures suggest that the young generations (Y and Z) do not make the most environmentally friendly purchase decisions. Rather, the older generations (Baby Boomers and Generation X) have been the most sustainable consumers for the past few decades (Wilska, 2002; Kuoppamäki, Wilska and Taipale, 2017; Ham *et al.*, 2021). Young people may have the greenest values and good intentions, but high product prices and the hedonistic pursuit of experiences (Kuoppamäki, Wilska and Taipale, 2017) may enhance unsustainable consumption among them (Ham *et al.*, 2021). Products that have been produced in an environmentally friendly way are often more expensive than non-green products (*e.g.*, fast fashion), and the desire for experiences may lead to unsustainable practices (*e.g.*, travelling). Lifestyles with real non-consumption practices are still rare. However, new trends are emerging among the young, such as preferring second-hand fashion and vegan food (Bedard and Tolmie, 2018).

The perceptions of what is sustainable and what should be done to increase sustainability in consumption vary in different theoretical approaches. The radical view emphasizes individual power and responsibility, whereas the reformist view relies on structural changes in society (Garner, 2000). The radical perspective aims to change the world by changing people or influencing the way they experience the world (Dryzek, 1997). Radical green movements emphasize the need to reduce all consumption. The reformist approach to green consumerism, on the other hand, relies on the theory of ecological modernization (*e.g.*, Spaargaren, 2011), which regards technical innovations as solutions to environmental problems. The role of a household is seen as effective, especially in minimizing waste, saving energy, recycling, preferring services over goods and promoting a sharing economy.

Another policy approach stream of thought on change of habits that has become popular among policymakers is the so-called nudge (Thaler and Sunstein, 2008) or choice-architecture approach. This approach requires policies, environments, and regulations to nudge individuals to make better choices, with desirable options given as defaults while not restricting the range of options (Keller, Halkier and Wilska, 2016). Nudging is one way of trying to close the gap between people's generally environmentally friendly attitudes and actual purchase behaviours. However, it has been argued that the nudge approach is too narrow. Many studies have suggested that there are several social, emotional, cognitive, and contextual reasons for the gap between green attitudes, intentions, and purchase behaviours (ElHaffar, Durif and Dube, 2020). Social practice theories expand the concept of nudging by suggesting that the motives behind consumer behaviour are complex because consumers are led by "routinised types of behaviour" (Reckwitz, 2002, p. 24). Thus, consumers should not be treated as conscious agents but as carriers of practices whose performance keeps such practices alive (Keller, Halkier and Wilska, 2016).

From the viewpoint of policy, technological innovations, and the persuasion of individuals to choose wiser behaviours are only partial solutions to the sustainability crises. The key solution lies in transforming social practices involving material goods and environments and people's competencies and willingness to do something about the problem (Shove, Pantzar and Watson, 2012; Keller, Halkier and Wilska, 2016). Thus, sustainability should be pursued in public governance, in individuals' everyday practices, in housing and transport, in modes of production and, above all, in the education of the young. In addition, the radical view of reducing all private and public consumption, presented by Dryzek (1997) should get more attention in affluent consumer societies.

Circular economy

The current consumption habits are threatening nonhuman nature. This is due to the fast-paced and ever-increasing production, transport, and consumption of goods, which cause high levels of raw material extraction, wastage, and carbon emissions. Human interference with nonhuman nature seems to be justified by the belief in human dominance over nature and supported by the view that natural resources are infinite. PW is not possible with the current degree and rate of consumption; therefore, the way we consume must be questioned, and new ways to fulfil human needs must be adopted. To some extent, CE could provide solutions for this transition (for CE, see Chapter 10).

The research on CE was previously technology- and engineering-oriented but has since moved towards business model aspects as CE research has increased rapidly in recent years (Sarja, Onkila and Mäkelä, 2021). However, the CE perspective on consumption and consumers has only recently been acknowledged, such as in studies on consumer acceptance of different CE products (Camacho-Otero, Boks and Pettersen, 2018), consumers' consumption behaviour in the CE context (Maitre-Ekern and Dalhammar, 2019) and consumers' CE-related knowledge and understanding (Korsunova, Horn and Vainio, 2021), whereas, the topics of non-consumption and refusing to consume in CE research are less explored.

The CE literature has recognized that CE is often understood as waste recycling (Merli, Preziosi and Acampora, 2018) or the trade of second-hand goods (Korsunova, Horn and Vainio, 2021). If CE is considered from such a narrow perspective, opportunities to challenge the fundamental issue of conspicuous consumption are evaded. CE should not be about producing goods more sustainably so that consumers could continue their conspicuous consumption. Without radical changes in consumption habits, CE solutions will not serve PW. Still, a lack of understanding, for instance, of the benefits or characteristics of CE products (Hobson *et al.*, 2021) and a lack of CE product availability or access can hinder CE product adoption. By overcoming these difficulties, perhaps the appreciation of goods will become higher: Once obtained, a product or service is valued more because efforts were made to get it (Nurmi, 2021, p. 53). Of course, the challenge should not be overwhelming, or consumers will be discouraged from pursuing more sustainable options.

From a consumption perspective, CE can connect with PW in practice by challenging consumption habits and demanding closer consideration to what kinds of goods are obtained. To realize more sustainable lifestyles, consumers should follow the CE principles of refusing, reducing, and repairing (Maitre-Ekern and Dalhammar, 2019) and learn to distinguish desires from actual needs. Moreover, consumers have to learn to appreciate pre-owned goods, access over ownership, and service-based solutions (Hobson *et al.*, 2021). While consumers are generally considered in business studies as one-dimensional buyers and users of products, the CE model offers them multiple roles, such as those of a buyer, user, maker, repairer, seller, sharer, and recycler (Korsunova, Horn and Vainio, 2021). This more active agency can help these citizen-consumers understand the need to create a positive impact through their participation and choices and can motivate them to try to create such an impact.

From the citizen-consumers' perspective, perhaps the most important change must take place in their mindsets. PW and CE principles can aid in the transition as they necessitate transformative changes in the knowledge bases and the ways goods arc valued. Moreover, humans' appreciation of nonhuman nature and an understanding of their dependence on it are needed.

Digitalization of consumption

The digitalization of consumption can transform sociocultural and technological systems that influence consumption. Digitalization has been identified as a driver of consumer behaviour via e-commerce, the Internet of Things, automation, personalization, and artificial intelligence (AI) (Sima *et al.*, 2020). This accelerates the extractive processes carried out by humans for consumption because it can make purchasing faster and easier. Digitalized consumption may make it challenging for people to see the consequences of their consumption as it makes their relationships with natural resources abstract and thus less traceable. This illuminates the role of humans in realizing digitalized consumption without necessitating other detrimental processes (*i.e.*, massive extraction of resources). While mainstream digitalized consumption has not nurtured sufficiency of humans' resource consumption (Gossen, Ziesemer and Schrader, 2019), which is needed for the survival of other species, numerous initiatives demonstrate determination to transit for sustainability and responsible consumption (Di Vaio *et al.*, 2020). This links sustainable marketing to PW through resource-use reconsideration.

Sustainable marketing has the potential to promote a sufficiency approach to (downscaling) resource consumption by encouraging the thorough reduction of resource use (Gossen, Ziesemer and Schrader, 2019). Using digitalization with the growing amount of data about customer needs, the new communication and distribution platform channels offer novel opportunities for promoting sufficient consumption. These platforms help connect specific consumer needs with the best-matched pre-owned and recycled goods (*e.g.*, in fashion web shops and mobile applications) or the closest zero-emission vehicles (*e.g.*, in electric scooter-sharing services). This enables consumption to involve fewer resources and enhance PW while forming an altruistic, trustworthy, and likeable brand image.

Example of using artificial intelligence for planetary well-being

AI pertains to autonomous and adaptive systems (Roos, 2019) that help users accomplish tasks normally requiring human intelligence (Huang and Rust, 2018). These systems operate using data, algorithms, and robust computers that help make sense of data (Roos, 2019), including consumer data (Huang and Rust, 2018). The impact of AI has been assessed against the accomplishment of 134 targets across the United Nations Agenda for Sustainable Development Goals (Vinuesa *et al.*, 2020), including *responsible consumption and production* (Di Vaio *et al.*, 2020).

Since 2009, AI applications have been increasingly used to conceptualize sustainable products, build a green society through renewable energy consumption, and help airports become resource-efficient and more environmentally friendly while cutting costs (Pusa, 2021), among others. This shows that marketing interventions can use data and digitally generated content for efficient use of resources that are vital for the needs of nonhuman species.

Before data technologies are applied, they need to be considered prudently and systemically. The advancement of data technologies calls for more critical evaluation rather than only increasing their convenience for human consumption or reducing the harm that they can cause. It is vital for PW that consumers are aware of data technologies' impacts on their consumption while such technologies are guiding them towards the most sustainable consumption and reduced consumption. Aside from governments' regulatory involvement in limiting unsustainable consumption through legislation and norms, a rigorous assessment of algorithms and consumer agency is critical. As AI is an emerging field, its algorithms are still limited in terms of upholding sustainable consumption. AI applications operate with predetermined product features, thus still limiting sustainable-product recommendations and options for consumers. Algorithm management is vital to ensure that consumption favours the most environmentally friendly products and services among the available options.

It is important to keep in mind that while AI applications can suggest the most environmentally friendly options within a certain product range, they have not yet been enabled to suggest recycling or non-consumption (when these are much more environmentally friendly). Thus, user education is critical in equipping people with the knowledge that they need to be independent and self-determined rather than reliant on and dominated by the evolving technology.

Informing consumers

To further reduce humans' impact on the nonhuman world, humans need to be provided with more credible information about and guidance towards sustainable consumption. Among the tools that can help consumers make better-informed choices are ecolabels.

Ecolabels are environmental claims that define, compile, test, and summarize products' environmental performance and present this in the easiest way possible to close the information gap between consumers and producers regarding products' environmental attributes (Gallastegui, 2002; Rex and Baumann, 2007). For companies, ecolabels are a benchmark for environmental improvement (Bratt *et al.*, 2011) and set stringent criteria that encourage eco-innovation beyond the regulatory requirements. The assumption is that in the long run, the repetition of incremental eco-innovations implemented by companies to meet the existing ecolabel criteria will result in more radical eco-innovations that will improve the state of the environment (Prieto-Sandoval *et al.*, 2016). The requirements that products or services must meet before they can use multi-criteria, third-party-certified ecolabels (Type 1) are a mechanism for integrating the PW approach.

Nevertheless, ecolabels are anthropocentric in the sense that their use does not aim to limit or question consumption, which can compromise PW. On the contrary, a product's ecolabel can justify its increased consumption. The growing popularity of the practice of marketing products based on their environmental attributes has resulted in the proliferation of ecolabeling schemes used by businesses, such as those in the food, textile, electronics, and tourism industries. In fact, there are over 450 ecolabels being administered privately, publicly, or by nongovernmental organizations, showing varying foci and levels of stringency and various administrative arrangements (Big Room Inc., 2021). This popularity of ecolabels poses a risk of their misuse by companies to greenwash their products by misleading consumers regarding their environmental practices within the company or the environmental performance of their products (Delmas and Burbano, 2011).

Conceptually, ecolabels are tools for showcasing the products with the best environmental performance, but there are limitations to evaluating their real-life impacts (Meis-Harris *et al.*, 2021). Hence, the possible contribution of ecolabels as a means of providing consumer information that supports the transition towards PW cannot be verified in real life. Because there is currently no consensus on the definition of "green product" and on how to determine whether a product can be regarded as such, the different ecolabeling schemes emphasize different aspects of sustainability performance. Although the ISO Type 1 ecolabels take a life cycle approach, other ecolabels focus on only one issue or entail companies' self-administered declarations, which may be based on varying assessment methods. To counter this lack of harmony among the objectives, requirements, and methods used by ecolabeling schemes, there is a growing idea that ecolabels must have common requirements and certification procedures to be able to jointly address global environmental challenges (Baumeister and Onkila, 2017; Iraldo, Griesshammer and Kahlenborn, 2020).

While it would be in line with the concept of PW to discourage consumption, all living organisms, including humans, do need to consume to ensure their well-being. Informing consumers about the impacts of their consumption choices through ecolabels can help them make better-informed choices, bringing us closer to the realization of PW.

Conclusion

Marketing is often accused of stimulating overconsumption (Gossen, Ziesemer and Schrader, 2019). Nevertheless, businesses are seeking ways not only to mitigate the adverse consequences of unsustainability but also to come up with solutions to the problem of making the production and consumption of goods and services acknowledge the PW criteria. This chapter discussed some solutions, ranging from small incremental improvements to more fundamental changes with significant impacts. Genuine sustainable and environmentally friendly consumption contributes to PW by reducing the resources used for consumption through the re-evaluation of the level of human needs (*ibid.*) or, in PW terminology, the relevant need satisfiers. CE introduces consumers to a new type of agency with multiple roles, values societal transformation and guides consumers' routinised practices, and ecolabeling could provide an assurance that product information is accurate and reliable, thus facilitating consumers' sustainable choices. While these are some ways that consumers can demonstrate respect for nature, Chapter 10 further reflects the role of business in PW.

Marketing can contribute to the efforts to create value for nature and humans by influencing consumers and public policymakers and promoting sustainability as a norm in society (Martin, 2013). There is a growing awareness among consumers, businesses, and policymakers of the adverse consequences of the current business and consumption practices on the planet. Effective communication and marketing tools, such as delivering accurate information through ecolabels and certificates and novel digital means utilizing AI, are necessary for a broader change to take place in consumers' and citizens' knowledge, values, and culture. The solutions presented in this chapter represent partial ways to transform towards PW. Marketing can also be used to create social media communities consisting of companies, consumers, and nature that support and nurture a way of life that respects nature. Effective models and examples of balancing human and nonhuman needs are required, and both businesses and consumers, as well as the education system, should be engaged in producing them.

Various incremental sustainability changes with marginal impacts are relatively easy for consumers and companies to adopt. Small steps are necessary to engage the larger masses of consumers and companies in the short term, and change is feasible if everyone (or at least the majority) participates. However, a radical reduction in natural resource consumption is needed to achieve PW. CE is a comprehensive business model that tackles the overconsumption of natural resources and the excessive waste problem. It not only changes businesses but also prompts and encourages consumers to move beyond being merely buyers and users of products and to adopt multiple roles in the production and consumption system.

Acknowledgements

The authors are grateful to all supporters for their contributions to the writing of this book chapter. They acknowledge financial support from the Kaute Foundation (grant year 2022) and from University of Jyväskylä (grant years 2022).

References

Aaker, J., Fournier, S. and Brasel, S.A. (2004) 'When good brands do bad', *Journal of Consumer Research*, 31(1), pp. 1–16. https://doi.org/10.1086/383419

Baumeister, S. and Onkila, T. (2017) 'An eco-label for the airline industry?', *Journal of Cleaner Production*, 142(4), pp. 1368–1376. https://doi.org/10.1016/j.jclepro.2016.11.170

BBC (2020) 'Ryanair rapped over low emissions claims', *BBC News*. Available at: https://www.bbc.com/news/business-51372780 (Accessed: 3 November 2021).

Bedard, S.A.N. and Tolmie, C.R. (2018) 'Millennials' green consumption behaviour: Exploring the role of social media', *Corporate Social Responsibility and Environmental Management*, 25(6), pp. 1388–1396. https://doi.org/10.1002/csr.1654

Big Room Inc. (2021). *Ecolabel Index*. Available at: www.ecolabelindex.com (Accessed: 18 November 2021).

Bratt, C. *et al.* (2011) 'Assessment of eco-labelling criteria development from a strategic sustainability perspective', *Journal of Cleaner Production*, 19, pp. 1631–1638. https://doi.org/10.1016/j.jclepro.2011.05.012

Camacho-Otero J., Boks C. and Pettersen I.N. (2018) 'Consumption in the circular economy: A literature review', *Sustainability*, 10(8), 2758. https://doi.org/10.3390/su10082758

Delmas, M. and Burbano, V. (2011) 'The drivers of greenwashing', *California Management Review*, 54(1), pp. 64–87. https://doi.org/10.1525/cmr.2011.54.1.64

Di Vaio, A. *et al.* (2020) 'Artificial intelligence and business models in the sustainable development goals perspective: A systematic literature review', *Journal of Business Research*, 121, pp. 283–314. https://doi.org/10.1016/j.jbusres.2020.08.019

Dietz, S. and Neumayer, E. (2007) 'Weak and strong sustainability in the SEEA: Concepts and measurement', *Ecological Economics*, 61, pp. 617–626. https://doi.org/10.1016/j.ecolecon.2006.09.007

Dryzek, J.S. (1997) *The Politics of the Earth: Environmental Discourses.* Oxford: Oxford University Press.

Dutta, S. and Pullig, C. (2011) 'Effectiveness of corporate responses to brand crises: The role of crisis type and response strategies', *Journal of Business Research*, 64(12), pp. 1281–1287. https://doi.org/10.1016/j.jbusres.2011.01.013

ElHaffar, G., Durif, F. and Dubé, L. (2020) 'Towards closing the attitude-intention-behavior gap in green consumption: A narrative review of the literature and an overview of future research directions', *Journal of Cleaner Production*, 275, 122556. https://doi.org/10.1016/j.jclepro.2020.122556

Gabler, C.B., Landers, V.M. and Richey, R.G. (2021) 'Benefits and challenges of developing an eco-social orientation: Implications for marketing practice', *European Journal of Marketing*, 55(4), pp. 1155–1176. https://doi.org/10.1108/EJM-05-2019-0400

Gallastegui, I. (2002) 'The use of eco-labels: A review of the literature', *European Environment*, 12, pp. 316–331. https://doi.org/10.1002/eet.304

Garner, R. (2000) *Environmental Politics: Britain, Europe and the Global Environment.* 2nd edn. London: MacMillan Pub. Ltd.

Geels, F.W. *et al.* (2015) 'A critical appraisal of sustainable consumption and production research: The reformist, revolutionary and reconfiguration positions', *Global Environmental Change*, 34, pp. 1–12. https://doi.org/10.1016/j.gloenvcha.2015.04.013

Gossen, M., Ziesemer, F. and Schrader, U. (2019) 'Why and how commercial marketing should promote sufficient consumption: A systematic literature review', *Journal of Macromarketing*, 39(3), pp. 252–269. https://doi.org/10.1177/0276146719866238

Ham, C.-D. *et al.* (2021) 'Greener than others? Exploring generational differences in green purchase intent', *International Journal of Market Research,* 64(3), pp. 376–396. https://doi.org/10.1177/14707853211034108

Hobson, K. *et al.* (2021) 'Consumption work in the circular economy: A research agenda', *Journal of Cleaner Production*, 321, 128969. https://doi.org/10.1016/j.jclepro.2021.128969

Huang, M.H. and Rust, R.T. (2018) 'Artificial intelligence in service', *Journal of Service Research*, 21(2), pp. 155–172. https://doi.org/10.1177/1094670517752459

Huber, F. *et al.* (2010) 'Brand misconduct: Consequences on consumer–brand relationships', *Journal of Business Research*, 63(11), pp. 1113–1120. https://doi.org/10.1016/j.jbusres.2009.10.006

Iraldo, F., Griesshammer, R. and Kahlenborn, W. (2020) 'The future of ecolabels', *The International Journal of Life Cycle Assessment*, 25, pp. 833–839. https://doi.org/10.1007/s11367-020-01741-9

Keller, M., Halkier, B. and Wilska, T.-A. (2016) 'Policy and governance for sustainable consumption at the crossroads of theories and concepts', *Environmental Policy and Governance*, 26(2), pp. 75–88. https://doi.org/10.1002/eet.1702

Korsunova, A., Horn, S. and Vainio, A. (2021) 'Understanding circular economy in everyday life: Perceptions of young adults in the Finnish context', *Sustainable Production and Consumption*, 26, pp. 759–769. https://doi.org/10.1016/j.spc.2020.12.038

Kortetmäki, T. *et al.* (2021) 'Planetary well-being', *Humanities and Social Sciences Communications*, 8, p. 258. https://doi.org/10.1057/s41599-021-00899-3

Kotler, P. (2011) 'Reinventing marketing to manage the environmental imperative', *Journal of Marketing*, 75(4), pp. 132–135. https://doi.org/10.1509/jmkg.75.4.132

Kuoppamäki, S.-M., Wilska, T.-A. and Taipale, S. (2017) 'Ageing and consumption in Finland: The effect of age and life course stage on ecological, economical and self-indulgent consumption among late middle-agers and young adults between 1999 and 2014', *International Journal of Consumer Studies*, 41(5), pp. 457–464. https://doi.org/10.1111/ijcs.12353

Lin-Hi, N. and Müller, K. (2013) 'The CSR bottom line: Preventing corporate social irresponsibility', *Journal of Business Research*, 66(10), pp. 1928–1936. https://doi.org/10.1016/j.jbusres.2013.02.015

Maitre-Ekern, E. and Dalhammar, C. (2019) 'Towards a hierarchy of consumption behaviour in the circular economy', *Maastricht Journal of European and Comparative Law*, 26(3), pp. 394–420. https://doi.org/10.1177/1023263X19840943

Martin, D. (2013) *Sustainable Marketing: Pearson New International Edition*. Pearson.

McDonagh, P. and Prothero, A. (2014) 'Sustainability marketing research: Past, present and future', *Journal of Marketing Management*, 30(11–12), pp. 1186–1219.

Meis-Harris, J. *et al.* (2021) 'What is the role of eco-labels for a circular economy? A rapid review of the literature', *Journal of Cleaner Production*, 306, 127134. https://doi.org/10.1016/j.jclepro.2021.127134

Merli, R., Preziosi, M. and Acampora, A. (2018) 'How do scholars approach the circular economy? A systematic literature review', *Journal of Cleaner Production*, 178, pp. 703–722. https://doi.org/10.1016/j.jclepro.2017.12.112

Nurmi, A. (2021) *Rakastan ja vihaan vaatteita*. Helsinki: Kustantamo S&S.

Ouyang, Z., Yao, C.N. and Hu, X. (2020) 'Crisis spillover of corporate environmental misconducts: The roles of perceived similarity, familiarity, and corporate environmental responsibility in determining the impact on oppositional behavioral intention', *Business Strategy and the Environment*, 29(4), pp. 1797–1808. https://doi.org/10.1002/bse.2474

Press, M. (2021) 'Developing a strong sustainability research program in marketing', *AMS Review*, 11, pp. 96–114. https://doi.org/10.1007/s13162-020-00185-6

Prieto-Sandoval, V. *et al.* (2016) 'ECO-labels as a multidimensional research topic: Trends and opportunities', *Journal of Cleaner Production*, 135, pp. 806–818. https://doi.org/10.1016/j.jclepro.2016.06.167

Pusa, M. (2021) *Finavia the optimal airport, Fourkind Helsinki*. Available at: https://www.fourkind.com/work/finavia-optimal-airport (Accessed: 12 June 2021).

Reckwitz, A. (2002) 'Toward a theory of social practices: A development in culturalist theorizing', *European Journal of Social Theory*, 5, pp. 243–263.

Rex, E. and Baumann, H. (2007) 'Beyond ecolabels: What green marketing can learn from conventional marketing', *Journal of Cleaner Production*, 15, pp. 567–576. https://doi.org/10.1016/j.jclepro.2006.05.013

Ritala, P., Albareda, L. and Bocken, N. (2021) 'Value creation and appropriation in economic, social, and environmental domains: Recognizing and resolving the institutionalized asymmetries', *Journal of Cleaner Production*, 290, 125796. https://doi.org/10.1016/j.jclepro.2021.125796

Roos, T. (2019) 'Elements of AI' [Course lecture]. University of Helsinki. Unpublished.

Sarja, M., Onkila, T. and Mäkelä, M. (2021) 'A systematic literature review of the transition to the circular economy in business organizations: Obstacles, catalysts and ambivalences', *Journal of Cleaner Production*, 286, 125492. https://doi.org/10.1016/j.jclepro.2020.125492

Shove, E., Pantzar, M. and Watson, M. (2012) *The Dynamics of Social Practice: Everyday Life and How It Changes*. London: Sage.

Sima, V. *et al.* (2020) 'Influences of the Industry 4.0 Revolution on the human capital development and consumer behavior: A systematic review. *Sustainability*, 12(4035), 4035. https://doi.org/10.3390/su12104035

Spaargaren, G. (2011) 'Theories of practices: Agency, technology, and culture: Exploring the relevance of practice theories for the governance of sustainable consumption practices in the new world-order', *Global Environmental Change*, 21, pp. 813–822. https://doi.org/10.1016/j.gloenvcha.2011.03.010

Thaler, R.H. and Sunstein, C.R. (2008) *Nudge: Improving Decisions about Health, Wealth, and Happiness*. New Haven, CT: Yale University Press.

Vinuesa, R. *et al.* (2020) 'The role of artificial intelligence in achieving the Sustainable Development Goals', *Nature Communications*, 11(1), 233. https://doi.org/10.1038/s41467-019-14108-y

Wilska, T.-A. (2002) 'Me, a consumer? Consumption, identities and lifestyles in today's Finland', *Acta Sociologica*, 45(3), pp. 195–210. https://doi.org/10.1080/00016990260257184

Xu, H., Bolton, L.E. and Winterich, K.P. (2021) 'How do consumers react to company moral transgressions? The role of power distance belief and empathy for victims', *Journal of Consumer Research*, 48(1), pp. 77–101. https://doi.org/10.1093/jcr/ucaa067

10

PLANETARY WELL-BEING AND SUSTAINABLE BUSINESS

A work in progress

Marileena Mäkelä, Valtteri A. Aaltonen, Stefan Baumeister, Irene Kuhmonen, Minna Käyrä, Tuuli Mäkinen, Annukka Näyhä, Tiina Onkila, Milla Sarja, Bhavesh Sarna and Johanna Suikkanen

Introduction[1]

Businesses account for a considerable part of human activity and thus have a significant negative impact on global environmental and social sustainability. To address these issues, the concept of sustainable business has been introduced. There are multiple definitions of sustainable business, but it is often understood to encompass the economic, social, and environmental dimensions of business practices (Dahlsrud, 2008; Sarkar and Searcy, 2016). It refers to voluntary actions (*ibid.*) that companies take beyond fulfilling legal requirements. Meeting the expectations of various stakeholders is also an important aspect of sustainable business (*ibid.*).

The sustainable business literature typically focuses on minimizing businesses' negative economic, social, and environmental impacts and rarely on increasing their positive impacts. The concept of planetary well-being has a different starting point, focusing on positive impacts and ensuring that ecosystems and organisms continue to thrive:

> Planetary well-being is a state in which the integrity of Earth system and ecosystem processes remains unimpaired to a degree that lineages can persist to the future as parts of ecosystems, and organisms (human and nonhuman) can realize their typical characteristics and capacities.
>
> *(Kortetmäki* et al., *2021, p. 4)*

The concept of planetary well-being was introduced to address the multitude of global environmental and social problems caused by human activity and shift the focus to a non-anthropocentric and systemic point of view. While recognizing the value of the existence of both human and nonhuman species, planetary well-being

DOI: 10.4324/9781003334002-14

also acknowledges that coexistence generates both synergies and conflicts. Furthermore, planetary well-being considers both environmental and social equality (see Kortetmäki *et al.*, 2021).

In this chapter, we critically analyse concepts, practices, and lines of thought related to sustainable business from the point of view of planetary well-being. In doing so, we address two questions: (1) How can current sustainable business concepts and practices contribute to promoting planetary well-being? (2) How should sustainable business concepts and practices be developed to meet the requirements of planetary well-being?

This chapter is structured as follows. First, we discuss three conceptual approaches to sustainable business, namely sustainability transition, circular economy, and degrowth. Second, we consider two practical examples of sustainable business: Sustainable business models and the role of employees as change agents. Finally, we present the conclusions drawn from our analysis.

Examples of conceptual approaches to sustainable business and planetary well-being

Sustainability transition

Over the past few decades, the concept of sustainability transition has been gaining a strong foothold among researchers exploring more sustainable modes of societal organization. Sustainability transitions can be defined as systemic processes that transform the structural character of society to address persistent sustainability problems (Rotmans, Kemp and Marjolein, 2001; Grin, Rotmans and Schot, 2010; Loorbach and Wijsman, 2013). The transition literature includes diverse streams, such as the socio-technical, socio-ecological, and socio-economic approaches (European Environmental Agency (EEA), 2018), each with its own vocabulary and emphasis but all relying on a systemic understanding of social change processes. These processes involve various spheres of human activity, such as production and consumption, material infrastructure and culture, technology and economy, and organizations and institutions. Transition studies thus make an important contribution to sustainable business research, in which the integration of whole-system approaches with organizational and management approaches is still in its infancy (Bansal and Song, 2017).

Processes considered to promote sustainability transition cover a broad range of initiatives, with some embracing radical, reformist approaches to social change and others being more incremental, primarily aiming at stepwise improvement of existing operations. However, the desired end results of transition processes are surprisingly vaguely covered in the literature (Meadowcroft, 2011; Patterson *et al.*, 2017). Indeed, the "sustainability" of sustainability transitions is often far from self-evident (Feola, 2020). Research on sustainability transitions tends to be anthropocentric, whereas the concept of planetary well-being represents an eco-centric approach to systemic change. Thus, not only does planetary well-being imply a radical departure from current anthropocentric trajectories, but it also requires different conceptualizations of social systems, their functions, and their aims.

Although the conceptual shifts required by planetary well-being thinking are not thoroughly discussed in the transition literature, some approaches to sustainable business, sustainability transitions, and ecological economics resonate with the concept of planetary well-being. Promoting planetary well-being requires reducing the scope of human operations instead of mere qualitative changes. As such, it requires rethinking the entire economic system to fulfil the promise of decoupling economic growth from material and resource use (Haberl *et al.*, 2020; Vadén *et al.*, 2020). Such a radical departure from the current socio-economic model is advocated by the concepts of circular economy (CE) and degrowth, which entail changes in both the quality and quantity of material flows and economic activities. Although the stance of the CE concept towards radical vs incremental systemic change has been debated (Kirchherr, Reike and Hekkert, 2017), it holds an undisputable promise for promoting planetary well-being. Degrowth, in turn, is a radical movement that questions the inevitability of economic growth and seeks alternative visions for the well-being of human societies. Although both concepts are thoroughly anthropocentric, they also provide signposts for addressing the burning question of how economies can be organized to promote planetary well-being. Next, we deal with CE and degrowth and their relations to planetary well-being in more detail.

Circular economy

It has been suggested that a more sustainable way to conduct business could be realized through CE practices. CE is regenerative and restorative by design (Ellen MacArthur Foundation, 2015). The concept was introduced to challenge the prevalent linear economy model, in which raw materials are wasted (Kirchherr, Reike and Hekkert, 2017). CE is based on reducing, reusing, and recycling materials, products, and components (*ibid.*) so that they remain in use for as long as possible. Thus, CE focuses on economic and environmental dimensions. However, social equity (*ibid.*) and human well-being are also important aspects of CE models (Murray, Skene and Haynes, 2017). In this section, we focus on CE from the point of view of sustainable business. Chapter 9 focuses on CE and consumption.

CE can support the transition towards planetary well-being by decoupling economic activity from resource depletion, which requires radically rethinking and replanning production and consumption processes to achieve a transition from linear models to circularity. This is attained by modifying the ways in which business is conducted by focusing on circulating materials, prolonging product lifetimes, and promoting service-based offerings (Ellen MacArthur Foundation, 2015). Concrete examples of this are designing for disassembly, improving repairability of products, utilizing recycled materials over virgin materials, and leasing products instead of selling them.

While CE has implications for directing business action towards planetary well-being, it also has multiple limitations. First, it still positions human and business actors at the core of thinking and treats nonhuman entities as "resources"—in other words, as unequal to humans (see Kortetmäki *et al.*, 2021). Second, although it provides moral grounds for future action in business by questioning the current linear economic model and overconsumption, as does the concept of planetary well-being, these remain mainly theoretical and cannot currently be actualized. Furthermore, using the rhetoric of CE entails risks: It does not support planetary well-being if it is aimed only at producing more to consume more. Moreover, to transform entire business logics to conform to the principles of planetary well-being, a complete rethinking of value production is required (Porter and Kramer, 2011). While CE changes the way in which value is created (as "waste" no longer exists, all materials have value because they should meet a demand in the larger loop of circularity), it fails to explain how nonhuman entities may also benefit from such changes. Thus, the question of value added—for example, for well-being of nonhuman species—remains open, as the concept is not yet implemented to its transformative potential, with its normative grounds in minimizing environmental impacts by learning from and mimicking nature, the model now serves mainly the efficiencies of business operations.

By advancing an understanding of well-being of nonhuman species as equal to human well-being, planetary well-being extends CE thinking beyond its limitations. By integrating the principle of equality of nonhuman entities, planetary well-being can help to strengthen and develop the central ideology of CE, which is centred on creating a system that is regenerative and restorative by design. This can naturally deepen and widen the ways in which CE changes are perceived, approached, and implemented in business. Moreover, it can lead to a rethinking of production and consumption systems to find ways to operate and produce that respect the opportunities of humans and nonhumans to achieve well-being. Such a fundamental change in CE thinking will inevitably influence the way in which CE is measured and managed within and between businesses.

Degrowth

Degrowth is a multidisciplinary research project and social movement that aims to shift the focus from pursuing constant economic growth to the well-being of humans and the planet (Kallis *et al.*, 2018). Promoters of degrowth argue that the logic of infinite growth leads to ecosystem collapse by overstepping the planetary boundaries (see *e.g.*, Rockström *et al.*, 2009; Hickel and Kallis, 2020). This logic creates a vicious cycle within the mainstream capitalist socio-economic system: Endless economic growth requires producing more and consuming more to maximize profit, sacrificing human health (society overworked and overstressed) and the environment (Herbert, 2018) in the process.

In practice, degrowth is concerned with how we can create a low-carbon and low-output economy that promotes well-being (Kallis, 2017) in a planned way.[2]

It is crucial to understand that this goes far beyond just reducing environmental impact. Degrowth can be described as a radical approach that advocates a democratically led reduction in production and consumption to achieve social justice and environmental sustainability (D'Alisa, Demaria and Kallis, 2014). This approach draws from the disciplines of economics, ecological economics, anthropology, social sciences, political science, and technological studies to combine their expertise in a single vision. Degrowth constitutes a critique but also offers proposals for addressing the shortcomings of the current socio-economic system (Demaria, 2020). Application of degrowth at organizational level is still marginal and it ranges from alternative organization forms (*e.g.*, social enterprises and growth-averse enterprises) to alternative organizing forms (*e.g.*, cooperatives and solidarity-based purchase groups). In the core of these proposals are abandonment of profit maximization, working to benefit the community, and localness.

However, the concept of degrowth is still characterized by theoretical and practical ambiguity (van den Bergh, 2011; Tokic, 2012) and is subject to multiple interpretations (van den Bergh, 2011; Wiefek and Heinitz, 2018). Although it emphasizes human and planetary well-being, degrowth is mainly discussed from an economic point of view. Therefore, its conceptualization is incomplete; environmental dimensions (*e.g.*, biodiversity loss and environmental pollution) are partly missing. This is contradictory, since the movement is based on the premise that the logic of infinite growth is the driving force behind environmental collapse.

Although the concept of degrowth is ambiguous and lacks consensus, some widely accepted notions can be identified. At the core of the concept lies the intention to promote nonhuman well-being along with human well-being. However, research has mainly focused on ways to minimize the negative impacts of production and consumption on humans. As degrowth aspires to change various political and socio-economic dimensions, it focuses on increasing human well-being by changing the ways in which we operate within society. However, if it is to promote planetary well-being, degrowth research should include environmental and sustainability sciences so that any proposals for changes to the current socio-economic system can directly consider processes that support life, well-being, and biodiversity. After all, degrowth is ecologically motivated critique of growth.

Practical examples of sustainable business from the point of view of planetary well-being

Can sustainable value creation and business models promote planetary well-being?

It is widely understood that current sustainability challenges cannot be solved with organization-centric business and value creation models, which focus on economic value creation for companies and their shareholders and customers (*e.g.*, Schaltegger, Hansen and Lüdeke-Freund, 2016). Sustainable business models (SBM) and sustainable value creation (SVC) aim to extend the traditional way of seeing value creation (Dentchev *et al.*, 2018; Lüdeke-Freund *et al.*, 2020). The key idea behind SBMs is that business models should incorporate sustainability concepts and look at value creation from a wider perspective that includes the interests and needs of various stakeholders (Dentchev *et al.*, 2018). Accordingly, SVC is typically seen as the

> integration of ecological, social and economic value creation with and for stakeholders. Such approaches take into account the negative impacts on ecological systems and human societies, and, as a logical consequence, the tensions and trade-offs between different forms of value creation and different stakeholders.
>
> *(Lüdeke-Freund* et al., *2020, p. 72)*

Despite their many advantages over traditional value creation and business models, SVC and SBMs still have several shortcomings. There is often insufficient emphasis on non-typical stakeholders (*e.g.*, nonhuman stakeholders), and analytical tools for measuring ("untraditional" or "hard to quantify") value creation in the business contexts are lacking. Furthermore, our understanding of the plurality of various stakeholder relationships and sources of value which can lead to "truly" SVC is limited (Lüdeke-Freund *et al.*, 2020). As Vladimirova (2019) notes, the fundamental question is what value is and for whom it should be created. Answering this question requires a better understanding of the forms of value that certain stakeholders aim to capture (Lüdeke-Freund *et al.*, 2020). All in all, value in SBMs is understood as a multirelational, multilevel, and multi-aspect concept, and further conceptualizing and empirical exploring of sustainable value and its creation processes are needed (Méndez-León, Reyes-Carrillo and Díaz-Pichardo, 2021). It is also important to consider the power relationships between various stakeholders—specifically unequal or asymmetrical distribution of power (Lüdeke-Freund *et al.*, 2020).

What do the issues presented above mean for planetary well-being? Can SBMs and the current modes of SVC facilitate planetary well-being? In our view, widely applied business models, though including many SBM elements, have rather limited potential to exert a significant positive influence on nonhuman well-being and planetary well-being more generally. To address the shortcomings discussed above, it is most important to recognize nature and nonhuman species as stakeholders with inherent rights to existence and well-being. Despite lacking the voice or power to express their needs as humans can, they cannot be ignored by human actors and stakeholders (see also Romero and Dryzek, 2021; Kortetmäki, Heikkinen and Jokinen, 2022). We should develop better ways of analysing SVC processes to enable the generation of "truly" sustainable value for nature and nonhuman species. Most societal transition processes are intertwined with power relationships (see, *e.g.*, Avelino and Wittmayer, 2016). Therefore, the question concerning the significance of SVC and SBMs for promoting planetary well-being is also closely related to the question of how humans use their power in relation to other humans, as well as in relation to nonhumans. This necessitates equal and transparent dialogue between various societal stakeholders (see, *e.g.*, Jonker *et al.*, 2020). SBMs with a broader systemic perspective and a deeper understanding of value creation can have a significant positive impact on the well-being of all species and planetary well-being more generally.

Can employees promote planetary well-being?

As discussed above, businesses explore the possibilities for transition from a traditional model to a more sustainable model—for example, through reorganization by adopting CE or degrowth. At the core of such changes are organizational members, namely managers and employees, who initiate, implement, and manage these changes. Here, "an employee" refers to all individuals employed by an organization, including managers of all levels. Naturally, the influence of organizational members differs according to their formal positions. For example, top managers have more power than shop floor employees. The role of employees in sustainable business has been recognized and researched (*e.g.*, Onkila and Sarna, 2022), thus making it relevant to planetary well-being studies in organizational context. In this section, we highlight selected aspects discussed in the literature (*i.e.*, employee agency, emotions, and attitudes) and interpret their implications for planetary well-being.

During such transitions, an organization as collectives and individuals participates in purposive actions to facilitate changes (Bos, Brown and Farrelly, 2013). It is important to understand the roles of individual employees and unions as agents of any kind of change. However, employees differ in cognitive, communicative, and behavioural aspects (Haack, Sieweke and Wessel, 2019). Thus, any organization developing a strategy for sustainability needs to understand the diversity of its employees to be able to integrate sustainability principles into their operations.

Employees may agree on the importance of sustainability but may have different views on the implementation of changes. Thus, agency plays an important role between the pre-established systems and employee actions in the implementation of the transition (Fischer and Newig, 2016). Employees make sense of and resolve emotional tensions around sustainability issues differently (Sarna, Onkila and Mäkelä, 2021). Hence, individual differences between employees (*e.g.*, different backgrounds, ambitions, value priorities, and material conditions) may lead to different attitudes towards sustainability. Because of diversity of opinions, employees may engage in sustainability action differently. In resolving emotional tensions related to sustainable business, employee self-identity constantly evolves when an organization takes action to address such crucial issues (Thomas and Davies, 2005; Brown, 2019). However, this is a time-consuming process affected by individuals' abilities.

Based on previous research on employees and organizations, the implementation of planetary well-being practices in organizations requires further studies on individual employees and their perceptions. Given that sustainability issues lead to complexities and tensions between employees (Hahn *et al.*, 2018), planetary well-being may have the same effect. However, we believe that planetary well-being, with its roots in the planetary boundaries, has even greater potential to provide organizations with a clearer and commonly joint value base. This can lead to redefining the entire concept of sustainable business by integrating the concept of nonhuman well-being. Thus, we need to study planetary well-being focusing on individual employees not only from the point of view of sustainable business but also in connection to organizational behaviour, agency, and psychology.

Conclusions and directions for future research

The first question that we sought to answer in this chapter is how current sustainable business concepts and practices can contribute to promoting planetary well-being. Although current concepts and practices have similarities to the concept of planetary well-being, they also have major shortcomings. The second question that we sought to answer is how current practices can be developed. In doing so, we highlight two important aspects of planetary well-being. First, the concept of planetary well-being effectively challenges the idea of continuous economic growth underlying the most of sustainable business practices. Second, the mainstream literature on sustainable business—for example, CE—and current alternative ways of organizing are closely aligned with anthropocentric approaches. This constitutes a fundamental limitation of business studies in terms of nonhuman species' well-being and planetary well-being.

While the concept of planetary well-being is relatively new, business studies addressing planetary boundaries and nonhuman life are not. However, business studies have typically had a rather limited focus with environmental issues. For example, Ergene, Banerjee, and Hoffman (2021) highlighted the "unsustainability" of business studies, although the environmental dimension has been increasingly considered since the early 2000s. According to them, this unsustainability lies in the epistemological roots of scholarship, which is dominated by abstract anthropocentric ideas and lacks critical reflexivity. Our chapter corroborates this claim. Although concepts such as sustainable business and CE offer the possibility for radical transformation, companies tend to cherry-pick those aspects that cause only incremental change in their operations to able the continuation of business-as-usual. In order to truly achieve planetary well-being, the whole economic system (not only individual companies) should shift the focus from economic perspective (*i.e.*, continuous economic growth) to environmental and social perspectives.

More attention should also be paid to the downstream effects of sustainable business initiatives. In this respect, planetary well-being can provide a systemic view. For example, the rebound effect means that gains in energy efficiency may be partially offset or even reversed by increased consumption (Ruzzenenti *et al.*, 2019; Sorrell, Gatersleben and Druckman, 2020). Leasing instead of selling, often promoted as a greener alternative, may sometimes increase life-cycle impacts (Agrawal *et al.*, 2012). Another potential issue is the waste-resource paradox: Circular innovations creating demand for a waste product may actually increase linear economy path dependencies (Greer, von Wirth and Loorbach, 2021). Addressing such complex interactions requires multidisciplinary approaches and more active public and governmental engagement (Ruzzenenti *et al.*, 2019; Ergene, Banerjee and Hoffman, 2021). Furthermore, studying the role of transition failures, a neglected area of research, is vital for purposeful systemic transitions (Turnheim and Sovacool, 2020).

This study has certain limitations. While the authors of this chapter are diverse in terms of gender and nationalities, our presentation is narrow, both culturally and in terms of academic disciplines as most of us evaluate business studies with business studies background. Furthermore, we addressed only a few sustainable business concepts and practices. We welcome a more thorough analysis of sustainable business from the perspective of planetary well-being.

Our study has both practical and research implications for sustainable business. Our analysis challenges all businesses to assess their core assumptions and values from a planetary well-being perspective. As Ergene, Banerjee, and Hoffman (2021) point out, business logic is dominated by profitability and shareholder wealth. Businesses should recognize the intrinsic value of nature. This means questioning businesses based on animal exploitation or natural resource overuse. Moreover, instead of solely focusing on minimizing their negative environmental impacts, companies should also focus on maximizing their positive impacts. For example, companies should focus on how they can promote biodiversity with their actions. Furthermore, planetary well-being requires businesses to reconsider ways of organizing. Large companies often rely on top-down approaches to sustainability, which limit employees' opportunities to act as change agents. We suggest three directions for future multidisciplinary sustainable business research:

1 Sustainable business studies should critically analyse (over)production and (over)consumption.
2 Sustainable business practices and tools should be developed in consideration of nonhuman species and nature more generally.
3 Employees' role as change agents should be further studied and supported.

Acknowledgements

Annukka Näyhä received financial support from the Academy of Finland ("Future-oriented collaborative business models as a remedy for the sustainability transition: Finnish forest-based sector as an empirical arena for the creation of a transition framework"; grant number 340756). Tiina Onkila, Marileena Mäkelä and, Milla Sarja received financial support from the Strategic Research Council of the Academy of Finland ("Circular economy catalysts: from innovation to business ecosystems"; grant number 320205). Tiina Onkila, Marileena Mäkelä, and Irene Kuhmonen received financial support from the Strategic Research Council of the Academy of Finland ("Biodiversity-respectful leadership"; grant number 345885). Irene Kuhmonen received financial support from the Ministry of Agriculture and Forestry of Finland ("The role and potential of the rural in a post-fossil society"; grant number VN/11093/2020). Minna Käyrä received financial support for a scholarship from the Finnish Cultural Foundation. Johanna Suikkanen received financial support for a scholarship from the KAUTE Foundation. Valtteri Aaltonen received financial support for a scholarship from the Wihuri Foundation.

Notes

1 This chapter is the result of a collective effort and intense discussions among the authors. All authors contributed to the work significantly and are listed in alphabetical order, except for the first author.
2 For example, the unplanned and abrupt reduction in social and economic activity caused by the COVID-19 outbreak was not degrowth (Rilovic *et al.*, 2020) but an unforeseen event with catastrophic economic and social consequences. Such abrupt collapses are exactly the type of events that the degrowth project seeks to prevent.

References

Agrawal, V.V. *et al.* (2012) 'Is leasing greener than selling?', *Management Science, 58*(3), pp. 523–533. https://doi.org/10.1287/mnsc.1110.1428

Avelino, F. and Wittmayer, J. M. (2016) 'Shifting power relations in sustainability transitions: A multi-actor perspective', *Journal of Environmental Policy & Planning, 18*, pp. 628–649. https://doi.org/10.1080/1523908X.2015.1112259

Bansal, P. and Song, H. (2017) 'Similar but not the same: Differentiating corporate sustainability from corporate responsibility', *Academy of Management Annals, 11*(1), pp. 105–149. https://doi.org/10.5465/annals.2015.0095

Bos, J.J., Brown, R.R. and Farrelly, M.A. (2013) 'A design framework for creating social learning situations', *Global Environmental Change, 23*(2), pp. 398–412. https://doi.org/10.1016/j.gloenvcha.2012.12.003

Brown, A.D. (2019) 'Identities in organization studies', *Organization Studies, 40*(1), pp. 7–22. https://doi.org/10.1177/0170840618765014

Dahlsrud, A. (2008) 'How corporate social responsibility is defined: An analysis of 37 definitions', *Corporate Social Responsibility and Environmental Management, 15*(1), pp. 1–13. https://doi.org/10.1002/csr.132

D'Alisa, G., Demaria, F. and Kallis, G. (eds.) (2014) *Degrowth: A Vocabulary for a New Era*. London: Routledge. https://doi.org/10.4324/9780203796146

Demaria, F. (2020) *Degrowth, Feminism and Pluriverse for a New Normal*. Available at: https://www.youtube.com/watch?v=nmCKKbgBcHM (Accessed: 17 March 2022).

Dentchev, N., *et al.* (2018) 'Embracing the variety of sustainable business models: A prolific field of research and a future research agenda', *Journal of Cleaner Production, 194*, pp. 695–703. https://doi.org/10.1016/j.jclepro.2018.05.156

EEA (2018) *Perspectives on Transitions to Sustainability*. EEA Report 25/2017. Luxembourg: Publications Office of the European Union. https://doi.org/10.2800/332443

Ellen MacArthur Foundation (2015) *Towards the Circular Economy: Business Rationale for an Accelerated Transition*. Available at: https://ellenmacarthurfoundation.org/towards-a-circular-economy-business-rationale-for-an-accelerated-transition (Accessed: 17 March 2022).

Ergene, S., Banerjee, S.B. and Hoffman, A.J. (2021) '(Un)sustainability and organization studies: Towards a radical engagement', *Organization Studies*, 42(8), pp. 1319–1335. https://doi.org/10.1177/0170840620937892

Feola, G. (2020) 'Capitalism in sustainability transitions research: Time for a critical turn?', *Environmental Innovation and Societal Transitions*, 35, pp. 241–250. https://doi.org/10.1016/j.eist.2019.02.005

Fischer, L. B. and Newig, J. (2016) 'Importance of actors and agency in sustainability transitions: A systematic exploration of the literature', *Sustainability*, 8(5), 476. https://doi.org/10.3390/su8050476

Greer, R., von Wirth, T. and Loorbach, D. (2021) 'The Waste-Resource Paradox: Practical dilemmas and societal implications in the transition to a circular economy', *Journal of Cleaner Production*, 303, 126831. https://doi.org/10.1016/j.jclepro.2021.126831

Grin, J., Rotmans, J. and Schot, J. (2010) *Transitions to Sustainable Development. New Directions in the Study of Long Term Transformative Change*. New York: Routledge. https://doi.org/10.4324/9780203856598

Haack, P., Sieweke, J. and Wessel, L. (2019) 'Microfoundations and multi-level research on institutions', in Haack, P., Sieweke, J. and Wessel, L. (eds.) *Microfoundations of Institutions*. Bingley: Emerald Publishing Limited, pp. 11–40. https://doi.org/10.1108/S0733-558X2019000065A005

Haberl, H., *et al.* (2020) 'A systematic review of the evidence on decoupling of GDP, resource use and GHG emissions, part II: Synthesizing the insights', *Environmental Research Letters*, 15(6), 065003. https://doi.org/10.1088/1748-9326/ab842a

Hahn, T., *et al.* (2018) 'A paradox perspective on corporate sustainability: Descriptive, instrumental, and normative aspects', *Journal of Business Ethics*, 148(2), pp. 235–248. https://doi.org/10.1007/s10551-017-3587-2

Herbert, J. (2018) *Degrowth Is the Radical Post-Brexit Future the UK Needs*. The Conversation, 19 November. Available at: https://theconversation.com/degrowth-is-the-radical-post-brexit-future-the-uk-needs-106964 (Accessed: 17 March 2022).

Hickel, J. and Kallis, G. (2020) 'Is green growth possible?', *New Political Economy*, 25(4), pp. 469–486. https://doi.org/10.1080/13563467.2019.1598964

Jonker, J., *et al.* (2020) *Collaborative Business Models for Transition*. TNO Report 2020 R11009. Den Haag: TNO. Available at: http://resolver.tudelft.nl/uuid:7361e81d-ad35-4ed2-affb-a6baff36de24 (Accessed: 17 March 2022).

Kallis, G. (2017) 'Radical dematerialization and degrowth', *Philosophical Transactions, Series A, Mathematical, Physical and Engineering Sciences*, 375, 20160383. https://doi.org/10.1098/rsta.2016.0383

Kallis, G., *et al.* (2018) 'Research on degrowth', *Annual Review of Environment and Resources*, 43, pp. 291–316. https://doi.org/10.1146/annurev-environ-102017-025941

Kirchherr, J., Reike, D. and Hekkert, M. (2017) 'Conceptualizing the circular economy: An analysis of 114 definitions', *Resources, Conservation & Recycling*, 127, pp. 221–232. https://doi.org/10.1016/j.resconrec.2017.09.005

Kortetmäki, T., *et al.* (2021) 'Planetary well-being', *Humanities and Social Sciences Communications*, 8, 258. https://doi.org/10.1057/s41599-021-00899-3

Kortetmäki, T., Heikkinen, A. and Jokinen, A. (2022) 'Particularizing nonhuman nature in stakeholder theory: The recognition approach', *Journal of Business Ethics*. https://doi.org/10.1007/s10551-022-05174-2

Loorbach, D. and Wijsman, K. (2013) 'Business transition management: Exploring a new role for business in sustainability transitions', *Journal of Cleaner Production*, 45, pp. 20–28. https://doi.org/10.1016/j.jclepro.2012.11.002

Lüdeke-Freund, F., *et al.* (2020) 'Sustainable value creation through business models: The what, the who and the how', *Journal of Business Models*, 8(3), pp. 62–90. https://doi.org/10.5278/jbm.v8i3.6510

Meadowcroft, J. (2011) 'Engaging with the politics of sustainability transitions', *Environmental Innovation and Societal Transitions*, 1, pp. 70–75. https://doi.org/10.1016/j.eist.2011.02.003

Méndez-León, E., Reyes-Carrillo, T. and Díaz-Pichardo, R. (2021) 'Towards a holistic framework for sustainable value analysis in business models: A tool for sustainable development', *Business Strategy and the Environment*, 31 (1), pp. 15–31. https://doi.org/10.1002/bse.2871

Murray, A., Skene, K. and Haynes, K. (2017) 'The circular economy: An interdisciplinary exploration of the concept and application in a global context', *Journal of Business Ethics*, 140, pp. 369–380. https://doi.org/10.1007/s10551-015-2693-2

Onkila, T. and Sarna, B. (2022) 'A systematic literature review on employee relations with CSR: State of art and future research agenda', *Corporate Social Responsibility and Environmental Management*, 29, pp. 435–447. https://doi.org/10.1002/csr.2210

Patterson, J., *et al.* (2017) 'Exploring the governance and politics of transformations towards sustainability', *Environmental Innovation and Societal Transitions*, 24, pp. 1–16. https://doi.org/10.1016/j.eist.2016.09.001

Porter, E.M. and Kramer, M.R. (2011) 'Creating shared value', *Harvard Business Review*, January-February, pp. 1–17.

Rilovic, A., *et al.* (2020) 'A degrowth perspective on the coronavirus crisis', *degowth.info Blog*, 23 November. Available at: https://www.degrowth.info/blog/a-degrowth-perspective-on-the-coronavirus-crisis (Accessed: 17 March 2022).

Rockström, J., *et al.* (2009) 'Planetary boundaries: Exploring the safe operating space for humanity', *Ecology and Society*, 14(2), p. 32.

Romero, J. and Dryzek, J.S. (2021) 'Grounding ecological democracy: Semiotics and the communicative networks of nature', *Environmental Values*, 30(4), pp. 407–429. https://doi.org/10.3197/096327120X16076972519089

Rotmans, J., Kemp, R. and Marjolein, V.A. (2001) 'More evolution than revolution: Transition management in public policy', *Foresight*, 3(1), pp. 15–31. https://doi.org/10.1108/14636680110803003

Ruzzenenti, F., *et al.* (2019) 'Editorial: The rebound effect and the Jevons' paradox: Beyond the conventional wisdom', *Frontiers in Energy Research*, 7, 90. https://doi.org/10.3389/fenrg.2019.00090

Sarkar, S. and Searcy, C. (2016) 'Zeitgeist or chameleon? A quantitative analysis of CSR definitions', *Journal of Cleaner Production*, 135, pp. 1423–1435. https://doi.org/10.1016/j.jclepro.2016.06.157

Sarna, B., Onkila, T. and Mäkelä, M. (2021) 'Rationality, experiences or identity work? Sensemaking of emotionally tense experiences of organizational sustainability', *Social Responsibility Journal*, 18(8), pp. 1692–1707. https://doi.org/10.1108/SRJ-05-2021-0205

Schaltegger, S., Hansen, E.G. and Lüdeke-Freund, F. (2016) 'Business models for sustainability: Origins, present research and future avenues', *Organization & Environment*, 29, pp. 3–10. https://doi.org/10.1177/1086026615599806

Sorrell, S., Gatersleben, B. and Druckman, A. (2020) 'The limits of energy sufficiency: A review of the evidence for rebound effects and negative spillovers from behavioural change', *Energy Research & Social Science,* 64, 101439. https://doi.org/10.1016/j.erss.2020.101439

Thomas, R. and Davies, A. (2005) 'Theorizing the micro-politics of resistance: New public management and managerial identities in the UK public services', *Organization Studies, 26*(5), pp. 683–706.

Tokic, D. (2012) 'The economic and financial dimensions of degrowth', *Ecological Economics,* 84, pp. 49–56. https://doi.org/10.1016/j.ecolecon.2012.09.011

Turnheim, B. and Sovacool, B. K. (2020) 'Exploring the role of failure in socio-technical transitions research', *Environmental Innovation and Societal Transitions,* 37, pp. 267–289. https://doi.org/10.1016/j.eist.2020.09.005

Vadén, T., *et al.* (2020) 'Decoupling for ecological sustainability: A categorisation and review of research literature', *Environmental Science & Policy,* 112, pp. 236–244. https://doi.org/10.1016/j.envsci.2020.06.016

van den Bergh, J.C.J.M. (2011) 'Environment versus growth—A criticism of 'degrowth' and a plea for 'a-growth'', *Ecological Economics,* 70, pp. 881–890. https://doi.org/10.1016/j.ecolecon.2010.09.035

Vladimirova, D. (2019) 'Building sustainable value propositions for multiple stakeholders: A practical tool', *Journal of Business Models,* 7(1), pp. 1–8. https://doi.org/10.5278/ojs.jbm.v7i1.2103

Wiefek, J. and Heinitz, K. (2018) 'Common good-oriented companies: Exploring corporate values, characteristics and practices that could support a development towards degrowth', *Management Revue,* 29(3), pp. 311–313. https://doi.org/10.5771/0935-9915-2018-3-311

PART IV

Rethinking human well-being

11

EUDAIMONIA AND TEMPERANCE

A pathway to a flourishing life

Miia Grénman, Outi Uusitalo, and Juulia Räikkönen

Introduction

Humankind has entered the Anthropocene Epoch, in which human activity is so massive that it leaves a lasting imprint on the entire planet and its systems. We also live in a time of transition, where the ecological crisis challenges our future on Earth. Profound questions regarding human and nonhuman flourishing are critical since human activities—particularly production and consumption—are among the root causes of the ongoing ecological crisis. Excessive consumption will eventually result in irrevocable damage, including the deterioration of human well-being and nonhuman nature (Amel *et al.*, 2017; Dasgupta, 2021; Díaz *et al.*, 2019; The Intergovernmental Science-Policy Platform on Biodiversity and Ecosystem Services (IPBES), 2019, 2020).

Nevertheless, humans are part of nature and depend on its systems. Recently, there has been a growing recognition that humans have a moral responsibility for future generations and biodiversity (Dasgupta, 2021; Díaz *et al.*, 2019; IPBES, 2019, 2020; Van Tongeren, 2003). Accordingly, the solutions lie in transforming human values and behaviour and shifting the prevailing sociocultural, political, and economic paradigms towards embracing enhanced visions of the "good life" (Amel *et al.*, 2017; Dasgupta, 2021; Díaz *et al.*, 2019; IPBES, 2019, 2020). These discussions often occur in the environmental philosophy—a discipline focusing on the ethical relationships between human beings and nature and the intrinsic value and moral status of the environment and its nonhuman components (Brennan and Lo, 2010; Van Tongeren, 2003).

What constitutes the good life is also a topical issue in current consumer research and positive psychology. Critical questions are whether and how material consumption and quality of life interrelate. These questions are further fuelled by the

DOI: 10.4324/9781003334002-16

ongoing ecological crisis that has raised new concerns about ethics[1] and individual and collective well-being (Mick *et al.,* 2012; Mick and Schwartz, 2012; Petrescu-Mag, Petrescu and Robinson, 2019). As a response, transformative consumer research (TCR) emerged from the need to improve human, societal, and environmental well-being, which refers to the state of human flourishing involving health, happiness, and prosperity to achieve a good life (Mick *et al.,* 2012). Similarly, positive psychology emerged to enrich the scientific study of human flourishing, primarily to articulate enhanced visions of the good life and what makes individuals, communities, and societies flourish (Seligman and Csikszentmihalyi, 2000).

The concept of planetary well-being suggests a non-anthropocentric systemic conceptualization of well-being on multiple scales of interaction (Kortetmäki *et al.,* 2021). This concept is based on understanding well-being as a system's functional integrity allowing continuation of its existence and realization its system-specific characteristics and capacities. Planetary well-being is defined as "a state in which the integrity of Earth system and ecosystem processes remains unimpaired to a degree that lineages can persist to the future as parts of ecosystems, and organisms (including humans) can realize their typical characteristics and capacities" (*ibid.*).

The needs-based approach is integral to planetary well-being because all organisms—human and nonhuman—have specific universal basic needs that must be satisfied to have a good life (*ibid.*). In understanding human needs, marketing and consumer research have primarily been built on humanistic psychology, especially on Abraham Maslow's (1943) motivational theory and hierarchy of needs, consisting of deficiency needs (basic and psychological) and growth needs (self-fulfilment). Notably, planetary well-being focuses on shared conditions for well-being that equal Maslow's basic needs (physiological and safety needs). After these shared conditions are fulfilled, planetary well-being acknowledges the existence of species-specific higher needs that, in humans, include psychological needs (love and belonging, esteem) and self-fulfilment needs (self-actualization).

In response, we extend the needs-based approach towards moral philosophy, transformative consumer research, and positive psychology by bringing Aristotelian eudaimonia and the virtue of temperance into the discussion as a path to a flourishing life for humans and nonhumans. Eudaimonia encompasses the aim to pursue a life of meaning, virtue, and excellence (Waterman, 2008). Eudaimonia equates to "living well," requiring that one identify one's virtues, cultivate them, and live according to them. According to a Neo-Aristotelian approach, humans should develop what is best within themselves and use those virtues to serve the common good: The well-being of others, society, and nonhuman nature (Mick *et al.,* 2012; Peterson, Park, and Seligman, 2005).

Aristotelian ideas lead us to examine how temperance (*i.e.,* the virtue of control over excess) can be achieved in everyday life, how humans can pursue the good life, and how temperance can foster human and nonhuman flourishing. Regarding planetary well-being, humans can achieve a good and fulfilling life by reducing materialistic desires, particularly consumption, that are irrelevant to basic human needs and well-being (Kortetmäki *et al.*, 2021). However, achieving subjective well-being with significantly less material consumption may be challenging, as, in Western consumer societies, individuals' self-definition and society's collective definition are still fuelled by ever-increasing production and consumption, transmitting the message that "the goods life" is the path to "the good life" (Petrescu-Mag, Petrescu and Robinson, 2019).

Based on this background, this chapter discusses planetary well-being from the premises of Aristotelian eudaimonia, regarding TCR and positive psychology as paradigmatic lenses to address individual, social, and environmental solutions. We elaborate on whether humans can be wise and live well, seeking meaning and temperance rather than prosperity in an economy driven by global responsibility regarding planetary limits. These considerations bear relevance to reflections on the relationships among material consumption, the good life, and planetary well-being. Yet, these considerations contribute to mainstream marketing and consumer research, where such viewpoints have largely been missing.

Aristotelian eudaimonia equates to living well

Conceptions of happiness and the "good life" have been central concerns for philosophers and great thinkers—from Aristotle's time, fourth century BCE, to the present (Kashdan, Biswas-Diener and King, 2008; Ryan and Deci, 2001). Originally, the concept of well-being evolved around two Western philosophical perspectives: Hedonism and eudaimonism. Hedonism posits that the pursuit of pleasure is the greatest good and that happiness is the totality of one's hedonic moments (Ryan and Deci, 2001). Conversely, eudaimonism holds that one should pursue a life of virtue and excellence by focusing on psychological well-being connected to meaningful and valuable actions in opposition to "vulgar" pleasure-seeking (Waterman, 2008). According to Aristotle's definition of eudaimonia, true happiness is found by leading a virtuous life and doing what is worth doing, meaning that functioning well and realizing human potential is the ultimate human goal (Ryan, Huta and Deci, 2008; Waterman, 2008).

Aristotle posited that living well requires one to identify one's virtues, cultivate them, and live according to them (Peterson, Park and Seligman, 2005). Virtue is a trait or quality deemed morally good and is thus valued as a foundation of principle and good moral being (Hursthouse, 1999). Aristotle defines virtue as the excellence in human character and the mean between extremes of deficiency and excess by which human beings can accomplish their greatest purpose: The highest good of eudaimonia or human flourishing[2] (Sanz and Fontrodona, 2019). This notion is embedded in the concept of eudaimonia: *Eu,* meaning "good or well," and *daimon,* meaning "true self" (Huta and Waterman, 2014). To live well, one must recognize and live in accordance with one's true self—to identify one's character strengths and choose goals providing personal meaning and purpose in life (Peterson, Park and Seligman, 2005; Ryan and Deci, 2001).

Living well consists of doing something intrinsically worthwhile rather than being in a certain state or condition, including activities actualizing the virtues of the rational part of the soul (Sanz and Fontrodona, 2019). Thus, Aristotelian eudaimonia is not conceived as a subjective state of feeling (*e.g.*, happiness) or condition (*e.g.*, life satisfaction) but as *a way of living* wherein one strives to improve by developing oneself through using one's virtues and potential, meaning when an individual is fully functioning. Similarly, contemporary psychological definitions consider eudaimonia a way of living in which individuals should first develop what is best within themselves and then use their skills and talents to serve the common good: The well-being of others and society (Mick *et al.,* 2012; Peterson, Park and Seligman, 2005). Many recent studies and examples indicate these skills and talents can be extended to the well-being of nonhuman nature (Dasgupta, 2021; Díaz *et al.,* 2019; IPBES, 2019, 2020).

The search for an understanding of human well-being has also extended to various fields of psychology. Interest in the hedonia–eudaimonia distinction has proliferated recently, especially in positive psychology, as many studies address well-being within these paradigms (Huta and Waterman, 2014; Kashdan, Biswas-Diener and King, 2008). Notably, while hedonism and eudaimonism are competing ethical perspectives addressing questions regarding the nature of the good life within philosophy, within positive psychology hedonic and eudaimonic traditions complement each other. Several researchers have argued that hedonic and eudaimonic well-being indicators tend to positively correlate and influence one another, implying they are not mutually exclusive but overlapping: Individuals high in hedonic and eudaimonic motives tend to experience the most well-being, known as human flourishing (Huta and Ryan, 2010; Huta and Waterman, 2014).

Virtue of temperance

For Aristotle, virtues represent "states of character," including practical wisdom, prudence, justice, fortitude, courage, liberality, magnificence, magnanimity, and temperance, which are tightly bound (Young, 1988). Temperance is considered one of the most important virtues and a crucial aspect of ethical behaviour (Sanz and Fontrodona, 2019). Aristotle defines temperance as a "moderation or observance of the mean with regard to pleasures" (Young, 1988). Accordingly, temperance is commonly understood as a certain *balance* or a *golden mean* to pursue pleasures and other appealing desires for an ethical purpose. Sanz and Fontrodona (2019) further noted that temperance represents three other vital characteristics: Temperance is the most elementary and fundamental virtue, a necessary condition for moral development, and is considered self-mastery.

The renaissance of Aristotelian virtue ethics and temperance can be found in various fields. In positive psychology, temperance is considered "the virtue of moderation and control over excess," especially regarding appetites related to food, drink, sex, and money (Peterson and Seligman, 2004). According to Peterson and

Seligman, temperance is best manifested through self-regulation (or self-control) in monitoring and managing one's emotions, motivations, and behaviour, protecting an individual against excess appetite and the excess and destabilization of certain emotions. Within TCR, temperance is viewed as helping people relocate production and consumption within sustainable boundaries, serving individual, collective, and environmental aims (Petrescu-Mag, Petrescu and Robinson, 2019). Moreover, environmental philosophy literature increasingly addresses temperance, suggesting temperance valuably contributes to environmental ethics in better understanding of how to interact with nature and our natural surroundings (Van Tongeren, 2003).

To this end, temperance is currently one of the most essential virtues not only because it promotes human flourishing (individual and collective) but because it sustains nonhuman flourishing as an end itself. Nevertheless, nonhuman flourishing is necessary to human beings as we are part of nature and depend on its systems (Gambrel and Cafaro, 2010; Petrescu-Mag, Petrescu and Robinson, 2019).

From temperance to sufficiency through societal transformation

Aristotelian virtue ethics leads us to discuss temperance in more detail concerning the doctrines of TCR. Due to the ongoing ecological crisis, global consumption must be dramatically reduced, requiring significant changes in human values and behaviour, as well as global business structures and policies (Díaz *et al.*, 2019; Gorge *et al.*, 2015; Petrescu-Mag, Petrescu and Robinson, 2019). Temperance can allow humans as well as societal, political, and economic structures to strike a balance between the well-being of human and nonhuman nature (Garcia-Ruiz and Rodriguez-Lluesma, 2014).

Various streams of literature within TCR reflect the core idea of temperance, yet different concepts are used to address this notion: Moderation, simplicity, and sufficiency. Garcia-Ruiz and Rodriguez-Lluesma (*ibid.*) discuss *moderation*, referring to the golden mean. The golden mean entails that underconsumption and overconsumption should be avoided to achieve the balance between these extremes. Gambrel and Cafaro (2010) address *simplicity* as a conscientious and restrained attitude toward materialism. This attitude dictates not only decreasing consumption but redirecting it towards nonmaterial consumption. By confining consumption within the planetary limits, humans simultaneously make conscious choices that can cultivate excellence in human character (Mick *et al.*, 2012; Peterson, Park and Seligman, 2005).

The concept of *sufficiency* emerged at the beginning of the 2000s, influenced by Ivan Illich's (1973) notion of "austerity," promoting an ecologically sustainable but socially enjoyable way of living (Gorge *et al.*, 2015). Gorge *et al.* (*ibid.*) discuss sufficiency to achieve a lifestyle nurturing human flourishing and the well-being of nonhuman nature. Compared to moderation or simplicity, sufficiency represents a more radical form of consumption limitation. Sufficiency calls for coercive measures, such as decreasing overconsumption, eventually lowering our standard of living.

Sufficiency is not considered a choice but a situation of adaptation and resilience. To this end, sufficiency refers to the consumption level fulfilling our basic needs and strongly challenges our current ways of consumption—or consumption itself.

A systemic transformation reaching the entire society is inevitable to address the current ecological crisis. An immediate need for fundamental system-level changes exists, as the human impact of life on Earth has sharply increased since the 1970s, driven by the demands of a growing population with rising income levels. Western societies, which maximize the flow of material contributions from nature to keep up with increasing consumption and a consumerist lifestyle, are built on conceptions and beliefs separating humans from nature and ignoring the planetary limits. Accordingly, humans must change their future trajectories through transformative action, addressing the social, economic, and technological root causes of nature's deterioration (Díaz *et al.,* 2019; IPBES, 2019).

The notion of *societal transformation* has become topical in academic discussions related to the recent ecological crisis (O'Brien, 2018; Sharma, 2007), including transforming values, beliefs, worldviews, and knowledge; the systems and structures, sociocultural, political, and economic relations; and technologies, practices, and behaviours (Schipper *et al.,* 2021). According to O'Brien (2018), societal transformation can occur in three embedded and interacting spheres: Personal (values and worldviews), political (systems and structures), and practical (technologies and behaviour). Individual and collective values and worldviews shape how the systems and structures are viewed and influence what types of technologies and behaviour are considered possible to achieve positive change.

Regarding the ecological crisis, the personal and practical spheres signify a shift in human values and behaviour from consumerism to the current quest for a good and meaningful life: Integrating meaning into life; striving for harmony and balanced living; embracing a more sustainable way of living, and valuing morality, ethics, and empathy—all highlighting the importance of Aristotle's timeless virtues (Grénman, 2019). By contrast, the political sphere denotes a shift from excessive production and unsustainable business structures to an increasing emphasis on societal and environmental responsibility addressing the planetary limits (*ibid.*; cf. Sharma, 2007).

Societal transformation requires sufficiency thinking, promote a good and meaningful life, and provide possibilities for a more ecologically sustainable way of living as the "ethics" of the good life instead of merely regarding sufficiency as a source of economic disadvantages, slower growth, and profit loss. Societal transformation can also lead to a *flourishing life* that considers and embraces human and nonhuman well-being by acknowledging Earth's limits.

Can humans be wise and live well?

Focusing on achieving a flourishing life through "functioning well" is common to Neo-Aristotelian eudaimonia and planetary well-being. The latter pursues the possibility of functioning well for all organisms by satisfying basic needs and acknowledging the intrinsic value of human and nonhuman well-being. Conversely, eudaimonia seeks optimal human functioning through virtues and excellence and doing something intrinsically worthwhile. In eudaimonia, functioning well refers to the quality of the activity; eudaimonia occurs when an individual is fully engaged in activities congruent with one's deeply held values (Ryan and Deci, 2001). While these activities may be effortful or challenging and include a negative effect in the short term, they often yield greater overall well-being for an individual and nonhuman nature in the long term (Mick *et al.,* 2012; Peterson, Park, and Seligman, 2005).

The severity of the ongoing ecological crisis challenges humanity to take urgent actions concerning transforming human values and behaviour: Moving from hedonic happiness to living well. This shift already occurs in Western societies while excessive material consumption continues expanding, leading to the critical question of whether humans have the wisdom and capacity to live well—to practise temperance and self-regulation for the greater good (Grénman, 2019; Mick and Schwartz, 2012). Culture and communities have crucial roles in encouraging and supporting individual choices through shared values, norms, and traditions. Societal and political priorities, decisions, incentives, and regulations can shape the cultural conditions where individuals can make their own choices towards sufficiency while avoiding societal marginalization (Gambrel and Cafaro, 2010; Gorge *et al.,* 2015).

In advancing the TCR approach, Mick and Schwartz (2012) discuss wisdom—a superior, complex, and desirable form of knowledge—by drawing from Aristotle's conception of practical wisdom. Practical wisdom is essential for organizing other virtues to pursue human flourishing and the common good. In this discussion, *balancing* is critical, reflecting Aristotle's emphasis on the golden mean: Wise solutions and behaviours that are not extreme but master large entities. Finding the right balance depends on one's values, the relative importance of their various interests, and the resulting consequences (*ibid.*). Due to the ongoing ecological crisis, balancing should no longer concern just the individual level but address the planetary one.

Balance is also central in temperance and sufficiency thinking. However, while temperance is practised through moderation and self-regulation (Peterson and Seligman, 2004; Sanz and Fontrodona, 2019), sufficiency is not considered a choice but a situation of adaptation (Gorge *et al.,* 2015). Thus, ethical discussion on whether humans should be persuaded or forced to transform their current way of living is necessary. Planetary well-being and sufficiency thinking call for reducing the current consumption level and secure life on Earth. Conversely, Aristotelian eudaimonia and temperance rely on special human characteristics: The ability to make moral judgments and practise moderation through self-regulation to become a moderate human being and serve the greater good.

Forming ethical character and basing one's actions on virtues necessitate taking responsibility for the well-being of other humans and nonhuman nature. Aligning with the TCR approach, living well implies adherence to humane values, building awareness of the consequences of one's decisions, and recognizing the capacity to make conscious choices, contrasting current consumption practices: Unnecessary habitual purchases, following the crowds, or passively adapting to the mainstream market's easy solutions. Due to the ecological crisis, humans must consider societal transformation to manage the major changes required. Likewise, not only transformative consumption but transformative markets and marketing are needed, given the scale of and time available for the needed changes. Mainstreaming the core idea of TCR to conventional marketing would imply that marketers replace fuelling material consumption with developing their business to serve individuals' pursuit of well-being and wise ways of living.

In the era of ecological crisis, we can sell the idea of refraining from consumption and trading our current standard of living for the good of the planet. By contrast, the TCR approach implies voluntarily returning to the basics and achieving the good life and human flourishing through eudaimonia. While the end goal of planetary well-being and eudaimonia is the same—a flourishing life—both "pathways" to achieve such a life require a renaissance of the virtue of temperance.

Acknowledgements

The authors received financial support from the Strategic Research Council of the Academy of Finland (Biodiversity-respectful leadership; grant number 345885)

Notes

1 Ethics refers to a set of standards of right and wrong indicating what people must do, distinguishing between acceptable and unacceptable behaviour (Petrescu-Mag, Petrescu and Robinson, 2019).
2 Notably, the Aristotelian view represents one sub-type of virtue ethics: not all virtue ethics approaches closely connect with human flourishing (Hursthouse, 1999).

References

Amel, E. *et al.* (2017) 'Beyond the roots of human inaction: Fostering collective effort toward ecosystem conservation', *Science*, 356(6335), pp. 275–279. https://doi.org/10.1126/science. aal1931

Brennan, A. and Lo, Y. (2010) *Understanding Environmental Philosophy*. Durham, NC: Acumen. https://doi.org/10.1017/UPO9781844654482

Dasgupta, P. (2021) *The Economics of Biodiversity: the Dasgupta Review*. London: HM Treasury.

Díaz, S. *et al.* (2019) 'Pervasive human-driven decline of life on Earth points to the need for transformative change', *Science*, 366(6471), pp. 1–10. https://doi.org/10.1126/science. aax3100

Gambrel, J.C. and Cafaro, P. (2010) 'The virtue of simplicity', *Journal of Agricultural and Environmental Ethics*, 23(1–2), pp. 85–108. https://doi.org/10.1007/s10806-009-9187-0

Garcia-Ruiz, P. and Rodriguez-Lluesma, C. (2014) 'Consumption practices: A virtue ethics approach', *Business Ethics Quarterly*, 24(4), pp. 509–531. https://doi.org/10.5840/beq20147313

Gorge, H. *et al.* (2015) 'What do we really need? Questioning consumption through sufficiency', *Journal of Macromarketing*, 35(1), pp. 11–22. https://doi.org/10.1177/027614671455393

Grénman, M. (2019) 'In quest of the optimal self - Wellness consumption and lifestyle—A superficial marketing fad or a powerful means for transforming and branding oneself?', *Annales Universitatis Turkuensis*, ser E47. Turku: University of Turku, Turku School of Economics.

Hursthouse, R. (1999) *On Virtue Ethics*. Oxford: Oxford University Press.

Huta, V. and Ryan, R.M. (2010) 'Pursuing pleasure or virtue: The differential and overlapping well-being benefits of hedonic and eudaimonic motives', *Journal of Happiness Studies*, 11(6), pp. 735–762. https://doi.org/10.1007/s10902-009-9171-4

Huta, V. and Waterman, A.S. (2014) 'Eudaimonia and its distinction from Hedonia: Developing a classification and terminology for understanding conceptual and operational definitions', *Journal of Happiness Studies*, 15(6), pp. 1425–1456. https://doi.org/10.1007/s10902-013-9485-0

Illich, I. (1973) *Tools for Conviviality*. New York: World Perspectives.

IPBES (2019) *Global Assessment Report on Biodiversity and Ecosystem Services of the Intergovernmental Science-Policy Platform on Biodiversity and Ecosystem Services.* Zenedo. https://doi.org/10.5281/zenodo.3831673

IPBES (2020) *Workshop Report on Biodiversity and Pandemics of the Intergovernmental Platform on Biodiversity and Ecosystem Services.* Zenedo. https://doi.org/10.5281/zenodo.4147317

Kashdan, T.B., Biswas-Diener, R. and King, L.A. (2008) 'Reconsidering happiness: The costs of distinguishing between hedonics and eudaimonia', *The Journal of Positive Psychology*, 3(4), pp. 219–233. https://doi.org/10.1080/17439760802303044

Kortetmäki, T. *et al.* (2021) 'Planetary well-being', *Humanities and Social Sciences Communications*, 8, 258. https://doi.org/10.1057/s41599-021-00899-3

Maslow, A.H. (1943) 'A theory of human motivation', *Psychological Review*, 50(4), pp. 370–396.

Mick, D.G. *et al.* (2012) 'Origins, qualities, and envisonments of transformative consumer research', in Mick, D.G., Pettigrew, S., Pechmann, C. and Ozanne, J.L. (eds.) *Transformative Consumer Research for Personal and Collective Well-Being.* New York: Routledge, pp. 3–24. https://doi.org/10.4324/9780203813256

Mick, D.G. and Schwartz, B. (2012) 'Can consumers be wise? Aristotle speaks to the 21st century', in Mick, D.G., Pettigrew, S., Pechmann, C. and Ozanne, J.L. (eds.) *Transformative Consumer Research for Personal and Collective Well-Being.* New York: Routledge, pp. 663–680. https://doi.org/10.4324/9780203813256

O'Brien, K. (2018) 'Is the 1.5 C target possible? Exploring the three spheres of transformation', *Current Opinion in Environmental Sustainability*, 31, pp. 153–160. https://doi.org/10.1016/j.cosust.2018.04.010

Peterson, C., Park, N. and Seligman, M.E. (2005) 'Orientations to happiness and life satisfaction: The full life versus the empty life', *Journal of Happiness Studies*, 6(1), pp. 25–41.

Peterson, C. and Seligman, M.E. (2004) *Character Strengths and Virtues: A Handbook and Classification.* New York: Oxford University Press.

Petrescu-Mag, R.M., Petrescu, D.C. and Robinson, G.M. (2019) 'Adopting temperance-oriented behavior? New possibilities for consumers and their food waste', *Journal of Agricultural and Environmental Ethics*, 32, pp. 5–26. https://doi.org/10.1007/s10806-019-09765-4

Ryan, R.M. and Deci, E.L. (2001) 'On happiness and human potentials: A review of research on hedonic and eudaimonic well-being', *Annual Review of Psychology*, 52(1), pp. 141–166.

Ryan, R.M., Huta, V. and Deci, E.L. (2008) 'Living well: A self-determination theory perspective on eudaimonia', *Journal of Happiness Studies*, 9(1), pp. 139–170. https://doi.org/10.1007/s10902-006-9023-4

Sanz, P. and Fontrodona, J. (2019) 'Moderation as a moral competence: Integrating perspectives for a better understanding of temperance in the workplace', *Journal of Business Ethics*, 155(4), pp. 981–994. https://doi.org/10.1007/s10551-018-3899-x

Schipper, E.L.F. *et al.* (2021) 'Turbulent transformation: Abrupt societal disruption and climate resilient development', *Climate and Development*, 13(6), pp. 467–474. https://doi.org/10.1080/17565529.2020.1799738

Seligman, M.E. and Csikszentmihalyi, M. (2000) 'Positive psychology: An introduction', *American Psychological Association*, 55(1), pp. 5–14.

Sharma, M. (2007) 'World wisdom in action: Personal to planetary transformation', *Kosmos*, pp. 31–35.

Van Tongeren, P. (2003) 'Temperance and environmental concerns', *Ethical Perspectives*, 10(2), pp. 118–128.

Waterman, A.S. (2008) 'Reconsidering happiness: A eudaimonist's perspective', *The Journal of Positive Psychology*, 3(4), pp. 234–252. https://doi.org/10.1080/17439760802303002

Young, C.M. (1988) 'Aristotle on temperance', *The Philosophical Review*, 97(4), pp. 521–542.

12

PSYCHOLOGICAL WELL-BEING AND PRO-ENVIRONMENTAL BEHAVIOUR

Kirsi Salonen, Katriina Hyvönen, Eleanor Ratcliffe and Jane-Veera Paakkolanvaara

Introduction

The adoption of environmentally friendly behaviour can have a major effect on reducing human impacts on the environment (Clayton *et al.*, 2015; Dietz *et al.*, 2009; Gardner and Stern, 2008). Hence, in an era in which multiple environmental crises are diminishing planetary well-being, it is crucial to promote pro-environmental behaviour without increasing immobilizing anxiety and avoidance. In this chapter we construct a view of nature as a part of human psychological functioning, one that combines mental well-being (including psychological needs) with pro-environmental behaviour. We also argue that supporting nature-connectedness and mental well-being among humans can facilitate pro-environmental behaviour; that is, we offer ways to promote both planetary and human well-being.

We consider mental well-being in line with the tripartite model of well-being that comprises psychological, emotional, and social well-being, and lack of mental health problems (Kokko *et al.*, 2013). Research has shown that humans who flourish along the lines of the tripartite model also tend to be healthy at the highest level (Keyes, 2005). Psychological well-being is a core feature of mental health; it is understood to include hedonic (enjoyment, pleasure) and eudaimonic (meaning, fulfilment) happiness, as well as resilience (coping, emotion regulation, healthy problem-solving) (*e.g.*, Tang, Tang and Gross, 2019). In this chapter we argue that the subjective experience of well-being is an essential part of improving planetary well-being, a concept that emphasizes the interconnectedness of human and non-human well-being.

Considering this interconnectedness, one first needs to comprehend certain features of the species-specific needs of humans, including manifold psychological needs that are integral to human well-being. For example, self-determination theory

DOI: 10.4324/9781003334002-17

notes the psychological needs required for optimal psychological well-being: Autonomy, competence, and relatedness (Deci and Ryan, 2000). *Autonomy* refers to the experience of choice and volition in one's behaviour, whereas *competence* involves the ability to bring about desired outcomes and feelings of effectiveness and mastery over one's environment. *Relatedness* reflects feelings of closeness and connection in one's everyday interactions *(ibid.)*. We suggest that relatedness in particular can promote perceptions and behaviours that are in line with the requirements of planetary well-being.

How, then, could such relatedness of psychological well-being and non-human nature be supported? Extensive literature in environmental psychology shows that non-human nature (including non-human nature in urban areas) supports human health and well-being (Berto, 2014; Bowler *et al.*, 2010; Hartig *et al.*, 2014; Ohly *et al.*, 2016). A large body of research on the topic of restorative environments shows that observing and/or engaging with non-human nature can provide affective, cognitive and behavioural benefits, including reductions in psychophysiological stress and increases in well-being (Twohig-Bennett and Jones, 2018; Wilkie and Davinson, 2021).

In the human–nature relationship, elements of non-human nature pertain both to concrete characteristics of nature, for instance presence of plants, trees, water (Ulrich *et al.*, 1991), and to perceived sensory dimensions, for instance species richness (Grahn and Stigsdotter 2010). These are relevant for restorative nature experiences and well-being (Hartig *et al.*, 1997; Ulrich *et al.*, 1991). From this perspective, human well-being is in part determined by nature-connectedness and exposure to nonhuman nature (*e.g.,* Brymer, Cuddihy and Sharma-Brymer, 2010; Mayer and Frantz, 2004).

There is an urgent need for interventions that promote planetary well-being. The needed transformation is not restricted to socio-technological solutions but requires the reshaping of human–nature relationships and restoring the view of humans and human minds as part of nature, not separate from it. Crucially, positive nature experiences—and in particular nature-connectedness achieved through emotional and social support—can promote both well-being and pro-environmental behaviour in humans. Pro-environmental behaviour is understood here as a range of behaviours that benefit the natural environment, enhance environmental quality, or harm the environment as little as possible (Steg and Vlek, 2009). A nature-based intervention called Act with Nature (AWN), introduced later in this chapter, is one possible method for supporting such behaviour and also promoting individual human well-being.

The human mind as part of nature

Psychology is the study of the human mind and behaviour (American Psychological Association (APA), 2015). The discipline embraces all aspects of the human experience—from the functions of the brain to the actions of communities, from child development to care for the aged. Psychology has typically focused on the effects of the social environment on the human mind and behaviour. Our view as eco- and environmental psychologists is that many mainstream psychological theories and approaches have helped to uphold the strict dichotomy between humans and nature (or the natural world)—or, at least, that these theories fail to sufficiently account for the interconnectedness of human and non-human well-being.

Yet the human-centred approach has been challenged within psychology too. Some theories and subdisciplines propose a more holistic view in which humans are part of the physical environment. We present three specialty areas in psychology that are relevant to our endeavours: *Environmental psychology* (*e.g.,* Stokols *et al.,* 2009), *gestalt therapy* (Perls, 1973), and *ecopsychology* (*e.g.,* Roszak, 1993; Winter and Koger, 2004). Although each provides valuable contributions, we argue that ecopsychology and its take on the concept of nature-connectedness is especially promising with respect to planetary well-being. The three specialty areas have a shared grounding in the idea, already discussed above, that human well-being (or lack thereof) is influenced by the physical environment, consciously or unconsciously. For example, environmental psychology proposes that humans have a species-typical propensity for psychological restoration in natural environments (*e.g.,* Kaplan and Kaplan, 1989) even though a person may not recognize this explicitly.

Environmental psychological theories of restoration in nature can be thought of as focusing mainly on attention restoration (Kaplan and Kaplan, 1989) or stress reduction (Ulrich, 1983). The concept of environmental self-regulation refers to more explicit use of physical settings—often favourite places—and relates experiences in nature more broadly to self-regulation (Korpela *et al.,* 2018). This means that a person consciously or unconsciously regulates (*e.g.,* facilitates, strengthens) their experiences (emotions, stress, coping, *etc.*) by means of the physical environment (*e.g.,* favourite places in nature). A concrete example of environmental self-regulation is going to a park or forest after a stressful workday and noticing the reduction in stress there.

Gestalt therapy's concept of organismic self-regulation is similar to environmental self-regulation. The central idea in gestalt therapy (Perls, 1973) is that a human being cannot be understood separately from its environment (Yontef and Fuhr, 2005). Humans are seen as organisms that are a part of nature, living in natural cycles of contact and withdrawal in relation to both physical and social environments (Crocker and Philippson, 2005). Human beings—like all other organisms in nature—regulate themselves in changing circumstances, including both internal changes related to bodily experiences and external changes related to the physical and social environment, that is, organismic self-regulation (Perls, Hefferline and Goodman, 1951). The environment becomes a bodily experience through sensory perceptions and is processed in human minds through complex cognitive and emotional schemes, which also include cultural and societal aspects. Expanding to a planetary well-being viewpoint, *all* living entities have various processes whose functioning and regulation is focal to well-being.

Ecopsychological views go even further. Ecopsychology's view of nature-connectedness unambiguously means that humans are part of nature (Brymer, Cuddihy and Sharma-Brymer, 2010) and that this interconnection explains the well-being effects of nature. Brymer, Cuddihy and Sharma-Brymer *(ibid.)* emphasize the depth and emotionality of nature-connectedness. According to them, in addition to psychological restoration (Kaplan and Kaplan, 1989; Ulrich *et al.*, 1991), non-human nature initiates deep reflections, provides opportunities for caring, and helps individuals to understand and experience being part of nature. Deep reflection in nature means, for example, that nature promotes self-awareness and acceptance. Non-human nature acts as a mirror that can reflect one's own thoughts and feelings. Interestingly, from a planetary well-being perspective, the concept of ecological unconsciousness (Roszak, 1993) is used in ecopsychology to argue that the state of the planet awakens feelings consciously and unconsciously.

Continuing within the ecopsychology approach, the comprehensive nature experience model (Salonen, 2020; Salonen, Kirves and Korpela, 2016) underlines that the perceived characteristics of nature are dependent on subjective emotions. Put simply, the characteristics that we see in nature are related to our subjective experiences. Further, nature-connectedness means here that there is no boundary separating a person's experience of self from that of non-human nature; the experience of self continues into nature and nature continues into the experience of self. Nature-connectedness is particularly experienced through close contact with natural elements and in relation to sheltering natural elements (*e.g.,* forests, trees).

Nature-connectedness and pro-environmental behaviour

In the following we examine more closely the conditions of environmentally friendly behaviour and take an in-depth view of the significance of nature-connectedness, including its relevance for supporting behavioural change. Planetary well-being requires overcoming the dualist dichotomies wherein humans and human societies are perceived as separate from nature. Nature-connectedness, thus, can help to address the environmental crises by promoting change in both behaviour and well-being.

Pro-environmental behaviour refers to the actions that individuals take to minimize environmental harm or to restore the natural environment (Anderson and Krettenauer, 2021; Brick, Sherman and Kim, 2017). A variety of different interventions and strategies have been developed to change human behaviour and reach sustainability goals. These involve changing factors that precede behaviour, for instance antecedent strategies such as information, education, and behavioural commitment strategy (*e.g.,* Geller, Winett and Everett, 1982). Previous research has shown that merely providing information or rewarding/punishing different behaviours is not sufficient to change individual behaviour (Schultz and Kaiser, 2012). In contrast, commitment strategies (*e.g.,* the participant commits to behavioural change) appear to be successful in encouraging pro-environmental behaviour (see Abrahamse *et al.*, 2005).

Variation in terms of individuals' nature-connectedness may affect their readiness and ability to engage in the desired behaviour change (Clayton, 2012). There is strong evidence that long-term nature-connectedness (*i.e.*, a deep relationship with nature and a sense of belonging to the wider natural community) (Mayer and Frantz, 2004) is an important predictor of pro-environmental behaviour (*e.g.,* Anderson and Krettenauer, 2021) and that it can explain nature's positive effects on well-being (Mayer and Frantz, 2004). The concept of nature-connectedness includes the idea of a subjective belongingness to nature (*ibid.*), which has been found to be a contributing factor for life satisfaction and subjective well-being (Cervinka, Röderer and Hefler, 2012; Mayer and Frantz, 2004) as well as for strengthening environmental responsibility (Mayer and Frantz, 2004).

In addition, social support can be helpful in strengthening pro-environmental behaviour. Modelling and providing information about the behaviour of others appears to be successful in supporting pro-environmental behaviour (Schultz *et al.*, 2007).

In sum, evidence-based interventions are urgently needed to support the well-being of humans during environmental crises and to facilitate desired pro-environmental behaviour change. To this end, we present an intervention that focuses on nature-connectedness but also applies commitment and social support to promote pro-environmental behaviour and well-being.

Act with nature: Intervention to promote nature-connectedness and pro-environmental behaviour

Act with Nature (AWN) is one of the several models and methodologies developed to promote nature-connectedness and pro-environmental behavioural change. In short, it is a working model for intervention that accounts for the role nature-connectedness and human well-being play in promoting pro-environmental behaviour. AWN is embedded within non-human nature. Participants are encouraged to recognize nature's significance for well-being and behaviour change, and to use the environment as support for psychological and environmental self-regulation (Korpela *et al.*, 2018). Through the intervention individuals learn to recognize, among other things, how their mood improves in nature, and that different nature elements enable different experiences. Through increased nature-connectedness, the participant can experience oneness with nature whereby nature becomes perceived as part of oneself (and oneself becomes a part of nature). Within the AWN approach, the well-being of humans and that of the surrounding non-human nature are both considered equally important.

AWN exercises take into account that changing a behaviour is a process that also includes mental changes. Different people have different levels of change readiness (see, *e.g.,* Norcross and Wampold (2018) on the transtheoretical model of behavioural change), meaning that that some participants may need more support for change than others. Nevertheless, the central idea is that behaviour changes do not require sacrifices with respect to human well-being.

AWN builds on a previous intervention, called Flow with Nature (FWN; Salonen *et al.*, 2018, 2020). Based on eco- and environmental psychology (*e.g.,* Mayer and Franz, 2004), FWN was developed to promote occupational well-being (Salonen *et al.* 2018) and to treat depression (Salonen *et al.*, 2022). The nature-based exercises of FWN have significant potential to promote pro-environmental behaviour, since participants reported stronger connectedness with nature and environmental responsibility during the intervention period (Salonen, 2020; Salonen *et al.*, 2018). FWN participants have shown positive well-being outcomes compared to control groups (Hyvönen *et al.*, 2023; Salonen *et al.*, 2022).

AWN techniques take into account research on pro-environmental behaviour (Brick, Sherman and Kim, 2017), as well as participant orientation to environmental attitudes (*e.g.,* Sparks, Ehret and Brick, 2022) and intentions (Rise, Thompson and Verplanken, 2003). For example, the participants decide themselves which concrete changes in behaviour they will commit to. It seems that behaviour change barriers/failures can result in strong feelings of disappointment, shame, and anxiety, which is why they are addressed in order to empower coping activities (*e.g.,* taking action to solve the problem causing one's mood), which in turn may help maintain the change in everyday life. These actions in everyday life help to maintain well-being and stabilize change. Consequently, the pro-environmental behaviour can be expected to continue even after the intervention.

AWN as a tool of intervention includes three separate stages in which the nature experiences, content of the exercises, and the intensity of social support varies. In the first stage, the aim is to strengthen nature-connectedness and environmental self-regulation, and to build experiences of safety and confidence through exercises focused on favourite places in nature. In the second stage, the aim is to address environment-related emotions and build psychological flexibility, which results in enhanced coping strategies (including environmental self-regulation). Participants become more aware of nature elements by reflecting on their own environment-related emotions and thereby acquire skills for psychological processing of change. In the third stage, the aim is to experiment with alternative ways of making changes and to affirm positive change in environmental behaviours.

AWN is an intervention method that seeks to facilitate behavioural change at individual and societal levels. At the core of the AWN intervention is a desire to support lifestyles that are respectful of nature's capacities and boundaries and that encourage respectful decisions about nature. Fundamental cultural and political changes in the structure of societies can be pushed forward through broad and collective behavioural changes in individuals. Put another way, while environmental crises and planetary well-being present great challenges for individuals and their behaviour patterns, intervention methods such as AWN can help address needed behavioural changes while simultaneously supporting the well-being of human individuals.

Conclusion

In this chapter we have argued for the promotion of psychological well-being from the perspective of eco- and environmental psychology. The chapter contributes a psychological perspective to the topic of planetary well-being, but does so in a way that reaches beyond the psychological perspective of the individual and beyond the problematic human/nature dichotomies that have long been mainstream in the field of psychology.

A truly integrated understanding of planetary well-being requires understanding of the conditions of human subjective well-being. The concepts and definitions used in this chapter to describe human nature and psychological well-being can be understood to be closely interconnected. They can be useful when analyzing human behaviour and promoting behavioural change for planetary well-being.

Deep behavioural change requires psychological well-being; well-being and behaviour are not separate aspects of human functioning. On the whole, when we humans perceive that there is no boundary between ourselves and the planet, and when we feel that we are one with our natural environment, it is much harder to destroy it.

References

Abrahamse, W. *et al.* (2005) 'A review of intervention studies aimed at household energy conservation', *Journal of Environmental Psychology,* 25(3), pp. 273–291. https://doi.org/10.1016/j.jenvp.2005.08.002

APA (2015) *About APA. Frequently asked questions about the American Psychological Association.* Available at: https://www.apa.org/support/about-apa?item=7 (Accessed: 17 January 2023).

Anderson, D.J. and Krettenauer, T. (2021) 'Connectedness to nature and pro-environmental behaviour from early adolescence to adulthood: A comparison of urban and rural Canada', *Sustainability,* 13(7), 3655. https://doi.org/10.3390/su13073655

Berto, R. (2014) 'The role of nature in coping with psycho-physiological stress: A literature review on restorativeness', *Behavioral Scieces,* 4(4), pp. 394–409. https://doi.org/10.3390/bs4040394

Bowler, D.E. *et al.* (2010) 'A systematic review of evidence for the added benefits to health of exposure to natural environments', *BMC Public Health,* 10(456). https://doi.org/10.1186/1471-2458-10-456

Brick, C., Sherman, D.K. and Kim, H.S. (2017) ''Green to be seen' and 'brown to keep down': Visibility moderates the effect of identity on pro-environmental behavior', *Journal of Environmental Psychology,* 51, pp. 226–238. https://doi.org/10.1016/j.jenvp.2017.04.004

Brymer, E., Cuddihy, T.F. and Sharma-Brymer, V. (2010) 'The role of nature-based experiences in the development and maintenance of wellness', *Asia-Pacific Journal of Health, Sport and Physical Education,* 1(2), pp. 21–27. https://doi.org/10.1080/18377122.2010.9730328

Cervinka, R., Röderer, K. and Hefler, E. (2012) 'Are nature lovers happy? On various indicators of well-being and connectedness with nature', *Journal of Health Psychology*, 17, pp. 379–388. https://doi.org/10.1177/1359105311416873

Clayton, S. (ed.) (2012) *The Oxford Handbook of Environmental and Conservation Psychology*. New York: Oxford University Press.

Clayton, S. *et al.* (2015) 'Psychological research and global climate change', *Nature Climate Change*, 5, pp. 640–646. https://doi.org/10.1038/nclimate2622

Crocker, S.F. and Philippson, P., (2005) 'Phenomenology, existentialism, and eastern thought in gestalt therapy', in Woldt, A.L. and Toman, S.M. (eds.) *Gestalt Therapy: History, Theory, and Practice*. London: Sage Publications Ltd, pp. 65–80. https://dx.doi.org/10.4135/9781452225661

Deci, E.L. and Ryan, R.M. (2000) 'The "what" and "why" of goal pursuits: Human needs and the self-determination of behavior', *Psychological Inquiry*, 11(4), pp. 227–268. https://doi.org/10.1207/S15327965PLI1104_01

Dietz, T. *et al.* (2009) 'Household actions can provide a behavioral wedge to rapidly reduce US carbon emissions', *Proceedings of the National Academy of Sciences*, 106(44), pp. 18452–18456. https://doi.org/10.1073/pnas.0908738106

Gardner, G.T. and Stern, P.C. (2008) 'The short list: The most effective actions U.S. households can take to curb climate change', *Environment: Science and Policy for Sustainable Development*, 50(5), pp. 12–25. https://doi.org/10.3200/ENVT.50.5.12-25

Geller, E.S., Winett, R.A. and Everett, P.B. (1982) *Environmental Preservation New Strategies for Behavior Change*. New York: Pergamon Press.

Grahn, P. and Stigsdotter, U. (2010) 'The relation between perceived sensory dimensions of urban green space and stress restoration', *Landscape and Urban Planning*, 94, pp. 264–275. https://doi.org/10.1016/j.landurbplan.2009.10.012

Hartig, T. *et al.* (1997) 'A measure of restorative quality in environments', *Scandinavian Housing & Planning Research*, 14, pp. 175–194. https://doi.org/10.1080/02815739708730435

Hartig, T. *et al.* (2014) 'Nature and health', *Annual Review of Public Health*, 35, pp. 207–228. https://doi.org/10.1146/annurev-publhealth-032013-182443

Hyvönen, K. *et al.* (2023) 'Effects of nature-based intervention in the treatment of depression: A multi-center, randomized controlled trial', *Journal of Environmental Psychology*, 85, 101950. https://doi.org/10.1016/j.jenvp.2022.101950

Kaplan, R. and Kaplan, S. (1989) *The Experience of Nature: A Psychological Perspective*. New York: Cambridge University Press.

Keyes, C.L. (2005) 'Mental illness and/or mental health? Investigating axioms of the complete state model of health', *Journal of Consulting & Clinical Psychology*, 73, pp. 539–548. https://doi.org/10.1037/0022-006X.73.3.539

Kokko, K. *et al.* (2013) 'Structure and continuity of well-being in mid-adulthood: A longitudinal study', *Journal of Happiness Studies*, 14, pp. 99–114. https://doi.org/10.1007/s10902-011-9318-y

Korpela, K.M. *et al.* (2018) 'Environmental strategies of affect regulation and their associations with subjective well-being', *Frontiers in Psychology*, 9(562). https://doi.org/10.3389/fpsyg.2018.00562

Mayer, F.S. and Frantz, C.M. (2004) 'The connectedness to nature scale: A measure of individual's feeling in community in nature', *Journal of Environmental Psychology*, 24, pp. 503–515. https://doi.org/10.1016/j.jenvp.2004.10.001

Norcross, J.C. and Wampold, B.E. (2018) 'A new therapy for each patient: Evidence-based relationships and responsiveness', *Journal of Clinical Psychology*, 74, pp. 1889–1906. https://doi.org/10.1002/jclp.22678

Ohly, H. *et al.* (2016) 'Attention Restoration Theory: A systematic review of the attention restoration potential of exposure to natural environments', *Journal of Toxicology and Environmental Health, Part B,* 19(7), pp. 305–343. https://doi.org/10.1080/10937404. 2016.1196155

Perls, F.S. (1973) *The Gestalt approach end eye witness to therapy.* New York: Bantman.

Perls, F.S., Hefferline, R.F. and Goodman, P. (1951) *Gestalt Therapy: Excitement and Growth in the Human Personality.* New York: Dell.

Rise, J., Thompson, M. and Verplanken, B. (2003) 'Measuring implementation intentions in the context of the theory of planned behavior', *Scandinavian Journal of Psychology,* 44(2). https://doi.org/10.1111/1467-9450.00325

Roszak, T. (1993) *The Voice of the Earth: An Exploration of Ecopsychology.* New York: Touchstone.

Salonen, K. (2020) *Kokonaisvaltainen luontokokemus hyvinvoinnin tukena [Comprehensive Nature Experience Supporting Well-Being].* Doctoral dissertation. Tampere: Tampere University. Available at: https://urn.fi/URN:ISBN:978-952-03-1563-4 (Accessed: 17 January 2023).

Salonen, K., Kirves, K. and Korpela, K. (2016) 'Kohti kokonaisvaltaisen luontokokemuksen mittaamista [Towards measuring comprehensive nature experience]', *Psykologia,* 5, pp. 324–342. Available at: https://urn.fi/URN:ISBN:978-952-03-1563-4 (Accessed: 17 January 2023).

Salonen, K. *et al.* (2018) 'Luontoympäristön yhteydet työhyvinvointiin ja työssä suoriutumiseen: kysely-, interventio- ja haastattelututkimuksen tuloksia [The associations of nature environment with occupational well-being and work performance: Results from survey, intervention, and interview studies]', *Jyväskylän yliopiston psykologian laitoksen julkaisuja,* 355. Available at: http://urn.fi/URN:ISBN:978-951-39-7539-5 (Accessed: 17 January 2023).

Salonen, K. *et al.* (2022) 'Flow with Nature -treatment group for depression: Participants' experiences', *Frontiers in Environmental Psychology,* 12. http://dx.doi.org/10.3389/fpsyg.2021.768372

Schultz, P.W. and Kaiser, F.G. (2012) 'Promoting pro-environmental behavior', in Clayton, S. (ed.) *The Oxford Handbook of Environmental and Conservation Psychology.* New York: Oxford University Press, pp. 556–580. https://doi.org/10.1093/oxfordhb/9780199733026.001.0001

Schultz, P.W. *et al.* (2007) 'The constructive, destructive, and reconstructive power of social norms', *Psychological Science,* 18(5), pp. 429–434. https://doi.org/10.1111/j.1467-9280.2007.01917.x

Sparks, A., Ehret, P. and Brick, C. (2022) 'Measuring pro-environmental orientation: Testing and building scales', *Journal of Environmental Psychology,* 81. https://doi.org/10.1016/j.jenvp.2022.101780

Steg, L. and Vlek, C. (2009) 'Encouraging pro-environmental behaviour: An integrative review and research agenda', *Journal of Environmental Psychology,* 29(3), pp. 309–317. https://doi.org/10.1016/j.jenvp.2008.10.004

Stokols, D. *et al.* (2009) 'Psychology in an age of ecological crisis: From personal angst to collective action', *American Psychologist,* 64(3), pp. 181–193. https://doi.org/10.1037/a0014717

Tang, Y-Y., Tang, R. and Gross, J.J. (2019) 'Promoting psychological well-being through an evidence-based mindfulness training program', *Frontiers in Human Neuroscience,* 13, 237. https://doi.org/10.3389/fnhum.2019.00237

Twohig-Bennett, C. and Jones A. (2018) 'The health benefits of the great outdoors: A systematic review and meta-analysis of greenspace exposure and health outcomes', *Environmental Research*, 166, pp. 628–637. https://doi.org/10.1016/j.envres.2018.06.030

Ulrich, R.S. (1983) 'Aesthetic and affective response to natural environment', in Altman, I. and Wohlwill, J. (eds.) *Behavior and the Natural Environment*. Boston, MA: Springer, pp. 85–125.

Ulrich, R.S. *et al.* (1991) 'Stress recovery during exposure to natural and urban environments', *Journal of Environmental Psychology*, 11, pp. 201–230. https://doi.org/10.1016/S0272-4944(05)80184-7

Wilkie, S. and Davinson, N. (2021) 'The impact of nature-based interventions on public health: A review using pathways, mechanisms and behaviour change techniques from environmental social science and health behaviour change', *Journal of the British Academy*, 9(s7), pp. 33–61. https://doi.org/10.5871/jba/009s7.033

Winter, D.D.N. and Koger, S. (2004) *The Psychology of Environmental Problems*. 2nd edn. Mahwah, NJ: Lawrence Erlbaum.

Yontef, G.M. and Fuhr, R. (2005) 'Gestalt Therapy Theory of Change', in Woldt, A.L. and Toman, S.M. (eds.) *Gestalt Therapy: History, Theory, and Practice*. London: Sage Publications Ltd, pp. 81–100. https://doi.org/10.4135/9781452225661

13

THE ECOSOCIAL PARADIGM IN SOCIAL WORK

Striving for planetary well-being

Ingo Stamm, Satu Ranta-Tyrkkö, Aila-Leena Matthies and Kati Närhi

Introduction

The chapter focuses on the planetary well-being concept from the perspective of social work and is structured in four main parts. First, we will briefly introduce social work as a practice-oriented profession and academic discipline that has many different forms globally. Second, we will describe the new paradigm of ecosocial work. Ecosocial work attempts to readjust the professions´ main emphasis on social problems of and between human beings to a position that puts humanity's dependence on the natural environment at its centre. Third, we will examine how the planetary well-being concept can be a fruitful addition to ecosocial work concepts and social work in general. Here we will focus on the implications of the planetary well-being concept for social work ethics. We argue that social work, as a human-centred profession and discipline, must strike a balance between critical anthropocentric and non-anthropocentric perspectives. In the fourth and final part, we discuss critically what ethical dilemmas could arise if the idea of planetary well-being would be fully implemented in social work practice. In conclusion, we identify planetary well-being as a useful addition to current discussions in social work.

Social work as an academic discipline and a practice-oriented profession

Social work simultaneously refers to many things: An academic discipline, a research-based, practice-oriented profession combined with a related service system, as well as social movements committed to the enhancement of human well-being. The groups and individuals that social work focuses on and collaborates with are often identified as vulnerable, oppressed, or living in poverty. In their own ways, from the premise

DOI: 10.4324/9781003334002-18

of collective responsibility, the different branches of social work aspire to promote social change, social cohesion, and empowerment. While many other professions and disciplines share similar ideals of social justice, the strong foundation in an ethical and moral discourse is a distinctive feature of social work (International Federation of Social Workers (IFSW), 2018; Witkin, 2003, p. 239).

With origins in the practices of both state and religion-based forms of organized care and support for those in need, social work has its roots in philanthropic work, community-organizing, and social movements. As an academic discipline, however, social work has only been formed globally over the last 50 years, with significant differences between countries. During this time, it has seen a long development of professionalization and an extension of its fields of action and responsibilities. Although an academic discipline in its own right, social work has interfaces with many other disciplines, such as psychology or social and public policy, and it employs theoretical and methodological inputs from other social and behavioural sciences. While social work has also been identified as part of social movements or as voluntary work, globally the trend has been a gradual professionalization of social work practice and academicization of social work education. Especially in the Nordic welfare states such as Finland, social work is closely entwined with the public system of welfare services.

As a profession, social work has its own ethical standards, manifested in international and national social work codes of ethics. According to the global definition of the social work profession (IFSW and International Association of Schools of Social Work (IASSW), 2014), the principles of social justice, human rights, collective responsibility, and respect for diversities are central to social work. On a general level, social workers cooperate with people in attempts to solve social problems and provide support for individuals and communities, ideally promoting social change on a structural and political level. Whatever the status and local organizational structures, social work is expected to encompass community work, health care services, and political processes for greater equality and inclusiveness of societies (*e.g.*, Ranta-Tyrkkö, 2010, p. 307). However, in the service infrastructures of modern welfare states, social workers are mainly directed to work at the micro level with individual service-users, and less on the community level.

The ecosocial paradigm in social work

The acknowledgement of the importance of the physical environment in social work can be traced back to its early beginnings as a profession and discipline (Närhi and Matthies, 2016; Stamm, 2021b; Staub-Bernasconi, 1989). During that time, in the late 19th century, urban or built environments started to be a concern for the forerunners of today's social workers. This included, among other issues, questions regarding air and water quality, waste removal, sanitation, and healthy food (*e.g.*, Waris, 2016). In the USA, these early, environmentally aware social workers, among them Jane Addams, often had strong links to the Chicago School of Sociology and especially urban sociology. They analyzed the living conditions of (migrant) workers in cities and developed methods and interventions to tackle problems of the urban environment in cooperation with the inhabitants. These methods and interventions led to a gradual improvement in the living conditions of the urban poor in industrialized countries. However, after World War II, in the globally hegemonic western social work, notions of the environment narrowed to perceiving it primarily as social, cultural, and economic, but excluding to a greater extent any connection to the natural environment (Närhi and Matthies, 2016).

Ecosocial work, overlapping with concepts such as environmental, ecological, or green social work, is built on the premise that humans are part of, and dependent on, the web of life on Earth. Hence, the human responsibility is to safeguard, and at a minimum not overly harm, the delicate balance of ecosystems and other complex interconnected systems that life on Earth depends on. Thus, ecosocial work has been critically questioning the growth-based economic foundation of the existing welfare states and social work (Matthies, 2001). For the time being, concurrent ecological crises, which are chiefly caused by extractivist overconsumption of natural resources, particularly by overconsuming population groups and economic sectors globally, endanger the continuity of many life forms, and in the long run humanity itself. While this alone challenges the ethical justification and meaningfulness of extractivist relationships with "nature" (Pihlström, 2020), it contradicts social work's mission to protect those who are vulnerable, marginalized, or in poverty. Rather, the environmental crises both deepen and cause new forms of vulnerability and marginalization (Ranta-Tyrkkö and Närhi, 2021). Furthermore, social work must deal with the possible negative consequences of environmental policies, such as rising energy poverty, for marginalized and vulnerable groups.

Ecosocial work strives to contribute to a profound and fair sustainability transition, as well as the widespread adoption of an ecosocial paradigm in social work and societies at large (Matthies and Närhi, 2017). Therefore, ecosocial work aspires to a deeper and transformative approach to sustainability in social work practice, including a critical evaluation of its own views of the world and subsequent reconfiguration of the place of humans within the natural world (Boetto *et al.*, 2020). The climate crisis and other life-threatening planetary scale environmental changes illustrate that human beings need to fundamentally reconfigure their relationship to planet Earth and its life forms. However, for modern social work, which stems largely from the same anthropocentric and modernist worldview as the current environmental problems, this presents a paradigmatic, and thus immense ontological, institutional, and practical challenge. Nonetheless, while still far from mainstream and not widely identified within the social work profession, recognition of and interest in ecosocial work has rapidly grown during the past two decades as a research area and theoretical development, having an increasing impact on education and practice developments (*ibid.*; Krings *et al.*, 2018; Matthies, Krings and Stamm, 2020; Ranta-Tyrkkö and Närhi, 2021).

The ecosocial framework has much in common with the critical, structural, indigenous, and feminist approaches in the field of social work, all of which carry a broad understanding of the person-in-environment concept and an interest in the dynamics of power (Coates, 2003; Coates and Gray, 2012; Närhi and Matthies, 2016). Moreover, they are linked with and contribute to currently evolving, interdisciplinary discussions on post-anthropocentric and posthuman (*e.g.*, Bozalek and Pease, 2021), as well as decolonizing social work (Clarke and Yellow Bird, 2021). Recognizing that even global change is made locally, the task of ecosocial work is to pursue a variety of locally meaningful pathways towards greater sustainability. In doing so, one of its priorities is to ensure that social work clients, and in general people with lesser resources and political and economic power, have both access to and a say over sustainable choices and lifestyles. In other words, sustainability and environmental justice can be considered as parallel and aligned principles of social work, together with human rights and social justice (see also Ife, 2018). Notwithstanding the clear need for a comprehensive systemic renewal, ecosocial work has heretofore proceeded mostly from within existing systems. Often, ecosocial work has meant promoting or downright organizing niches of fairer and more sustainable everyday practices, income earning possibilities, relationships, and well-being.

Ecosocial work identifies on a practical level, first, a strong link between social and environmental problems, because marginalized groups often suffer from both environmental and social injustice. Second, regarding solutions, the ecosocial framework brings the social and the environmental dimension together. This means, among other things, that nature can be seen as a resource that could be (re)discovered by social workers, for example, by recognizing and utilizing the healing power of the natural environment and animal companions, such as in various forms of nature and/or animal-assisted care. Moreover, various activities have been organized, for example, around re- and upcycling, to provide both sustainable income opportunities and to promote resource-sparing ways of life. Third, ecosocial work involves an obligation to social workers, together with their clients, to contribute to more sustainable societies, which can mean considering planetary well-being as a new goal of the profession (*cf.*, Stamm, 2021a). This proposed obligation can be identified independent of the social work approach. It can play a role in individual, clinical social work, in group-based or community approaches but also in structural or political social work aspiring for change at societal and policy levels (Boetto, 2017; Närhi and Matthies, 2018).

Planetary well-being and its relationship with the ecosocial paradigm in social work

As a goal, planetary well-being overlaps in numerous ways with the objectives of ecosocial work. Emphasizing the integrity of the Earth system and ecosystem processes as the foundation of life, it brings together both social, humanistic, and natural scientific knowledge. In line with the concept of planetary well-being

(Kortetmäki *et al.*, 2021), proponents of ecosocial work often stipulate a shift from an anthropocentric worldview to an ecocentric (or simply ecosocial) one (*cf.*, Gray and Coates, 2012; Powers and Rinkel, 2019; Rambaree, Powers and Smith, 2019). Social work further relies heavily on needs theories and emphasizes their connections to human rights and social justice. The focus on systems and processes, inherent in the planetary well-being concept as a precondition for the satisfaction of needs, is also familiar to social work (*e.g.*, Hollstein-Brinkmann and Staub-Bernasconi, 2005). However, the focus usually remains on the individual person, and systems are often used to describe various aspects of the social environment of a social work client, such as the family system, the work life system or the cultural or religious system that a person is embedded in. Finally, the planetary well-being approach addresses the problem of global inequality, which is an important issue for social work globally. However, for the time being, social work is largely stuck in national frameworks that do not support and instead actually hinder global views and problem-solving (Ranta-Tyrkkö, 2017, p. 115).

The overlap between the concept of planetary well-being and the ecosocial paradigm in social work is already manifested in the concept of well-being. The term is highlighted in the current global definition of the social work profession. The last sentence of this global focal point for social workers states: "Underpinned by theories of social work, social sciences, humanities and Indigenous knowledge, social work engages people and structures to address life challenges and enhance well-being" (IFSW and IASSW, 2014). As with the term environment, in social work the notion of well-being is mostly understood as human well-being, emphasizing human needs (Gamble, 2012). However, based on the assumption that well-being is a fundamentally important concept of social work, many scholars and advocates of the ecosocial paradigm have made attempts to further develop the understanding of well-being in social work (Peeters, 2016; Powers, Rinkel and Kumar, 2021). Peeters, for example, argues that in times of the ecological crisis the idea that well-being follows from high material prosperity must be revised. The emphasis should be on the quality of human relationships and the relationship with nature (Peeters, 2016, p. 178). Other scholars suggest the introduction of concepts such as holistic or mutual well-being, or "true well-being for the Web of Life" (Powers, Rinkel and Kumar, 2021, p. 5). To strive for holistic well-being in social work would mean to shift towards a non-anthropocentric, or ecocentric worldview (*cf.*, Rambaree, Powers and Smith, 2019). The guiding principle for such a worldview would be ecological justice, which seeks to preserve the integrity of the natural world, among other things, and ascribes to nonhuman nature an intrinsic value irrespective of its value for human beings (Gray *et al.*, 2013, p. 321). The underlying ethical principle is the equality of all living beings (Sterba, 2014).

The concept of environmental justice can be seen as subordinated or anthropocentric because it adheres to a human perspective, emphasizing distributional, representational, and procedural justice (*cf.*, Kivimaa *et al.*, 2021; Schlosberg, 2007). Environmental justice is a concept strongly connected to the US-American context, where it originated in the Black civil rights movement. Later, it also incorporated other marginalized groups that faced both racism and environmental hazards at the same time (Krings and Copic, 2020). In the context of the climate crisis, environmental justice has been incorporated into the concept of climate justice. Given that the different effects of global warming on different countries and peoples are well documented, climate justice points to imbalances in bearing the brunt of the climate crisis both within and between nation states.

Globally, people living in poverty are commonly affected more harshly by the changing climate, with the impact of extreme weather conditions, such as heat waves or floods, as well as by climate change mitigation measures, such as increasing energy costs. In social work, increasing numbers of scholars insist on taking these effects more seriously and integrating them in assessments and the methods of social work practitioners. Both principles, environmental and ecological justice, follow the same direction but simultaneously deviate in some regards. Both go beyond the traditional notions of social justice in social work, which do not consider relations to the natural environment, and both ascribe an intrinsic value to the natural world. Combined with the principle of sustainability, environmental justice must also be widened (as intergenerational justice) to accommodate the needs and rights of future people (Stamm, 2021b).

In summary, the concept of planetary well-being and the ecosocial paradigm in social work share a lot of common ground. This includes a holistic view on well-being, which goes beyond human needs and seeks to achieve ecological justice. At least in theory, also global inequalities are highlighted in both approaches. The question of whose needs should be fulfilled individually to abolish inequalities among humans, while at the same time considering the well-being of other forms of life, remains open. These dilemmas are partly discussed in the next section.

Challenges in applying the planetary well-being concept in social work

To apply the planetary well-being concept in social work would mean to reconsider social work ethics. In global social work statements on ethics, as well as in national codes of ethics in general, human rights and social justice are laid down as the main principles. In practice, however, much of the ethical deliberation focuses on worker–client relations in an implicitly national context (Ranta-Tyrkkö, 2017). The planetary well-being concept, as the more specific ecosocial paradigm, would stipulate to go beyond these traditional principles and values of social work, and to build bridges to the natural environment and recognize its value for social work. In environmental ethics, which the planetary well-being concept is partly based on, these two perspectives are identified as anthropocentric and non-anthropocentric ethics (Boylan, 2014; Light and Rolston, 2003). For social work, as a human-centred profession and discipline, striking a balance between the (moral) anthropocentric and the non-anthropocentric perspectives seems crucial.

Sterba (2014) argues that a reconciliation between anthropocentric and non-anthropocentric ethics is possible. His line of reasoning is of value also for social work and its connection to the planetary well-being concept. As a starting point, he acknowledges the intrinsic value of all species but he argues that in certain circumstances the value of human beings, or in other words the well-being of humans, can be prioritized. He introduces three principles that could be seen as common ground between the two described ethical perspectives, allowing a reconciliation between both:

1 A Principle of Human Defence: Actions that defend oneself and other human beings against harmful aggression are permissible even when they necessitate killing or harming animals or plants (Sterba, 2014, pp. 164–166).
2 A Principle of Human Preservation: Actions that are necessary for meeting one's basic needs or the basic needs of other human beings are permissible even when they require aggressing against the basic needs of animals and plants (*ibid.*).
3 A Principle of Disproportionality: Actions that meet nonbasic or luxury needs of humans are prohibited when they aggress against the basic needs of animals and plants (*ibid.*).

Even though his argumentation is challenged by other environmental ethics scholars (*cf.*, Steverson, 2014), it can serve as a starting point for a revised social work ethic that would still focus on human well-being but acknowledge the intrinsic value of the natural world as well. Regarding the third principle, there has been a related debate in social work theory (Staub-Bernasconi, 2018). Apart from the needs of animals and plants, an important question is what basic and luxury needs are. In social work this difference has also been discussed using the terms *needs* versus *wishes* (*ibid.*). Some scholars oppose the idea of any objective needs. Ife, for example, suggests that needs are "by their very nature, value-laden" (Ife, 2012, p. 126). They depend, according to Ife, to a great extent on individual views of the clients of social work as well as on the values of social workers themselves. Without having the space to elaborate the theoretical foundations and standpoints of the debate here, it could be concluded based on Sterba's argumentation that social work would, in the future, not only have to differentiate between basic and luxury needs of humans but would have to consider the needs of the natural world as well (where only basic needs exist). Notably, in the planetary well-being framework, only basic needs are referred to as needs.

Taking the position that the needs of the natural world could be allowed to be subordinated only if basic human needs are at stake could pave the way for a critical anthropocentrism in social work (Grunwald, 2016). The task of reconciliation between (moral) anthropocentric and non-anthropocentric ethics can also be used for linking environmental and ecological justice. On a general level, both concept-pairs share a common ground. We argue that for social work theory and social work ethics a better understanding of these concepts and their overlap is needed.

This could then serve as a basis for discussions on the concrete implications of the planetary well-being concept for social work.

The implications or challenges for social work practice are manifold. First, it must be stated that social workers take action based on certain mandates. Traditionally, the common understanding was that of a double mandate between support and control: One by the state, which was associated with the term *control*, and the second one coming from the clients, which represented *support*. Social workers in this respect had to balance and handle tensions between the two tasks—supporting and controlling. Swiss social work scholar, Staub-Bernasconi, has added a third mandate to these. She argues for a self-given, professional mandate that is based on both social work's scientific knowledge base and an ethical foundation. The latter consists mainly of social work's main principles of human rights and social justice and is broadly laid down in international and national ethic statements and codes (Staub-Bernasconi, 2016, 2018). In recent years, an extension or adjustment of the third mandate, to include the natural environment and sustainability goals, has been suggested (Stamm, 2021b). However, a direct mandate from plants or animals cannot be given. All three mandates might only implicitly include a consideration of the intrinsic value of the nonhuman nature. To date, however, this component has been rarely discussed.

While some social work codes of ethics already mention environmental justice as a principle, the concept as such is left undefined and without operationalizing for social work practice. This makes it hard for social workers in the current situation to know what they could or should do in regard to environmental justice or promoting the well-being of nonhuman nature. Moreover, as they are trained to consider human well-being, knowledge about other species or the natural environment is usually not part of their education. When some social workers or social work organizations nonetheless pay attention to the natural environment, the reasoning behind this is usually that it is integral to the social environment of the clients. The above notwithstanding, many social workers, professional and non-professional, are very likely to be concerned with the well-being of nonhuman nature but lack knowledge of how to take it into account and promote it in their own work (Ranta-Tyrkkö and Närhi, 2021).

Part of a classical social work diagnosis is an assessment phase, in which a problem is identified together with the clients. Such an assessment can have different components, such as looking at the needs, rights, and resources of clients (*cf.*, Arnegger, 2005). Based on the assessment, generally certain goals are set, linked with methods to achieve them. In individualized forms of social work, the natural environment might play a role, but only when it comes to environmental hazards or amenities. This can mean a combined form of social and environmental or ecological justice from the perspective of individual problems.

Regarding the above-mentioned principle of disproportionality, in most cases the needs of social work clients can be considered basic needs. However, the implementation of the planetary well-being concept might be more likely to be successful in social work on the community level or in structural social work. Here, planetary processes and systems can be considered when assessing problems and possible solutions. This could also include the life situation of more affluent people, who might overconsume natural resources and who are usually not considered representatives of social work clients. In a community, such as a village, small city, or neighbourhood, it is common to balance different needs and interests of various individuals or groups. Moreover, it would be possible to combine social work on the community level with a consideration of the needs of nonhuman species. For example, an animal population which might be "part" of the community, as well as the ecosystem in a broader sense.

Conclusion

In this chapter, we introduced social work as an academic discipline and a research-based, practice-oriented profession and as part of social movements. During the last 20 years the rise of a new ecosocial paradigm has evolved in social work. It coincides in many aspects with the concept of planetary well-being and it can be used as another reference point to highlight the interconnectedness between human beings, other species and the ecosystem of planet earth. It can further remind social workers not only to consider and differentiate between basic needs and wishes (of people living today and in the future), but also to pay attention to the needs of nonhuman life on earth. Social work cannot remain on the more abstract level of systems and processes only, because it is involved in the daily lives of individuals, families, and groups and their social problems, a situation which makes such a holistic view an immense challenge. In terms of environmental ethics, it might mean striking a balance between (moral or critical) anthropocentric and non-anthropocentric viewpoints. Though the concept of planetary well-being has its limits, it is a useful steppingstone for social work to use for looking beyond traditional ethics and practices. It can help social workers and their clients to reconsider their role regarding the well-being of other species and entire ecosystems.

Acknowledgements

The authors thank Amy Krings for her valuable comments on earlier drafts of the text. The authors did not receive any additional funding.

References

Arnegger, M. (2005) 'Soziale Arbeit als Menschenrechtsprofession in der diagnostischen Praxis', *Neue Praxis*, 6, pp. 682–694.

Boetto, H. (2017) 'A transformative eco-social model: Challenging modernist assumptions in social work', *British Journal of Social Work*, 47, pp. 48–67. https://doi.org/10.1093/bjsw/bcw149

Boetto, H. *et al.* (2020) 'Raising awareness of transformative ecosocial work: Participatory action research with Australian practitioners', *International Journal of Social Welfare*, 29(4), pp. 300–309. https://doi.org/10.1111/ijsw.12445

Boylan, M. (ed.) (2014) *Environmental Ethics.* 2nd edn. Malden, MA: Wiley Blackwell.

Bozalek, V. and Pease, B. (eds.) (2021) *Post-Anthropocentric Social Work: Critical Posthuman and New Materialist Perspectives*. London and New York: Routledge.

Clarke, K. and Yellow Bird, M. (2021) *Decolonizing Pathways towards Integrative Healing in Social Work*. London and New York: Routledge.

Coates, J. (2003) *Ecology and Social Work: Toward a New Paradigm*. Halifax: Fernwood Pub.

Coates, J. and Gray, M. (2012) 'The environment and social work: An overview and introduction', *International Journal of Social Welfare*, 21(3), pp. 230–238. https://doi.org/10.1111/j.1468-2397.2011.00851.x

Gamble, D.N. (2012) 'Well-being in a globalized world: Does social work know how to make it happen?', *Journal of Social Work Education*, 48(4), pp. 669–689. https://doi.org/10.5175/JSWE.2012.201100125

Gray, M. and Coates, J. (2012) 'Environmental ethics for social work: Social work's responsibility to the nonhuman world: Environmental ethics for social work', *International Journal of Social Welfare*, 21(3), pp. 239–247. https://doi.org/10.1111/j.1468-2397.2011.00852.x

Gray, M., Coates, J. and Hetherington, T. (2013) *Environmental Social Work*. 1st edn. New York: Routledge.

Grunwald, A. (2016) *Nachhaltigkeit verstehen: Arbeiten an der Bedeutung nachhaltiger Entwicklung*. München: oekom.

Hollstein-Brinkmann, H. and Staub-Bernasconi, S. (eds.) (2005) *Systemtheorien im Vergleich: was leisten Systemtheorien für die Soziale Arbeit? Versuch eines Dialogs*. Wiesbaden: VS Verl für Sozialwissenschaften.

Ife, J. (2012) *Human Rights and Social Work. Towards Rights-Based Practice*. 3rd edn. Cambridge: University Press.

Ife, J. (2018) 'Social work and human rights – The 'human', the 'social' and the collapse of modernity', in Spatscheck, C. and Steckelberg, C. (eds.) *Menschenrechte und Soziale Arbeit. Konzeptionelle Grundlagen, Gestaltungsfelder und Umsetzung einer Realutopie*. Opladen and Toronto: Barbara Budrich, pp. 21–35.

IFSW (2018) *Global Social Work Statement of Ethical Principles*. Available at: https://www.ifsw.org/global-social-work-statement-of-ethical-principles/ (Accessed: 14 December 2022).

IFSW and IASSW (2014) *Global Definition of Social Work. Commentary Notes for the Global Definition of Social Work*. Available at: https://www.ifsw.org/what-is-social-work/global-definition-of-social-work/ (Accessed: 14 December 2022).

Kivimaa, P. *et al.* (2021) 'How to consider Justice in Climate Policy? Discussion Paper', The Finnish Climate Change Panel, 5/2021. Available at: https://www.ilmastopaneeli.fi/wp-content/uploads/2021/12/Finnish-Climate-Change-Panel_how-to-consider-justice-in-climate-policy_publication-5-2021.pdf (Accessed: 14 December 2022).

Kortetmäki, T. *et al.* (2021) 'Planetary well-being', *Humanities and Social Sciences Communications*, 8, 258. https://doi.org/10.1057/s41599-021-00899-3

Krings, A. and Copic, C. (2020) 'Environmental justice organizing in a gentrifying community: Navigating dilemmas of representation, issue selection, and recruitment', *Families in Society: The Journal of Contemporary Social Services*, 102(2), pp. 154–166. https://doi.org/10.1177/1044389420952247

Krings, A. *et al.* (2018) 'Environmental social work in the disciplinary literature, 1991–2015', *International Social Work*, 63(3), pp. 275-290. https://doi.org/10.1177/0020872818788397

Light, A. and Rolston, H. (eds.) (2003) *Environmental Ethics: An Anthology*. Malden, MA: Blackwell Pub.

Matthies, A.-L. (2001) 'Perspectives of eco-social sustainability in social work', in Matthies, A-L., Närhi, K. and Ward, D. (eds.) *The Eco-Social Approach in Social Work*. Jyväskylä: Sophi, pp. 127–152.

Matthies, A.-L., Krings, A. and Stamm I. (2020) 'Research-based knowledge about social work and sustainability', *International Journal of Social Welfare*, 29(4), pp. 297–299. https://doi.org/10.1111/ijsw.12462

Matthies, A.-L. and Närhi, K. (eds.) (2017) *The Ecosocial Transition of Societies. The Contribution of Social Work and Social Policy*. New York: Routledge.

Närhi, K. and Matthies, A.-L. (2016) 'Conceptual and historical analysis of ecological social work', in McKinnon, J. and Alston, M. (eds.) *Ecological Social Work*. Hampshire: Palgrave, pp. 21–38.

Närhi, K. and Matthies, A.-L. (2018) 'The ecosocial approach in social work as a framework for structural social work', *International Social Work*, 61(4), pp. 490–502. https://doi.org/10.1177/0020872816644663

Peeters, J. (2016) 'A safe and just space for humanity: The need for a new concept of wellbeing', in McKinnon, J. and Alston, M. (eds.) *Ecological Social Work*. Hampshire: Palgrave, pp. 177–196.

Pihlström, S. (2020) 'Ilmastonmuutos eksistentiaalisena uhkana', in Kyllönen, S. and Oksanen, M. (eds.) *Ilmastonmuutos ja filosofia*. Helsinki: Gaudeamus, pp. 297–316.

Powers, M. and Rinkel, M. (2019) 'Overview. Social work promoting community and environmental sustainability, within and beyond the UN Sustainable Development Goals: A degrowth critique', in Rinkel, M. and Powers, M. (eds.) *Social Work Promoting Community and Environmental Sustainability: A Workbook for Global Social Workers and Educators*. Rheinfelden: IFSW, pp. 24–35.

Powers, M., Rinkel, M. and Kumar, P. (2021) 'Co-creating a 'Sustainable New Normal' for social work and beyond: Embracing an ecosocial worldview', *Sustainability*, 13(19), 10941. https://doi.org/10.3390/su131910941

Rambaree, K., Powers, M. and Smith R.J. (2019) 'Ecosocial work and social change in community practice', *Journal of Community Practice*, 27(3–4), pp. 205–212. https://doi.org/10.1080/10705422.2019.1660516

Ranta-Tyrkkö, S. (2010) *At the Intersection of Theatre and Social Work in Orissa, India: Natya Chetana and Its Theatre*. Acta Universitatis Tamperensis 1503. Tampere: Tampere University Press. http://urn.fi/urn:isbn:978-951-44-8003-4

Ranta-Tyrkkö, S. (2017) 'Sosiaalityön tulevaisuuden etiikka epävarmuuden ja ympäristökriisien maailmassa', in Enroos, R., Mäntysaari, M. and Ranta-Tyrkkö, S. (eds.) *Mielekäs tutkimus: näkökulmia sosiaalityön tutkimuksen missioihin*. Tampere: Tampere University Press, pp. 113–138. http://urn.fi/URN:ISBN:978-952-03-0606-9

Ranta-Tyrkkö, S. and Närhi, K. (2021) 'Striving to strengthen the ecosocial framework in social work in Finland', *Community Development Journal*, 56(4), pp. 608–625. https://doi.org/10.1093/cdj/bsab030

Schlosberg, D. (2007) *Defining Environmental Justice: Theories, Movements, and Nature*. Oxford: Oxford University Press. https://doi.org/10.1093/acprof:oso/9780199286294.001.0001

Stamm, I. (2021a) 'Ecosocial work and services for unemployed people: The challenge to integrate environmental and social sustainability', *Nordic Social Work Research*. https://doi.org/10.1080/2156857X.2021.1975154

Stamm, I. (2021b) *Ökologisch-kritische Soziale Arbeit. Geschichte, aktuelle Positionen und Handlungsfelder.* Opladen, Berlin and Toronto: Barbara Budrich. https://doi.org/10.2307/j.ctv1prssqj

Staub-Bernasconi, S. (1989) 'Soziale Arbeit und Ökologie 100 Jahre vor der ökologischen Wende', *Neue Praxis*, 19(4), pp. 283–309.

Staub-Bernasconi, S. (2016) 'Social work and human rights—Linking two traditions of human rights in social work', *Journal of Human Rights and Social Work*, 1(1), pp. 40–49. https://doi.org/10.1007/s41134-016-0005-0

Staub-Bernasconi, S. (2018) *Soziale Arbeit als Handlungswissenschaft: Soziale Arbeit auf dem Weg zu kritischer Professionalität.* 2nd edn. UTB Soziale Arbeit 2786. Opladen and Toronto: Budrich. https://doi.org/10.36198/9783838547930

Sterba, J.P. (2014) 'Reconciling anthropocentric and nonanthropocentric environmental ethics', in Boylan, M. (ed.) *Environmental Ethics*. 2nd edn. Malden, MA: Wiley Blackwell, pp. 163–175.

Steverson, B.K. (2014) 'On the reconciliation of anthropocentric and nonanthropocentric environmental ethics', in Boylan, M. (ed.) *Environmental Ethics*. 2nd edn. Malden, MA: Wiley Blackwell, pp. 176–186.

Waris, H. (2016) *Työläisyhteiskunnan syntyminen Helsingin Pitkänsillan pohjoispuolelle I-II*. Helsinki: Into.

Witkin, S. (2003) 'Päämääränä hyvän tekeminen. Pohdintoja ihmisoikeuksista ja etiikasta sosiaalityössä', in Laitinen, M. and Pohjola, A. (eds.) *Sosiaalisen vaihtuvat vastuut*. Jyväskylä: PS-kustannus, pp. 237–253.

PART V

Fostering transformation towards planetary well-being

14

EXTINCTION RISK INDICES FOR MEASURING AND PROMOTING PLANETARY WELL-BEING

Mikael Puurtinen, Kaisa J. Raatikainen, Jenna Purhonen, Nerea Abrego, Panu Halme, Janne S. Kotiaho, and Merja Elo

Introduction

The impact of human actions on Earth system and ecosystem processes has increased to a level that threatens the existence of diverse life-forms on the planet and harms human well-being. The leading direct drivers of ecosystem degradation and biodiversity loss are conversion of natural ecosystems for agricultural, urban, and other uses (*e.g.*, forestry), direct exploitation of populations on both land and sea, climate change, pollution, and transport of species outside their natural ranges (Intergovernmental Science-Policy Platform on Biodiversity and Ecosystem Services (IPBES), 2019).

Scientists widely agree that halting, and ultimately reversing, the negative trends in ecosystem degradation will require transformative changes across economic, social, political, and technological structures within and across nations (*ibid.*; Leclere *et al.*, 2020; Leadley *et al.*, 2022). However, navigating such transformative changes involves setting common goals and targets as well as managing the competing interests of different stakeholders (Harrop, 2011). In this chapter, we use existing biodiversity goals and targets as a point of departure and focus on one family of indices whose qualities we find particularly effective in guiding action and tracking progress towards planetary well-being.

To date, global efforts to halt ecosystem degradation and biodiversity loss have been unsuccessful. Nonetheless, most world governments have agreed to pursue the conservation of biological diversity by signing the 1992 UN Convention on Biological Diversity (CBD). In 2002, governments further agreed "to achieve by 2010 a significant reduction of the current rate of biodiversity loss", but this goal was not achieved (Morgera and Tsioumani, 2010). After failing to meet the 2010 target, governments across the globe approved the Strategic Plan for Biodiversity

DOI: 10.4324/9781003334002-20

2011–2020. The plan included 20 Aichi Biodiversity Targets and aimed to "take effective and urgent action to halt the loss of biodiversity" (CBD, 2010). Again, not one of the Aichi Biodiversity targets has been met in full (CBD, 2020).

The repeated failures in global biodiversity conservation have given rise to a debate on how the goals and targets of multilateral environmental agreements should be formulated to allow national implementation and monitoring of progress. For example, Butchart, Di Marco, and Watson (2016) found that the above-mentioned 20 Aichi targets in general suffer from ambiguity, lack of quantifiable elements, complexity, and redundancy, which together makes it difficult to stimulate and quantify progress. Green *et al.* (2019) found that more progress was made towards Aichi targets with elements that were measurable, realistic, unambiguous, and scalable, suggesting that such target qualities may make it easier for governments to interpret and translate into policies and actions. In December 2022, after four years of negotiations over the implementation intricacies of biodiversity goals and targets (Leadley *et al.*, 2022), governments adopted the Kunming-Montreal Global Biodiversity Framework and 23 action-oriented global targets to facilitate urgent action over the decade ending 2030 (CBD, 2022a). During the negotiations, particular attention was paid to the specificity and measurability of the targets.

Regardless of the above-mentioned associations between target qualities and ease of implementation, it is good to note that measurable targets in and of themselves do not guarantee success. A fitting example of this is Aichi target 12 from the 2010 CBD agreement: "By 2020 the extinction of known threatened species has been prevented and their conservation status, particularly of those most in decline, has been improved and sustained". Despite the relative ease of quantifying species extinctions and conservation status, these targets were not met, and the conservation status of species actually worsened between 2010 and 2020 (CBD, 2020). The successor of Aichi target 12 is the combination of Kunming-Montreal target 4 and goal A, which together produce a similar albeit slightly more ambitious and measurable version of the Aichi target: By 2030 we should "halt human induced extinction of known threatened species" and "by 2050, extinction rate and risk of all species are reduced tenfold" (CBD, 2022a).

The key problem in multilateral environmental agreements seems to be the difficulty of getting countries to commit to clearly defined targets with assigned responsibilities for necessary actions. While the 2015 Paris Agreement to hold the increase in global average temperature to well below 2°C above pre-industrial levels has fostered climate action, the action has not, at least to date, been sufficient to reach the target (Boehm *et al.*, 2022). One reason for this is that the agreement does not specify who should do what and how much; instead, countries independently decide their nationally determined contributions towards achieving the global target.

Lack of assignability or responsibility is also prevalent in the target and goal setting of the Convention on Biological Diversity. Concerning the Aichi targets, it states that "[p]arties are invited to set their own targets within this flexible framework, taking into account national needs and priorities, while also bearing in mind national contributions to the achievement of the global targets". Almost the same escape clauses are embedded in the text of the Kunming-Montreal targets: "Actions to reach these targets should be implemented … taking into account national circumstances, priorities and socioeconomic conditions". Thus, the agreements do not bind each and every party to take action, but the responsibility is diluted among all signatories.

Agreeing on clear responsibilities is obviously difficult in multilateral agreements. Yet without clear responsibilities the chances of achieving the targets are low. Maxwell *et al.* (2015) pointed out that in contentious issues with diverging stakeholder interests—like the protection of biodiversity—signatories find it easier to agree on targets that are worded ambiguously, are difficult to measure, or are so ambitious that they are clearly unachievable. Even though the signatories of the Convention on Biological Diversity are obliged to develop, implement, and report national biodiversity strategies and action plans that significantly contribute towards the global biodiversity agenda, it has simply proven to be too easy for the parties to wriggle out of the obligations due to the ambiguous goals and targets for which there are no quantifiable indicators.

In this chapter, we suggest that eliminating the human-induced extinction risk of all species is the ultimate goal of promoting planetary well-being, and argue that Red List Indices, which are based on the International Union for Conservation of Nature (IUCN) methodology for assessing species extinction risk, provide good indicators for monitoring and quantifying progress towards this goal. We first explain the links between planetary well-being and species extinction risk, then describe the relevant methodologies for extinction risk assessment and the Red List Index, and close by elucidating the benefits of the Red List Index as an indicator for monitoring success of global biodiversity policy and progress towards planetary well-being.

Linking planetary well-being and extinction risk

The relationship between planetary well-being and extinction risk of species and populations originates from the very definition of planetary well-being as

> a state in which the integrity of Earth system and ecosystem processes remains unimpaired to a degree that lineages can persist to the future as parts of ecosystems, and organisms (human and nonhuman) can realize their typical characteristics and capacities.
>
> *(Kortetmäki* et al.*, 2021)*

Thus, the essence and aim of planetary well-being is securing the integrity of ecosystem processes and the persistence of lineages (*i.e.*, groups of organisms with a shared genetic ancestry, distinct from other such groups). In the case of sexually reproducing organisms, species and populations constitute lineages at global and local scales, respectively. Before going into the details on how the persistence of lineages into the future can be quantified, let us explain why it is incorporated into the definition of planetary well-being in the first place.

The inclusion of the persistence of lineages in the definition of planetary well-being arises from three dimensions: Normative, systemic, and practical. First, the concept of planetary well-being is normative: It considers the well-being of both humans and nonhumans as intrinsically valuable and extends the scope of moral considerability to lineages and even to ecosystems. The survival of lineages is seen as a goal in itself (Chapter 2). Wiping out the outcomes of eons of evolutionary history and their future potential, that is, driving lineages to extinction, is considered immoral.

Second, the concept of planetary well-being is systemic: It is understood that life on Earth is a set of interlinked, interdependent systems, where the well-being of any system (*i.e.*, the functional integrity of the system) is dependent on the functioning of many other systems (Kortetmäki *et al.*, 2021). Lineages of living organisms are integral parts of the larger system of life on Earth. Hence, even if we may have difficulties in cataloguing and measuring the integrity of all Earth system and ecosystem processes, we can be confident that safeguarding lineages also serves to safeguard Earth system and ecosystem processes. The logic also works in reverse: If we see that lineages are at risk of disappearing from ecosystems, we have good reasons to believe that some ecosystem processes are failing to provide for the needs of those lineages. Lineages are thus essential parts of larger systems, and the risk of loss of lineages can be seen as an indication of larger system failure.

Third, planetary well-being is meant to be a practical concept for facilitating action and transformative change. This means that we should be able to assess the state of planetary well-being, identify the necessary actions to improve it, and quantify the progress towards planetary well-being. We suggest that assessments of extinction risks for species and populations—which are estimates of lineage persistence and thus directly relevant for planetary well-being—offer just that: An ideal database for derivation of indicators with which we can monitor the development of extinction risk of species. In addition to indicating the risk of extinction, these assessments also include information about the main direct threats that must be mitigated to actively reduce and eliminate the risk of extinction.

The IUCN Red List of Threatened Species

The IUCN Red List of Threatened Species (hereafter Red List) is a methodology for assessing the extinction risk of species with clearly defined science-based criteria. The methodology has been developed since the 1960s in numerous different expert groups, and it is the most objective, comprehensive, and commonly used approach for evaluating the risk of extinction at global, regional, and national levels (Mace *et al.*, 2008; IUCN, 2012a,b).

The IUCN Red List classification utilizes data of past, current, and projected population sizes and geographic ranges to assign species to extinction risk categories (see Figure 14.1). By 2023, the global extinction risk of more than 150,000 species has been assessed.[1] Because extinction risk assessment requires a considerable amount of work and adequate data regarding the ecology, distribution, and population size of species, assessments have been carried out mainly for well-studied species, especially vertebrates.

The IUCN Red List employs five categories of extinction risk, corresponding to increasing risk of impending extinction, ranging from Least Concern (LC) to Critically Endangered (CR). In addition, species that have disappeared from their past natural range, either regionally or globally, are placed in one of the appropriate Extinct categories: Regionally Extinct (RE), Extinct in the Wild (EW), or Extinct (EX). For instance, if a species has less than 50 mature individuals left, or its population has reduced by ≥80% over ten years or three generations (whichever is longer), the species is classified as Critically Endangered. This corresponds

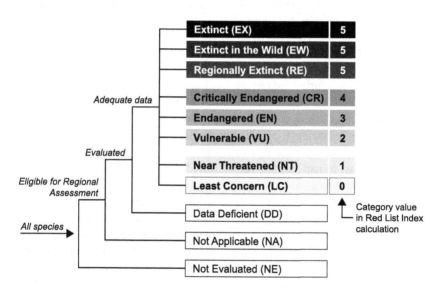

FIGURE 14.1 IUCN Red List assessments assign evaluated species to extinction risk categories (or to the Data Deficient category when there is insufficient data to assess extinction risk). The regional Red Lists have two categories that are not present in the global Red List: Not Applicable (NA) and Regionally Extinct (RE). A species is listed as Not Applicable if it occurs in the focal region but has been excluded from the regional Red List for a specific reason, and is listed as Regionally Extinct if it is now extinct in the region but still occurs in its natural range outside the region. The Red List Index (RLI) is a summary statistic portraying the mean risk of extinction for a species utilizing the category weight portrayed in the figure (see main text for further details).

roughly to at least a 50% chance of extinction in the following ten years or three generations, whichever is longer (IUCN, 2012b).

In addition to classifying species according to their risk of extinction, the Red List includes data on direct threats to species survival, following a comprehensive standard lexicon (*i.e.*, systematic classification) (Salafsky *et al.*, 2008). Direct threats are those proximate human activities or processes (*e.g.*, livestock farming and ranching, urban sprawl, or logging) that currently have, have had or will have an impact on species endangerment. The data on direct threats allows general comparisons of threat types with respect to biodiversity loss (*e.g.*, IPBES, 2019, p. 253). For each threat, the Red List assessment identifies whether it is past, current, or likely to occur in the future ("timing"); the proportion of the total population affected ("scope"); as well as the overall declines caused by the threat ("severity") (https://www.iucnredlist.org/resources/threat-classification-scheme). Altogether, this information can be used to identify actions that can help to mitigate threats to species survival (see *e.g.*, Kyrkjeeide *et al.*, 2021).

The IUCN Red List evaluates the global status of species, but exclusive focus on global extinction risk does not give sufficient attention to protection of biodiversity outside global biodiversity hotspots (Purvis, 2020). Therefore, the IUCN system for assessing extinction risk has been developed for regional and national levels, with appropriate modifications for dealing with non-native species and species that do not regularly breed in the focal area (IUCN, 2012a). Indeed, regional and national Red Lists offer valuable information for conservation at the relevant level of jurisdiction, which in the implementation phase of global biodiversity policies is generally countries (Kyrkjeeide *et al.*, 2021). While "region" and "regional" can refer to geographic units above or below the national level, in what follows we refer, for brevity, to national and regional Red Lists as national Red Lists and to regions as countries.

National Red List assessments are especially valuable for countries that cover only a small part of a species' range and have few endemic species, that is, species that occur only in that country (*e.g.*, Finland, see Raimondo *et al.*, 2022). Within their borders such countries can do relatively little direct conservation work, such as protection, management, and restoration, to influence the global risk of extinction (however, the impacts of transborder effects via for instance pollution or damming of rivers should not be dismissed). Nonetheless, such countries are responsible for the survival of populations within their own borders. National Red Lists are developed in particular to assess the likelihood of survival of populations within the borders of countries. Of specific importance in national Red Lists is the Regionally Extinct category, which is used for species that are now extinct from the country but still occur in their natural range outside the country. National Red Lists thus manifest the disappearance of populations from a country that often would not be evident in the global Red List. However, it is also possible for a species to be stable within a country yet declining in other parts of its range. In this case, the status of the species may be better in the national Red List than in the global Red List. Such species should be given particular attention at the national level because of their significance for the species' global status (IUCN, 2012a). To facilitate such consideration, it might be worthwhile in the national Red List assessments to always report the global Red List status alongside the national one.

While the global and national Red Lists are arguably the most objective and thorough sources for data on extinction risk, they are not all-encompassing. The assessed species are biased towards terrestrial ecosystems and vertebrates, while for instance insects, plants, and fungi are underrepresented. Also, coverage is poorer in the global South, where biodiversity is richer, reflecting the state of ecological knowledge in general (Bachman *et al.*, 2019). However, there are ongoing efforts to fill in the data gaps.

Red List Index (RLI)

To gain an overall idea of the state of biodiversity, the wealth of data in the Red Lists can be compiled into an index. The Red List Index (RLI) is a statistic that indicates the mean risk of extinction for a group of species (*s*) at any given time (*t*). It is calculated as:

$$RLI_t = 1 - \frac{\sum_s W_{c(s,t)}}{W_{max} \cdot N}$$

where the category weights (W_c) of all included species (*s*) at time (*t*) are summed and then divided by the product of the number of included species (*N*) and the maximum category weight ($W_{max} = 5$) (see Figure 14.1) (Butchart *et al.*, 2007).

The RLI takes values between zero and one: Zero means that all included species are extinct, one means that all included species are in the Least Concern category. The Red List Index thus gives a simple and intuitive measure of the risk of extinction for the group of included species.

If eliminating the human-induced extinction risk of all species is considered the ultimate goal of promoting planetary well-being, the deviation of RLI values from one would serve as a specific and quantifiable indicator of how far we are from achieving that goal. Moreover, RLI values calculated for the same set of species diachronically are ideal for monitoring progress over time because changes can be interpreted as signifying improving or deteriorating planetary well-being. Perhaps it is worth mentioning here that for the purpose of monitoring progress, only those changes in extinction risk category where the reason for the change is genuine (*i.e.*, threats, distribution or population size have changed) should be included; non-genuine category changes (*e.g.*, due to improved knowledge, revised taxonomy, or changes to classification criteria) should not be included (IUCN, 2023c).

The global RLI is calculated from the global Red List and currently includes only mammals, birds, amphibians, corals, and cycads (IUCN, 2023a). However, even if it were comprehensive across taxa, the global Red List Index alone would not be a very good indicator of planetary well-being. This is because most of the world's biodiversity is located in the tropics, and a comprehensive global RLI would thus effectively be a description of the state of tropical biodiversity. In other words, degradation of ecosystems in less biodiverse regions, like boreal forests, would not be detected in the global RLI. This is an undesirable feature, as planetary well-being is about integrity of ecosystem processes and persistence of lineages irrespective of the species richness of the region. However, Red List Indices compiled at the national level can be good indicators of planetary well-being, as we will argue below.

There are two ways to calculate country-specific RLIs, and they produce results that can be interpreted differently. The first way, "disaggregated global RLI", uses global Red List assessments to derive global extinction risk and adjusts each species' contribution to the country-specific index by weighting it by the fraction of the species' distribution occurring within the country (Rodrigues *et al.*, 2014; Raimondo *et al.*, 2022). Disaggregated global RLIs for each country are available on the IUCN Red List website (see IUCN, 2023b). However, as was discussed above in the context of national and global Red Lists, the disaggregated global RLI as an indicator of planetary well-being suffers from the characteristic that it is a poor biodiversity indicator for countries that cover only a small part of the species' ranges and have few endemic species.

The second way to calculate country-specific RLI is to conduct national Red List assessments (see above) and compile a "national RLI" for the assessed species. Investment in national RLI is worthwhile as it is a better indicator of species conservation status in any given country compared to global or disaggregated global RLI. Conducting national species assessments also builds capacities and knowledge for designing appropriate conservation actions and provides the needed opportunity to monitor the impacts of conservation measures taken nationally (Raimondo *et al.*, 2022). For biodiverse countries in particular, another option is to conduct assessments on a sample of a few hundred or more species per taxonomic group. When conducted correctly, such "sampled RLI" method has been shown to be able to detect trends that can be extrapolated beyond the conservation status of the sampled species (Baillie *et al.*, 2008; Henriques *et al.*, 2020). Perhaps it is worth mentioning here that despite its usefulness, national RLIs cannot be mathematically compiled into a global RLI. Specifically, it would not be appropriate to take an average of national RLIs to track global progress towards planetary well-being: Such calculation could mask biodiversity loss in megadiverse countries under the better performance of countries that are less biodiverse but more numerous. Instead, global progress could be tracked by nations showing improvement in their country-specific RLI.

Conclusions

In order to improve planetary well-being it is critical to be able to measure it (see Chapter 15). Above, we have explained why species extinction risk is a good indicator of planetary well-being, and how this risk can be estimated in practice with the IUCN Red List assessments and associated Red List Indices. The Red List can also be used to identify the direct threats that need to be mitigated in order to move towards planetary well-being.

Our arguments in the chapter provide support for the Red List Index to be maintained as a headline indicator in the monitoring framework of the Kunming-Montreal Global Biodiversity Framework (CBD, 2022b). Headline indicators of the monitoring framework are explained to be the minimum set of indicators that capture the overall scope of the goals and targets of the Kunming-Montreal global biodiversity framework.

We believe that disaggregating the current Kunming-Montreal Global Biodiversity Framework target (*i.e.*, halting human-induced extinction of known threatened species by 2030 and reducing the extinction rate and risk of extinction of all species tenfold by 2050) to the national level would provide the much-needed assignment of responsibility to the agreement. In line with the argument presented by the IPBES in its assessment report on land degradation and restoration (Kohler *et al.*, 2018, pp. 61–65), such disaggregation could be considered fair in the sense that it sets the same baseline for all countries: The aim for each country would be to ensure that all native species, including those that are currently Regionally Extinct, reach the status of Least Concern. This would share the burden of conservation and restoration more evenly between the higher-income countries, which have degraded ecosystems and have lost species more in the past, and the lower-income countries, where biodiversity and ecosystems may be less degraded relative to their natural state.

The disaggregation of targets to the level (national, subnational, or supranational) where policy is designed, implemented, and monitored does not diminish our common responsibility for planetary well-being at the global level. Efforts to improve national RLI should not be designed in such a way as to undermine planetary well-being in other countries (*e.g.*, by sourcing natural resources from other countries in a way that harms biodiversity there). In contrast, trade policies could be adjusted to make use of national or disaggregated global RLIs to favour countries that are showing improvement. While the current global trade laws do not allow origin-specific discrimination, trade agreements allow room for encouraging and rewarding production processes that help improve RLI values, and non-state actors could also use the RLI information in procurement and subcontracting agreements. Moreover, we contend that the current trade system needs to be changed to stop subjugating planetary well-being to free trade.

A popular mnemonic from management theory suggests that goals and targets should be SMART: specific, measurable, assignable, realistic, and time-related (Doran, 1981). Interestingly, the original Meaning of "A" as "assignable—specify who will do it" has changed in biodiversity literature either to "ambitious" (Maxwell *et al.*, 2015; Green *et al.*, 2019; Hughes, Qiao and Orr, 2021), "achievable" (Wood, 2011), or "agreed" (Burgass *et al.*, 2021). Whether the meaning of "A" has been changed intentionally or by accident in literature is not clear, but this surely has been a misstep. Even though assignable targets may be challenging to agree on, they have a much higher chance of delivering than ambitious targets without a responsible actor. National RLIs, by reintroducing assignability to multilateral agreements, could function as the foundation for genuinely SMART targets for improving planetary well-being.

Note

1 There are approximately 1.2 million identified species in the world, and perhaps around 7 million unidentified species, of which the great majority are insects.

References

Bachman, S.P. *et al.* (2019) 'Progress, challenges and opportunities for Red Listing', *Biological Conservation*, 234, pp. 45–55. https://doi.org/10.1016/j.biocon.2019.03.002

Baillie, J.E.M. *et al.* (2008) 'Toward monitoring global biodiversity', *Conservation Letters*, 1(1), pp. 18–26. https://doi.org/10.1111/j.1755-263X.2008.00009.x

Boehm, S. *et al.* (2022) *State of Climate Action 2022*. Berlin, Cologne, San Francisco, CA, and Washington, DC: Bezos Earth Fund, Climate Action Tracker, Climate Analytics, Climate-Works Foundation, NewClimate Institute, the United Nations Climate Change High-Level Champions, and World Resources Institute. https://doi.org/10.46830/wrirpt.22.00028.

Burgass, M.J. *et al.* (2021) 'Three key considerations for biodiversity conservation in multilateral agreements', *Conservation Letters*, 14(2), e12764. https://doi.org/10.1111/conl.12764

Butchart, S.H.M., Di Marco, M. and Watson, J.E. (2016) 'Formulating smart commitments on biodiversity: Lessons from the Aichi Targets', *Conservation Letters*, 9(6), pp. 457–468. https://doi.org/10.1111/conl.12278

Butchart, S.H.M. *et al.* (2007) 'Improvements to the Red List Index', *PLoS One*, 2(1), e140. https://doi.org/10.1371/journal.pone.0000140

CBD (2010) *The Strategic Plan for Biodiversity 2011–2020 and the Aichi Biodiversity Targets*. UNEP/CBD/COP/DEC/X/2. Available at: https://www.cbd.int/decision/cop/?id=12268 (Accessed: 1 January 2023).

CBD (2020) *Global Biodiversity Outlook 5*. Montreal: Secretariat of the Convention on Biological Diversity. Available at: https://www.cbd.int/gbo5 (Accessed: 1 January 2023).

CBD (2022a) *Kunming-Montreal Global Biodiversity Framework*. CBD/COP/DEC/15/4. Available at: https://www.cbd.int/doc/decisions/cop-15/cop-15-dec-04-en.pdf (Accessed: 1 January 2023).

CBD (2022b) *Monitoring Framework for the Kunming-Montreal Global Biodiversity Framework*. CBD/COP/DEC/15/5. Available at: *https://www.cbd.int/doc/decisions/cop-15/cop-15-dec-05-en.pdf* (Accessed: 1 January 2023).

Doran, G.T. (1981) 'There's a SMART way to write management's goals and objectives', *Management Review*, 70(11), pp. 35–36.

Green, E.J. *et al.* (2019) 'Relating characteristics of global biodiversity targets to reported progress', *Conservation Biology*, 33(6), pp. 1360–1369. https://doi.org/10.1111/cobi.13322

Harrop, S.R. (2011) '"Living In Harmony With Nature'? Outcomes of the 2010 Nagoya Conference of the Convention on Biological Diversity', *Journal of Environmental Law*, 23(1), pp. 117–128. https://doi.org/10.1093/jel/eqq032

Henriques, S. *et al.* (2020) 'Accelerating the monitoring of global biodiversity: Revisiting the sampled approach to generating Red List Indices', *Conservation Letters,* 13(3), e12703. https://doi.org/10.1111/conl.12703

Hughes, A.C., Qiao, H. and Orr, M.C. (2021) 'Extinction targets are not SMART (specific, measurable, ambitious, realistic, and time bound)', *BioScience,* 71(2), pp. 115–118. https://doi.org/10.1093/biosci/biaa148

IPBES (2019) *Global Assessment Report on Biodiversity and Ecosystem Services of the Intergovernmental Science-Policy Platform on Biodiversity and Ecosystem Services.* Bonn: IPBES Secretariat. https://doi.org/10.5281/zenodo.3831673

IUCN (2012a) *Guidelines for Application of IUCN Red List Criteria at Regional and National Levels.* Version 4.0. Gland: IUCN. Available at: https://portals.iucn.org/library/node/10336 (Accessed: 1 January 2023).

IUCN (2012b) *IUCN Red List Categories and Criteria: Version 3.1.* 2nd edn. Gland and Cambridge: IUCN. Available at: https://portals.iucn.org/library/node/10315 (Accessed: 1 January 2023).

IUCN (2023a) *Red List Index.* Available at: https://www.iucnredlist.org/assessment/red-list-index (Accessed: 1 January 2023).

IUCN (2023b) *IUCN Red List. Advanced Search.* Available at: https://www.iucnredlist.org/search (Accessed: 1 January 2023).

IUCN (2023c) *Reasons for Changing Category.* Available at: https://www.iucnredlist.org/assessment/reasons-changing-category (Accessed: 1 January 2023).

Kohler, F. *et al.* (2018) 'Chapter 2: Concepts and perceptions of land degradation and restoration', in Montanarella, L., Scholes, R. and Brainich, A. (eds.) *The IPBES Assessment Report on Land Degradation and Restoration.* Bonn: Secretariat of the IPBES, pp. 53–134. https://doi.org/10.5281/zenodo.3237392

Kortetmäki, T. *et al.* (2021) 'Planetary well-being', *Humanities and Social Sciences Communications,* 8(1), 258. https://doi.org/10.1057/s41599-021-00899-3

Kyrkjeeide, M.O. *et al.* (2021) 'Bending the curve: Operationalizing national Red Lists to customize conservation actions to reduce extinction risk', *Biological Conservation,* 261, 109227. https://doi.org/10.1016/j.biocon.2021.109227

Leadley, P. *et al.* (2022) 'Achieving global biodiversity goals by 2050 requires urgent and integrated actions', *One Earth,* 5(6), pp. 597–603. https://doi.org/10.1016/j.oneear.2022.05.009

Leclere, D. *et al.* (2020) 'Bending the curve of terrestrial biodiversity needs an integrated strategy', *Nature,* 585(7826), pp. 551–556. https://doi.org/10.1038/s41586-020-2705-y

Mace, G.M. *et al.* (2008) 'Quantification of extinction risk: IUCN's system for classifying threatened species', *Conservation Biology,* 22(6), pp. 1424–1442. https://doi.org/10.1111/j.1523-1739.2008.01044.x

Maxwell, S.L. *et al.* (2015) 'Being smart about SMART environmental targets', *Science,* 347(6226), pp. 1075–1076. https://doi.org/10.1126/science.aaa1451

Morgera, E. and Tsioumani, E. (2010) 'Yesterday, today, and tomorrow: Looking afresh at the convention on biological diversity', *Yearbook of International Environmental Law,* 21(1), pp. 3–40. http://dx.doi.org/10.2139/ssrn.1914378

Purvis, A. (2020) 'A single apex target for biodiversity would be bad news for both nature and people', *Nature Ecology & Evolution,* 4(6), pp. 768–769. https://doi.org/10.1038/s41559-020-1181-y

Raimondo, D. *et al.* (2022) 'Using Red List Indices to monitor extinction risk at national scales', *Conservation Science and Practice,* 5(1), e12854. https://doi.org/10.1111/csp2.12854

Rodrigues, A.S.L. *et al.* (2014) 'Spatially explicit trends in the global conservation status of vertebrates', *PLoS One,* 9(11), e113934. https://doi.org/10.1371/journal.pone.0113934

Salafsky, N. *et al.* (2008) 'A standard lexicon for biodiversity conservation: Unified classifications of threats and actions', *Conservation Biology,* 22(4), pp. 897–911. https://doi.org/10.1111/j.1523-1739.2008.00937.x

Wood, L. (2011) 'Global marine protection targets: how SMART are they?', *Environmental Management,* 47(4), pp. 525–535. https://doi.org/10.1007/s00267-011-9668-6

15

A PLANETARY WELL-BEING ACCOUNTING SYSTEM FOR ORGANIZATIONS

Sami El Geneidy and Janne S. Kotiaho

Introduction

Unsustainable land use and overexploitation of natural resources to produce the consumables necessary to satisfy the needs and desires of humankind has compromised ecosystem integrity to a degree that in many places ecosystems are losing their ability to support the diversity of life (Intergovernmental Science-Policy Platform on Biodiversity and Ecosystem Services (IPBES), 2018; Willemen *et al.*, 2020). Incremental changes in our production and consumption practices are unlikely to alleviate this state of affairs (Díaz *et al.*, 2019; IPBES, 2019), and we need to figure out ways to make considerable, even transformative changes that truly support the transition towards planetary well-being (Kortetmäki *et al.*, 2021).

We humans organize our everyday lives through organizations, be they private businesses or public services such as hospitals or education institutions. To understand organizations' role in enhancing or diminishing planetary well-being, we need to be able to identify and quantify the environmental impacts (*e.g.*, greenhouse gas emissions or biodiversity loss) their operations are causing. Although vital, such understanding alone is unlikely to facilitate the necessary transformative changes in production and consumption practices. Therefore, we argue here that a value-transforming integration of financial and environmental accounting and reporting is critical for ensuring that the environmental impacts really influence the management decisions of organizations.

As Schaltegger and Burritt (2000, p. 21) put it:

> Conventional financial accounting provides the most important information management system for any company because it links all company activities with performance and expresses these in the form of a single unit

DOI: 10.4324/9781003334002-21

of account—money—which can be used as a basis for comparing available alternatives.

Financial accounting is generally recognized to be an objective information management system, but we often fail to notice how much power it actually holds in creating the premises and boundaries of an organization. It is the financial accounts that, for example, define what are included or excluded in assets and liabilities and how profit and loss are calculated, which consequently defines the size, health, structure, and performance of the organization (Hines, 1988). We do not dispute the usefulness of the conventional financial accounting. However, we do note that the convention of only including information related to flows of money neglects the more complex web of impacts organizations have on society and the environment, both of which are not customarily expressed as money within the boundaries of the organization. Indeed, conventional financial accounting has largely failed to steer organizations towards environmentally and societally sustainable decision-making (Laine *et al.*, 2020; Maas, Schaltegger and Crutzen, 2016; Nicholls, 2020; Veldman and Jansson, 2020).

Environmental accounting has been developed to make visible the impacts an organization has on the environment (Bracci and Maran, 2013; Schaltegger and Burritt, 2000; Unerman, Bebbington and O'dwyer, 2018). In their review on the history of academic work on environmental accounting, Russell, Milne, and Dey (2017) explain that before the 1990s the focus was on extending accounting systems so that traditional accounts could include environmental impacts beyond market transactions. Dominant themes were identifying, measuring, counting, and ultimately monetizing environmental costs and benefits, and then drawing them into the conventional financial accounts of organizations. Russell, Milne, and Dey (*ibid.*) make the observation that during the past two decades this stream of scholarly investigation has dwindled, and that monetizing the environment in financial accounts has not caught on. The case today is still that financial decision-making does not value negative or positive environmental impacts (Nedopil, 2022). Nevertheless, monetizing nature, despite widespread criticism of the notion (*e.g.*, Redford and Adams, 2009; Spash, 2015), appears to be a growing practice (Russell, Milne and Dey, 2017), with at least about 100 different solutions applied across the world (Hein, Miller and De Groot, 2013; Kotiaho *et al.*, 2016; Nedopil, 2022).

Environmental and social issues are profoundly complex; so too is the matter of accounting for them (Gray, 2001). Therefore, it is unsurprising that we have faced serious challenges when attempting to integrate environmental and social, never mind sustainability, impacts into conventional financial accounting. Predominantly the challenges seem to relate to issues of whether such impacts can be quantified (Gray, 2010; Norman and MacDonald, 2004; Pava, 2007). For example, Norman and MacDonald (2004) considered it to be a specious promise that we could ever measure, calculate, audit and report an organizations environmental and social performance with the same rigour and detail as we can disclose its financial performance.

Although scholarly efforts to integrate environmental accounts with financial ones may have dwindled (Russell, Milne and Dey, 2017), non-financial disclosures and environmental accounts have become increasingly common. However, there is ample evidence that such non-financial environmental accounting remains isolated within organizations, and that even when it is included in reporting, it commonly remains unexploited in management decisions (Bracci and Maran, 2013; Maas, Schaltegger and Crutzen, 2016; Saravanamuthu, 2004; Veldman and Jansson, 2020). This observation indicates that simply mainstreaming environmental accounting across organizations is not enough. We think that a deep value-transforming integration of financial and environmental accounting is required to ensure that the disclosed environmental impacts capture the attention of the senior executives of the organizations. In other words, the depth of the integration needs to be such that the environmental accounts actually transform the value of the financial accounts.

Recently, Nicholls (2020) proposed that integrating financial, environmental, and social accounting should be a public policy solution. Before public policy can be implemented, however, some capacity building regarding how such integration might be done in practice is still needed. Although several methodologies towards integration of financial and environmental accounting have been developed (Maas, Schaltegger and Crutzen, 2016; Vallišová, Černá and Hinke, 2018; Veldman and Jansson, 2020; empirical case studies: Alvarez, Blanquer and Rubio, 2014; Larsen *et al.*, 2013; Thurston and Eckelman, 2011), generalized applications for the integration remain scarce. This is especially the case for applications that highlight environmental impacts by transforming the value of the financial accounts at the organization level.

Here we will first focus on how environmental impacts can be identified and quantified by utilizing financial accounts and environmentally extended input-output databases. Our perspective is slightly different from previous attempts to integrate environmental and financial accounts (Russell, Milne and Dey, 2017) in that initially we do not directly monetize nature. Rather, we quantify the environmental impacts (*e.g.*, biodiversity loss) caused by the money spent in an organization and thus disclose its environmental performance through the financial accounts.

What should be noted, however, is that even when the environmental impacts are disclosed through the financial accounts (and thus, in principle, the environmental impacts are indirectly monetized), the disclosure itself does not transform the value of the financial accounts. To facilitate value transformation, which we consider to be critical for ensuring that the environmental impacts really influence the management decisions, we need to create money-based incentives for the senior executives. We believe that executives will pay attention when causing environmental damage costs money (or enhancing the state of the environment pays off) and will consequently begin to avoid and reduce the negative environmental impacts of their organizations and thus support the transition towards planetary well-being. Therefore, in the proposed planetary well-being accounting system we will include an example in which biodiversity offsetting is used to concretely transform the value of the financial accounts. Noting that the financial performance of organizations is communicated through impact statements and balance sheets, we suggest that reporting as well should be developed towards integrated financial-environmental impact statements.

Integrating financial and environmental accounting

Conventional financial accounting is an efficient system with respect to what it was made for: Tracking the financial flows of consumption (expenses and investments) and production (sales and revenue) within an organization. In other words, anything an organization consumes and produces should be visible in its financial accounts and all of its operations are at least indirectly touched upon by financial accounting. Therefore, financial accounts provide a promising platform for a deep value-transforming integration of financial and environmental accounts.

Integrating financial and environmental accounting basically requires that when an organization accounts for the impacts of its financial transactions, it should simultaneously account for the environmental impacts associated with those transactions. While the financial accounts might hold information about the price and type of a good or service, additional tools and information are needed to quantify the environmental impacts because they are currently not visible in conventional financial transactions. What is in particular needed is detailed information about the identity of products and services, which is not always readily available in current financial accounts. Thus, development work regarding what kind of information is reported in financial accounts, and particularly in receipts of transactions, needs to be undertaken so that information allowing the environmental impacts to be quantified becomes available. Information about the physical quantities and specific types of goods and services is vital for quantitative environmental accounting. What would help the process would be to require producers in all the steps of the supply chain to report on the environmental impacts of the goods and services they provide, so that the same information can be used further along the supply chain when the products are consumed by other organizations or end users.

Negative environmental impacts can be quantified in various ways but two methodologies stand out in the context of assessing environmental impacts of organizations: Environmentally extended input-output analysis (EEIOA) and life cycle assessment (LCA). Similar to any methodology, the accounts need first to be identified, meaning it needs to be determined what kinds of products or services the financial transactions in the accounts refer to. As already stated, the current financial accounting and reporting system does not necessarily need detailed information about the products and services, and therefore, in some cases, this identification is difficult or even impossible to complete (Bracci and Maran, 2013). After the account identification, a suitable methodology for the assessment of each account's environmental impact can be chosen, based on whether the transactions of the specific account can best be quantified in terms of financial or physical units.

Generally, environmental impacts of financial accounts can be assessed by using EEIO databases, such as EXIOBASE, Eora, GTAP, and WIOD (for an introduction to the techniques, see Kitzes, 2013; Leontief 1970). For example, the biodiversity impact of procured information technology supplies can be assessed through an EEIO database by converting the unit of money spent in an organization (situated in a given country) into square meters of land used (in different ecosystems in different regions of the world) to produce the supplies. Land use can then be further converted into biodiversity impacts by utilizing another, for example LC-Impact, database (Verones *et al.*, 2020; El Geneidy *et al.*, 2021a,b; El Geneidy, Baumeister and Kotiaho, n.d.).

While EEIO operates predominantly on financial transactions, LCA databases, such as ecoinvent, LCA Commons and ELCD, can be used to assess the environmental impacts of different goods based on their physical consumption. An example of physical consumption better amenable to LCA than to EEIO methodology is the amount of megawatt hours of electricity consumed by an organization. More generally, physical consumption information about travel- and energy-related accounts is often readily available (El Geneidy *et al.*, 2021b; Larsen *et al.*, 2013), and consequently LCA-based approaches are more likely to deliver accurate results on environmental impacts than utilization of EEIO-based approaches on financial transactions alone.

A hybrid EEIO-LCA approach combines the strengths of both methodologies (Crawford *et al.*, 2018; Suh *et al.*, 2004; for applications see *e.g.*, El Geneidy *et al.*, 2021b; Larsen *et al.*, 2013; Marques *et al.*, 2017), and it may be that in the future we will see a stronger merger of the two approaches. It is worth noting that the process can be easily automated after the initial link between financial and environmental accounts has been constructed.

Even though the methodologies for assessing environmental impacts through both financial and physical consumption are already relatively well understood, from a practitioner's point of view the methods for utilizing financial accounts to calculate the environmental impacts of an organization are not yet readily available. In addition, information, especially about environmental impacts of physical consumption of goods, is in many cases still lacking, and this information is generally a prerequisite for LCA-based approaches. Also, while EEIO methodologies allow analysis of environmental impacts of different consumption sectors, they often cannot yet differentiate between two or more different products of the same sector (Stadler *et al.*, 2018).

Outlining financial-environmental impact statements

Once the the link between financial and environmental accounts has been established, we can start developing a financial-environmental impact statement. These can then be utilized to communicate the financial as well as environmental performance of the organization to the management of the organization, to other decision-makers such as investors, and to stakeholders such as non-governmental organizations.

In financial accounting, relevant information is generally compiled in an income (or impact) statement and a balance sheet. An income statement describes the performance of an organization over a certain period with key figures such as revenue and expenses (Chen, 2022). A balance sheet on the other hand shows the assets and liabilities of an organization at a specific point of time, that is, what the organization owns and owes (Fernando, 2022). Here we use the income statement as a model because, after scrutinizing both, we concluded that it is the impact statement that contains most of the information needed for accounting the negative environmental impacts of an organization. Nevertheless, in the future it might also be useful to develop a balance sheet to allow accounting of the cumulative negative and positive environmental impacts the operations of an organization cause. Current financial impact statements only capture the flows of produced capital, but as Dasgupta (2021) has argued, we need to shift towards a system where the impact statement of an organization also captures the flows of natural capital (as well as human capital, which is not in the scope of the current chapter). In Table 15.1 we present an outline of the potential content of the financial-environmental impact statement following the guidelines of the International Financial Reporting Standards (IFRS) on the contents of a conventional financial income statement.

In Figure 15.1 we illustrate the overall idea of how natural capital is utilized and passed from one organization to another to create human and produced capital.

TABLE 15.1 Potential content for the financial-environmental impact statement of an organization

	Financial impact	Environmental impact
Sales/downstream impact	Sales from operations	Negative and/or positive environmental impacts of the goods and services produced
Expenses/upstream impact	Expenses from operations	Negative environmental impacts of the goods and services consumed
Offsets	Financial value of offsets used to balance the negative environmental impacts	The quantity of offsets procured to balance the negative environmental impacts
Net impact	The net income (sales – expenses – offsets)	The net environmental impact (negative impacts – offsets)

We have included expenses from offsets to transform the value of the financial accounts. It is almost certain that even after careful avoidance of emissions and ecosystem degradation, not all negative environmental impacts can be evaded and hence organizations aiming for carbon neutrality and/or no net loss of biodiversity will have to resort to purchasing offsets.

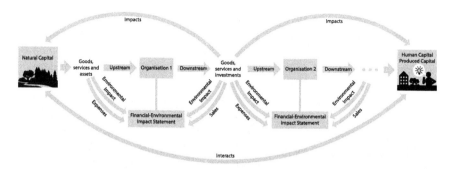

FIGURE 15.1   Visualization of financial and environmental flows relevant for the financial-environmental impact statement of an organization.

Assets any organization uses are called capital goods and have been classified into three different categories: Natural, human, and produced capital (*e.g.*, Dasgupta, 2021). Natural capital is directly consumed as upstream goods and services in Organization 1, which are in turn transformed and sold as downstream goods and services to Organization 2 or used to create produced capital. From the perspective of Organization 2, goods and services from Organization 1 are upstream goods and services that are again transformed and used further along the supply chain as different products and services. Consuming natural capital to create produced capital generally has a negative impact on the environment either by causing emissions or reducing biodiversity. Organizations can also procure assets from natural capital or provide investments to other organizations or to produced capital. Finally, the goods and services satisfy the needs of organizations or individuals and contribute to human and produced capital, which in turn can interact with natural capital.

Concluding remarks: The imperative of transforming financial value

If environmental information is not afforded the same value as financial information in decision-making, it can easily be ignored. In such situations the integration of financial and environmental accounting and reporting will not be sufficient to transform the operations of organizations and organizations will not become sensitive to the influence they have on planetary well-being. Indeed, our main thesis throughout this chapter has been that to truly make a difference in decision-making, environmental impacts uncovered by the integration of financial and environmental accounting and reporting need to transform the financial value.

Some initiatives are already piloting the financial valuation of environmental impacts, for example the so-called environmental profit and loss accounts (Høst-Madsen *et al.*, 2014; Schmidt and de Saxcé, 2016) and the social cost of carbon approach (Nordhaus, 2017). However, the valuation has not been deeply integrated into the financial accounts such that it would directly influence, that is transform, the financial value. The environmental information has generally been presented only as additional information alongside conventional financial information (Nicholls, 2020). In the worst cases such reporting has been used to exploit the concept of sustainability to back up the dominant financial discourses of development and growth (Zappettini and Unerman, 2016).

It may be that integrating environmental and financial accounting, and especially transforming financial value based on environmental impacts, is an issue that is best tackled by public policy (Nicholls, 2020). Important steps towards this goal have already been taken, for instance in the European Union (EU) with the adoption of the Corporate Sustainability Reporting Directive (CSRD) which builds upon an earlier Non-Financial Reporting Directive (Council of the EU, 2022a). In addition, the EU aims to scale up sustainable investments by classifying the sustainability criteria of economic activities for investors (European Commission, 2022a). While the EU taxonomy will include mandatory reporting requirements (connecting to the CSRD), it is up to the businesses to decide whether they want to apply for eligibility within the investment regime, and up to investors to decide whether they want to direct investments based on sustainability criteria. That said the possible adoption of a carbon border adjustment mechanism that puts a tax on certain goods imported to the EU based on their assessed climate impact (Council of the EU, 2022b) will also influence the financial accounting values of supply chains in organizations. Furthermore, some progressive corporations and financial institutions are actually calling for governments of the world to legislate mandatory disclosure of nature-related impacts and dependencies for businesses (Business for Nature, Capitals Coalition and CDP, 2022). Unfortunately, it seems that the current political initiatives aim to entrench the existing trend of environmental accounting as a separate aspect of corporate reporting, and we do not yet see any meaningful steps towards value-transforming integrated financial and environmental accounting.

As the value-transforming integration of financial and environmental accounting outlined here can be replicated in any organization with standardized financial accounts, we conclude that such integration offers a platform that could be used to initiate a truly transformative change in the management of organizations, one that supports the transition towards planetary well-being. We note, however, that the mere existence of the platform does not guarantee that the integrated reporting or the value transformation will be adopted by organizations. Indeed, there is evidence that voluntary reporting is not as effective as mandatory reporting (Crawford and Williams, 2010; see also Gray, 2001; Hess, 2007; Koehler, 2007; Wu and Babcock, 1999), and that value-transforming economic instruments to protect biodiversity, including biodiversity offset programs, do not and cannot operate without robust regulation and state involvement (Boisvert, 2015; Koh, Hahn and Boonstra, 2019; Koh, Hahn and Ituarte-Lima, 2017; Kujala *et al.*, 2022; Vatn, 2015). Therefore, we adopt the view that strong public oversight might be needed and offer two suggestions. First, make the integration of financial and environmental accounting mandatory for all organizations with financial disclosure obligations. Second, make the environmental impacts salient to the senior executives of the organizations by transforming the value of financial accounts on the basis of environmental impacts. This can be done for example by introducing mandatory biodiversity offsetting schemes (see *e.g.*, Moilanen and Kotiaho, 2018, 2021), new environmental protection taxes and subsidies, or some other instruments that have the potential to transform the value of the financial accounts. Perhaps it is worth noting that we are currently witnessing a shift away from policies that use offsets to balance environmental impacts, and moving towards political interventions that aim for net positive environmental impacts (Leclère *et al.*, 2020; Moilanen and Kotiaho, 2021; the Convention on Biological Diversity (CBD), 2022).

In this chapter, we focused exclusively on the integration of financial and environmental accounting. With a methodology analogous to the one outlined here for the accounting of environmental impacts of organizations, it might be possible to begin to quantitatively account at least some of the social impacts of the financial accounts of organizations. Quantitative accounting of both environmental and social impacts of financial accounts would be in line with the current political development in the EU towards a Corporate Sustainability Due Diligence Directive (European Commission, 2022b). Whether mechanisms such as offsets or taxes and subsidies can be innovated to transform the value of the financial accounts based on social impact accounts remains to be seen. Although we think the deep value-transforming integration of environmental accounts with financial accounts as outlined here is a critical step forward, the integration of social impacts and human capital is also needed. Once this step is taken, we may be close to a truly transformative planetary well-being accounting system.

References

Alvarez, S., Blanquer, M. and Rubio, A. (2014) 'Carbon footprint using the Compound Method based on Financial Accounts. The case of the School of Forestry Engineering, Technical University of Madrid', *Journal of Cleaner Production*, 66, pp. 224–232. https://doi.org/10.1016/j.jclepro.2013.11.050

Boisvert, V. (2015) 'Conservation banking mechanisms and the economization of nature: An institutional analysis', *Ecosystem Services*, 15, pp. 134–142. https://doi.org/10.1016/j.ecoser.2015.02.004

Bracci, E. and Maran, L. (2013) 'Environmental management and regulation: Pitfalls of environmental accounting?', *Management of Environmental Quality: An International Journal*, 24, pp. 538–554. https://doi.org/10.1108/MEQ-04-2012-0027

Business for Nature, Capitals Coalition and CDP (2022) *Make It Mandatory: the case for mandatory corporate assessment and disclosure on nature*. Available at: https://www.businessfornature.org/make-it-mandatory-campaign (Accessed: 27 January 2023).

CBD (2022) *Kunming-Montreal Global Biodiversity Framework*. CBD/COP/DEC/15/4. Available at: https://www.cbd.int/doc/decisions/cop-15/cop-15-dec-04-en.pdf (Accessed: 27 January 2023).

Chen, J. (2022) *Income Statement: How to Read and Use It*. Available at: https://www
.investopedia.com/terms/i/incomestatement.asp (Accessed: 27 January 2023).

Council of the EU (2022a) 'Council gives final green light to corporate sustainability
reporting directive', press release, 28 November. Available at: https://www.consilium.
europa.eu/en/press/press-releases/2022/11/28/council-gives-final-green-light-to-
corporate-sustainability-reporting-directive/ (Accessed: 27 January 2023).

Council of the EU (2022b) 'Council agrees on the Carbon Border Adjustment Mechanism
(CBAM)', press release, 15 March. Available at: https://www.consilium.europa.eu/en/
press/press-releases/2022/03/15/carbon-border-adjustment-mechanism-cbam-council-
agrees-its-negotiating-mandate/ (Accessed: 27 January 2023).

Crawford, E.P. and Williams, C.C. (2010) 'Should corporate social reporting be voluntary or
mandatory? Evidence from the banking sector in France and the United States', *Corporate
Governance: International Journal of Business in Society*, 10(4), pp. 512–526. https://
doi.org/10.1108/14720701011069722

Crawford, R.H. *et al.* (2018) 'Hybrid life cycle inventory methods – A review', *Journal
of Cleaner Production*, 172, pp. 1273–1288. https://doi.org/10.1016/J.JCLEPRO.
2017.10.176

Dasgupta, P. (2021) *The Economics of Biodiversity: The Dasgupta Review*. London: HM
Treasury. Available at: https://assets.publishing.service.gov.uk/government/uploads/
system/uploads/attachment_data/file/962785/The_Economics_of_Biodiversity_The_
Dasgupta_Review_Full_Report.pdf (Accessed: 27 January 2023).

Díaz, S. *et al.* (2019) 'Pervasive human-driven decline of life on Earth points to the need
for transformative change', *Science*, 366, eaax3100. https://doi.org/10.1126/science.
aax3100

El Geneidy, S. *et al.* (2021a) *Sustainability for JYU: Jyväskylän yliopiston ilmasto- ja
luontohaitat*. Wisdom Letters, 2/2021. Available at: https://jyx.jyu.fi/bitstream/
handle/123456789/75182/1/wisdom_letters_2-21_valmis_230421_web.pdf (Accessed:
27 January 2023).

El Geneidy, S. *et al.* (2021b) 'The carbon footprint of a knowledge organization and emission scenarios for a post-COVID-19 world', *Environmental Impact Assessment Review*,
91, 106645. https://doi.org/10.1016/j.eiar.2021.106645

El Geneidy, S., Baumeister, S. and Kotiaho, J.S. (n.d.) 'Value-transforming integration of
financial and environmental accounting in organizations' [Manuscript in preparation].

European Commission (2022a) *EU Taxonomy for Sustainable Activities*. Available at: https://
finance.ec.europa.eu/sustainable-finance/tools-and-standards/eu-taxonomy-sustainable-
activities_en (Accessed: 27 January 2023).

European Commission (2022b) 'Just and sustainable economy: Commission lays down
rules for companies to respect human rights and environment in global value chains',
press release, 23 February. Available at: https://ec.europa.eu/commission/presscorner/
detail/en/ip_22_1145 (Accessed: 27 January 2023).

Fernando, J. (2022) *Balance Sheet: Explanation, Components, and Examples*. Available at:
https://www.investopedia.com/terms/b/balancesheet.asp (Accessed: 27 January 2023).

Gray, R. (2001) 'Thirty years of social accounting, reporting and auditing: what (if anything)
have we learnt?', *Business Ethics: A European Review*, 10, pp. 9–15. http://dx.doi.
org/10.1111/1467-8608.00207

Gray, R. (2010) 'Is accounting for sustainability actually accounting for sustainability… and
how would we know? An exploration of narratives of organisations and the planet', *Accounting, Organizations and Society*, 35, pp. 47–62. https://doi.org/10.1016/j.aos.2009.04.006

Hein, L., Miller, D.C. and De Groot, R. (2013) 'Payments for ecosystem services and the financing of global biodiversity conservation', *Current Opinion in Environmental Sustainability*, 5(1), pp. 87–93. https://doi.org/10.1016/j.cosust.2012.12.004

Hess, D. (2007) 'Social reporting and new governance regulation: the prospects of achieving corporate accountability through transparency', *Business Ethics Quarterly*, 17(3), pp. 453–476. https://doi.org/10.5840/beq200717348

Hines, R.D. (1988) 'Financial accounting: In communicating reality, we construct reality', *Accounting, Organizations and Society*, 13, pp. 251–261. https://doi.org/10.1016/0361-3682(88)90003-7

Høst-Madsen, N.K. *et al.* (2014) *Novo Nordisk's Environmental Profit and Loss Account 2014*. The Danish Environmental Protection Agency. Available at: https://www2.mst.dk/udgiv/publications/2014/02/978-87-93178-02-1.pdf (Accessed: 27 January 2023).

IPBES (2018) Summary for policymakers of the assessment report on land degradation and restoration of the Intergovernmental Science-Policy Platform on Biodiversity and Ecosystem Services. Zenodo. https://doi.org/10.5281/zenodo.3237411

IPBES (2019) Summary for policymakers of the global assessment report on biodiversity and ecosystem services of the Intergovernmental Science-Policy Platform on Biodiversity and Ecosystem Services. Zenodo. https://doi.org/10.5281/zenodo.3553579

Kitzes, J. (2013) 'An introduction to environmentally-extended input-output analysis', *Resources*, 2(4) pp. 489–503. https://doi.org/10.3390/resources2040489

Koehler, D.A. (2007) 'The effectiveness of voluntary environmental programs—A policy at a crossroads?', *Policy Studies Journal*, 35, pp. 689–722. https://doi.org/10.1111/j.1541-0072.2007.00244.x

Koh, N.S., Hahn, T. and Boonstra, W.J. (2019) 'How much of a market is involved in a biodiversity offset? A typology of biodiversity offset policies', *Journal of Environmental Management*, 232, pp. 679–691. https://doi.org/10.1016/j.jenvman.2018.11.080

Koh, N.S., Hahn, T. and Ituarte-Lima, C. (2017) 'Safeguards for enhancing ecological compensation in Sweden', *Land Use Policy*, 64, pp. 186–199. https://doi.org/10.1016/j.landusepol.2017.02.035

Kortetmäki, T. *et al.* (2021) 'Planetary well-being', *Humanities and Social Sciences Communications*, 8, p. 258. https://doi.org/10.1057/s41599-021-00899-3

Kotiaho, J.S. *et al.* (2016) *Framework for Assessing and Reversing Ecosystem Degradation – Report of the Finnish Restoration Prioritization Working Group on the Options and Costs of Meeting the Aichi Biodiversity Target of Restoring at least 15 Percent of Degraded Ecosystems in Finland.* Reports of the Ministry of the Environment, 15en. Helsinki. Available at: https://julkaisut.valtioneuvosto.fi/bitstream/handle/10024/74862/YMre_15en_2016.pdf?sequence=1&isAllowed=y (Accessed: 27 January 2023).

Kujala, H. *et al.* (2022) 'Credible biodiversity offsetting needs public national registers to confirm no net loss', *One Earth*, 5, pp. 650–662. https://doi.org/10.1016/j.oneear.2022.05.011

Laine, M. *et al.* (2020) 'Special issue editorial: Social and environmental account/ability 2020 and beyond', *Social and Environmental Accountability Journal*, 2245. https://doi.org/10.1080/0969160X.2020.1733631

Larsen, H.N. *et al.* (2013) 'Investigating the carbon footprint of a university – The case of NTNU', *Journal of Cleaner Production*, 48, pp. 39–47. https://doi.org/10.1016/j.jclepro.2011.10.007

Leclère, D. *et al.* (2020) 'Bending the curve of terrestrial biodiversity needs an integrated strategy', *Nature*, 585, pp. 551–556. https://doi.org/10.1038/s41586-020-2705-y

Leontief, W. (1970) 'Environmental repercussions and the economic structure: An input-output approach', *The Review of Economics and Statistics*, 52, pp. 262–271. https://doi.org/10.2307/1926294

Maas, K., Schaltegger, S. and Crutzen, N. (2016) 'Integrating corporate sustainability assessment, management accounting, control, and reporting', *Journal of Cleaner Production*, 136, pp. 237–248. https://doi.org/10.1016/j.jclepro.2016.05.008

Marques, A. *et al.* (2017) 'How to quantify biodiversity footprints of consumption? A review of multi-regional input–output analysis and life cycle assessment', *Current Opinion in Environmental Sustainability*, 29, pp. 75–81. https://doi.org/10.1016/j.cosust.2018.01.005

Moilanen, A. and Kotiaho, J.S. (2018) 'Fifteen operationally important decisions in the planning of biodiversity offsets', *Biological Conservation*, 227, pp. 112–120. https://doi.org/10.1016/j.biocon.2018.09.002

Moilanen, A. and Kotiaho, J.S. (2021) 'Three ways to deliver a net positive impact with biodiversity offsets', *Conservation Biology*, 35, pp. 197–205. https://doi.org/10.1111/cobi.13533

Nedopil, C. (2022) 'Integrating biodiversity into financial decision-making: Challenges and four principles', *Business Strategy and the Environment*, early view. https://doi.org/10.1002/bse.3208

Nicholls, J.A. (2020) 'Integrating financial, social and environmental accounting', *Sustainability Accounting, Management and Policy Journal*, 11(4), pp. 745–769. https://doi.org/10.1108/SAMPJ-01-2019-0030

Nordhaus, W.D. (2017) 'Revisiting the social cost of carbon', *PNAS*, 114, pp. 1518–1523. https://doi.org/10.1073/pnas.1609244114

Norman, W. and MacDonald, C. (2004) 'Getting to the bottom of 'Triple Bottom Line'', *Business Ethics Quarterly*, 14, pp. 243–262. http://dx.doi.org/10.2307/3857909

Pava, M.L. (2007) 'A response to 'getting to the bottom of 'triple bottom line''', *Business Ethics Quarterly*, 17(1), pp. 105–110. http://dx.doi.org/10.2307/27673160

Redford, K.H. and Adams, W.M. (2009) 'Payment for ecosystem services and the challenge of saving nature', *Conservation Biology*, 23, pp. 785–787. https://doi.org/10.1111/j.1523-1739.2009.01271.x

Russell, S., Milne, M.J. and Dey, C. (2017) 'Accounts of nature and the nature of accounts: Critical reflections on environmental accounting and propositions for ecologically informed accounting', *Accounting, Auditing & Accountability Journal*, 30, pp. 1426–1458. https://doi.org/10.1108/AAAJ-07-2017-3010

Saravanamuthu, K. (2004) 'What is measured counts: Harmonized corporate reporting and sustainable economic development', *Critical Perspectives on Accounting*, 15(3), pp. 295–302. https://doi.org/10.1016/S1045-2354(03)00063-7

Schaltegger, S. and Burritt, R. (2000) *Contemporary Environmental Accounting: Issues, Concepts and Practice.* 1st edn. London: Routledge. https://doi.org/10.4324/9781351282529

Schmidt, J.H. and de Saxcé, M. (2016) *Arla Foods Environmental Profit and Loss Accounting 2014.* The Danish Environmental Protection Agency. Available at: http://eng.mst.dk/media/176132/arla-foods-epl.pdf (Accessed: 27 January 2023).

Spash, C.L. (2015) 'Bulldozing biodiversity: The economics of offsets and trading-in nature', *Biological Conservation*, 192, pp. 541–551. https://doi.org/10.1016/j.biocon.2015.07.037

Stadler, K. *et al.* (2018) 'EXIOBASE 3: Developing a time series of detailed environmentally extended multi-regional input-output tables', *Journal of Industrial Ecology*, 22(3), pp. 502–515. https://doi.org/10.1111/jiec.12715

Suh, S. *et al.* (2004) 'System boundary selection in life-cycle inventories using hybrid approaches', *Environmental Science and Technology*, 38, pp. 657–664. https://doi.org/10.1021/es0263745

Thurston, M. and Eckelman, M.J. (2011) 'Assessing greenhouse gas emissions from university purchases', *International Journal of Sustainability in Higher Education*, 12, pp. 225–235. https://doi.org/10.1108/14676371111148018

Unerman, J., Bebbington, J. and O'dwyer, B. (2018) 'Corporate reporting and accounting for externalities', *Accounting and Business Research*, 48(5), pp. 497–522. https://doi.org/10.1080/00014788.2018.1470155

Vallišová, L., Černá, M. and Hinke, J. (2018) 'Implementation of sustainability aspects in the financial reporting system: An environmental accounting standard', *Economic Annals,* XXI, 173(9–10), pp. 55–59. https://doi.org/10.21003/ea.V173-09

Vatn, A. (2015) 'Markets in environmental governance. From theory to practice', *Ecological Economics*, 117, pp. 225–233. https://doi.org/10.1016/j.ecolecon.2014.07.017

Veldman, J. and Jansson, A. (2020) 'Planetary boundaries and corporate reporting: The role of the conceptual basis of the corporation', *Accounting, Economics and Law: A Convivium*, 20180037. https://doi.org/10.1515/ael-2018-0037

Verones, F. *et al.* (2020) 'LC-IMPACT: A regionalized life cycle damage assessment method', *Journal of Industrial Ecology*, 24(6), pp. 1201–1219. https://doi.org/10.1111/jiec.13018

Willemen, L. *et al.* (2020) 'How to halt the global decline of lands', *Nature Sustainability*, 3, pp. 164–166. https://doi.org/10.1038/s41893-020-0477-x

Wu, J. and Babcock, B.A. (1999) 'The relative efficiency of voluntary vs mandatory environmental regulations', *Journal of Environmental Economics and Management*, 38(2), pp. 158–175. https://doi.org/10.1006/jeem.1999.1075

Zappettini, F. and Unerman, J. (2016) "Mixing' and 'Bending': The recontextualisation of discourses of sustainability in integrated reporting', *Discourse and Communication*, 10(5), pp. 521–542. https://doi.org/10.1177/1750481316659175

16

FINANCIAL SYSTEM IN STEERING THE ECONOMY TOWARDS PLANETARY WELL-BEING

Kari Heimonen, Juha Junttila and Heikki Lehkonen

Introduction

This chapter discusses the possible ways in which the financial system might steer economic production towards planetary well-being. Following Dasgupta (2021), we define planetary well-being as the natural capital (nature, biosphere), a self-regenerative part of the Earth that is occupied by living organisms—that is, we, the human race, are stakeholders in it. In economic terms, nature works as an asset that provides us with food, water, and shelter; regulates our climate and disease; and improves our mental well-being by offering spiritual fulfilment and recreation opportunities. Biodiversity (*i.e.*, diversity of life) allows nature to be productive, resilient, and adaptable, and any threat to biodiversity, such as external use of natural resources, poses a threat to nature and should also be regarded as jeopardizing economic prosperity. The chapter connects excessive use of natural resources to the standard asset pricing framework and discusses the roles that financial institutions (banks) as well as debt and equity funding (direct funding channels) play in the global transition towards less harmful production. Finally, the chapter emphasizes the important role that the central bank plays in resolving the incompatibility between economic development and planetary well-being through the banking system and financial markets.

The decline of natural capital challenges the traditional concept of welfare in terms of Gross Domestic Product (GDP). An increase in GDP generates higher economic welfare when measured purely in GDP/per capita for humans in a way that significantly overlooks the roles played by natural capital, biodiversity, and human well-being (see Kortetmäki *et al.*, 2021). Since the development of the Solow-Swan model, economic growth models have considered GDP per capita growth to be the product of goods and services provided using productive capital,

DOI: 10.4324/9781003334002-22

human capital, and technology (see *e.g.*, Romer, 2019). Natural capital has played no role in this setup, and thus economic well-being and planetary well-being have been somewhat pitted against one another. Natural capital has no well-defined price, and the relevant resources (such as the seas and air) are considered "public", common-pool resources. Hence, no pricing mechanism exists that would steer the monetary market values of natural resources to equal their correct value (*i.e.*, the shadow price, or accounting value, as defined by Dasgupta (2021)). Consequently, revenues from exploitation of these resources significantly exceed the costs stemming from their use for nature, given that the prices do not accurately value their negative effects, particularly in the long term (*e.g.*, for oil, gas, and coal). Definition of the natural capital's correct price and value is a notoriously difficult task that requires policy actions and market interventions aimed at correcting externalities and filling the gaps in the missing market mechanism.

Nature catastrophes, such as floods and heatwaves, have alerted the world's population to the consequences ensuing from the unregulated use of natural resources. For example, increasing CO_2 emissions and the effects of global warming are hazardous and costly in terms of both environmental and human well-being as well as GDP growth and financial stability (see, *e.g.*, Alogoskoufis *et al.*, 2021; Colacito, Hoffmann and Phan, 2019; European Central Bank (ECB), 2020). Accordingly, in 2021, the European Central Bank launched action plans that incorporated considerations of climate change in the implementation of its monetary policy.

Concerns about the negative effects of economic growth on the environment are not new (see, *e.g.*, Bastien-Olvera and Moore 2021, 2022). At a time when the globally produced capital per capita has doubled and human capital per capita (*e.g.*, investments in education and other human-related investments on improvement in labour productivity) has increased by 13%, natural capital stock has decreased by approximately 40% (Dasgupta, 2021; Managi and Kumar, 2018). Nations with high GDP/capita use considerably more natural resources than poorer countries for their final consumption needs, whereas the growth rate of natural resources use is highest amongst the fastest-growing economies and in countries most recently integrated into international trade (Kacprzyk and Kuchta, 2020). Hartley, van den Bergh, and Kallis (2020) noted the differences in the development of wealth between rich, global North and poor, global South countries. For convergence, poorer Southern countries require greater economic growth than rich Northern countries, but such growth must be achieved with as little detriment to planetary well-being as possible. Natural capital relates to the debates about *green growth,* defined as "fostering economic growth and development, while ensuring that natural assets continue to provide the resources and environmental services on which our well-being relies" (Organization for Economic Co-operation and Development (OECD), 2022).

However, no empirical evidence on resource use exists to support green growth theory (Hickel and Kallis, 2020; Ward *et al.*, 2016). For example, Hickel and Kallis (2020) argue that it is not possible to introduce the necessary absolute decoupling, whereby the environmentally harmful variable is stable or decreasing while the economic driving force (*e.g.*, GDP) is growing on a global scale against a background of continued economic growth. Hence, policy makers should put more effort in strategies other than the existing green growth-based policy strategies in the immediate future.

As alternatives for green growth, Mastini, Kallis, and Hickell (2021) analyzed two prominent climate change mitigation narratives: The Green New Deal and degrowth (zero-level or even negative real economic growth). In the former, the role that energy systems and markets play is essential because the idea is to advocate a plan to co-ordinate and finance a large-scale overhaul of the energy system. Some regard the positive real economic growth rate over time as the core element in financing this transition and claim that the Green New Deal will further stimulate growth (Pollin, 2018). As a completely contradictory alternative, proponents of degrowth (see, *e.g.*, Buch-Hansen and Koch, 2019) maintain that growth makes it more difficult to accomplish transition to ecologically sustainable economies. However, these two approaches agree on the *importance of public investments for financing* the transition of industrial policies towards the economy's decarbonization, socializing the energy sector to allow longer investment horizons, and expanding the welfare state to increase social protection (Mastini, Kallis and Hickell, 2021).

Which are the economic forces that can help to minimize production costs to natural capital? We focus on a mechanism wherein the financial allocations to nature-friendly capital guide production in such a way that the negative side effects experienced by the environment are minimized, natural resources can be regenerated, and decoupling may take place. The financial system must channel financial resources from lender-savers who have a surplus of funds to borrower-spenders who have funding shortages. Given that capital is always required in the production of goods or services, financial institutions, and markets function as arteries of the modern economies' production by evaluating the expected returns of investment and financing viable projects. The central banks are tasked with guaranteeing the stable functioning of the entire financial system, implying that the central banks are powerful institutions in the process whereby capital is steered towards environment-enhancing production. Moreover, strong evidence indicates that private investors wish investment opportunity providers to consider sustainability in their instrument supply (the United Nations Environment Programme Finance Initiative (UNEP FI) and Principles for Responsible Investment (PRI), 2019).

This chapter discusses the ways in which the price of financial investments in productive capital that steers real economic production has the potential to preserve and even enhance natural capital. These financial resources' prices operate via production and Dasgupta's (2021) Impact Equation which relates the use of natural resources to biosphere regeneration. The capital market should increase the investment costs (*i.e.*, cost of capital) of activities that dilute planetary well-being to such an extent that they are substituted with a capital allocation towards production that are more conducive to planetary well-being. Capital markets are physical or nonphysical spaces in which investors trade on assets (*e.g.*, stocks, bonds, currencies) with longer-term holding periods. Market prices are determined according to asset supply and demand and should reflect expectations of both the asset's future values and their uncertainty. For an individual company, expectations regarding the company's and the relevant industry's performance form the basis of the price; for the market in general, however, prices are driven by expectations regarding overall economic development. Although anyone can participate in asset markets as an owner, large institutional investors, and funds—together with governments and central banks in particular—exert the greatest impact on stronger market movements. The role played by standard instruments (*e.g.*, taxonomy, taxation, fees, *etc.*) is inarguably essential here, but we suggest that central banks in particular will play a vital role in this process in the near future.

The nature-friendly capital market allocates capital into production, which uses fewer natural resources and enables nature to regenerate the biosphere. In terms of standard macro-finance thinking, the need for these changes in investment behaviour clearly entails renewed thinking about the expected or required rates of returns on investment. Future financial market-based activities should take into account, for example, the need to reduce inequality of wealth between the global economy's poor Southern and rich Northern parts (see, *e.g.*, Hartley, van den Bergh and Kallis, 2020) and simultaneously achieve the ultimate target of GDP's absolute decoupling from resource use and carbon emissions, although this would necessitate the acceptance of lower levels of returns together with higher levels of risk in the financial investments. The sections that follow thoroughly describe the current status of the ideas, instruments, and mechanisms that are most relevant to achieving these changes.

Impact Equation and price of capital

Planetary well-being and Impact Equation

The aggregate-level exploitation of natural resources comprises a combination of the exploitation of individual natural assets with different characteristics. Dasgupta (2014) presents the total natural capital resources $S(t)$ at time t as a sum over individual natural assets, including all types. Production can occur with any non-zero values of natural resources (S), capital (K) and labour (L) inputs. Dasgupta (2021) additionally introduced the biosphere's regeneration rate (G), which is a real accounting value given as a function of the stock of biosphere S (*i.e.*, $G = G(S)$)—that is, G is the rate at which the biosphere regenerates natural resources on a sustainable basis. The *Impact Equation* (IE) demonstrates the relationship between the regeneration rate of the biosphere's stock, G, and the aggregate demand of natural resources—the global ecological footprint, Ny / α. Here, N is the world population and y is the output, so y/N reflects the economic activity per capita. α is the efficiency parameter $(\alpha_z + \alpha_x) / (\alpha_z \, \alpha_x)$, which takes into account how biosphere's goods and services are converted into the GDP (α_x) and the extent to which the biosphere is transformed by global waste products (α_z) (Dasgupta, 2021, p. 116).

Impact Equality follows when these are equal, *i.e.*, $Ny/\alpha = G(S)$. If the resource supply $G(S)$ exceeds the demand, the supply of natural capital increases. When the aggregate demand for natural resources exceeds the supply, a decrease in natural capital and *Impact Inequality* ensues, where

$$Ny/\alpha > G(S)$$

Financial system has the means to affect the IE's demand and supply sides by directing funds towards various economic activities and impacting consumer preferences by reducing financial flows to activities that exert adverse impacts on the biosphere while supporting the opposite (affecting y). Moreover, it enables investment in the research and development of technologies that can enhance the efficiency with which natural assets are exploited (α). On the supply side, channelling financial flows in a way that increases natural assets directly (*e.g.*, via restoration and conservation of natural capital) improves the natural capital regeneration rate (*i.e.*, S and G; *ibid.*).

For example, to mitigate the impact inequality, investment in physical capital and technologies that use fewer natural resources (*e.g.*, less energy-intensive machinery) or cause less pollution must be increased. Furthermore, not only is the technological progress an essential factor in economic growth but technological improvements increase efficiency (*i.e.*, the value of α). The greater the α, the smaller the demand exerted on the biosphere at a given level of production. Increased α could further compensate for the impact associated with population growth, N. New technology would also replace older technologies, resulting in lower production costs per unit.

Planetary well-being and the price of capital

In theory, for any investment project—whether physical (*e.g.*, factory) or financial (stocks or bonds)—and for any investor—whether public, private, or non-profit—the decision to invest should be based on the discounted present value (*DPV*) of the investment, which is the discounted sum of all its future values (*FV*):

$$DPV_t = \frac{FV_{t+1}}{1+r} + \frac{FV_{t+2}}{(1+r)^2} + \frac{FV_{t+3}}{(1+r)^3} + \ldots = \sum \frac{FV_{t+i}}{(1+r)^i},$$

where the expected rate of return (r) used to discount the accruing future values (FV, *e.g.*, dividends for stocks or coupon payments for coupon-paying bonds) consists of both the compensation that investors require to delay their consumption (*i.e.*, the time value of money) and the risk premium (*e.g.*, for higher credit default probability). In equilibrium, the discounted present value (*DPV*) should equal the price of the asset. That is, the higher the future values, other things equal, the more profitable the investment project today is and the higher its price is. The higher the risks associated with the investment, the more compensation investors demand for it and the lower the present value. When the price is higher than the *DPV*, the investment does not take place. This mechanism should also drive the capital allocations of natural capital-related investments.

All policy actions affecting the future values and/or discount rate exert an impact on the investment's profitability and can either direct capital to or from nature-enhancing investments and support or hamper less environmentally harmful production. For example, owing to the failure to correctly evaluate nature, markets are unable to price the exploitation of natural capital correctly. The standard suggestion is that policy makers should intervene to compensate for this. In financial system, this could take the form of, for example, limited collateral value of nature-detrimental investment, nature-related taxonomy, green bond rating or any other policy that generates extra costs on nature-detrimental investment capital. Mathematically, this leads to the definition $r_{S,PW} = r_S + r_{S,\text{intervention}}$, where r_S is the cost of using S, $r_{S,\text{intervention}}$ is the intervention-related extra cost and $r_{S,PW}$ captures the total negative impacts on natural capital. This decreases the *DPV* of those investments, implying declines in investments to both the environmentally harmful production and to the exploitation of natural resources. Similarly, actions contributing to increased *FV* and reduced *r* will lead to higher financial flows to the project. That is, the intervention can also be regarded as a negative tax rate or subsidy to the cost of capital for environmentally friendly, green industry investments, in which the use of natural resources does not threaten the environment, leading to the enhancement of nature-friendly production.

Financial system and natural capital

Risks and natural capital

The role that financial system plays, as reflected in the natural capital literature, remains in its early phases. Existing studies have focused primarily on the valuation of Environmentally, Socially, and Governance (ESG) actions and policies, calculation of the social cost of carbon and climate risks. However, owing to the multifaceted interplay between nature and production, no universally accepted framework for incorporating nature-related risks into economic models has yet been developed.

Koumbarakis *et al.* (2020) propose that in financing the climate change-related real investment projects, financial institutions are most exposed in light of their credit risk and connection to financed firms' physical, transition, and litigation risks due to the environmental change. More specifically, the financial institutions must confront *credit risk* because they include in the asset side of their balance sheets the exposures to projects (*i.e.*, loans given to their customers) that may cause them to default on their obligations. *Physical risks* refer to the severe disruptions or collapses of ecosystems leading to supply chain interruptions caused by property damage, business disruption, loss of production, and/or via stranded assets. These reduce both the debt-servicing capacity and the collateral values of the financial institution. If the damages to the collateral are not insured, the financial burden may be transferred onto other market participants, further increasing the credit exposures. The realization of sudden extreme physical risks may even result in bank defaults (Dasgupta, 2021; Schüwer, Lambert and North, 2019). Moreover, *transition risks* stem from the adoption of environmentally friendly operations and business models. Government policies and direct subsidies can contribute to technological advances that promote biodiversity, while changing consumer preferences impose a pressure to move away from environmentally detrimental operations. Finally, *litigation risks* relate to the liability issues taken against the firms responsible for the realization of physical and transition risks (*e.g.*, biodiversity loss) due to the firm's production decisions (Abdelli *et al.*, 2021). To understand the overall risk dimension imposed by the changes in natural capital, the firm's entire value chain must be investigated. In any case, the risks are ultimately related to the price of capital. The higher the risks, the higher the r (return) required from the firm/investment.

Financing natural capital

Governments play an important role in the development of less environmentally harmful production that can also support the positive development of natural capital. They do not merely provide regulation; they also aim to correct for market failures surrounding natural capital pricing. As they are maximizing long-term social well-being, they can also participate in long-term projects with low and risky expected financial returns. With their main toolbox, which consists of budgets as well as tax policies and legislation, governments can channel financial flows, impact the incentive structures, and undertake financial de-risking to increase private financial flows to assets supporting natural capital (United Nations Development Program (UNDP), 2020). Taxes, fees, and charges can help to reflect the social value of natural assets in market prices, whereas subsidies can be used to enhance and support actions that benefit the environment while limitations to harmful subsidies impact the industries that pollute and cause significant environmental damage. Other public instruments for natural capital include payments for ecosystem services (*e.g.*, payments for carbon storage, biodiversity conservation, and watershed services); climate and biodiversity offsets that direct funds towards projects that aim to compensate nature's losses; and direct fundraising for natural asset investments.

However, governments cannot do all the heavy lifting as, from the finance perspective, in industrialized, market-based economies, private funding is significantly greater than public finance (Bank for International Settlements (BIS), 2020). Private investments are an extremely powerful machine for development that should henceforth be harnessed for nature. Private financial investments in natural capital are typically regarded as a sub-set of financial investments in broader investment categories, such as "sustainable" and "green" finance. "Sustainable" investment defines a large category for approaches to investment behaviour wherein non-financial factors also guide the selection and management of investments (Suttor-Sorel and Hercelin, 2020). The "green finance" label encompasses green bonds, sustainability-linked loans, private equity funds in supporting biodiversity, environmental impact bonds, and other sources, such as insurance products as the forms of mechanisms and instruments (Deutz *et al.*, 2020; OECD, 2020). Carbon markets (or emissions trading schemes) are another potential mechanism for supporting conservation and restoration projects (von Unger and Emmer, 2018) and, thus, natural assets (see, *e.g.*, Dasgupta 2021, Figure 20.2).

However, financial investments in natural capital remain scarce due to three key factors. First, these investments have not proven particularly profitable. Second, even globally, projects that enhance natural capital are often too small to attract financial investment (Huwlyer, Käppeli and Tobin, 2016), which affects their riskiness and the time required to set up each project (Cooper and Trémolet, 2019; World Bank, 2020). Third, standardized data and transparency on financial investments are lacking. For potential investors, it is difficult to make investment decisions in the absence of information about expected returns and impact. Nature-related risks will be realized over lengthy time horizons, and these risks may be ignored and overshadowed by the much shorter time horizon of risks to financial players. Lack of information and information asymmetry regarding the outcome of the investments have also been identified as barriers to private finance's provision of sufficient investment in natural capital (G20 Sustainable Finance Study Group, 2018). However, some mechanisms have already been developed with the aim of overcoming these problems. *Blended Finance* uses public finance to mobilize sources of private funding as governments provide both grants and guarantees to cover or reduce the risks related to loans and equities. Typically, it covers potential first losses, provides grants for initial finance and venture funding, and undertakes result-payments or provides technical assistance. Blended finance mechanisms can signal to investors the financial returns of a project, de-risk it and develop proof-of-concept (Dasgupta, 2021). Another alternative, *spatial finance,* utilizes information derived from the independent assessment of the location of the company's or country's assets and infrastructure using ground data, remote sensing observations and modelled insights (World Bank and World Wide Fund for Nature (WWF), 2020). This lends greater substance to the use of, for example, ESG information in the investment decisions by utilizing, for example, satellite data to measure all the sustainability-related characteristics of the relevant entity's assets.

The EU Taxonomy for sustainable activities represents a recent European action (European Commission, 2022). It has been designed as a tool for investors, companies, issuers, and project promoters to use in advancing the transition to a low-carbon, resilient, and resource-efficient economy. It is a classification system that establishes a list of environmentally sustainable economic activities. Sustainable activities should not exert significant environmental harm and must make a substantive contribution to one or more of the following six environmental objectives: (1) Climate-change mitigation; (2) climate-change adaptation; (3) sustainable protection of water and marine resources; (4) transition to a circular economy; (5) pollution prevention and control; and (6) protection and restoration of biodiversity and ecosystems.

Natural capital and central banks

The development of regulation and institutional arrangements governing the supply of financial resources to nature-enhancing projects is evidently eminent. Both public and private funding sources are required to ensure a sustainable shift from Impact Inequality to Equality, but the role that financial system plays is ultimately bounded by broader government and regulatory policies to correct for institutional failures. Since governments have been unable to fully internalize the externalities stemming from previous institutional failures, such as the failure to meet the Paris Agreement 2015 emission reduction targets globally and the accompanying target of retaining global warming below 1.5°C, financial system cannot incorporate these costs into pricing and therefore into credit allocation and lending decisions. To mitigate this situation, central banks should be given a more robust role in the near future.

The central banks have recognized the effects of global warming, natural disasters, biodiversity, and natural capital loss in light of the potential threats that they pose to economic, financial, and price stability. Boneva, Ferrucci, and Mongelli (2021) have emphasized the need for central banks to tackle the climate change, both to safeguard their ability to conduct monetary policy smoothly, deliver on their mandates, and to ensure that they remain resilient to emerging climate-related financial risks. As banks' banks, central banks may assume a more substantial role in the fight against the biodiversity loss that poses environmental risks on a systemic level, with non-linear consequences and tipping points (Abdelli *et al.*, 2021).

Masciandaro and Russo (2022) focus on the trade-offs that central banks would face were they to begin tackling especially climate change more aggressively and note that the selection of instruments available to central banks to mitigate climate-related risks overlaps considerably with those already used in relation to their monetary and macroprudential mandates. They argue that central banks' effectiveness here depends on their degree of independence from governments' climate preferences and on their ability to calibrate their "green" easing, either monetary and/or regulatory, on the realized abatement level and emissions.

From a supervisory perspective, central banks have already begun to monitor the banks in terms of their effects on Climate and Environmental (C&E) risks.

The ECB's (2021) report of 112 significant euro-area banks revealed that none of the institutions are even close to fully aligning their practices with the supervisory C&E risk management expectations. Although some have already taken steps towards adapting their practices to reflect C&E risks, most remain in the early stages of development. As the challenges related to the integration of C&E risks into banks' operations are constantly evolving, the ECB is committed to continuing its dialogue with these institutions and aims to play a substantial role in the enhancement of C&E risk management practices in the near future.

Finally, central banks' role in enhancing the efficiency of funding channels regarding especially the greening of financial system has increased recently. Eliet-Doillet and Maino (2022) report that the announcement of the July 2021 ECB's Monetary Policy Strategy Review had a significant effect on the pricing and issuance of green bonds in the Eurozone: ECB-eligible green bonds' prices increased together with the amount of issued green bonds. Hence, ECB's action seemed to have a positive effect on increasing funding of green projects in the euro area.

Debt, equity, and natural capital

All dimensions of sustainability have received greater attention from investors in recent decades. Investors demand ethical portfolio allocations and prioritize social responsibility in their decisions. Krueger, Sautner, and Starks (2020) reveal that active institutional investors believe climate change has significant financial implications. JP Morgan has stated that the value of socially responsible investment is up 200% from the previous decade and was worth almost $22.8 trillion in 2018. The numbers of both ESG-themed funds and assets under their management have tripled in the last seven years (JP Morgan, 2018). Most importantly, investors prioritize the protection of their own reputations, followed by their moral/ethical obligations and legal/fiduciary duties. However, suitable investment opportunities, risk management, and asset owners' preferences follow closely.

Green bonds can work as an indirect medium to also attract the equity capital required for environment-supporting production. Aside from bank loans, firms can finance their operations by issuing bonds and/or stocks. Investors buying corporate bonds lend money for the company which, in return, promises to pay back interest on the principal and the principal itself when the bonds mature. On the other hand, equity capital provides funds for firms in exchange for stocks. Shareholders own parts of the firms and are entitled to a portion of their earnings in form of dividends and have a voting right in shareholders' meetings. The higher the price of a stock, the lower the cost of capital for the firm when it issues new stocks. The connection between green bonds and firms' equity valuations has been identified in recent findings implying that an issuance of the green bonds attracts positive media attention and functions as a signalling device. Given that only firms with the most efficient green projects commit to the process, the issuance of green bonds signals the environmental project's positive values, leading to higher stock prices and lower equity capital costs for the firm (Daubanes, Mitali and Rocher, 2022).

The banking sector and bond markets have already begun to reduce the capital costs for sustainable loans. Kempa, Moslener, and Schenker (2021) suggest that renewable energy firms might initially face higher debt costs but that these have decreased in recent years in comparison to others. Similar changes have occurred among economies with more developed banking sector and stringent environmental policies. According to JP Morgan, 65% of all socially responsible investments are focusing on bond markets. Firms issuing green bonds pledge finance for environmentally friendly projects, such as clean and renewable energy or energy storage investments (Giglio, Kelly and Stroebel, 2021).

The green bonds trade at a premium and offer lower yields than otherwise similar, non-green bonds (Baker et al., 2018; Zerbib, 2019). This signals the inclusion of non-financial utility related to investing in green bonds, stemming from environmental concerns. Bonds issued by governments and supranational institutions and very large issues of corporate bonds together with third-party certificates signal credibility, leading to reduced debt costs (Kapraun et al., 2021). These premia are modest but non-negligible. Stock (2021) advocates a shift in the emphasis in sustainability discussion to sectoral level policies with the idea of permanently reducing the cost of debt for funding the nature-enhancing projects of real investments.

Sustainable equity financing is currently considered less profitable than investments in traditional assets, but Bauer, Ruof, and Smeets (2021) argue that investors are also willing to sacrifice part of the returns for the social good. Pástor, Stambaugh, and Taylor (2021, p. 550) state that "green assets have low expected returns because investors enjoy holding them and because green assets hedge climate risk". Hence, the lower expected returns verify non-pecuniary compensations or that the nature-supporting assets are regarded as safer investments with respect to environmental and regulatory risks. To attract more market-based funding, environment-supporting production should offer higher returns with similar or lower risks than the alternatives and should be able to signal this to the investors.

Conclusions

This chapter has discussed financial system's ability to steer investments towards production that will ensure the Earth's natural capital (nature, biosphere), a self-regenerative part of the planet. We propose that planetary well-being-oriented sustainable economic production of this nature occurs via the financial exclusion of non-environmentally friendly investments that tilt investment and resources towards more sustainable production. In addition to the obvious substantial role played by governments, the financial intermediation system—through both the indirect (banking) and direct (market-based) channels—and the central banks, in setting the rules and as active market participants, are vital in steering the economy towards planetary well-being-preserving production.

The sustainability-related criteria in finance, together with the emergence of green bonds, and the newly introduced European taxonomy in investments are directing the future of real economic production towards more planetary well-being-friendly production. However, the long-term nature of planetary well-being and valuation uncertainties also call for changes in traditional thinking. In planetary well-being-oriented projects, investors must be willing to accept higher long-term risks that are not necessarily compensated with higher returns. To ensure funding in these circumstances, the standard thinking is that supporting public policies are also required in terms of direct subsidies and tax allowances. However, experiences from the central banks' role in the recent crises (the GFC 2007–2009 and the COVID-19 pandemic) lend support to central banks' abilities to also enhance the funding available for planetary well-being projects. Among other standards, the internationally agreed financial standards, such as the Basel III and IV capital adequacy rules for banks and the Insurance Capital Standard, could also be applied to biodiversity-related financial risks. The central banks and financial supervisors should fundamentally integrate the environmental risks into macro- and micro-prudential supervision. They should also address carefully the environmental risks on their own balance sheets and request enhanced disclosure from the financial sector (as is envisaged by the work of the Taskforce on Nature-related Financial Disclosures). Furthermore, they should speed up the adaptation of international financial standards to properly take into account the new cross-cutting dimensions into traditional financial risk management, ensuring the necessary coordination and convergence of practices among the relevant institutions.

It is our hope that, in the very near future, finance will facilitate the perennial integrity of Earth and ecosystem processes without serious conflicts with economic well-being.

Acknowledgements

Authors are thankful for the financial support of the paper which contributes to the activities of the OP Research Foundation's Group on Financial Institutions.

References

Abdelli, M. *et al.* (2021) *Nature's Next Stewards. Why Central Bankers Need to Take Action on Biodiversity Risk?* Zürich: WWF-Switzerland. Available at: https://wwfint.awsassets.panda.org/downloads/wwf_report_nature_s_next_stewards_14_july_2021.pdf (Accessed: 23 November 2022).

Alogoskoufis, S. *et al.* (2021) 'Climate related risk to financial stability', *ECB Financial Stability Review*. Available at: https://www.ecb.europa.eu/pub/financial-stability/fsr/special/html/ecb.fsrart202105_02~d05518fc6b.en.html (Accessed: 23 November 2022).

Baker, M. *et al.* (2018) 'Financing the response to climate change: The pricing and ownership of US green bonds', *NBER Working Paper*, 25194. Available at: https://

www.brookings.edu/wp-content/uploads/2018/07/Wurgler-J.-et-al..pdf (Accessed: 23 November 2022).

Bastien-Olvera, B.A. and Moore, F.C. (2021) 'Use and non-use value of nature and social costs of carbon', *Nature Sustainability*, 4, pp. 101–108. https://doi.org/10.1038/s41893-020-00615-0

Bastien-Olvera, B.A. and Moore, F.C. (2022) 'Climate impacts on natural capital: Consequences for the social costs of carbon', *Annual Review of Resource Economics*, 14, pp. 515–542. https://doi.org/10.1146/annurev-resource-111820-020204

Bauer, R., Ruof, T. and Smeets, P. (2021) 'Get real! Individuals prefer more sustainable investments', *The Review of Financial Studies*, 34, pp. 3976–4043. https://doi.org/10.1093/rfs/hhab037

BIS (2020) *Annual Economic Report*. Available at: https://www.bis.org/publ/arpdf/ar2020e.pdf (Accessed: 23 November 2022).

Boneva, L., Ferrucci, G. and Mongelli, F.P. (2021) 'To be or not to be 'green': How can monetary policy react to climate change?', *ECB Occasional Paper Series*, 285.

Buch-Hansen, H. and Koch, M. (2019) 'Degrowth through income and wealth caps?', *Ecological Economics*, 160, pp. 264–271. https://doi.org/10.1016/j.ecolecon2019.03.001

Colacito, R., Hoffmann, B. and Phan, T. (2019) 'Temperature and growth: A panel analysis of the United States', *Journal of Money, Credit and Banking*, 51(2–3), pp. 313–368. https://doi.org/10.1111/jmcb.12574

Cooper, G. and Trémolet, S. (2019) *Investing in Nature: Private Finance for Nature-Based Resilience*. London: The Nature Conservancy and Environmental Finance. Available at: https://www.nature. org/content/dam/tnc/nature/en/documents/TNC-INVESTING-INNATURE_Report_01.pdf (Accessed: 23 November 2022).

Dasgupta, P. (2014) 'Measuring the wealth of nations', *Annual Review of Resource Economics*, 6(1), pp. 17–31. https://doi.org/10.1146/annurev-resource-100913-012358

Dasgupta, P. (2021) *The Economics of Biodiversity: The Dasgupta Review*. London: HM Treasury.

Daubanes, J.X., Mitali, S.F. and Rocher, J-C. (2022) 'Why do firms issue green bonds?', *MIT CEEPR Working Paper Series*, 2022–011. Available at: https://ceepr.mit.edu/wp-content/uploads/2022/01/2022-001v2.pdf (Accessed: 23 November 2022).

Deutz, A. *et al.* (2020) *Financing Nature: Closing the Global Biodiversity Financing Gap*. The Paulson Institute, the Nature Conservancy, and the Cornell Atkinson Center for Sustainability. Available at: https://www.paulsoninstitute.org/wp-content/uploads/2020/09/FINANC-ING-NATURE_Full-Report_Final-Version_091520.pdf (Accessed: 23 November 2022).

ECB (2020) *Guide on Climate-Related and Environmental Risks. Supervisory Expectations Relating to Risk Management and Disclosure*. Frankfurt am Main: ECB. Available at: https://www.bankingsupervision.europa.eu/ecb/pub/pdf/ssm.202011finalguideonclimate-relate dandenvironmentalrisks~58213f6564.en.pdf (Accessed: 23 November 2022).

ECB (2021) *The State of Climate and Environmental Risk Management in the Banking Sector. Report on the Supervisory Review of Banks' Approaches to Manage Climate and Environmental Risks*. Frankfurt am Main: ECB. Available at: https://www.bankingsupervision.europa.eu/ecb/pub/pdf/ssm.202111guideonclimate-relatedandenvironmentalrisks ~4b25454055.en.pdf (Accessed: 23 November 2022).

Eliet-Doillet, A. and Maino, A. (2022) 'Can unconventional monetary policy contribute to climate action?', *Swiss Finance Institute Research Paper Series*, 22–35. https://dx.doi.org/10.2139/ssrn.4090616

European Commission (2022) *EU Taxonomy for Sustainable Activities*. Available at: https://ec.europa.eu/info/business-economy-euro/banking-and-finance/sustainable-finance/eu-taxonomy-sustainable-activities_en (Accessed: 23 November 2022).

G20 Sustainable Finance Study Group (2018) *Sustainable Finance Synthesis Report*. Available at: G20_Sustainable_Finance_Synthesis_Report_2018.pdf (g20sfwg.org) (Accessed: 23 November 2022).

Giglio, S., Kelly, B. and Stroebel, J. (2021) 'Climate finance', *Annual Review of Financial Economics*, 13(1), pp. 15–36. https://doi.org/10.1146/annurev-finanical-102620-103311

Hartley, T., van den Bergh, J. and Kallis, G. (2020) 'Policies for equality under low or no growth: Model inspired by Piketty', *Review of Political Economy*, 32(2), pp. 243–258. https://doi.org/10.1080/09538259.2020.1769293

Hickel, J. and Kallis G. (2020) 'Is green growth possible?', *New Political Economy*, 25(4), pp. 469–486. https://doi.org/10.1080/13563467.2019.1598964

Huwlyer, F., Käppeli, J. and Tobin, J. (2016) *Conservation Finance from Niche to Mainstream: The Building of an Institutional Asset Class*. Credit Suisse Group AG and McKinsey Center for Business and Environment. Available at: https://www.rockefellerfoundation.org/wp-content/uploads/conservation-finance-en.pdf (Accessed 23 November 2022).

JP Morgan (2018) 'Sustainable investing is moving mainstream', 20 April. Available at: https://www.jpmorgan.com/insights/research/esg (Accessed: 23 November 2022).

Kacprzyk, A. and Kuchta, Z. (2020) 'Shining a new light on the environmental Kuznets curve for CO2 emissions', *Energy Economics*, 87, pp. 1–10. https://doi.org/10.1016/j.eneco.2020.104704

Kapraun, J. *et al.* (2021) '(In)-credibly green: Which bonds trade at a green bond premium?', *Proceedings of Paris December 2019 Finance Meeting EUROFIDAI - ESSEC*. https://dx.doi.org/10.2139/ssrn.3347337

Kempa, K., Moslener, U. and Schenker, O. (2021) 'The cost of debt of renewable and non-renewable energy firms', *Nature Energy*, 6, pp. 135–142. https://doi.org/10.1038/s41560-020-00745-x

Kortetmäki, T., *et al.* (2021) 'Planetary well-being', *Humanities & Social Sciences Communications*, 8, 258. https://doi.org/10.1057/s41599-021-00899-3

Koumbarakis, A. *et al.* (2020) *Nature Is Too Big to Fail. Biodiversity: The Next Frontier in Financial Risk Management*. Zürich: PWC. Available at: https://wwfint.awsassets.panda.org/downloads/nature_is_too_big_to_fail_en_web.pdf (Accessed: 23 November 2022).

Krueger, P., Sautner, Z. and Starks, L.T. (2020) 'The importance of climate risks for institutional investors', *Review of Financial Studies*, 33, pp. 1067–1111. https://doi.org/10.1093/rfs/hhz137

Managi, S. and Kumar, P. (2018) *Inclusive Wealth Report 2018: Measuring Progress Towards Sustainability*. New York: Routledge. https://doi.org/10.4324/9781351002080

Masciandaro, D. and Russo, R. (2022) 'Central banks and climate policy: Unpleasant trade-offs? A principal–agent approach', *BAFFI CAREFIN Centre Research Paper*, 2022–181. https://dx.doi.org/10.2139/ssrn.4139124

Mastini, R., Kallis, G. and Hickell J. (2021) 'A Green New Deal without growth?', *Ecological Economics*, 179, 106832. https://doi.org/10.1016/j.ecolecon.2020.106832

OECD (2020) *A Comprehensive Overview of Global Biodiversity Finance*. OECD Environment Directorate. Available at: https://www.oecd.org/environment/resources/biodiversity/report-a-comprehensive-overview-of-global-biodiversity-finance.pdf (Accessed: 23 November 2023).

OECD (2022) *Green Growth and Sustainable Development*. Available at: https://www.oecd.org/greengrowth/ (Accessed: 23 November 2022).

Pástor, L., Stambaugh, R.F. and Taylor, L.A. (2021) 'Sustainable investing in equilibrium', *Journal of Financial Economics*, 142(2), pp. 550–571. https://doi.org/10.1016/j.jfineco.2020.12.011

Pollin, R. (2018) 'De-growth vs a green new deal', *New Left Review*, 112, pp. 5–25. Available at: https://newleftreview.org/issues/ii112/articles/robert-pollin-de-growth-vs-a-green-new-deal (Accessed: 23 November 2022).

Romer, D. (2019) *Advanced Macroeconomics*. 5th edn. New York: McGraw Hill Economics.

Schüwer, U., Lambert, C. and Noth, F. (2019) 'How do banks react to catastrophic events? Evidence from Hurricane Katrina', *Review of Finance*, 23(1), pp. 75–116. https://doi.org/10.1093/rof/rfy010

Stock, J. (2021) 'Driving deep decarbonization: As green economy costs drop, we should shift emphasis from economy-wide carbon prices to sectoral policies', *IMF: Finance & Development*, 58(3), pp. 12–15.

Suttor-Sorel, L. and Hercelin, N. (2020) *Nature's Return: Embedding Environmental Goals at the Heart of Economic and Financial Decision-making*. Finance Watch Report. Available at: https://www.finance-watch.org/wp-content/uploads/2020/05/Natures-Return_Finance-Watch-Report_May2020.pdf (Accessed: 22 November 2022).

UNDP (2020) *Moving Mountains: Unlocking Private Capital for Biodiversity and Ecosystems*. New York: UNDP. Available at: https://www.biofin.org/knowledge-product/moving-mountains-unlocking-private-capital-biodiversity-and-ecosystems http://www.biodiversityfinance.org/(Accessed: 22 November 2022).

UNEP FI and PRI (2019) *Fiduciary Duty in 21st Century*. Available at: https://www.unepfi.org/wordpress/wp-content/uploads/2019/10/Fiduciary-duty-21st-century-final-report.pdf (Accessed: 22 November 2022).

von Unger, M. and Emmer, I. (2018) *Carbon Market Incentives to Conserve, Restore and Enhance Soil Carbon*. Arlington, VA: Silvestrum and the Nature Conservatory. Available at: https://www.nature.org/content/dam/tnc/nature/en/documents/Carbon-Market-Incentives-Report.pdf (Accessed: 22 November 2022).

Ward, J.D. *et al.* (2016) 'Is decoupling GDP growth from environmental impact possible', *PLoS One*, 11(10), e0164733. https://doi.org/10.1371/journal.pone.0164733

World Bank (2020) *Mobilizing Private Finance for Nature*. Washington, DC: The World Bank Group. Available at: https://thedocs.worldbank.org/en/doc/916781601304630850-0120022020/original/FinanceforNature28Sepwebversion.pdf (Accessed: 23 November 2022).

World Bank and WWF (2020*) Spatial Finance: Challenges and Opportunities in a Changing World*. Washington, DC: World Bank. Available at: http://hdl.handle.net/10986/34894 (Accessed: 23 November 2022).

Zerbib, O. (2019) 'The effect of pro-environmental preferences on bond prices: Evidence from green bonds', *Journal of Banking and Finance*, 98, pp. 39–60. https://doi.org/10.1016/j.jbankfin.2018.10.012

17

TOWARDS CULTURAL TRANSFORMATION

Culture as planetary well-being

Aino-Kaisa Koistinen, Kaisa Kortekallio, Minna Santaoja and Sanna Karkulehto

Introduction

Culture is often mentioned as the fourth pillar of sustainability, alongside its social, ecological, and economic dimensions. Whereas "social", "ecological", and "economic" are relatively clearly distinguished concepts and attributes of sustainability, "cultural sustainability"—let alone the of concept "culture"—remains vaguer (Soini and Birkeland, 2014; Sabatini, 2019). Culture is, indeed, an elusive and multidimensional concept that can include everything from Hollywood films to heritage sites and lifestyles—not to mention divisions into "high" and "low" culture or mainstream and sub-cultures. Culture can thus be defined in multiple ways. According to cultural studies scholar Raymond Williams (1985, p. 64), there are three common definitions: (1) "[A] general process of intellectual, spiritual and aesthetic development"; (2) "a particular way of life, whether of a people, a period, a group, or humanity in general"; and (3) "the works and practices of intellectual and especially artistic activity".

Williams' third understanding of culture has become the most common. This is a concept of culture as visual and fine arts, literature, music, theatre, architecture, films, games, concerts, and performances—and institutions such as libraries and museums that foster these practices. Quite often culture is understood more broadly as ways of life that encompass intellectual/artistic activity as well as habits, lifestyles, traditions, beliefs, values, and worldviews (see also Pirnes, 2009; Dessein *et al.*, 2015, p. 21). Understood broadly, culture is part of the life of every human being—or even, culture is *human life* in all its aspects. Cultural practices, understood as shared habitual and customary ways of life, shape human lives, and culture as ways of life is simultaneously shaped by the practices and activities of individuals.

DOI: 10.4324/9781003334002-23

Building on and rethinking culture and cultural sustainability in the framework of planetary well-being, this chapter outlines how culture can be regarded as planetary well-being. In their influential report, Dessein *et al.* (2015) define cultural sustainability in terms of three roles that reflect the multidimensionality of culture as a concept. The first role, (1) culture *in* sustainable development, defines culture as something with intrinsic value (*i.e.*, valuable "as such"). This can refer to individual artworks, architecture, or heritage sites. When culture is seen as the fourth pillar in sustainability discourse, it is understood in line with this first definition. The second role, (2) culture *for* sustainable development, frames culture as a mediator for sustainability, with the capacity to frame, contextualize, and balance the requirements of social, ecological, and economic aspects of sustainability. This can encompass for example films, literary works, and visual art that carry messages relevant to sustainability. The third and most comprehensive role, (3) culture *as* sustainable development, refers to culture as a broader shift towards more sustainable lifestyles and worldviews.

Culture *in* sustainable development corresponds roughly to the narrower understanding of culture as intellectual or artistic activities, whereas the second and third roles refer to the broader understanding of culture as ways of life. The different roles and definitions are interlinked and overlapping, and the two first roles of culture—culture *in* and *for* sustainability—are at least partly nested in culture *as* sustainable development. According to Dessein *et al.* (*ibid.*), culture, in the broadest sense, forms a foundation for sustainable development and can even be considered the most important dimension of sustainability. Recognizing culture as an overarching concern in sustainability thinking, in all its forms, may allow culture and sustainability to intertwine in ways that can help dissolve the tensions between social, economic, and ecological sustainability.

In this chapter, we suggest that in the current ecological and well-being crises, cultural transformation has to denote a process towards *planetary well-being*, in which the well-being and needs of humans, other species, and ecosystems are considered both intrinsically important and interlinked. By *cultural transformation,* we refer to a large-scale change in shared knowledges, lifestyles, traditions, beliefs, morals, laws, customs, values, institutions, and worldviews, and how they are practised in everyday life. Large-scale cultural transformation requires simultaneous work and changes on different levels of society, from individual to institutional and structural. As cultural practices are renewed in everyday actions, they are open to change, and the changes may give rise to broader cultural transformations.

Cultural transformation—including changing unsustainable production and consumption patterns—needs to be considered with respect to multiple levels of society (*e.g.*, Raatikainen *et al.*, 2021). In other words, culture as a whole—what is considered meaningful and how life is organized based on that—needs to transform. To put it simply, we suggest that cultural transformation is critical for achieving planetary well-being, and the required cultural transformation can be called *culture as planetary well-being*. We emphasize that a narrower understanding of culture as intellectual and artistic activity is relevant in this transformation. We focus specifically on the potential of contemporary art in evoking and developing planetary thinking and action. The potential of arts and literature to influence or transform people, for either good or bad, has been widely researched (*e.g.*, Keen, 2007; Fialho, 2019; Lähdesmäki and Koistinen, 2021; Schneider-Mayerson, 2021). More broadly, imagination—or symbolic meaning-making—has been considered one of the key drivers of cultural practices, including social cooperation, and thus the formation of societies. By evoking imagined entities such as gods, nation-states, and theoretical concepts, human communities can explain and organize events and dynamics that are not readily available to their senses (Thrift, 2008, pp. 158–159).

As an example of how art can contribute to cultural transformation and promote culture as planetary well-being, we examine the art exhibition *Siat—Pigs* (henceforth *Pigs*; 2021) by the internationally renowned Finnish artist duo Gustafsson&Haapoja.[1] The exhibition highlighted the simultaneous societal presence and absence of pigs by exploring the experiences of a nonhuman animal commonly reduced to a mere resource for human exploitation (see also Bolman, 2019). Furthermore, the exhibition discussed how pigs are connected to class struggles, industrialization, global capitalism, environmental crises, and colonialism by emphasizing the poor working and living conditions on pig farms and in slaughterhouses. The exhibition was considered controversial by some, as it was interpreted as criticism towards the treatment of pigs in animal husbandry. We argue that the exhibition engaged in culturally transformative imagination by underlining the human and nonhumans' vulnerable, interconnected lives. By doing so in the context of animal husbandry, it also invited cultural negotiation on what forms of work and livelihood are viable in sustainable societies. The empirical case allows us to address culture as planetary well-being on different scales, from the perceptions of an individual visitor to the broader societal contexts of the artwork.

Art and the shared vulnerability of humans and nonhumans

In September 2021, *Pigs* opened in the Kunsthalle exhibition space in Seinäjoki, a town of approximately 65,000 residents in a farming region, Western Finland. The exhibition was held in three interconnected exhibition rooms. It included a sound installation *Waiting Room* (2019), consisting of a 16-channel recording of pigs' voices (recorded the night before they were slaughtered), set up in a dim-lit hall, and two videos. *Untitled (Alive)* (2021) portrays the life of a pig called Paavo, saved from slaughter, and since living in an animal shelter. *No Data* (2021) is a collage-like piece based on online data concerning the global pig industry.[2] The video brings together the use of pigs and the conditions of animal industry workers through often overlapping black and white images (primarily as negatives) of the pig industry, such as slaughterhouses and their surroundings, and fragments of text (in both English and Finnish). It includes a synthetic soundscape with a dark undertone that the visitors could listen to through headphones.

The exhibition developed on the themes expressed in Gustafsson&Haapoja's previous exhibitions, such as *The Museum of the History of Cattle* (2014) or *Museum of Nonhumanity* (2016–), that criticized the role of museums as institutions and spaces for preserving only human history and cultural heritage without recognizing the role of nonhuman animals in history and culture. In *Pigs*, Gustafsson&Haapoja called attention to the well-being of both humans and nonhumans by presenting the visitors with the experiences of pigs and pig industry workers, both suffering from poor living and working conditions. Thus, the exhibition was thematically intertwined with global contexts and critical questions on ecological, economic, and social sustainability and well-being on a planetary scale.

The sound installation *Waiting Room* consisted of speakers playing pigs' voices and nothing else, but it was framed by an exhibition text in the room leading to the sound installation, stating that the pigs were recorded on their last night before slaughter. The minimalist setting of the exhibition room highlighted the effect of the voices: There was not much else that the visitor could focus on (see Figure 17.1). The visitor was thus forced to encounter the pigs in a manner to which most city-dwelling museum-goers are not accustomed—that is, by their overwhelming auditive presence. The lack of visual representation of the pigs also emphasized the simultaneous absence and presence of pigs in society that the exhibition sought to address. Scholars such as Carol J. Adams (2010) and Timothy Pachirat (2011, p. 3; see also Creed, 2017, p. 114) have noted the cultural invisibility of animals reared for their meat: The animals become products, meat, and the actual living and dying animals are concealed from sight. The pigs' voices even seeped through the headphones when viewing the videos in the other rooms, thus contributing to the viewing experience. The fact that the voices were recorded on their last night before slaughter highlighted the pigs' vulnerability and dependency on humans and confronted the visitor with questions such as the pigs' possible awareness of their approaching death.

The visual absence of the pigs in *Waiting Room* was in stark contrast to the video *Untitled (Alive)* displayed in the preceding room—even the title of the video serves as a counterpoint to the soon-to-be-dead animals. The video was captured by attaching a camera with a harness to the pig called Paavo, now living in an animal shelter. The camera was attached to Paavo's neck, so his ears and snout were visible from the back (see Figure 17.2). In this sense, the video not only offers a visual representation of a pig (that was lacking in *Waiting Room*) but invites the viewers to see the world through the eyes of one. Unlike the pigs in the sound installation, Paavo is roaming freely on the farm, sniffing and digging the ground, napping, and receiving human caresses. Watching the video, it is easy to describe Paavo as a happy hog who gets to act according to his species-specific behaviour. The video portrays him as an individual, not as a resource to be consumed.

In the exhibition catalogue, Gustafsson&Haapoja describe the video *No Data* as "an attempt to examine what kind of world is created by animal husbandry".[3] They also note the difficulty in attempting to grasp the whole picture of pig husbandry,

FIGURE 17.1 *Waiting Room.* Copyright: Jenni Latva. Courtesy of Kunsthalle Seinäjoki.

FIGURE 17.2 *Untitled (Alive).* Screenshot. Courtesy of Kunsthalle Seinäjoki.

where the well-being of both humans and nonhumans is connected to bacteria, feed production, and industrial infrastructure. The name *No Data* thus highlights the enormous scale and inaccessibility of the animal industry. The fragmented poetics of the video communicates this scale and inaccessibility: The viewers are presented with changing images and texts that do not provide enough data to see the whole (see Figure 17.3). The effect is further emphasized by the fragmented nature of the presented texts, as the following excerpts illustrate:

> the bloodier incidents really bothered her, she said, such as when a new hire caught his

> an employee working on a sanitation crew pushed a button after removing parts from the upper of a machine. the employee then placed his foot into a

> a worker was reaching to pick up a box of clear a jam when his jacket became caught in a roller. As he tried to pull out, his

The fragments leave the sentences open, allowing viewers to fill in the gaps. The promise of "bloody incidents" in the first fragment invites viewers to assume that the omitted texts would contain something violent for the workers. It is noteworthy that *No Data* also encompasses the experiences of the pig farmers in the fragment: "Farms facing distress have relied on short-term loans".[4] The precarious conditions of the pig industry workers discussed in the video thus extend to the farmers. Precarity is commonly understood as uncertainty of employment and human livelihood within the global capitalist economy (see, *e.g.*, Precarias a la deriva, 2009, pp. 100, 387). In the era of ecosocial crises, precarity has become an existential question about the possibility of future human and nonhuman life on Earth. In this precarious condition, humans and pigs are both culprits of environmental disasters via complex ecological and economic interlinkages, and simultaneously the victims of conditions.

The fragmented texts borrow their aesthetics from poetry. Discussing the possibility of writing the life of another meat animal, the cow, Jessica Holmes (2021) connects poetry to activism in its potential to lend voices to those who are silenced, "in part due to its capacity to embody loss, fragmentation, and absence". Thus, "poems offer alternative methods of seeing or bearing witness to, remembering and assigning value to individual subjects" (*ibid.*, p. 229). Within the context of the *Pigs* exhibition, the poetic language of *No Data* invited the viewers to bear witness to the vulnerabilities and interconnected lives of pigs and pig industry workers, habitually rendered invisible by the sheer logistics of technological civilization.

It is often claimed that the potential of art and literature to instigate societal changes lies in their capacity to allow people to grasp the experiences, feelings, and emotions of others, including nonhuman animals (Rifkin, 2010, p. 312; Creed, 2017, pp. 123–124; Weik von Mossner, 2017; Lähdesmäki and Koistinen, 2021). In *Pigs*, the visitors were invited to share some parts of the experiences of both pigs and pig industry workers. In *No Data*, the fates and well-being of both humans and nonhumans are deeply entangled, speaking of their shared vulnerability and precarity. The images and texts depict conditions that are hazardous and deadly for both—and even for the broader natural environment that is affected by pig industrial waste. Some of the fragments also underline the role of immigrants as pig industry workers in poor conditions, highlighting how some humans are in more precarious situations than others (see Butler, 2004).

FIGURE 17.3 The fragmented poetics of *No Data*. Copyright Jenni Latva. Courtesy of Kunsthalle Seinäjoki.

In the case of the voice installation and the text fragments of *No Data*, *Pigs* can also be interpreted as "giving voice" to cultural "others". The idea of speaking for others may be contested in the case of humans, since instead of "speaking for" one might instead need to listen to others capable of speaking for themselves (*e.g.*, marginalized, indigenous, or racialized people; see Montero-Sieburth, 2020). However, as the texts in *No Data* represent the words of actual workers, the artists are borrowing their own words to speak for them, which emerges as a form of listening. When it comes to nonhumans, "speaking for" becomes somewhat problematic, and the possibility of human beings representing nonhumans via language has been criticized (Karkulehto *et al.*, 2020; MacCormack, 2020, p. 56, pp. 79–80). That said, in human legislation and cultural practices, nonhuman animals need humans to speak for them, but this "speaking for" always requires listening to nonhumans first. The sound installation *Waiting Room* can be interpreted as inviting the visitors to listen to the pigs as living, breathing, and sometimes noisy animals. It is not always possible to concretely listen to nonhumans, but listening can be understood as turning human attention to nonhumans and their experiences.

Approaching the experiences of others through arts and literature has been argued to lead to empathy towards other people (*e.g.*, Keen, 2007; Fialho, 2019) and perhaps even to other species (*e.g.*, Creed, 2017, p. 19; Weik von Mossner, 2017, pp. 1–16)—even though it cannot, of course, be argued that this is always the outcome of reading literature or experiencing art (Lähdesmäki and Koistinen,

2021). It can, however, be claimed that the *Pigs* exhibition used the imaginative potential of art to expose museum-goers to the experiences and living/working conditions of both humans and animals in the pig industry.[5] Depending on the viewer, this may have been an affective and emotional experience that involved empathetic feelings towards the pigs and meat industry workers and reveals the more-than-human vulnerability, injustices, and (political) struggle in the industrialized, neoliberal, and postcolonial market economy.

Art and the changing meanings of work

The site of the exhibition brought another level to the discussion on the animal industry. Until the 1980s, the building was used as a cowshed, with a slaughterhouse and a meat processing plant in its immediate vicinity. Kunsthalle Seinäjoki's exhibitions address issues arising from its location on the intersection of urban and rural contexts. The animal industry is still an important livelihood in the region, and Gustafsson&Haapoja wanted to bring the exhibition to discuss the future of food production on-site. The exhibition hit a pressure point at the intersection of local livelihoods, animal ethics, and sustainable transformation of (food) culture. In November 2021, *Pigs* attracted a lot of media attention. After two middle school classes from the nearby town of Kurikka had visited the exhibition, the mayor of Kurikka forbade further elementary school classes from visiting it. Parents, many of them pig farmers themselves, had contacted the mayor. The ban was based on the claim that the exhibition gave too one-sided an image of pig husbandry. According to the head of the local education and culture department, the decision aimed to protect children from offensive content (Koivuranta and Ahola, 2021).

The media debate that followed the ban on school visits questioned whether the mayor had the authority to intervene in the curriculum. After all, animal welfare has been part of the Finnish school curriculum since 2016, although it varies significantly how this is implemented in schools. In an interview (Mäenpää, 2021), the exhibition curator claimed that people who had not even seen the exhibition gave too scandalous an image of it. According to the curator, many of the people who had seen the exhibition said that they were rather positively disappointed than shocked, as everything was presented in a sensitive manner. The local pig farmers, for their part, took the exhibition as part of a broader attack on their livelihood, even though the exhibition did not directly comment on local pig husbandry. What was forgotten in the media discussions around the exhibition was that *No Data* also highlights the precarious situation of pig industry workers, as discussed above.

The farmers' reaction to the exhibition stresses the need for reimagining and transforming livelihoods and work for planetary well-being in ways that no one is left behind, even when the transformation becomes a site of heated cultural negotiation and political struggle. We suggest that the imaginative potential of art can be used to transform the normalized perceptions of work, as made visible by the *Pigs* exhibition and the media discussions it spurred. Especially in the video *No Data*, pig industry workers' precarious experiences and vulnerability can be interpreted on the larger scale of planetary well-being, including both human and nonhuman beings in critical discussions on ecological, economic, and social sustainability. In these contexts, it is interesting that ecological crises are often discussed in terms of consumption—both on the level of individual consumer choices and the multilateral political negotiations and agreements for sustainability—but not so often in terms of work. Nevertheless, most environmental harm is connected to some kind of work, and work causes many social and environmental injustices.

Work, like culture, is a multifaceted concept, both a noun and a verb. Work may refer, for instance, to the effort of converting matter into a desired form, or to the diverse ways people contribute to society in exchange for salary or goods— or to services, charity, and care that people offer or share without any monetary exchange. Along with numerous changing practices regarding what we eat, how we produce energy, and how mobility is organized, the transformation entails fundamental cultural changes concerning work. Many occupations will become obsolete, whereas many new professions will be formed. At best, individuals and communities would receive sufficient economic, social, and psychological support when transitioning to new livelihoods, and the cultural transformation could leave more time for care, societal participation, and cultural practices such as art (*cf.*, BIOS, 2019; Järvensivu and Toivanen, 2018). The ongoing cultural transformation of work requires a new kind of political economy, including novel solutions for income that could facilitate meaningful lifestyles, economic, ecological, and social sustainability, and planetary well-being.

The conflict raised by the *Pigs* exhibition can be perceived as a conflict of values that entails a wicked moral choice: Should society prioritize the well-being of pigs or the current livelihoods of farmers? The exhibition was probably perceived as offensive as it showed pigs as individuals with desires that the visitors could and should empathize with. The moral conflict was highlighted in *No Data* by presenting the viewer with images and texts featuring the ill-being of pigs, followed by a question that brings to the fore the anthropocentrism of pig husbandry: "Raising pigs on concrete—is it right for me?" Here, the well-being of pigs remains concealed, and the focus remains on the human farmers: No one is asking whether it is right for the pigs to raise them on concrete. Regardless of our moral preference, the persuasive power of art matters for the public discussion about pigs and farm workers—and this discussion may, then, ultimately affect the material living conditions of both.

Upon opening of the *Pigs* exhibition in September 2021, Gustafsson&Haapoja organized a seminar discussing pigs in society.[6] They had invited several experts from different fields to address the topic: An animal welfare representative, a researcher of regenerative agriculture, an animal rights lawyer, and an activist secretly shooting videos on animal farms. The seminar posed the question of how to live more ethically with nonhuman animals while acknowledging the problematic position of the farmers. In light of the seminar, the media debate on the exhibition oversimplified it by constructing a bias between local livelihoods and animal welfare. Laura Gustafsson recognized how farmers are caught between a rock and a hard place, as they are bound to the current production system by agricultural subsidies and an emphasis on the efficiency and growth of the agricultural sector. Galina Kallio, a researcher in regenerative agriculture, described the many ways producers are already experimenting with re-organizing food production. "Invisible work" done by humans and ecosystems is not explicit in political talk, market prices, or official statistics but nevertheless increases the well-being of both humans and ecosystems. Currently, these new forms of organizing work transpire mainly outside formal organizations (see also Kallio, 2018), but making them visible through art and research may make different ways of organizing livelihood more widely available to producers.

In farms where forms of regenerative agriculture are already practised, relationships between humans and nonhuman animals such as pigs are configured very differently from the "conventional" industrial pig husbandry. The animals on the farm do work—they may contribute, for instance, by keeping the grass short and processing it into manure, thus recycling nutrients back to the soil. They do not exist only to be killed and eaten, and they get to live according to their species-specific and individual needs. Working for the well-being of the ecosystems, animals, and humans could provide farmers with new meaningful livelihoods and work.

The *Pigs* exhibition and the seminar exemplify art's potential to invite the visitors to imagine a transformation towards more sustainable living. It shows the potential of art in raising questions about planetary well-being and making visible the subordinate role of many, especially nonhuman, others in culture and society. While the exhibition may have contributed to the cultural transformation towards planetary well-being by questioning the justification of industrial meat production and related work, it also showed how daunting the transformation may be. Pig farmers have been accusing urban dwellers and green politicians of aiming to reduce meat production without understanding where domestic meat comes from and how the animals are treated. During the exhibition, however, the farmers strongly opposed the artists' attempt at educating audiences about pig farming practices—and, as the media debate shows, even deemed the topic unsuitable for their children. The farmers appeal for their right to practise their legal livelihood, but the debate goes deeper. By questioning the morality of industrial animal husbandry, art challenges the farmers' identities, exposing their vulnerability by drawing parallels between the suffering of the pigs and of the animal industry employees.

The example highlights how art's affective and political impact can be considered threatening. This potential threat is intimately connected to art's capacity to imagine the perspectives of others—even of people and creatures usually considered aliens or enemies. In transitioning to culture as planetary well-being, such concerns should be addressed by listening to the voices of all concerned—consumers or producers, pigs or farmers, artists or politicians.

Conclusion: Culture as planetary well-being

Cultural transformation is a matter of both visions and practices. It encompasses the imagination of what planetary well-being would look like in more-than-human societies and the ongoing realization of such visions as concrete actions. Sometimes, promoting cultural transformation entails paying attention to cultural practices that already contribute to planetary well-being. In this chapter, we have sought to highlight the work of societally engaged artists such as Gustafsson&Haapoja. As our examination of *Pigs* shows, Gustafsson&Haapoja's work invites broad audiences to rethink how their lives are entangled with the lives of others—human and nonhuman.

The power of cultural productions, like art, lies in the possibility of creating such visions of planetary well-being. More broadly, culture as ways of life has the potential to shift the emphasis from current consumer culture and its practices to planetary well-being. Planetary well-being is based on "needs-based, nonsubjective conceptions of human well-being", meaning the fulfilment of human needs such as "the need for physical and mental health, for relationships, and for autonomy in action and thought" within planetary boundaries (Kortetmäki *et al.*, 2021, p. 5). When art brings us to realize and rethink our material embeddedness in the lives of others and our shared vulnerability, it can deepen our understanding of what these needs are—for ourselves and others.

Moreover, art can help fulfil social and psychological needs in ways that are less destructive to ecosystems. Enjoying and practising art and cultural products can enhance mental health (Fancourt and Finn, 2019), for example, by supporting one's experience of living a meaningful life (*e.g.*, Thiele, 2013, pp. 168–193; Aholainen *et al.*, 2021). The sense of meaning is essential in inspiring people to work for the greater good of the community, which may extend to the broader environment (Thiele, 2013, pp. 168–193; Salonen and Bardy, 2015, p. 9). The sense of meaning may also lessen the need to consume material goods and inspire hope for a sustainable future (Salonen and Bardy, 2015, p. 4, 12). In this sense, the potential of art to bring meaning to life should not be overlooked.

It should be acknowledged that art is not independent of unsustainable material conditions (see Parikka, 2018; Brennan *et al.*, 2019). The ecological footprints of cultural productions and practices vary greatly. Compared to energy-intensive digital media services, large music festivals, or big Hollywood films, smaller-scale practices such as drawing and writing, meditation, dancing, or loaning books from the library have a significantly lower ecological footprint. Sustainability is a growing concern for the cultural sector (*e.g.*, Brennan *et al.*, 2019). Acknowledging their current ecological impact, many cultural organizations have begun to reimagine and reconstruct their working practices.

In our vision of culture as planetary well-being, engagement with art contributes to social and ecological sustainability by providing opportunities for reflection, creativity, connection, and enjoyment. Working towards culture as planetary well-being could involve what botanist and Potowatomi philosopher Robin Wall Kimmerer (2020, p. 336) calls "biocultural restoration". Kimmerer uses the term "culture" in the broad sense, as complete ways of life. In their view, biocultural restoration means that local people restore damaged lands and ecosystems, such as former mining areas or polluted rivers, which in turn contributes to the restoration of cultures that value respectful and reciprocal relations to the land:

> Like other mindful practices, ecological restoration can be viewed as an act of reciprocity in which humans exercise their caregiving responsibility for the ecosystems that sustain them. We restore the land, and the land restores us.

As we have argued in this chapter, engagement with art may be essential to such restoration. Not only can it alert us to the destructive ways of contemporary cultural practices but it can also orient us towards culture as planetary well-being.

Notes

1 Laura Gustafsson and Terike Haapoja.
2 These works were accompanied by English and Finnish translations of the texts seen in *No Data*; Laura Gustafsson's essay on Paavo, the pig from *Untitled (Alive)*; and an exhibition catalogue, which includes a brief description of the exhibition and discusses the use and well-being of pigs in Finnish society. For our examination, the first author took notes upon visiting the exhibition. We also collected media coverage of the exhibition from diverse electronic outlets. In addition, the research material includes some related videos and a recording from a seminar organized in connection with the exhibition. We are grateful to Gustafsson&Haapoja and Kunsthalle Seinäjoki for providing the needed materials and to Gustafsson for providing information on the source materials for *No Data*.
3 Translated by Koistinen.
4 Translated by Koistinen from the Finnish transcript that accompanied the video.
5 Museum-goers' reactions to exhibitions are difficult to predict (see Landkammer, 2018; Sommer and Klöckner, 2019), and exhibitions may therefore not produce the expected effect. People tend to visit museums to strengthen—rather than challenge—their own values and beliefs, and demographic factors may have an effect on the choice of the museum/exhibition (Smith, 2021, pp. 3, 161–174). Museums have also been critiqued for catering to elite audiences (*e.g.*, Hall, 2008; Dixon, 2016; Turunen and Viita-aho, 2021). The media discussion around *Pigs* nevertheless highlights the potential of museums "to expand beyond their walls" (Turunen, 2020, p. 1022; see also Kros, 2014), reaching people not interested in visiting the physical museum space.
6 The seminar was part of a series entitled Art and the Rural Gathering, organized at Kunsthalle Seinäjoki.

References

Adams, C.J. (2010) *The Sexual Politics of Meat: A Feminist-Vegetarian Critical Theory.* 20th anniversary edn. New York: Continuum.

Aholainen, M. *et al.* (2021) 'Miten taide vaikuttaa? Kulttuurisia näkökulmia hyvinvointiin ja terveyteen', *Lääkärilehti* 76(9), pp. 564–568. Available at: https://www.laakarilehti.fi/tieteessa/katsausartikkeli/miten-taide-vaikuttaa-kulttuurisia-nakokulmia-hyvinvointiin-ja-terveyteen/?public=29e7a5eeae789608f35becb2cc8ef7a4 (Accessed: 26 August 2022).

BIOS (2019) *Ecological Reconstruction.* Available at: https://eco.bios.fi/ (Accessed: 26 August 2022).

Bolman, B. (2019) 'Carnivorous anatomies art and being beasts', in Karkulehto, S., Koistinen, A.-K. and Varis, E. (eds.) *Reconfiguring Human, Nonhuman and Posthuman in Literature and Culture.* New York: Routledge, pp. 163–181. https://doi.org/10.4324/9780429243042

Brennan, M. *et al.* (2019) 'Do music festival communities address environmental sustainability and how? A Scottish case study', *Popular Music*, 38(2), pp. 252–275. https://doi.org/10.1017/S0261143019000035

Butler, J. (2004) *Precarious Life: The Powers of Mourning and Violence.* London and New York: Verso.

Creed, B. (2017) *Stray. Human–Animal Ethics in the Anthropocene.* Sydney: Power Books.

Dessein, J. *et al.* (2015) *Culture in, for and as Sustainable Development. Conclusions from the COST ACTION IS1007 Investigating Cultural Sustainability.* Jyväskylä: University of Jyväskylä. Available at: https://jyx.jyu.fi/handle/123456789/50452 (Accessed: 26 August 2022).

Dixon, C. (2016) *The 'Othering' of Africa and Its Diasporas in Western Museum Practices.* PhD Thesis. University of Sheffield. Available at: https://etheses.whiterose.ac.uk/17065/ (Accessed: 26 August 2022).

Fancourt D. and Finn S. (2019) *What Is the Evidence on the Role of the Arts in Improving Health and Well-Being? A Scoping Review.* Health Evidence Network synthesis report 67. Copenhagen: WHO Regional Office for Europe 2019. Available at: https://apps.who.int/iris/handle/10665/329834 (Accessed: 26 August 2022).

Fialho, O. (2019) 'What is literature for? The role of transformative reading', *Cogent Arts & Humanities*, 6, pp. 1–16. https://doi.org/10.1080/23311983.2019.1692532

Hall, S. (2008) 'Un-settling 'the Heritage', Re-imagining the post-nation. Whose heritage?' *Third Text,* 13(49), pp. 3–13. https://doi.org/10.1080/09528829908576818

Holmes, J. (2021) 'Writing the cow: Poetry, activism, and the texts of meat', in White, J. and Whitlock, G. (eds.) *Life Writing in the Anthropocene.* New York: Routledge, pp. 228–241. https://doi.org/10.1007/978-3-030-77973-3

Järvensivu, P. and Toivanen, T. (2018) 'Miten järjestää työ ja työllisyys ekologisen jälleenrakennuksen aikakaudella?', in Suoranta, A. and Leinikki, S. (eds.) *Rapautuvan palkkatyön yhteiskunta.* Tampere: Vastapaino, pp. 44–61.

Kallio, G. (2018) *The Visible Hands: An Ethnographic Inquiry into the Emergence of Food Collectives as a Social Practice for Exchange.* Aalto University publication series Doctoral dissertations, 170/2018. Available at: https://aaltodoc.aalto.fi/handle/123456789/34034 (Accessed: 26 August 2022).

Karkulehto, S. *et al.* (2020) 'Reconfiguring human, nonhuman and posthuman: Striving for more ethical cohabitation', in Karkulehto, S., Koistinen, A.-K., and Varis, E. (eds.) *Reconfiguring Human, Nonhuman and Posthuman in Literature and Culture.* New York: Routledge, pp. 1–19. https://doi.org/10.4324/9780429243042

Keen, S. (2007) *Empathy and the Novel.* Oxford: Oxford University Press.

Kimmerer, R.W. (2020) *Braiding Sweetgrass. Indigenous Wisdom, Scientific Knowledge and the Teachings of Plants.* London: Penguin Books.

Koivuranta, R. and Ahola, S. (2021) 'Kurikan kaupunki perui yläkoululaisten vierailut sikoja ja lihateollisuutta käsittelevään näyttelyyn, syynä nuorten suojelu: 'Joidenkin kestokyvyt alkavat olla rajoilla'', *Helsingin Sanomat*, Kulttuuri & Kuvataide, 4 November. Available at: https://www.hs.fi/kulttuuri/art-2000008381115.html (Accessed: 26 August 2022).

Kortetmäki, T. et al. (2021) 'Planetary well-being', *Humanities and Social Sciences Communications*, 8, 258. https://doi.org/10.1057/s41599-021-00899-3

Kros, C. (2014) 'Tainted heritage? The case of the Branly museum', *International Journal of Heritage Studies*, 20(7–8), pp. 834–850. https://doi.org/10.1080/13527258.2013.860393

Lähdesmäki, T. and Koistinen, A.-K. (2021) 'Explorations of linkages between intercultural dialogue, art, and empathy', in Maine, F. and Vrikki, M. (eds.), *Dialogue for Intercultural Understanding: Placing Cultural Literacy at the Heart of Learning*. Cham: Springer, pp. 45–58. https://doi.org/10.1007/978-3-030-71778-0_4

Landkammer, N. (2018). 'The museum as a site of unlearning? Coloniality and education in ethnographic museums, a study focusing on Germany, Austria and Switzerland', in Endter, S., Landkammer, N. and Schneider, K. (eds.) *The Museum as a Site of Unlearning: Materials and Reflections on Museum Education at the Weltkulturen Museum*, pp. 2–23. Available at: https://another-roadmap.net/articles/0003/4909/the-museum-as-a-site-of-unlearning-nora-landkammer.pdf (Accessed: 26 August 2022).

MacCormack P. (2020) *Ahuman Manifesto. Activism for the End of the Anthropocene*. London: Bloomsbury Academic.

Mäenpää, T. (2021) 'Seinäjoen taidehallin Siat-näyttelyn kävijämäärässä nähtävissä selvää nostetta runsaan keskustelun ja kohun keskellä', Yle Uutiset, 18 November. Available at: https://yle.fi/a/3-12192810 (Accessed: 23 January 2023).

Montero-Sieburth, M.A. (2020) 'Who gives 'Voice' or 'Empowers Migrants' in participatory action research? Challenges and solutions', *Migration Letters,* 17(2), pp. 211–218. https://doi.org/10.33182/ml.v17i2.806

Pachirat, T. (2011) *Every Twelve Seconds: Industrialized Slaughter and the Politics of Sight*. New Haven, CT and London: Yale University Press.

Parikka, J. (2018) 'Medianatures', in Braidotti, R. and Hlavajova, M. (eds.) *Posthuman Glossary*. London: Bloomsbury, pp. 251–253.

Pirnes, E. (2009) 'Cultural policy in the sectoral trap—but how to escape it', *Nordisk Kulturpolitisk Tidskrift* 2/2009, pp. 155–174.

Precarias a la deriva (2009) *Hoivaajien kapina. Tutkimusmatkoja prekaarisuuteen [A la deriva por los circuitos de la precariedad femenina]*. Helsinki: Like and Tutkijaliitto.

Raatikainen, K.J. et al. (2021) 'Pathways towards a sustainable future envisioned by early-career conservation researchers', *Conservation Science and Practice*, 3(9), e493. https://doi.org/10.1111/csp2.493

Rifkin, J. (2010) *The Empathic Civilization. The Race to Global Consciousness in a World in Crisis*. New York: Polity Press.

Sabatini, F. (2019) 'Culture as fourth pillar of sustainable development: Perspectives for integration, paradigms of action', *European Journal of Sustainable Development* 8)3, pp. 31–40. https://doi.org/10.14207/ejsd.2019.v8n3p31

Salonen, A.O. and Bardy M. (2015) 'Ekososiaalinen sivistys herättää luottamusta tulevaisuuteen', *Aikuiskasvatus*, 35(1), pp. 4–15. https://doi.org/10.33336/aik.94118

Schneider-Mayerson, M. (2021) 'Does climate fiction make a difference?' *Literary Hub*, 16 December. Available at: https://lithub.com/does-climate-fiction-make-a-difference/ (Accessed: 26 August 2022).

Smith, L. (2021) *Emotional Heritage. Visitor Engagement at Museums and Heritage Sites.* London and New York: Routledge.

Soini, K. and Birkeland, I. (2014) 'Exploring the scientific discourse on cultural sustainability', *Geoforum*, 51, pp. 213–223. https://doi.org/10.1016/j.geoforum.2013.12.001

Sommer, L.K. and Klöckner, C.A. (2019) 'Does activist art have the capacity to raise awareness in audiences?—A study on climate change art at the ArtCOP21 Event in Paris', *Psychology of Aesthetics, Creativity, and the Arts*, 15(1), pp. 60–67. https://doi.org/10.1037/aca0000247

Thiele, L.P. (2013) *Sustainability*. Cambridge: Polity Press.

Thrift, N. (2008) *Non-Representational Theory. Space/Politics/Affect*. London: Routledge.

Turunen, J. (2020) 'Decolonising European minds through Heritage', *International Journal of Heritage Studies*, 26(10), pp. 1013–1028. https://doi.org/10.1080/13527258.2019.1678051

Turunen, J. and Viita-aho, M. (2021) 'Kriittisen museon mahdottomuus? Gallen-Kallelan Afrikka-kokoelman uudelleentulkinnat 2000-luvulla', in Koivunen, L. and Rastas A. (eds.) *Marginaalista museoihin*. Tampere: Vastapaino, pp. 93–113.

Weik von Mossner, A. (2017) *Affective Ecologies: Empathy, Emotion, and Environmental Narrative*. Columbus: The Ohio State University Press. https://doi.org/10.2307/j.ctv11hpszq

Williams, R. (1985) *Keywords: A Vocabulary of Culture and Society*. Oxford: Oxford University Press.

18

EDUCATION FOR PLANETARY WELL-BEING

Valtteri A. Aaltonen, Mikko Hiljanen, Heidi Layne, Anna Lehtonen, Meri Löyttyniemi, Niina Mykrä, Anu S. Virtanen and Hannu L.T. Heikkinen

Education is the key to transforming practices[1]

The ongoing global crises are the motivation for the concept of planetary well-being (Kortetmäki *et al.*, 2021). These crises can be regarded as being nested in one another (Heikkinen *et al.*, 2023; Kaukko *et al.*, 2021). The most discussed of these nested crises are the climate emergency and the global loss of biodiversity, but the global tangle of crises also includes social and economic crises, like the social justice gap between the global North and the global South, and health crises, like global pandemics (*e.g.*, Johnson *et al.*, 2020; Kaukko *et al.*, 2021). To be able to solve these nested crises, humans must learn to act in a new way; in other words, humanity needs to make a rapid shift from unsustainable practices to sustainable ones. The term *green transition* has increasingly been used to describe this shift (*e.g.*, Bianchi, 2020), the urgency of which has been recognized worldwide.

Learning and education play a key role in the green transition. However, in order to change prevailing practices, learning and education need to be understood in a new way. Traditionally, education has socialized new generations to conventional practices and ways of thinking. Given the present circumstances, reproducing prevailing practices and habitual belief systems is no longer defensible; rather, education should promote new kinds of practices and new ways of thinking. Education should, in other words, promote *transformative learning* that aims for something unprecedented (Mezirow, 1994; O'Sullivan, Morrell and O'Connor, 2002; Wals, 2011). Transformative learning means bringing about such a fundamental change that it transforms a person's psyche, forming a new kind of identity; it is a shift of consciousness that dramatically and permanently alters the human way of being in the world. Such a profound transformation involves experiencing a deep, structural shift in the basic premises of thought, feeling, and action.

DOI: 10.4324/9781003334002-24

To enable such a transformation, we must first critically examine the prevailing practices and reflect on their underlying beliefs. One fundamental belief system that makes us reproduce previous practices in a path-dependent manner is our human-centred worldview, in other words our anthropocentrism. The concept of *education for planetary well-being* advocates a more-than-human view, or rather a planetary view, as the basis for education—one which manifests as a dialogic relationship between humans and the rest of nature. The current paradigm of socialization—that is, societal continuity and reliability based on educating new generations with required knowledge and skills (Värri, 2018)—appears to be inadequate to securing planetary well-being. For example, according to Ruuska (2017), higher education reproduces the current drastically unequal economic systems, which exacerbates the ecological crises. This notwithstanding, in recent decades, numerous initiatives and frameworks have been introduced in order to address this problem. These initiatives, which we refer to as current frameworks, have been helpful but have not been sufficient to effect fundamental change. Nonetheless, in our view, some of these ideas are germane to the concept of *education for planetary well-being* and therefore germane to our present purposes.

The key question is how to put into practice a form of education that promotes the necessary transformative learning and renewal of practices and that maintains a planetary state in which "organisms (including humans) can realize their typical characteristics and capacities" (Kortetmäki *et al.*, 2021, p. 4). To answer this question, we suggest the concept of *education for planetary well-being* as a framework that could bring together important existing educational themes and ideas with a new, more focused stance. *Education for planetary well-being* refers to the processes of upbringing, teaching, and learning that enable individuals and communities to promote the well-being of the planet and its inhabitants, which we refer to as life on Earth (consisting of nonhuman and human life in the biosphere and its ecosystems as well as the geophysical Earth systems). *Education for planetary well-being* promotes transformative learning and empowers individuals and societies to make responsible choices in terms of life on Earth. It focuses on learning about the interconnectedness of all life on Earth and the importance of preserving the liveable planet into the future, emphasizing the need to advance toward this goal.

The undercurrents of education for planetary well-being

Humanism, instrumental rationality, and dualism

A considerable number of the problems of our time (in education systems built on "Western" beliefs) stem from anthropocentric thinking, which attributes the greatest value to that which is good for humans. In other words, the actions and activities that yield benefits for humans are seen as worth pursuing foremost. This worldview does not necessarily take into consideration what is good for the rest of nature.

Quite the contrary: Very often humans have acted in a way that undermines the well-being of the rest of nature.

The origin of these problems can be traced back to the birth of the Enlightenment and humanism. A decisive change in thinking was the shift towards Cartesian dualism in the sixteenth century, based on the philosopher René Descartes' concept that the human mind is separate from the world outside of it; that is, humans are conscious "subject" and the rest of the world is regarded as an "object" of human thought and action. The transition to Cartesian dualism was also on the background of the Enlightenment project. Originally a European philosophical movement that began at the end of the seventeenth century, the influence of the Enlightenment has continued into modern times, especially with regard to its emphasis on rationality and knowledge (Horkheimer and Adorno, 1972). In humanism, what is good for humans is thought to have the highest absolute value. A phrase by Protagoras of Ancient Greece was quoted as the motto of humanism: *Homo mensura*—the human being is the measure of everything (Hietalahti, 2022; Niiniluoto, 2015).

The Enlightenment and humanism thus share the assumption that all life on Earth exists *for* humans. One of their guiding principles was that humans should free themselves from the power of the natural forces. The greatest achievement of the Enlightenment era was thought to be that the human species had managed to subjugate nature and other lifeforms on Earth to its own use with the help of human reason. In other words, everything on Earth was deemed to be of instrumental value for the benefit of humans specifically: Since the Enlightenment, the value of nature has been measured from the perspective of how it increases human well-being and wealth. The Age of Enlightenment has thus been seen as the triumph of *instrumental rationality*. Education has further reproduced and developed the idea that humans should use their reason to subdue natural resources for their own advantage (Horkheimer and Adorno, 1972).

Posthumanist thinking has emerged as a counter-movement to this tradition (Hietalahti, 2022). Posthumanism assumes that the continuation of life on this planet is of higher value than the life of one particular species, *Homo sapiens*. Posthumanism has developed from various philosophical origins and has expanded in many directions, and it is not a unified school of thought. It is rather an umbrella term that challenges anthropocentric ways of thinking and redefines the idea of what it means to be human and how humans (should) relate to their material and mediated environment (Ennser-Kananen and Saarinen, 2022).

The concept of planetary well-being is based on a similar criticism of human-centred thinking typical of posthumanism. In the definition of planetary well-being, the highest value, according to our interpretation, is not attributed to human well-being exclusively but rather to achieving a planetary state in which organisms, including humans, can realize their typical characteristics and capacities. Therefore, the concept of planetary well-being can be considered a natural continuation of the discussion that has taken place within posthumanist theorization in terms of its critique of Cartesian dualism, instrumental rationality, and anthropocentric humanism.

Consequently, *education for planetary well-being* is also based on this thinking. It is not our intention to claim that *education for planetary well-being* is the only educational approach that is based on non-anthropocentrism and the critique of instrumental rationality, as there are also other approaches in the field of education that share these assumptions to varying degrees. These current frameworks are introduced in the upcoming section to present the earlier and current stages and concepts in the field of education that have paved the way for developing the concept of *education for planetary well-being* introduced in this chapter.

The historical background of the current frameworks

There are a number of approaches in the field of education whose common denominators are sustainability, protection of nature, and consideration of the natural environment. We call these approaches current frameworks. They consist of different initiatives, literature, and terms related to environmental and social responsibility as well as intergenerational justice in the context of education. Such current frameworks are presented here firstly as a historical continuum. These current frameworks offer a kind of mirror against which we outline the idea of *education for planetary well-being*.

According to Bianchi (2020), the historical development of initiatives and literature of the field has undergone three phases. Originating in the 1960s, the first phase is characterized by the impact of Rachel Carson's book *Silent Spring* (1962) and others whose work preceded the environmental movements and the tradition of environmental education. The environmental education tradition embraced ecological arguments without conceits and eschewed anthropocentrism (Robottom, 1992). While these developments were the foundation for the first international UN conference on environmental issues, organized in Stockholm in 1972, these principles did not influence the framework and key term that was to dominate environmental policy in the coming decades: Sustainable development. According to *Our Common Future* (World Commission on Environment and Development (WCED), 1987, p. 16): "Humanity has the ability to make development sustainable to ensure that it meets the needs of the present generation without compromising the ability of future generations to meet their own needs". Although the legacy of sustainable development and its emphasis on intergenerational justice has had significant influence in the world, ultimately it was founded on anthropocentric humanism and can be seen as directly continuing the Enlightenment project, albeit in a slightly toned-down form.

The second phase was framed around the UN Rio conference in 1992 and the adoption of Agenda 21, a non-binding sustainable development action plan that pushed educational policies towards skills and values linked to social, developmental, and environmental justice. This is the explicit educational foundation for the sustainable development tradition, currently present in the United Nations Educational, Scientific and Cultural Organization (UNESCO) framework (Laurie *et al.*, 2016). According to UNESCO (2017), learning about sustainability must prepare students and learners of all ages to find solutions for the challenges of today and the future. Education should be transformative and should allow citizens to make informed decisions and take individual as well as collective action to change our societies and care for the planet.

The third phase is the era after the World Summit for Sustainable Development that took place in Johannesburg in 2002. This event served as the impetus for the Decade of Education for Sustainable Development (2005–2014), which emphasized lifelong learning and spurred initiatives worldwide. That project was followed by the UN Global Action Programme (2015–2019), which aimed to intensify the initiatives of Education for Sustainable Development and set Sustainable Development Goals (SDGs), a framework adopted by the UN in 2015 which, in addition to providing general guidance for sustainable change, places an explicit focus on the quality of and conditions for education (SDG 4) (Bianchi, 2020, p. 11). Currently, the UN Global Action Programme is being followed up by UNESCO's Education for Sustainable Development as part of its 2030 programme, which aims to bring about the personal and societal transformation that is needed to achieve sustainable development worldwide (Bianchi, 2020; UNESCO, 2022).

Sustainable development and sustainability are ubiquitously present in educational policy discourse, but it is not always clear what these terms mean. Bianchi (2020, p. 10) sums up the recent policy focus on sustainable development and sustainability as follows:

> Sustainability and sustainable development are often used interchangeably, despite their conceptual difference. In reference to the UNESCO definitions, sustainability is best described as a long-term goal, such as attaining a more sustainable world; while sustainable development, like the term suggests, refers to the many processes and pathways to achieve development.

The "take-home message" of Bianchi is that it makes a difference whether we discuss sustainability or sustainable development, and that this choice has consequences for education. As indicated by Matero and Arffman (see Chapter 7), the concept of sustainable development has been interpreted in different ways during its relatively short history, depending on the context in which it is used. However, often it has been connected to the idea of continuous economic growth, especially by the Organization for Economic Co-operation and Development (OECD) and the European Union. Economic growth as a policy goal is difficult to align with planetary well-being as it has been previously linked to overconsumption of materials, ecosystem destruction, inequality in human societies, and the general destruction of life on Earth (see Kortetmäki *et al.*, 2021). Hence, the concept of sustainable development too can be regarded as a direct heir of the Enlightenment tradition and the belief in human progress based on instrumental rationality.

Sustainable development-related frameworks are globally influential in the field of education to the extent that they can even be referred to as a paradigm, delineating the set of concepts and beliefs that prefigure public debate during a particular period of time. The ambiguity of sustainable development can be seen in the ambivalence surrounding how the concept is interpreted and used by different scholars. Therefore, some educational researchers consciously avoid using the term sustainable development or are sceptical of the concept of sustainability. However, there are also approaches that use the word sustainability but still want to distinguish themselves from the idea of continuous growth implied by the concept of sustainable development. Further still, there are some frameworks in the field of education that make no reference at all to either of these concepts (*e.g.*, Bianchi, 2020; Connelly, 2007; Jickling and Wals, 2008; Snaza *et al.*, 2014).

Next, we briefly introduce some well-known and commonly used frameworks as alternatives to the prevailing sustainable development paradigm, that is, alternatives that support the idea of *education for planetary well-being*. The concept of *sustainability as education*, as defined by Stephen Sterling (2001, 2010) and Arjen Wals (2006, 2015), who are among the earliest and most central authors representing the move, called for holistic behavioural change and transformative learning. Sterling's (2001) original distinction between sustainability as education and *education for sustainable development* highlights that the latter was framed to raise awareness without challenging the existing institutions and status quo. Sustainability as education, instead, requires a profound change in one's worldview, switching from a dualistic, hierarchical worldview to systems understanding and relational sustainability competences.

Global Citizenship Education Otherwise (Andreotti, 2015; Stein and Andreotti, 2021) criticizes the framework of the taken-for-granted Eurocentric knowledge system in regard to how, for example, Sustainable Development Goals are framed and understood as global goals by the United Nations. The education for global citizenship promotes the transition from a singular universal belief or knowledge to an approach of listening and including counternarratives on knowledge in the curriculum. In this approach, education is viewed as a dialogue that considers diverse historical, political, and knowledge foundations (Andreotti, 2015).

In the Nordic countries, the concept of *eco-social education* (or *eco-social Bildung*) is one of the more influential current frameworks that calls for transformation by stressing the acute need for prioritizing diversity of life on Earth in the value system. Eco-social education has been part of the public debate for more than a decade, and it is explicitly mentioned, for example, in the national core curriculum of Finland (Finnish National Board of Education, 2014; Halinen, 2018; Lehtonen, Salonen and Cantell, 2018). Eco-social education emphasizes ecology, takes climate crises seriously, and considers planetary boundaries (Rockström *et al.,* 2009) instead of the economy as the basis for social and economic well-being (Salonen and Konkka, 2015).

Ecojustice education (Martusewicz, Edmundson and Lupinacci, 2011, p. 9) highlights "the necessary interdependent relationship of humans with the land, air, water, and other species with whom we share this planet". Ecojustice education calls for critical awareness of the unequal power dynamics related to binaries (*e.g.*, men/women, white/other, European/other, culture/nature, reason/emotion, science/local), indigenous knowledges, and how these inequalities are sustained across different languages and means of communication. The theoretical foundations of ecojustice education include ecofeminism and neo-agrarianism, with a shared dedication to a feminist ethic of care for ecological social justice and posthumanism (*ibid.*).

Other examples of approaches that avoid using the term "sustainable development" are *environmental education*, in its advanced mode, (Reid *et al.*, 2021) and the hybrid concept of *environmental and sustainability education* (Wals, Weakland and Corcoran, 2017). Both of these can be regarded as taking a critical stance toward anthropocentrism. Additionally, we acknowledge that critical approaches to human-centred education have also been raised by posthumanist writers (*e.g.*, Morris, 2015; Snaza *et al.*, 2014). Overall, posthuman education has wider perspectives in its critic of humanism in education, such as colonialism and complex relations not only between humans and nonhuman animals, but also technology.

Criticism of anthropocentrism can be seen as a distinguishing factor according to which education for sustainability can be divided into two different types of approaches: Weak and strong (Connelly, 2007). The *weak* form is associated with continuous technological development and economic growth, or, at best, so-called ecological modernization (*ibid.*, p. 270) emphasizing efficiency in energy use and recycling of materials. The weak approach also includes an assumption about sustainable development benefitting all humanity, but, in reality, the approach accepts drastic inequalities between different human communities, such as the division between the global North and global South. Education for sustainability in the *strong* sense, in contrast, could be translated as *eco-socialism* (*ibid.*) with an emphasis on a just transition toward the well-being of all life on Earth, which aligns well with the concept of planetary well-being.

Based on the review above, we conclude that our concept of *education for planetary well-being* builds on the ideas raised by many of the current frameworks. In many respects, *education for planetary well-being* agrees with the mentioned frameworks; it advocates non-anthropocentric and posthumanist thinking as well as sustainability in the strong sense. However, it is more explicit in instilling the educational approach with the encompassing idea of planetary well-being as a state in which all organisms, including humans, can realize their typical characteristics and capacities.

Dialogue as an ontological and pedagogical principle

Our conceptualization of *education for planetary well-being* is rooted in a dialogic relationship between humans and other lifeforms on Earth, one in which it is assumed that human well-being is built in dialogue with the rest of nature.

Dialogue can be identified implicitly in many of the current frameworks, such as in sustainability as education, global citizenship education otherwise, and ecojustice education. In *education for planetary well-being*, however, the dialogical way of being is central and explicitly present, drawing from Buber's (2004) dialogical philosophy and posthumanism (Braidotti, 2013, 2019).

The opposite of a dialogical relationship is a monologic (and an instrumental) relationship. The monological relationship is based on the aforementioned dualistic assumption that nature is understood as an object separate from humans and as an instrument for human well-being. In a dialogical relationship, humans are viewed as one of the species living in a given ecological niche of the Earth system and as largely dependent on and connected to different ecosystems and various forms of life on Earth. It is only through the interaction of species in and between ecosystems, including human societies, that well-being occurs (see Kortetmäki *et al.*, 2021, p. 3). The dialogic approach provides an ontological basis for the concept of *education for planetary well-being*.

As an ontological principle, dialogue can be regarded as a human way of being where the relations between beings are more fundamental than the beings themselves and where the ethical aspect of these relations is emphasized. Beings are understood to be constructed through these relationships, which are characterized by interconnectedness, diversity, and respect for alterity. The nature of this ontological "in-betweenness" has been aptly described by Martin Buber (2004) as two basic modes of existing, representable as word-pairs: *I–it* and *I–Thou*. According to Buber, the monological I–it relationship is characterized by the experience of a detached object and a concept of oneself as an isolated subject of experience that defines another being according to one's interests. According to Buber, one can be truly human only in a dialogical relation between I and Thou, where the other is encountered openly without any restricting classification. Hence, as a true "other", Thou has an inherent value.

Applied to the planetary well-being concept, this means that both humans and the rest of nature have an absolute value, or rather, that human dignity is best realized through the recognition of the dignity of nature. In this case, human beings are not seen as separate from the rest of the world, but as embodied being who co-exists through senses and affects. These ideas of co-existence and interdependence are also typical of posthumanism. For example, Braidotti (2019) calls to become aware of human embodiment and accountability to the way one affects and is affected in the dynamic web of human and nonhuman relations.

Education for planetary well-being requires dialogic consideration and an empathic understanding of other species' needs also in the pedagogical practice. Dialogical practice is a way of learning new, posthuman, and even planetary ways to relate to other species (see Davies and Renshaw, 2020; Saur and Sidorkin, 2018). However, the needs of different species are often conflicting and evoke challenging ethical questions that should be acknowledged and discussed (Valtonen, 2022). Posthumanism offers a view of pedagogy that emphasizes a critical awareness of the highly unequal power relations between humans and Earth's "others" and embodied and sentient being (Braidotti, 2019). Participation in a collective dialogic practice is a moral phenomenon focused on the nature of our identity and existence as humans (Wegerif, Mercer and Major, 2020) and on how we are connected to the well-being of the whole planet.

Dialogue as pedagogical practice is based on the collaborative construction of knowledge through interaction between learner and teacher. The dialogical principle is an alternative to monological teaching's mere transmission of knowledge from a teacher to a learner. In dialogical teaching, learners are not regarded as objects of a teacher but rather as active subjects of knowledge construction. In this sense, one could say that *education for planetary well-being* is essentially based on constructivist learning (Tynjälä and Gijbels, 2012).

According to Alexander (2020), dialogic talk is understood to be collective, affirmative, and reciprocal. This means that learners and teachers address learning tasks together and are able to express their ideas. It is also crucially important to listen to others and profoundly explore alternative viewpoints. Ideally, dialogue is deliberative, cumulative, and purposeful. Based on dialogue, something new emerges. However, this does not mean that learning goals cannot be set in dialogic teaching. Quite the opposite, dialogical learning can be structured towards a specific learning outcome. In the context of planetary well-being, the dialogue should focus on personal meaning-making, emphasizing strong sustainability, planetary boundaries, and social justice.

Dialogical teaching in terms of *education for planetary well-being* calls for humility and empathetic openness to alterity in our human way of relating to all life on Earth. Dialogue thus enables transformative learning instead of a socialization to current practices and belief systems: It promotes a structural shift in the basic premises of thought, feeling, and action that can fundamentally alter the human way of being in the world (Mezirow, 1994; O'Sullivan, Morrell and O'Connor, 2002; Wals, 2011).

A new measure for humanity: Responsibility for planetary well-being

This chapter has explored how planetary well-being appears in the context of education in relation to other frameworks, and how planetary well-being could be promoted in education through dialogue. *Education for planetary well-being* aligns with many of the current approaches, embracing transformative learning towards social change, aiming for humanity to live in balance with other lifeforms on Earth and within the limits of the planet. It can be viewed as the culmination of these developments, offering a new stepping stone for reaching a shared goal: The well-being of all inhabitants on planet Earth.

The main argument of this chapter is that what is good for humans can no longer be regarded as the guiding premise for education; instead, what is good for all life on Earth should become the new rule. Therefore, a new theorem of *education for planetary well-being* is introduced to replace the motto of humanism, *homo mensura* or human is the measure of everything. Now, in accordance with posthumanist thinking, the guiding theorem can be turned into *natura mensura* or nature is the measure of everything (Niiniluoto, 2015). It is evident that a shift in pedagogy is needed, away from the perspective of humanistic anthropocentrism and towards posthumanism with an emphasis on the well-being of both human and nonhuman lifeforms.

Nevertheless, the transition from classical humanism to a posthumanist and planetary perspective does not mean that humans should not be the central focus of education. Humankind must reclaim its name as *Homo sapiens*, the wise human. Accordingly, our proposal for a basic theorem of *education for planetary well-being* is the following: *Responsibility for planetary well-being is the new measure of humanity.* It is worth pointing out that this theorem does not undermine human dignity, rather the opposite. By following this principle, human beings could paradoxically demonstrate their greatness by admitting their smallness before nature, or rather *within* nature. This new motto for humanity would be the starting point of *planetary wisdom*, which is a human ability that enables and promotes planetary well-being, and thus helps us to build a world worth living in.

Acknowledgements

The writing of this chapter has been supported by the following research funding: Academy of Finland, Wisdom in Practice project, funded under grant agreement 351238 for Hannu L.T. Heikkinen, Niina Mykrä, and Anu S. Virtanen; European Union's Green Deal/Horizon 2020 Research and Innovation Programme, ECF-4CLIM project, funded under grant agreement 10103650 for Hannu L.T. Heikkinen, Niina Mykrä, and Anna Lehtonen; Jyväskylä University School of Business and Economics, Grant for doctoral research for Meri Löyttyniemi; Ministry of Education and Culture of Finland, KESTO project, funded under grant agreements OKM/239/523/2020 and OKM/117/523/2020 for Hannu L.T. Heikkinen and Anu S. Virtanen; Wihuri Foundation, grant for doctoral research for Valtteri A. Aaltonen.

Note

1   This chapter is the result of a collective effort and intense discussions among the authors. All authors contributed to the work significantly and are listed in alphabetical order, except for the first and the last author.

References

Alexander, R. (2020) *A Dialogic Teaching Companion.* London: Routledge.
Andreotti, V. (2015) 'Global citizenship education otherwise. Theoretical and pedagogical insights', in Abdi, A.A., Schultz, A. and Pillay, T. (eds.) *Decolonizing Global Citizenship Education.* Rotterdam: Brill Sense, pp. 221–229.

256 Valtteri A. Aaltonen et al.

Bianchi, G. (2020) *Sustainability Competences*. EUR 30555 EN. Luxembourg: Publications Office of the European Union. https://doi.org/10.2760/200956

Braidotti, R. (2013) *The Posthuman*. London: Polity.

Braidotti, R. (2019) *Posthuman Knowledge*. Cambridge: Polity Press.

Buber, M. (2004) *I and Thou*. London: Continuum.

Carson, R. (1962) *Silent Spring*. Boston, MA: Houghton Mifflin.

Connelly, S. (2007) 'Mapping sustainable development as a contested concept', *Local Environment*, 12(3), pp. 259–278. https://doi.org/10.1080/13549830601183289.

Davies, K. and Renshaw, P. (2020) 'Who's talking? (and what does it mean for 'us'): Provocations for beyond Humanist dialogic pedagogies', in Mercer, N., Wegerif, R. and Major, L. (eds.) *The Routledge International Handbook of Research on Dialogic Education*. London: Routledge. pp. 38–49. https://doi.org/10.4324/9780429441677

Ennser-Kananen, J. and Saarinen, T. (eds.) (2022) *New Materialist Explorations into Language Education*. Cham: Springer. https://doi.org/10.1007/978-3-031-13847-8

Finnish National Board of Education (2014) *National Core Curriculum for Basic Education*. Helsinki: Finnish National Board of Education.

Halinen, I. (2018) 'The new educational curriculum in Finland', *Improving the quality of childhood in Europe*, 7, pp. 75–89.

Heikkinen, H. *et al.* (2023) 'Miten muuttaa käytäntöjä ihmisen ja luonnon kannalta kestäviksi? Ekososiaalinen sivistys käytäntöarkkitehtuuriteorian valossa [How to change practices to sustainable from the perspective of human and nature? Eco-social education in the light of the theory of practice architectures]', *Kasvatus*, 54(1), pp. 64–76.

Hietalahti, J. (2022) *Ihmisyyden ytimessä. Filosofisen humanismin idea [In the Core of Humanity. The Idea of Philosophic Humanism]*. Helsinki: Gaudeamus.

Horkheimer, M. and Adorno, T.W. (1972) *Dialectic of Enlightenment*. New York: Seabury Press.

Jickling, B. and Wals, A.E.J. (2008) 'Globalization and environmental education: Looking beyond sustainable development', *Journal of Curriculum Studies*, 40(1), pp. 1–21. https://doi.org/10.1080/00220270701684667

Johnson, C. *et al.* (2020) 'Global shifts in mammalian population trends reveal key predictors of virus spillover risk', *Proceedings of Royal Society B Biological Sciences*, 287, 20192736. https://doi.org/10.1098/rspb.2019.2736

Kaukko, M. *et al.* (2021) 'Learning to survive amidst nested crises: Can the coronavirus pandemic help us change educational practices to prepare for the impending eco-crisis?', *Environmental Education Research*, 27(11), pp. 1559–1573. https://doi.org/10.1080/13504622.2021.1962809

Kortetmäki, T. *et al.* (2021) 'Planetary well-being', *Humanities and Social Sciences Communications*, 8, p. 258. https://doi.org/10.1057/s41599-021-00899-3

Laurie, R. *et al.* (2016) 'Contributions of education for sustainable development (ESD) to quality education: A synthesis of research', *Journal of Education for Sustainable Development*, 10(2), pp. 226–242. https://doi.org/10.1177/0973408216661442

Lehtonen, A., Salonen, A.O. and Cantell, H. (2018) 'Climate change education: A new approach for a world of wicked problems', in Cook, J. (ed.) *Sustainability, Human Well-Being, and the Future of Education*. Cham: Palgrave Macmillan, pp. 339–374. https://doi.org/10.1007/978-3-319-78580-6

Martusewicz, R.A., Edmundson, J. and Lupinacci, J. (2011) *EcoJustice Education. Towards Diverse, Democratic, and Sustainable Communities*. London: Routledge.

Mezirow, J. (1994) 'Understanding transformation theory', *Adult Education Quarterly*, 44(4), pp. 222–232. https://doi.org/10.1177/074171369404400403

Morris, M. (2015) 'Posthuman education and animal interiority', in Snaza, N. and Weaver, J. (eds.) *Posthumanism and Educational Research*. London: Routledge, pp. 43–55.

Niiniluoto, I. (2015) *Hyvän elämän filosofiaa [Philosophy of the Good Life]*. Helsinki: Suomalaisen kirjallisuuden seura.

O'Sullivan, E., Morrell, M., and O'Connor, M.A. (2002) *Expanding the Boundaries of Transformative Learning. Essays on Theory and Practice*. New York: Palgrave.

Reid, A. *et al.* (2021) 'Scientists' warnings and the need to reimagine, recreate, and restore environmental education', *Environmental Education Research*, 27(6), pp. 783–795. https://doi.org/10.1080/13504622.2021.1937577

Robottom, I. (1992) *Environmental Education: Practice and Possibility*. Melbourne: Deakin University.

Rockström, J. *et al.* (2009) 'Planetary boundaries: Exploring the safe operating space for humanity', *Ecology and Society*, 14(2), p. 32. Available at: http://www.ecologyandsociety.org/vol14/ iss2/art32/ (Accessed: 6 January 2023).

Ruuska, T. (2017) *Reproduction of Capitalism in the 21st Century: Higher Education and Ecological Crisis*. PhD dissertation. Aalto University School of Business. Available at: https://aaltodoc.aalto.fi/handle/123456789/26627 (Accessed: 6 January 2023).

Salonen, A.O. and Konkka, J. (2015) 'An ecosocial approach to well-being: A solution to the wicked problems in the era of Anthropocene', *Foro de Educación*, 13(19), pp. 19–34.

Saur, E. and Sidorkin, A.M. (2018) 'Disability, dialogue, and the posthuman', *Studies in Philosophy and Education*, 37, pp. 567–578. https://doi.org/10.1007/s11217-018-9616-5

Snaza, N. *et al.* (2014) 'Toward a posthuman education', *Journal of curriculum theorizing*, 30(2), pp. 39–55.

Stein, S. and Andreotti, V. (2021) 'Global citizenship otherwise', in Bosio, E. (ed.) *Conversations on Global Citizenship Education: Research, Teaching and Learning*. London: Routledge, pp. 13–36.

Sterling, S. (2001) *Sustainable Education: Re-Visioning Learning and Change*. Schumacher Briefings, no. 6. Bristol: Green Books.

Sterling, S. (2010) 'Transformative learning and sustainability: Sketching the conceptual ground', *Learning and Teaching in Higher Education*, 5(11), pp. 17–33.

Tynjälä, P., and Gijbels, D. (2012) 'Changing world: Changing pedagogy', in Tynjälä, P., Stenström, M-L. and Saarnivaara, M. (eds.) *Transitions and Transformations in Learning and Education*. Dordrecht: Springer, pp. 205–222. https://doi.org/10.1007/978-94-007-2312-2

UNESCO (2017) *Education for Sustainable Development Goals: Learning Objectives*. Paris: UNESCO. Available at: https://unesdoc.unesco.org/ark:/48223/pf0000247444 (Accessed: 23 December 2022).

UNESCO (2022) *Berlin Declaration on Education for Sustainable Development; Learn for Our Planet: Act for Sustainability*. UNESCO World Conference on Education for Sustainable Development 2021. Programme and meeting document. Available at: https://unesdoc.unesco.org/ark:/48223/pf0000381228 (Accessed: 23 December 2022).

Valtonen, V. (2022) *Kanssakuljeskelua: Monilajisen kasvatuksen teoreettisia ja pedagogisia lähtökohtia [Walking with: Theoretical and Pedagogical Contributions of Multispecies Education]*. PhD dissertation. University of Helsinki. Available at: http://urn.fi/URN:ISBN:978-951-51-8531-0 (Accessed: 23 December 2022).

Värri, V-M. (2018) *Kasvatus ekokriisin aikakaudella [Education in the era of ecocrisis]*. Tampere: Vastapaino.

Wals, A.E.J. (2006) 'The end of ESD … the beginning of transformative learning—emphasizing the E in ESD', in Cantell, M. (ed.) *Proceedings of the Seminar on Education for Sustainable Development*. Helsinki: Finnish UNESCO Commission, pp. 42–59.

Wals, A.E.J. (2011) 'Learning our way to sustainability', *Journal of Education for Sustainable Development*, 5(2), pp. 177–186. https://doi.org/10.1177/097340821100500208

Wals, A.E.J. (2015) 'Beyond unreasonable doubt. Education and learning for socio-ecological sustainability in the Anthropocene', Inaugural address, 17 December, Wageningen University. Available at: https://edepot.wur.nl/365312 (Accessed: 6 January 2023).

Wals, A.E.J., Weakland, J. and Corcoran, P.B. (2017) 'Introduction', in Corcoran, P.B., Weakland, J. and Wals, A.E.J. (eds.) *Envisioning Futures for Environmental and Sustainability Education*. Wageningen: Wageningen Academic Publishers, pp. 19–30. https://doi.org/10.3920/978-90-8686-846-9

WCED (1987) *Our Common Future [Brundtland report]*. A/42/427. Geneva: United Nations General Assembly. Available at: https://digitallibrary.un.org/record/139811?ln=en (Accessed: 6 January 2023).

Wegerif, R., Mercer, N. and Major, L. (2020) 'Introduction', in Mercer, N., Wegerif, R. and Major, L. (eds.) *The Routledge International Handbook of Research on Dialogic Education*. London: Routledge, pp. 1–8. https://doi.org/10.4324/9780429441677

INDEX

Note: **Bold** page numbers refer to tables; *italic* page numbers refer to figures and page numbers followed by "n" denote endnotes.

Printed in the United States
by Baker & Taylor Publisher Services